D0848737

THE CODE OF CAPITAL

The Code of Capital

How the Law Creates Wealth and Inequality

Katharina Pistor

PRINCETON UNIVERSITY PRESS

PRINCETON AND OXFORD

Requests for permission to reproduce material from this work
should be sent to permissions@press.princeton.edu

Published by Princeton University Press
41 William Street, Princeton, New Jersey 08540
6 Oxford Street, Woodstock, Oxfordshire OX20 1TR

press.princeton.edu

LCCN: 2018965763
ISBN 978-0-691-17897-4

British Library Cataloging-in-Publication Data is available

Editorial: Joe Jackson and Jackie Delaney
Production Editorial: Nathan Carr
Production: Jacquie Poirier
Publicity: Caroline Priday and James Schneider
Copyeditor: Karen Verde

This book has been composed in Adobe Text Pro and Gotham

Printed on acid-free paper. ∞

Printed in the United States of America

10 9 8 7 6 5 4 3 2 1

To Carsten

CONTENTS

Preface   ix

1   Empire of Law   1

2   Coding Land   23

3   Cloning Legal Persons   47

4   Minting Debt   77

5   Enclosing Nature's Code   108

6   A Code for the Globe   132

7   The Masters of the Code   158

8   A New Code?   183

9   Capital Rules by Law   205

Notes   235

Index   279

The idea for this book has been with me for quite some time. It first emerged when, in the fall of 2007, the global financial system began to teeter toward the abyss. The speed of the unfolding crisis left little time for deep thinking, but once the eye of the storm had passed, I, along with many others, sought to discover what might explain finance's stupendous expansion in recent decades, and what accounted for its steep fall. Together with collaborators from different disciplines, I aimed to unpack the institutional structure of different segments of financial markets, one at a time. To me, the most revelatory part of our findings was how familiar the basic building blocks of the financial system looked, notwithstanding the fanciful assets that had been created more recently and the system's unparalleled complexity. Everywhere we probed a little deeper, we found the core institutions of private law: contract, property, collateral, trust, corporate, and bankruptcy law. They had powered the expansion of markets in financial assets, but, as it turned out, they were also key determinants in their undoing. When actual returns on these assets started falling behind expected returns, asset holders enforced their legal entitlements: they made good on the collateral calls, credit lines, repo contracts, and bankruptcy safe harbors, and in doing so, they helped deepen the crisis. Some still got out in time, but many others found themselves with assets that no one would take, except the central banks of select countries.

Having identified the core modules of our complex financial system, I began to trace their roots back in time. I investigated the evolution of property rights, of simple debt instruments, the various forms of pledges and gages that were used to collateralized debt obligations, the evolution of the use and the trust, the corporate form and the history of bankruptcy, the critical juncture when decisions over life and death in economic life are made. The more I read, the more I was convinced that what had started as an investigation into global finance had led me to the fountain of wealth, the making of capital.

This book is the result of that journey. Capital, I argue in this book, is coded in law. Ordinary assets are just that—a plot of land, a promise to be paid in the future, the pooled resources from friends and family to set up a new business, or individual skills and know-how. Yet every one of these assets can be transformed into capital by cloaking it in the legal modules that were also used to code asset-backed securities and their derivatives, which were at the core of the rise of finance in recent decades. These legal modules, namely contract, property rights, collateral, trust, corporate, and bankruptcy law, can be used to give the holders of some assets a comparative advantage over others. For centuries, private attorneys have molded and adapted these legal modules to a changing roster of assets and have thereby enhanced their clients' wealth. And states have supported the coding of capital by offering their coercive law powers to enforce the legal rights that have been bestowed on capital.

This book tells the story of the legal coding of capital from the perspective of the asset: land, business organizations, private debt, and knowledge, even nature's genetic code. I do not trace every turn in the evolution of the law, the twists and tweaks that were necessary to ensure that the old coding techniques would fit the new asset. For lawyers, these details are immensely gratifying, but for outsiders they add a level of detail and complexity that is not necessary to grasp the basic idea about how law creates wealth as well as inequality. Moreover, there exists a rich literature that traces the evolution of select legal institutions, such as the trust, the corporate form, or collateral law. Readers who wish to follow up on this will find some guidance in the citations provided in the notes. I ask for understanding from the legal historians and experts on the relevant legal domains for the simplifications I felt compelled to make to ensure that the book would be accessible to non-lawyers. These are the readers I had in mind while writing the book, readers who might not ever have opened a book about the law for fear that it would be too dry and complicated, or perhaps just not relevant. I have tried to make the legal institutions not only accessible, but also interesting and relevant for current debates about inequality, democracy, and governance. The law is a powerful tool for social ordering and, if used wisely, has the potential to serve a broad range of social objectives; yet, for reasons and with implications that I attempt to explain, the law has been placed firmly in the service of capital.

Many people have accompanied me on my journey to write this book. My colleagues at Columbia Law School encouraged me to write a book, not just an article, when I first presented my ideas at a faculty workshop four years ago. My students at Columbia Law School are always the first ones on whom I try out my new ideas. They are smart and forthright in their ideas and critiques, and I have learned a ton from them over the years, teaching them, as it were, the intricacies of corporate law, financial assets and their regulation, but also the role of law in development outside the capitalist economies of the West. I have also enormously benefited from conversations with former students and alums who are successful practitioners. Some even joined me in my teaching endeavors and shared insights with me and my students that are available only to insiders of the practice of law.

The book also greatly benefited from the research projects and workshops that were held under the auspices of the Center on Global Legal Transformation, which I direct at Columbia Law School. I am most grateful to the funders, in particular the Institute for New Economic Thinking (INET) and the Max Planck Society jointly with the Alexander von Humboldt Foundation.

Writing a book can be a rather lonely endeavor. Luckily, I was given many opportunities to share early ideas and test them on different audiences. Among these were the Buffett Institute at Northwestern University, Chinese University of Hong Kong, ETH Zurich, Goethe University in Frankfurt, Humboldt University of Berlin, Interdisciplinary Center Herzliya in Tel Aviv, KU Leuven (where I had the honor of giving the Dieter Heremans Fund Lectures in Law and Economics in 2016), the London School of Economics, Oxford University, Tel Aviv University Faculty of Law, as well as participants at annual meetings of the Global Conference on Economic Geography, the Global Corporate Governance Institute, and WINIR, the World Interdisciplinary Network for Institutional Research. The comments and feedback I received at these venues from colleagues and students helped to clarify my arguments and saved me from many errors and wrong turns.

I was also fortunate to have many close colleagues and friends who cheered me along the way. My late colleague, Robert Ferguson, instilled me with the sense that I was onto something; I only wish I could have shared the final result with him. Carol Gluck reviewed my book proposal and urged me to keep my sight on the present and not lose myself in the past, which was a real temptation. Bruce Carruthers, Jean Cohen, Hanoch Dagan, Tsilly Dagan, Horst Eidenmüller, Tom Ginsburg (and his students), Maeve Glass, Martin Hellwig, Jorge Kamine, Cathy Kaplan, Dana Neacsu, Delphine Nougayrède, Casey Quinn, Annelise Riles, Bill Simon, Wolfgang Streeck, Massimiliano Vatiero, and Alice Wang all read and commented on individual chapters or earlier versions of the entire manuscript. The final product is so much the better because of their constructive critiques, and I am most thankful for the time and attention they have given to it.

I am also immensely grateful to two anonymous reviewers, who offered their own thoughts and advice on how best to strengthen the book's arguments and make sure that it lived up to its ambition to reach a broader audience. Of course, I remain solely responsible for any and all remaining errors.

Many thanks to my editor, Joe Jackson, who gave me all the freedom I wanted, but stood ready whenever I needed advice on how to improve the book's structure or its narrative. I was blessed with Kate Garber as faculty assistant, who helped improve my English, and pointed out where my writing style was too convoluted to make sense even to a mind as sharp as hers. Thanks also to the librarians at Columbia Law School, who tirelessly searched for materials I needed, and to Karen Verde, who polished the final manuscript with great care.

I am dedicating this book to my husband, Carsten Bönnemann. He shared my enthusiasm for this project from the outset and has been my sounding board throughout the entire writing process. He never complained that the book was encroaching on our time to-gether, even though it did on the many occasions when we were together but my mind was wandering, when yet another opportunity to teach students or to speak to overseas audiences about the book's core arguments drew me away from him, or when, in its final stages, it even accompanied us on our summer vacation. He was my most critical reader, asked the most probing questions, and pushed me to bring my arguments to their logical conclusion, even at the risk of alienating potential allies or friends. Most important, he reminded me time and again that there is life beyond a book. Danke.

THE CODE OF CAPITAL

1

Empire of Law

It looks like an elephant's head: the line that represents the growth rate and the amount of wealth captured by different income groups globally between 1980 and 2017; fittingly, it is called the "elephant curve."[1] The broad forehead holds 50 percent of the world's population; over the past 35 years they captured a paltry 12 percent of growth in global wealth. From the forehead a curve leads down toward the trunk and from there, steeply up to the raised tip. The trunk is where "the one percent" sit; they hold 27 percent of the new wealth, more than double the amount held by the people clustered together on the elephant's forehead. The valley between the forehead and the trunk is where lower-income families in the advanced Western market economies are bundled together, the "squeezed bottom 90 percent" of these economies.[2]

It was not meant to be this way. The 1980s witnessed a surge in economic and legal reforms in developed and emerging markets alike that prioritized markets over government in allocating economic resources, a process that was further galvanized by the disappearance of the iron curtain and the collapse of socialism.[3] The idea was to create conditions by which everyone would prosper. Individual initiative protected by clear property rights and credible contract enforcement would, so the argument went, ensure that scarce resources would be allocated to the most efficient owner, and this in turn would increase the pie to the benefit of all. The playing field may not have been leveled, but the prevailing wisdom was that by freeing individuals from the shackles of state tutelage, all would eventually benefit.

Thirty years later, we are not celebrating prosperity for all, but instead are debating whether we have already, or not quite, reached levels of inequality that were last seen before the French Revolution, and this in countries that call themselves democracies, with their commitment to self-governance based on majoritarian, not elite, rule. It is hard to reconcile these aspirations with levels of inequality that smack of the Ancien Régime.

Of course, there has been no shortage of explanations. Marxists point to the exploitation of labor by capitalists.[4] Globalization skeptics argue that excessive globalization has deprived states of the power to redistribute some of the gains capitalists make through social programs or progressive taxation.[5] Finally, a novel interpretation holds that in mature economies capital grows faster than the rest of the economy; whoever has amassed wealth in the past, therefore, will expand it further, relative to others.[6] These are at least partly plausible explanations, but they fail to address the more fundamental question about the genesis of capital:[7] How is wealth created in the first place? And, relatedly, why does capital often survive economic cycles and shocks that leave so many others adrift, deprived of the gains they had made earlier?

The answer to these questions, I suggest, lies in capital's legal code. Fundamentally, capital is made from two ingredients: an asset, and the legal code. I use the term "asset" broadly to denote any object, claim, skill, or idea, regardless of its form. In their unadulterated appearance, these simple assets are just that: a piece of dirt, a building, a promise to receive payment at a future date, an idea for a new drug, or a string of digital code. With the right legal coding, any of these assets can be turned into capital and thereby increase its propensity to create wealth for its holder(s).

The roster of assets that are coded in law has changed over time and will likely continue to do so. In the past, land, firms, debt, and know-how have all been coded as capital, and as this list suggests, the nature of these assets has changed along the way. Land produces foodstuff and shelter even in the absence of legal coding, but financial instruments and intellectual property rights exist only in law, and digital assets in binary code, for which the code itself *is* the asset. And yet, the legal devices that have been used for coding every one of these assets have remained remarkably constant over time. The most important ones are contract law, property rights, collateral law, trust, corporate, and bankruptcy law. These are the *modules* from which capital is coded. They bestow important attributes on assets and thereby privilege its holder: *Priority*, which ranks competing claims to the same assets; *durability*, which extends priority claims in time; *universality*, which extends them in space; and *convertibility*, which operates as an insurance device that allows holders to convert their private credit claims into state money on demand and thereby protect their nominal value, for only legal tender can be a true store of value, as will be further explained in chapter 4.[8]

Once an asset has been legally coded, it is fit for generating wealth for its holder. The legal coding of capital is an ingenious process without which the world would have never attained the level of wealth that exists today; yet the process itself has been largely hidden from view. Through this book I hope to shed light on how law helps create both wealth and inequality. Tracing the root causes of inequality has become critically important not only because rising levels of inequality threaten the social fabric of our democratic systems, but also because conventional forms of redistribution through taxes have become largely toothless. Indeed, shielding assets from taxes is one of the most sought-after coding strategies that asset holders covet. And lawyers, the code's masters, are paid extraordinary fees to place them beyond the reach of creditors, including the tax authorities, with the help of these states' own laws.[9]

How assets are selected to be legally coded as capital, by whom, and for whose benefit are questions that cut to the core of capital and the political economy of capitalism. Yet, there are few, if any, answers to these questions in the literature. The reason is that most observers treat law as a sideshow when in fact it is the very cloth from which capital is cut. This book will show how and by whom ordinary assets are turned into capital and will shed light on the process by which lawyers can convert just about any asset into capital. The wealthy often claim special skills, hard work, and the personal sacrifice they themselves or their parents or forefathers have made as justifications for the wealth they hold today. These factors may well have contributed to their fortunes. Yet, without legal coding, most of these fortunes would have been short-lived. Accumulating wealth over long stretches of time requires additional fortification that only a code backed by the coercive powers of a state can offer.

It is often treated as a coincidence that the economic success that separates modern economies from millennia of much lower growth rates and much greater volatility of wealth closely tracks the rise of nation-states that rely on law as their primary means of social ordering.[10] Many commentators herald the advent of private property rights, seen as a critical restraint on state power, as the key explanation for the rise of the West.[11] Yet, it may be more accurate to attribute this to the state's willingness to back the private coding of assets in law, and not only property rights in the narrow sense, but also other legal privileges that confer priority, durability, convertibility, and universality on an asset. Indeed, the fact that capital is linked to and dependent on state power is often lost in debates about market economies. Contracts and property rights support free markets, but capitalism requires more—the legal privileging of some assets, which gives their holders a comparative advantage in accumulating wealth over others.[12]

Uncovering the legal structure of capital also helps solve the puzzle Thomas Piketty presented in his seminal book, *Capital in the Twenty-First Century*.[13] In advanced economies, he showed, the average rate of return on capital exceeds the average rate of economic growth ($r>g$). Piketty did not explain this puzzle, but settled on documenting its remarkable empirical regularity. Yet his own data offer important cues for solving it. In a chapter entitled "The

Metamorphoses of Capital," Piketty shows that rural land was the most important source of wealth until the early twentieth century.[14] Shares, bonds, and other financial assets as well as urban housing have since replaced it.

The analysis offered in this book will show that the metamorphosis of capital goes hand in hand with grafting the code's modules onto ever new assets, but also, from time to time, stripping some assets of key legal modules: rural land, the major source of private wealth for centuries, had long benefited from greater durability as compared to other assets, but lost this privilege in the UK and elsewhere in the late nineteenth century. By that time, corporations had become widely used legal modules not only for organizing industry, but as incubators of wealth. The corporate form, together with trust law, is also one of the key legal devices for emitting financial assets, from shares to derivatives. Last but not least, intellectual property rights have been on the rise over the last few decades and account for the lion's share of the market valuation of many firms today.

Decoding capital and uncovering the legal code that underpins it regardless of its outward appearance reveals that not all assets are equal; the ones with the superior legal coding tend to be "more equal" than others. The gist of this argument has been made before by the late legal historian, Bernard Rudden. He captured the essential role of law in fashioning assets that confer power and wealth on their holders in the following quote:

> The traditional concepts of the common law of property were created for and by the ruling classes at a time when the bulk of their capital was land. Nowadays the great wealth lies in stocks, shares, bonds and the like, and is not just movable but mobile, crossing oceans at the touch of a key-pad in the search for a fiscal utopia. (. . .) In terms of legal theory and technique, however, there has been a profound if little discussed evolution by which the concepts originally devised for real property have been detached from their original object, only to survive and flourish as a means of handling abstract value. The feudal calculus lives and breeds, but its habitat is wealth not land.[15]

In this book, I will show that the "feudal calculus" is indeed alive and kicking, including in democratically governed societies that pride themselves on guaranteeing everyone equality before the law—only that some can make better use of it than others. It operates through the modules of the legal code of capital, which, in the hands of sophisticated lawyers, can turn an ordinary asset into capital. Not the asset itself, but its legal coding, protects the asset holder from the headwinds of ordinary business cycles and gives his wealth longevity, thereby setting the stage for sustained inequality. Fortunes can be made or lost by altering an asset's legal coding, by stripping some modules from an asset, or by grafting them onto a different asset. We will see this play out in the rise and decline of landed wealth; the adaptation of legal coding techniques to firms; the conversion of loans into tradable financial assets that can be converted into cash at the doors of central banks; and, finally, in the rise of know-how as capital. For each of these assets, the legal coding ultimately determines their capacity to bestow wealth on their holders. It also provides them with a powerful defense against challengers: "But it's legal."

Law's Guiding Hand

The legal code of capital may be invisible to the casual observer, but that does not make it less real. Some may find it easier to believe in the market's "invisible hand" immortalized by Adam Smith, than to spend their time decoding capital's legal structures.[16] And yet, changes in the legal structure have fundamentally altered the conditions for Smith's invisible hand to do its work. As is well known, Smith argued that the pursuit of individual self-interest will inevitably benefit society. Often ignored is the mechanism that powers the invisible hand. "Every individual," Smith explained, "endeavours to employ his capital as near home as he can, and consequently as much as he can in the support of domestic industry; provided always that he can thereby obtain the ordinary, or not a great deal less than the ordinary profits of stock."[17] Why so? Because "he can know better the character and situation of the persons whom he trusts, and if he should happen to be deceived, *he knows better the laws of the country from which he must seek redress*."[18] Whereas conventional wisdom attributes the operation of the invisible hand to the market, it might just as well be read as a reference to the quality of the rules of the game where business is conducted. The invisible hand does its job under weak institutions; it becomes superfluous once institutions are in place that allow economic agents to enforce their rights and interests anywhere.

Today's entrepreneurs no longer need to seek redress at home, and the fate of their wealth is no longer tied to the communities they left behind. Instead, they can choose among many legal systems the one they prefer, and enjoy its benefits even without physically moving themselves, their business, their goods, or assets to the state that authorized that law. They can code capital as they choose in domestic or foreign law by opting into another country's contract law, or by incorporating their business in a jurisdiction that offers them the greatest benefits in the form of tax rates, regulatory relief, or shareholder benefits. Opting out of one and into a different legal regime leaves only a paper or digital trail but will not compromise the code's power as long as there is at least one state that is willing to back it.

This is so because, since Smith's writing more than two hundred years ago, an empire of law has been built that is made primarily of domestic law but remains only loosely tied to specific states or their citizens. States have actively torn down legal barriers to entry and offered their laws to willing takers and have thereby made it easier for asset holders to pick and choose the law of their liking. Most states recognize foreign law not only for contracts but also for (financial) collateral, corporations, and the assets they issue; they use their coercive powers to enforce it, and they allow domestic parties to opt into foreign law without losing the protections of local courts. The phenomenal expansion of trade, commerce, and finance globally would have been impossible without legal rules that enable asset holders to carry their local rules with them, or, if they prefer, to opt into foreign law. Dislodging the modules of capital from the legal systems that begot them has fostered the creation of wealth by holders of capital, the ones along the elephant's trunk, but it has also contributed to a highly skewed distribution of wealth for others without access to sophisticated coding strategies.

Realizing the centrality and power of law for coding capital has important implications for understanding the political economy of capitalism. It shifts attention from class identity and class struggle to the question of who has access to and control over the legal code and its masters: the landed elites; the long-distance traders and merchant banks; the shareholders of corporations that own production facilities or simply hold assets behind a corporate veil; the banks who grant loans, issue credit cards, and student loans; and the non-bank financial intermediaries that issue complex financial assets, including asset-backed securities and derivatives. The craftsmanship of their lawyers, the code's masters, explains the adaptability of the code to the ever-changing roster of assets; and the wealth-creating benefits of capital help explain why states have been only too willing to vindicate and enforce innovative legal coding strategies.

With the best lawyers at their service, asset holders can pursue their self-interests with only few constraints. They claim freedom of contract but overlook the fact that in the last instance, their freedoms are guaranteed by *a state*, though not necessarily their home state. Not every state, however, is equally accommodating for coding capital. Two legal systems dominate the world of global capital: English common law and the laws of New York State.[19] It should come as no surprise that these jurisdictions also harbor the leading global financial centers, London and New York City, and all of the top one hundred global law firms. This is where most capital is coded today, especially financial capital, the intangible capital that exists only in law.

The historical precedent for global rule by one or several powers is empire.[20] Law's empire has less need for troops; it relies instead on the normative authority of the law, and its most powerful battle cry is "but it is legal." The states these citizens constitute as "we, the people" readily offer their laws to foreign asset holders and lease their courts to enforce foreign law as if it were home-grown, even if this deprives them of tax revenue or the ability to implement the policy preferences of their own citizens.[21] For the global capitalists, this is the best of all worlds, because they get to pick and choose the laws that are most favorable to them without having to invest heavily in politics to bend the law their way.

Like most empires of the past, the empire of law is a patchwork; it consists not of a single global law, but of select domestic laws that are knit together by rules, including conflict-of-law rules that ensure the recognition and enforcement of these domestic laws elsewhere, as well as select international treaty law.[22] The decentered nature of the law that is used to code global capital has many advantages. It means that global commerce and finance can thrive without a global state or a global law; and it allows those in the know to pick and choose the rules that best suit their or their clients' interests. In this way, the empire of law severs the umbilical cord between the individual's self-interest and social concerns. The legal decoding of capital reveals Smith's invisible hand as a substitute for a reliable legal code—visible even if often hidden from sight, and with a legal infrastructure firmly in place that is global in scope—that is no longer serving its purpose. Effective legal protection almost anywhere allows private self-interest to flourish without the need to return home to benefit from local institutions. Capital coded in portable law is footloose; gains can be made and pocketed anywhere and the losses can be left wherever they fall.

The Enigma of Capital

Capital is a term we use constantly, but its meaning remains obscure.[23] Ask any person on the street and she will probably equate capital with money. But as Marx has explained in the introductory chapter to *Das Kapital*, money and capital are not the same.[24] Rather, in his view capital is produced in a process that includes the exchange of goods for money and the extraction of surplus from labor.

In fact, the term capital was in use long before Marx immortalized the concept. The social historian Fernand Braudel traces it back to the thirteenth century, when it was used to denote interchangeably a fund of money, goods, or money rented out for interests,[25] at least where this was permissible.[26] Definitions abound, even today, as

Geoffrey Hodgson has shown in a careful review of the literature.[27] To some, capital is a tangible object, or "physical stuff."[28] To this day, many economists and accountants insist that capital must be tangible; if you can't touch it, it ain't capital.[29] To others it is one of the two factors of production; or just an accounting variable.[30] And to Marxists, capital is at the heart of fraught social relations between labor and its exploiters who own the means of production, which gives them the power to extract surplus from labor. The historiography of capitalism does not offer much clarity either. Some historians confine the "age of capital" to the period of heavy industrialization; others, however, have pushed the concept back in time, to periods of agricultural or commercial capitalism.[31] Our own post-industrial age has been labeled alternatively the age of financial or global capitalism.

What makes the concepts of capital and capitalism so confusing is that the outward appearance of capital has changed dramatically over time, as have the social relations that underpin it. Against this background, one might even question whether it makes sense to bundle historical epochs that differ so fundamentally from one another under a single rubric of "capitalism." In this book, I will take the position that we can, indeed that we should do so, but to justify this we need to dig deeper and understand the making of capital itself.

To start with, it is critical to note that capital is not a thing; neither can it be pinned down to a specific period of time, a political regime, or just one set of antagonistic social relations as between the proletariat and the bourgeoisie.[32] These manifestations of capital and capitalism have changed dramatically, yet capital's source code has remained almost unchanged throughout. Many of the legal institutions we still use today to code capital were first invented in the time of feudalism, as Rudden observed in the quote provided earlier in this chapter.

Marx noted already that ordinary objects must undergo some transformation before they can be traded in exchange for money to set in motion a process by which profits are made. He labeled this process commodification, a necessary but, as we will see, not a sufficient step in the coding of capital, and he also recognized the possibility of commodifying labor. Karl Polanyi disagreed with Marx about classifying land, labor, or money as commodities. Only items that are *"produced* for the market" qualify as commodities, he argued, and none of these assets are.[33] Polanyi was correct that commodification is man-made, but he erred on the nature of this transformation at the hands of humans: not a physical production process, but legal coding is key. For commodification alone, two of the code's attributes will do: priority and universality. However, to attain the utmost legal protection, durability or convertibility must be added to the mix. Capitalism, it turns out, is more than just the exchange of goods in a market economy; it is a market economy in which some assets are placed on legal steroids.[34]

Contrary to Polanyi and many economists today, even humans can be coded as capital. This is at odds with neoclassical accounts that describe the production function as the sum of capital (K) and labor (L), the two factors of production, which together produce goods, or Q.[35] This equation treats both K and L as quantities, the price of which is determined by their relative scarcity. It ignores the power of the legal code. In fact, with a little bit of legal engineering, L can easily be turned into K. Many a freelancer, for example, has discovered that she can *capitalize* her labor by establishing a corporate entity, contributing her services to it in kind and taking out dividends as the corporation's shareholder in lieu of a salary—thereby benefiting from a lower tax rate.[36] The only input to this entity is human, but with some legal coding, it has been transformed into capital. Defining capital as non-human is also at odds with the rise of property rights in ideas and know-how, such as patents, copyrights, and trademarks, often collectively referred to as "intellectual property rights." What else are they but the legal coding of human ingenuity?

Another reason why humans are often excluded from the definition of capital is that they cannot offer themselves as collateral and thereby monetize their own labor.[37] But as I have just shown, they can contribute their labor as capital to a firm. Law is malleable, and it is easy to mold human labor as an in-kind contribution. Moreover, when slavery *was* legal, slaves were not only owned; they were widely used as collateral to secure loans—in the United States this was often done by investors from the Northern, slave-free states, who thereby helped sustain an inhumane system, even as they condemned it in public.[38] As a result, when slavery was finally abolished and the formerly enslaved men, women, and children were set free, their former owners lost what to them had been a valuable economic asset.[39] Of course, their economic loss pales against the fate their former slaves had suffered at their hands, which at the time was sanctioned by the inhumane recognition and enforcement of property rights in humans.[40] The point is that the history of slavery illustrates the power (not the morality!) of the legal code in the making and taking of capital, but also of human dignity.

To fully appreciate the versatility of capital, we have to move beyond simple classifications and understand how capital obtains the qualities that distinguish it from other assets. Economists in the "old" institutionalist tradition have come close, but their contributions have largely been forgotten.[41] Thorstein Veblen, for example, suggested that capital is an asset's "income-yielding capacity."[42] And in his seminal book *The Legal Foundations of Capitalism,* John Commons defined capital as "the present value of expected beneficial behavior of other people."[43] In his account, law takes center stage in enhancing the reliability of others' expected behavior. As he documented, in the late nineteenth century, US courts extended the notion of property rights from the right to use an object at the exclusion of others to protect asset holders' expectations to future returns. Once this was done, these expectations could not only be taxed; they could be exchanged and re-invested, and violators of these interests, including the state, could be charged with compensation for damages.[44]

Bringing this line of argument to its logical conclusion, Jonathan Levy defines capital as "legal property [that is] assigned a pecuniary value in expectation of a likely future pecuniary income."[45] In short, capital is a *legal* quality that helps create and protect wealth. This book will shed light on how exactly the critical legal attributes are grafted onto assets and the work that key legal institutions, the code's modules, have done for centuries in creating new capital assets.

Once we recognize that capital owes its wealth-creating capacity to its legal coding, we can see that in principle, any asset can be turned into capital. Viewed in this light, there is nothing new about the "new capitalism."[46] Capitalism's changing face, including its most recent turn to "financialization," can be explained by the fact that old coding techniques have migrated from real assets, such as land, to what economists like to call legal fictions: assets that are protected by corporate or trust veils, and intangibles that are created in law.[47]

Capital's Legal Attributes

In law, the term "code" is typically used for voluminous books that compile legal rules. Prominent examples are the big codifications of the nineteenth century, such as the French and German civil and commercial codes.[48] I use the term to show how certain legal institutions have been combined and recombined in a highly modular fashion to code capital. Looking back, the most important modules that were used for this purpose, but by no means the only ones, were contracts, property, collateral, the law of trusts and corporations, as well as bankruptcy law. How these modules operate will be explored in greater detail in the chapters to come. For now, it is sufficient to understand that these modules bestow critical attributes on an asset and thereby make it fit for wealth creation, namely priority, durability, convertibility, and universality.

Priority rights operate like an ace in a game of cards—ranking claims and privilege over weaker titles. Having priority rights is critical for a creditor when the debtor suffers economic ruin and all her creditors will descend on her assets at once. This is when owners can request their property, and secured creditors are able to pull out the assets they have secured and sell them to recover their loss, whereas the unsecured creditors have to settle for the leftovers. Property rights confer title to an owner and allow her to remove an asset she owns from the pool of assets that are in the possession of a bankrupt debtor, no matter how loudly other creditors might protest. Collateral law works in a similar way. The holder of a mortgage, pledge, or other security interest may not have full title to the asset, but she has a stronger right than creditors without such protection,

i.e., the *unsecured* creditors.[49] Bankruptcy can therefore be called
the acid test for the legal rights that have been created long before
bankruptcy loomed.

Hernando de Soto, a life-long advocate for bringing property
rights to the poor, has suggested that these rights can turn "dead
land" into "life capital," because owners can mortgage their land or
other assets to obtain investment capital.[50] And yet, this is only half
of capital's full story. Without additional legal safeguards, debtors
risk losing their assets to creditors if and when they default on their
payments, even if this happens through no fault of their own. History
books are filled with cases of debtors who have lost not only their
family silver, but their shirts to creditors in times of severe economic
downturns. Asset holders who wish to turn their assets into lasting
wealth therefore crave not just priority, but also durability.

Durability extends priority claims in time. Legal coding can extend the life span of assets and asset pools, even in the face of competing claimants, by insulating them from too many creditors. As
long as it was not allowed to seize all the land of a debtor, even if it
had been mortgaged, land could serve as a reliable source of wealth,
which could be transferred from generation to generation. Not just
any firm, but the ones that are organized as legal entities, can have
an indefinite life span; short of putting them to death by liquidation,
they can operate forever and incubate wealth for a changing roster
of owners or shareholders. Creditors of the corporation itself can
seize its assets should it default on a loan; but, as we will see, the
corporation's own shareholders cannot gain access to these assets,
and neither can the shareholders' personal creditors.[51] Because of
its ability to shield its assets from all but its direct creditors, even
its own shareholders, the corporation has become one of the most
enduring institutions of capitalism.

The third attribute is universality, which not only ensures that
priority and durability will affect the parties who agreed to be bound
by them, but that these attributes will be upheld against anybody,
or *erga omnes* in Latin legalese. Universality sheds a crucial light on
the nature of capital and its relation to state power. A simple agreement between two parties can exert influence only between the two

contracting parties, but it cannot bind others. It takes a powerful third party to extend priority and durability rights against the world such that others will yield.

Convertibility is the final attribute of capital's code; it gives asset owners an explicit or implicit guarantee to convert their assets into state money when they can no longer find private takers. Convertibility presumes the right to freely transfer an asset. In the past, even simple debt obligations had to be performed by the original parties to the contract. But convertibility adds another dimension to the simple right to transfer (or assign) legal obligations: it gives asset holders access to state money, the only asset that can retain its nominal value (not necessarily its real value, as the history of inflation documents).[52] The reason is that the money states issue as legal tender is backed by the coercive powers of that state, including the power to unilaterally impose liabilities on others, i.e. its citizens. This is what turns state money into a reliable store of value and explains its unique status among attempts to create private money, the private debt that is coded in law, or more recently, the cryptocurrencies that use digits instead.[53] For financial assets, convertibility is more important than durability, indeed, is an effective substitute. It allows the holders of these assets to lock in past gains at a time when other market participants no longer value them.

State, Power and Capital

The code of capital is a legal code; it owes its power to law that is backed and enforced by a state. We may negotiate contracts with others and we may treat them as binding, whether or not they would be enforceable in a court of law. We may even find an arbiter to resolve any disputes that might threaten the full implementation of a commitment we made in the past. If the world consisted only of such simple deals, law would be trivial, even superfluous;[54] and for lawyers, such a world would be rather boring.

Things become more interesting (and more realistic) only in the face of competing claims to the same asset. Individuals buy or lease cars, rent an apartment or mortgage a house, receive salaries, buy bonds or shares, and deposit money in a bank account. Entrepreneurs buy input, hire employees, rent premises, make investments, enter into contracts for electricity and water, owe taxes, collect money from selling goods, and pay back loans to creditors. As long as every obligation is met and every bill paid as it becomes due, many legal issues remain invisible. They come to the surface with a vengeance, however, when the individual or entity at the center of this web of claims falls behind; when liabilities mount, asset values decline, and it becomes apparent that not all claimants will get what they had contracted for at the outset. When insolvency looms, insisting on contract enforcement is no longer an answer; instead, it is time to decide who gets how much and in what order.

Absent such a decision, the first creditor who arrives on the scene is likely to take it all—a practice that was common before the invention of bankruptcy law. Its purpose was to avoid a run on the debtor's assets, a market failure that in most cases destroys any chance of reorganization or the efficient reallocation of the debtor's assets.[55] Most bankruptcy codes today impose a simple rank order. Owners can take out their assets, secured creditors can pull the collateral from the pool and sell it to obtain satisfaction, and unsecured creditors get the leftovers on a pro-rata basis.

In the best of worlds, creditors with weaker rights as compared to others would yield voluntarily. Creditors who are in danger of losing, however, may not be so inclined. Enforcing priority rights effectively involves more than finding a solution to a coordination game; someone must stand in for, and, if necessary, execute these rights. In fact, modern economies are built around a complex network of legal rights of different standing that are backed by coercive state power.[56]

When trade and commerce take place primarily within tightly knit communities, formal law enforcement may not be needed. Everybody in that community will know who has better rights; after all, this is how things have always been done. As long as most members of the group continue to abide by established norms, there will be little need for complex legal systems, courts, and enforcement powers. However, when trade and commerce extend beyond the boundaries of established spheres of exchange where norms and entrenched hierarchies are known to all, a different mode of social ordering becomes necessary, one that is capable of upholding stronger claims even against strangers.[57] States and state law are examples of such institutions, and they have been critical for the rise of capitalism.

To be sure, law may not always succeed in garnering respect, and states may at times lack the resources to make enforcement credible. In many societies law is not perceived to be legitimate and compliance tends to be weak. Many countries that received their formal legal system by imposition during the era of colonization and imperialism tend to have weaker legal institutions than countries that developed their formal legal institutions internally.[58] Under such conditions, the modules of the code will not produce lasting wealth effects. Instead, private wealth will be guarded by physical force, stacked in foreign bank accounts, or coded in foreign law with foreign courts standing by to back it.[59]

Law is a powerful social ordering technology; it has been used for centuries to scale social relations beyond close-knit communities and to assure strangers that they can risk transacting with one another to the tune of billions of dollars without ever having to come face to face. This is so because law that is backed by the threat of coercive enforcement increases the likelihood that the commitments that private parties made to one another and the privileges they obtained will be recognized and enforced without regard to preexisting social ties or competing norms and that these legal claims will even be respected by strangers. What exactly gives law this scaling power? This question has concerned social and legal theorists for generations.[60] One answer to this question is that law is backed by the coercive powers of a state; another reason is law's capacity to focus collective expectations that minimize deviant behavior and encourage decentralized, private enforcement.

Max Weber explained the power of law by invoking the state's monopoly over the means of coercion.[61] Through its courts, bailiffs, and police forces, states enforce not only their own commands, but also private property rights and the binding commitments private parties make to one another. This does not mean that state power is omnipresent. As long as the threat of coercive law enforcement is sufficiently credible, voluntary compliance can be achieved without mobilizing it in every case.[62] Others have argued that systems of law can evolve in the absence of coercive state power.[63] People have been governing themselves since long before the emergence of modern nation-states. All it takes for effective self-governance is a central authority that is capable of proclaiming a binding interpretation of rules and principles. With this in place, enforcement can be left to private parties, because they have powerful self-interests to help others to enforce their claims in accordance with known and respected norms, knowing they might need similar support in the future. Private parties may not have sheriffs or prisons at their disposal, but they can shame, shun, and expel members from the group.

This coordination game, however, is likely to work best in settings where all market participants have comparable assets and interests. In capitalist systems, however, not all assets are equal; some asset holders have better rights than others. When the rank order of competing claims is in dispute, relying on others to protect one's own claims now, against a vague promise to reciprocate at some future date, is unlikely to work. The more diverse the assets and the more uneven their distribution, the greater the need for coercive law enforcement, and thus for states and their coercive powers. Herein lies the deeper reason for why states and capital are joined at the hip.

The fact that capital has become global does not refute the argument that state power is central for capitalism. For capital's global mobility is a function of a legal support structure that is ultimately backed by states. Many states have committed themselves under their own domestic law, or in international treaties, to recognize the priority rights that were created under foreign law. They regularly enforce foreign law in their own courts and lend their coercive powers to executing the rulings of foreign courts or arbitration tribunals. This legal infrastructure is the backbone for global capitalism and explains why today's merchants no longer have to venture home to protect their spoils.

An Exorbitant Privilege

The story about capital and its legal code is complicated, as the legal modules that are used are complex and hidden in arcane statutory or case law and the plot frequently develops behind the closed doors of large law firms, with only a rare airing in a court of law or parliament. The legal code confers attributes that greatly enhance the prospects of some assets and their respective owners to amass wealth, relative to others—an exorbitant privilege.[64] Choosing the assets and grafting onto them the legal attributes of priority, durability, universality, and convertibility is tantamount to controlling the levers for the distribution of wealth in society.

This account contradicts the standard argument that capitalist economies are defined by free markets that allocate scarce resources efficiently and that prices reflect the fundamental value of assets.[65] Many legal scholars have already drawn attention to the fact that the operation of the market hinges on legal institutions that facilitate price discovery.[66] I go a step further and argue that the legal coding accounts for the value of assets, and thus for the creation of wealth and its distribution. This should be only too apparent with respect to financial assets and intellectual property rights that do not exist outside the law. However, it is also true for simpler assets that were used as the prototypes for legal coding, such as land or pools of assets held together in firms.

States and state law are central to the coding of capital. States have not only dismantled existing rights and privileges to make room for the power of market forces, as Polanyi has pointed out.[67] Capital and capitalism would not exist without the coercive powers of states.[68] States often do not, in fact they need not, control the legal coding process itself. Indeed, at the frontiers where new capital rights are minted day by day in the offices of law firms, states take a back seat. But states provide the legal tools that lawyers use; and they offer their law enforcement apparatus to enforce the capital that lawyers have crafted. Not all coding strategies will go unchallenged, and some of them will be struck down at a future date. Many, however, will never be scrutinized and others will survive the challenge; and the few that are eventually struck down often have already produced fortunes for their holders.

The ability to graft the code's modules onto an ever-changing roster of assets makes lawyers the true masters of the code of capital. In principle, anybody has access to lawyers and their coding skills, but the market for legal services ensures that only the best-paying clients can hire the most skillful among them. The specifics about how assets are selected for legal coding are rarely scrutinized. The common depictions of law as stable, almost sacrosanct, immunize from the public eye the work that is done more and more in private law firms, and less and less in parliaments or even courtrooms.

The states' willingness to recognize and enforce privately coded capital, indeed to foster it by recognizing innovative coding strategies and the expansion of asset classes that can be legally coded as capital, may seem puzzling. Many a state has fallen for the promise that expanding the legal options for some, including offering them exemptions from general laws and other legal privileges, will enlarge the pie and offer greater prosperity for all. They frequently realize only later that the trickle is often rather small. More important, most of the benefits from capital do not trickle down; they trickle up to capital holders who repatriate their gains or place them behind the legal shields other jurisdictions afford them to protect their wealth from tax and other creditors.[69]

Another explanation is that states themselves have more to gain than to lose from privileging capital by backing the private coding efforts that create it. States benefit from economic growth, because it boosts their tax revenue and allows them to raise debt finance. The fate of governments in democracies in particular has been tied ever more closely to their governments' ability to produce growth. Growth rates, and the rise of stock markets, not the distribution of wealth or indices of human development, have become the standard measures for adjudicating success or failure of elected governments—in itself an indicator of the enormous cognitive sway capital has over polities. Yet, as many states have realized, the power of the tax sword has been blunted by sophisticated legal coding strategies that can hide assets from their reach. Even more generally, promoting the interests of capital first and foremost boosts private, not necessarily national, wealth and thereby fosters inequality.[70] To see why this is so, we need to decode the legal structures of capital.

Summary and Outlook

In this introductory chapter, I have outlined the major themes of this book: Capital is coded in law, and, more specifically, in institutions of private law, including property, collateral, trust, corporate, bankruptcy law, and contract law. These are the legal modules that bestow critical legal attributes on the select assets that give them a comparative advantage over others in creating new and protecting old wealth. Once properly coded, capital assets enjoy priority and durability, are convertible into cash, or legal tender, and, critically, these attributes will be enforced *against the world*, thereby attaining universality. This works because states back and, if necessary, coercively enforce the legal code of capital, whether or not they had a direct hand in choosing the coding strategy for the asset in question.

Recognizing that capital is made, and not simply the product of superior skills, shifts attention to the processes by which different assets are slated for legal coding and to the states that endorse relevant legal modules and offer their coercive powers to enforce them. As I will show, this process is both decentralized and, in only seeming contradiction, increasingly global. Private attorneys perform most of the work on behalf of their clients, and states, for their part, offer their own legal systems as a menu from which private parties get to pick and choose. As a result, many polities have lost the ability to control the creation and distribution of wealth.

In the following chapters, I will illustrate this argument by showing how different asset classes have been coded as capital, starting with land (chapter 2) and moving on to firms (chapter 3), debt (chapter 4), and know-how (chapter 5). This survey sets the stage for unpacking the legal order that sustains global capitalism in the absence of a global state or a global legal system (chapter 6) and for exploring the rise of the global legal profession, the masters of the code (chapter 7). While law has been the foremost coding technique for the past several centuries, it is no longer the only contender for claims across time and space; the digital code has become a close competitor. However, as I will argue in chapter 8, its greatest powers will likely come not from offering an alternative to the legal code, but from using the legal code as a shield to protect private gains.

The questions of access to and the distribution of legal coding powers will be raised throughout the book, but they are taken up more fully in the book's final chapter, entitled "Capital Rules by Law." There I will argue that the coding of capital occurs typically in a much more decentralized fashion than Marxists would have it. Asset holders do not need to capture the state directly, much less win class struggles or revolutions; all they need is the right lawyers on their side who code their assets in law. This highly fragmented way of deciding how wealth is distributed in society raises fundamental political and normative questions. After all, law is the predominant means by which democracies govern themselves; yet the law they furnish is used by private parties, the holders of capital assets and their lawyers, to advance their private interests. As the code of capital has become portable, it has taken over the space that was once occupied by the invisible hand. The creeping erosion of the legitimacy of states and their laws in the face of growing inequality is a direct result of this structural bias that is rooted in the legal code of capital. The increasing threat to law's legitimacy may turn out to be capital's greatest threat yet.

2

Coding Land

The Maya peoples of Belize scored a legal victory at the country's Supreme Court in 2007, when the court recognized their collective land use practice as a property right that was protected by the constitution.[1] The case offers a glimpse into the making of property rights and highlights the critical role courts often play in vindicating practices as law—if only after centuries of denials and decades of legal battle. The legal battle of the Maya against their own government also shows that the question of which claims are worthy of property rights protection does not precede but is imbued with state power.[2] As will become apparent, the Maya had to learn the bitter but not uncommon lesson that, absent the state's willingness to back their claims, their legal victory was at best a partial one; and at worst toothless. Finally, the case illustrates that states are not neutral when it comes to whose interests in an asset shall be given priority; promises of future gains are more likely to find their blessing than claims that assert self-governance or seek to ensure environmental sustainability.

Land has played an outsized role for much of human history, as a source of sustenance and for our cultural identity, along with social, economic, and political life. Even today, billions of people still literally live off the land, harvesting its fruit, grazing animals, and using the water it carries and its underground resources.[3] Rural land constituted the most important source of wealth even in industrializing countries into the early twentieth century.[4] Since then, intangibles, including financial assets and intellectual property rights, have outpaced land in the creation of wealth, but these assets use the same legal modules that were first tried and tested for coding land as capital.

This chapter unpacks the development of the basic techniques for coding capital that were first used for land and later transposed to other assets. By coding land as private property, individuals could capture its monetary value at the expense of others. Landowners, however, soon discovered that these priority rights might not protect them against their own creditors; they needed to add durability to priority to protect land as their family wealth and they found lawyers who set up a trust or corporate entity to which assets could be transferred, and thereby protected from various groups of creditors. But the story of the Maya and their quest to legally code their claims to the land also holds the promise that legal coding might be used for purposes other than private wealth maximization; as the reasoning of the highest court of Belize suggests, property rights can take many shapes and forms, and they might just as well be used to protect collective use rights and sustainable practices.

From Usage to Legal Title

The Earth's surface is an abundant resource for humans and other living beings. It is part of nature and, unlike financial assets, legal persons, or intellectual property, it has existed since before humans conquered the Earth.[5] Human conquest has taken different forms over the millennia, subjecting land to occupation, cultivation, excavation, construction, and, last but not least, legal coding. When competing groups fought over access to the same land, they often fought over land itself. Legal dispute settlement offers an alternative and perhaps more peaceful way to clarify priority rights, although the results can be as brutal as physical conquest; indeed, legal battles over land have often gone hand in hand with the battles on the ground.

The dispute between the Maya and the government of Belize pitted indigenous peoples with a long history of occupancy on the land that is now part of the state of Belize against the country's government. At the heart of the dispute was the fact that the government had granted concessions to logging and mining companies without consulting the Maya or offering them any compensation for the losses they incurred as a result. The Maya and their legal representatives—a law clinic from a US law school[6]—claimed that they had a superior right to the land and that by granting concessions to investors to exploit the land's natural resources, the government had violated their property rights. The Maya, however, had no formal title to the land. The question for the court to decide was whether informal occupancy and established collective use practices over centuries qualified as a property right under the country's constitution.

The constitution of Belize provides that every person has a right to "protection from arbitrary deprivation of property";[7] and further, that "no property of any description shall be compulsorily acquired except by or under a law" that stipulates the principles for reasonable compensation and grants recourse to the courts, and only for a public purpose.[8] This language resembles the Fourteenth Amendment of the US Constitution, which states that no person "shall be deprived of life, liberty or property, without due process of law."[9] Neither constitution, however, defines what property *is*, and these two are by no means exceptions. Most countries' constitutions presume property rights but don't define them, and it is rare to find so much as a reference to who, within the constitutional order, has the power to define new property rights or alter existing ones.[10]

The Maya claimed that their centuries-old use practices gave them priority rights to their land, which they should be able to use as they wished. They offered evidence that their ancestors had already lived by similar rules that governed access by members of their community to the land and its resources. This basic governance structure had remained intact for centuries, notwithstanding dramatic changes, including their dislocation and decimation under colonial rule. Perhaps these use practices did not look like the private property rights that are typically used to turn simple assets into capital in capitalist systems. But nowhere in the Belize Constitution does it say that property rights have to take a specific form; i.e., that only rights that are purposefully installed to produce future returns rather than, say, to ensure the sustenance of a people and the sustainability of their environment, is a defining feature of property.

The court organized its inquiry into three parts: first, it inquired into the nature of the relations the Maya had to the land; second, it asked whether these relations had in fact survived colonial conquest, first by the Spanish and later by the British; and finally, it turned to the question of whether the claimed right was in fact a property right under the country's post-independence constitution. Because the Maya asserted property rights, they had to prove their case. Anthropologists were flown in to testify about the practices of the Maya today and in the past, and historians parsed the difference between sovereignty and private property rights. The fact that the Maya had used the land subject to "unwritten customary rules and values that form part of the social, cultural, and political organization of our communities" was not really in dispute.[11] The real question was whether the government of Belize could claim superior rights and therefore had the legal power to grant concessions to mining companies on the Maya's land without their approval and without compensation for taking their land.

The government of Belize argued that whatever claims the Maya might have had in the distant past, British colonial conquest had put an end to them. Colonial conquest had undone not only their sovereignty, but also their property rights. As the legal successor to the British Crown, the state of Belize therefore now held the exclusive right to all land that had not been formally titled, which gave it the power to grant logging and mining concessions as it wished.[12] This is quite a case to be made by a government of a country that acquired independence only in 1981, but the argument had some legal appeal, because under international law Britain and other Western powers have forged over centuries, sovereignty indeed passes hands when power is transferred.[13] Nonetheless, it did not prove to be a winning argument, because the court drew a line between territorial sovereignty and private property.[14] There were no records showing that the British Crown explicitly over-ruled preexisting individual or collective rights to land. A complete reordering of preexisting property rights in occupied territories, according to the court, would have required some purposeful act, and this was not apparent. The fact that the Crown had granted concessions to some (British) mining companies on those terri-tories without much regard to preexisting rights, even that it had reassumed control over the land in question after such companies had gone bankrupt, was deemed insufficient for proving an intent to alter property rights on the ground.

This then set the stage for assessing the legal quality of the Maya's claims to their land. The court framed its argument by citing a case of the Privy Council from 1921 about a land dispute in Nigeria, another former colony of Great Britain. The Privy Council has its origins in the old King's Council; its Judicial Committee serves as the highest court of appeal for members of the British Commonwealth that still accepted its jurisdiction after independence. Belize did so until 2010, when it delegated the power of judicial oversight to the Caribbean Court of Justice instead.

As the Privy Council opined in its 1921 ruling,

There is a tendency, operating at times unconsciously, to render that title conceptually in terms which are appropriate only to systems which have grown up under English law. But this ten-dency has to be held in check. [. . .] [A] community may have the possessory title to the common enjoyment of a usufruct, with customs under which its individual members are admitted to en-joyment, and even to a right of transmitting the individual enjoy-ment as members by assignment inter vivos or by succession. To ascertain how far this latter development of right has progressed involves the study of the history of the particular community and its usages in each case. Abstract principles fashioned a priori are of but little assistance and are as often as not misleading.[15]

Property rights, in other words, come in many different forms, and it falls to courts to discern their specific contents and meaning by observing actual practices rather than imposing their own pre-conception. With this in mind, the Belize Supreme Court proceeded to describe the legal nature of the land use practices, based on accounts that were provided by the expert witnesses. The Maya's land practices were "of a usufructuary nature" and comprised the right to "occupy the land, farm, hunt and fish thereon, and to take for their own use and benefit the fruits and resources thereof."[16] These rights were held not individually, but in community.

But did this amount to a property right under the country's constitution? In search of an answer to this question, the court turned to the preamble of the Belize Constitution. The state shall protect the "identity, dignity and social and cultural values" of all peoples of Belize, it says. In addition, the court cited other constitutional provisions, including protections against discrimination, and finally, it turned to the country's statute on property law. Property, this statute declares, "includes any *thing* in action and any interest in real and personal property."[17] The Maya's use rights, the court reasoned, fit into an "interest in real property," but the definition is so open-ended that one wonders what does *not* constitute a property right.

The point of following the court's reasoning in some detail here is to illuminate the process by which property rights are made into law—typically not in a top-down fashion by statute, not even by constitutional law. Rather, they are negotiated case by case by matching actual practices to legal concepts. The process of legal reasoning is much more open-ended than conventional claims about the benefits of "clear property rights" would have us believe, and typically involves multiple sources of law.[18] Some arguments may be more persuasive than others, and in many cases, there can be more than one right answer. Legal scholars in the realist and critical legal studies tradition made this point long ago.[19] Whether this means that law is but a disguise for the exercise of naked power is debated to this day. But one need not adopt such a radical position to see that the fashioning of property rights in law is a complex process that is pregnant with value judgments and power.

In the case of the Maya, the Supreme Court of Belize bent to the calls for justice for indigenous peoples that had, at long last, received UN backing with an international convention adopted in 1989.[20] With an open mind to their plight, it consulted case law of the Privy Council, the Inter-American Commission on Human Rights (IACHR), as well as that of other courts in Australia, New Zealand, and Canada, which were dealing with similar legal issues contemporaneously. With the exception of the decisions of the Privy Council, these decisions were not binding on the Belize court, and the court made clear that it used them only in an advisory capacity. Still, there is little doubt that they influenced the court's interpretation of Belize law and the Belize Constitution.

After extensive hearings, the court handed a legal victory to the Maya, but the government of Belize simply ignored the ruling of its own supreme court and continued to encourage mining on their lands. The Maya won a battle but were unable to win the war against their own government, on the legal protection of which their own priority rights depended.

Turning Land into Private Property

The Maya desired legal protection of their rights to the land, but the notion of individualized private property was an alien concept for them. Their claims to their land followed a different logic, one of common use, of managing access to and protecting the land and its resources as the foundation for their way of life. They certainly had no intention of turning their land into capital and extracting its monetary value. It is one of the paradoxes of history that they sought protection in property rights, the same legal modules that landlords in England had used half a millennium earlier, not to protect but to destroy a similar set of collective rights, the commons.

The enclosure of the commons started in the early 1500s, with the Enclosure Acts that Parliament enacted only between 1720 and 1840 marking the tail end of the movement.[21] Estimates suggest that by 1600 most arable land in England was already enclosed, leaving only about 24 percent of land that was still held in common, most of which was wasteland.[22] To understand the enclosure of land, we therefore must go beyond the big Enclosure Acts and take a closer look at the legal and physical enclosure battles that preceded them.

Under feudalism, land was not freely alienable but rather assigned in exchange for military and other services and political loyalty. The transfer of land conferred specific use rights, not full title, including the right to the fruits of the land and jurisdiction over the peasants who tilled it. Neither landlords nor tenants, much less peasants, could transfer the land at their free will. Transfer upon death was subject to mandatory primogeniture rules, giving priority to the first-born son. Neither could land be repossessed by creditors, not even secured creditors. Creditors could claim the fruits of the land, but under the *writ of elegit*, a statute dating back to 1285, they could claim at most half of the land, and even this only for as long as it took for the fruits of the land to cover past debt.[23]

These restrictions did not exist because alternatives were unknown. Early English treaties compiled prior to the Norman conquest followed the Roman legal tradition, which treated land just like other objects of property rights.[24] In Roman law a property right was considered an absolute right that included the right to use, possess, and alienate an asset. However, following the Norman conquest, legal practice in England increasingly ignored these treaties. For two centuries, from 1290 to 1490, the terms "property" and "ownership" dropped out of the vocabulary in court cases concerning land, even as these terms continued to be used for "chattel," that is, goods and animals. Rights to land were neither unified nor absolute; there were only "greater" or "higher" rights, and only the king could claim an *absolute* right to the land. Yet, already by the end of the 1600s, a remarkable change had taken place. "A grand rule was emerging: *whoever* had the 'general' or 'absolute' property in a thing could assert the interest against everyone in the world, and whoever had the 'special' property (like a specific use right or collateral), could assert it against everyone but the 'general' or 'absolute' owner."[25]

This legal transformation of the law of realty occurred in lockstep with the enclosure movement, in which landlords asserted absolute rights over the land they had earlier shared with the commoners—the peasants who tilled the land or grazed their cattle on it.[26] In pursuit of their exclusive rights, the landlords built hedges and fences, and petitioned local courts claiming title based on first use. The commoners responded by tearing down the same hedges and fences, ploughing over the land the landlords had set aside for grazing sheep, and also petitioning the courts.

Both sides faced substantial legal uncertainty. There were no titles or title registries—England introduced a voluntary land registry only in 1881 and made it mandatory as late as 1925.[27] The whole battle therefore was about whose claim to the land the courts would recognize as superior and on what grounds. Both sides relied on custom and legal tradition. Long-term occupancy and continued land use could sway a court to recognize a superior right; conversely, the failure of the commoners to challenge changing use patterns for too long could be read as yielding to superior rights held by others. Legal battles were therefore not an alternative to the landlords' attempt to hedge and fence what they claimed to be theirs, nor were the commoners' breaking them; the physical and legal battles over the land went hand in hand.

Courts did not always side with the landlords who spearheaded the enclosure movement. Some cases lingered in courts for decades and spanned generations as the rulings swung back and forth between landlords and commoners.[28] In the long run, though, landlords prevailed in court, and this ultimately gave them the upper hand on the grounds as well. For their part, the commoners were not oblivious to legal strategies and often had lawyers representing them. In the end, however, they suffered from several disadvantages. The landlords described the commoners as rioters who stood in the way of new land use practices that promised not only greater returns for them, but, so they claimed in a move that rings familiar even today, prosperity for all.

The common law courts heard some of the cases; however, most disputes were taken to the Star Chamber, a late thirteenth century spinoff from the King's Council, which later morphed into the chancery courts. These courts were freed from the rigidities of the common law and, instead, ruled in equity, that is, on broad principles of justice, and since the reign of Elizabeth I (1558–1603), they were increasingly used as a corrective to the common law courts. Unlike the common law courts with their jury trials, the chancery courts followed a written procedure. Neither plaintiff nor defendant appeared in court, and instead were examined by a clerk of the court in London or by a commissioner in the country. While this may have compensated for lack of literacy on the part of many commoners, it also left them at the mercy of clerks and commissioners who portrayed them in the court filings.

Finally, landlords may well have had the better lawyers on their side. Lawyers who served private clients were known in England since the thirteenth century, but a true legal profession did not come about until the late sixteenth century. Statistical data are incomplete and are available only for some institutions but are indicative of a broader trend. Between the 1590s and the 1630s, the number of lawyers called to the bar at the Inns of Court, for example, increased by 40 percent; and between 1578 and 1633, the number of attorneys enrolled in the court of Common Pleas increased from 342 to 1,383, that is, by a factor of four. Equally important, many lawyers came from the same social ranks as their future clients and invariably shared with them a common worldview.[29]

The successful enclosure of the land created the conditions for an emerging land market—a radical change in societies that had revolved around stable relations to land, which provided sustenance and also served as the foundation of political and economic power. Land sales rose steadily since the late 1500s and by 1610 were 250 percent higher than 50 years earlier.[30] Part of this can be attributed to the Crown seizing land owned by monasteries, churches, and bishops and throwing it on the market after its rupture with the pope; but the legal enclosures of land and its increasing use for commercial purposes played a critical role as well.

The legal and doctrinal battles over private property rights in land continued for much of the seventeenth century. Most treaties on property rights continued to assert that the king was the only one to have absolute rights, but some treaties began to prepare the grounds for private individuals to claim similar powers for themselves.[31] By the early 1800s, a digest of case law concluded that "an absolute proprietor hath an absolute Power to dispose of his Estate as he pleases, subject only to the Laws of the Land."[32] A new legal concept of absolute private property rights was born.

This new legal concept has since conquered the world. First, it was taken to the colonies and later it became the blueprint for economic policy advice by the World Bank and other agencies.[33] Wherever English settlers went, there were already "first" people with their own long-standing relations to the land, but nowhere did they encounter the legal concept of private property rights to land. The Crown claimed territorial sovereignty in "settlers' colonies" of North America, Australia, and New Zealand, but territorial sovereignty did not necessarily alter existing rights to the land. Still, legal uncertainty left ample room for settlers to pursue aggressive land acquisition and occupation strategies with the expectation that their claims would eventually be recognized as full legal title.[34]

The Crown sought to balance the possible costs of warfare with the benefits of settlement. To this end, it often entered into treaties with indigenous peoples to demarcate the territory that was left to their autonomous governance. Fearing anarchy and disorder from disputes between settlers and the indigenous peoples that would drag British soldiers into prolonged conflicts, it at times prohibited settlers from venturing beyond these agreed boundaries. However, it either lacked the power and resources to effectively enforce these demarcations or it simply acquiesced in the settlers' land-grabbing tactics. Settlers and land hunters (both individuals and companies), for their part, had strong incentives to gain control over land either by squatting or by cutting land deals with locals.[35] Still, the nature of the right they received in such deals was often vigorously disputed; the settlers claimed absolute property rights, whereas the indigenous peoples asserted that they had only parted with some type of "use rights."

Just like the battle over land enclosures in England in the sixteenth century, many disputes between European settlers and the indigenous peoples ended up in court. In New Zealand, for example, special courts were established to resolve land disputes. They were typically chaired by an English judge, with three chiefs representing indigenous peoples serving on the bench as well. Records from these events are sparse, and it is unlikely that all disputes were won by the settlers. Still, the overall balance tipped in their favor, not least because they relied on two legal arguments: discovery and improvement. The reasoning went as follows: First Peoples had no notion of individual ownership. They may claim prior use over the European settlers, but they could not possibly be said to "own" the land in any legal sense. In contrast, the Europeans *discovered* the land and *improved* it.[36] By switching from seniority, a principle that landowners had invoked regularly in their legal battles with the commoners back home, to discovery and improvement, the presumption of legal title shifted from the First Peoples to the settlers.

The most elaborate statement of the "discovery doctrine" can be found in a US Supreme Court ruling of 1823 in *Johnson v. M'Intosh*. Justice Marshall wrote at the time that

> the United States . . . have unequivocally acceded to that great and broad rule by which its civilized inhabitants now hold this country. They hold, and assert in themselves, the title by which it was acquired. They maintain, as all others have maintained, that discovery gave an exclusive right to extinguish the Indian title of occupancy either by purchase or by conquest; and gave also a right to such a degree of sovereignty, as the circumstances of the people would allow them to exercise.[37]

By virtue of this court ruling, America's First Peoples had become squatters of the land of which they had been the first, and until not too long ago, the only occupants. Soon thereafter, Congress enacted the Indian Removal Act of 1830.[38] American Indians were forced into reservations, and their land was carved up into plots that were zoned and titled into individualized property rights ready to be used for monetary gain; the Indians' land was turned into capital. *M'Intosh* was later overruled, but by that time the fate of the Indian peoples in the United States had been sealed. One of the greatest "conquests by law" had been achieved by altering the cause for recognizing a superior right: discovery and improvement extinguished first in time claims. Discovery and improvement became the winning arguments for settlers who had bet all along that aggressive capture would give them title eventually; similar practices later brought about the "second enclosure movement," this time not of land, but of knowledge.[39]

Protecting the Spoils

Having rights empowers individuals and groups; and the "right to have rights" is inextricably linked to belonging to a legal order backed by a state.[40] By the same token, rights come with strings attached, with obligations and liabilities. This quid pro quo is also at the heart of the argument that private property is efficient: only a private owner is said to fully incorporate the costs of using her asset and thus make the most efficient use of it.[41] After all, she will bear the losses of overuse. Of course, owners prefer to enjoy the benefits of ownership without bearing its costs and they have employed lawyers to help them have their cake and eat it too.

After having secured formal title over the land, English landlords enjoyed exclusive use rights, which were further fortified through legislation that made poaching, breaching hedges, and cutting down trees a felony punishable by death—and without clergy.[42] The landlords were now free to use the land for private gains by herding sheep and selling the wool for profit into textile production; or by growing crops that could be sold to city dwellers. To finance their new ventures, and sometimes only to increase their consumption, they mortgaged their land to creditors. This gave them access to funding, but it also put their new property rights at risk.

Like other forms of collateral, a mortgage gives a creditor additional security in the event the debtor defaults on his loan, in which case the creditor may try to seek satisfaction from the secured asset. In *The Merchant of Venice*, William Shakespeare immortalized the nature of collateral in a rather grizzly fashion. In the play, Antonio asks the merchant Shylock for a bridge loan; his own capital is tied up in a ship that is approaching Venice, but he wants to help out a friend who needs cash immediately to woo the wealthy heiress Portia to marry him. As soon as the ship arrives on shore, he will return the money. Being certain that the illiquidity of funds he is currently experiencing is only temporary, Antonio accepts the condition Shylock demands. Should he fail to repay the loan within 30 days, Shylock shall have the right to carve out from Antonio's body one pound of flesh.

Against all odds, Antonio's ship capsizes, and his liquidity problem turns into an insolvency problem. Antonio has no choice but to default on the loan and Shylock insists on enforcing his collateral, a revenge for Antonio's frequent anti-Semitic tirades against him. The Duke refuses to intervene: a deal is a deal. This is when Portia, disguised as a *doctor of laws*, appears on the scene and uses the skills of legal interpretation to spare Antonio's life.[43] "This bond doth give thee here no jot of blood. The words expressly are 'a pound of flesh'," but no more.[44] Shylock, she suggests, has the right to take his "bond,"

> But in the cutting it, if thou dost shed
> One drop of Christian blood, thy lands and goods
> Are by the laws of Venice confiscate
> Unto the state of Venice.[45]

The English landowners who had mortgaged their land did not face death when their creditors came after them; but they feared for their newly amassed wealth, which they wished to pass on to the next generation. They found willing helpers in the country solicitors who used an old legal institution, the entail, to prevent the family estate from being "sold, mortgaged, or dispersed at will."[46] To the outside world, nothing changed; but the rights to their estate, the land and the family mansion, were recoded. The head of the household was turned from an owner into a life tenant of a family estate that was entailed to his first-born son. The life tenant held the estate on behalf of future generations and therefore could not possibly transfer the right to seize all the property to a creditor. Under the old feudal writ of elegit from 1285, enacted in a very different political and economic order, creditors could seize at most half of the land. The entail turned land from a commodity that could be freely sold into a keep-safe for family wealth. Not modern principles of property rights, but the combination of individual priority rights with medieval-style legal privileges, made these rights durable and thereby turned land into private wealth, or capital.

The attraction of this legal scheme is apparent in statistics that show that by the middle of the nineteenth century, between one-half and two-thirds of all the land in England was entailed and as such subject to strict family settlement.[47] Writing in 1866, the news magazine, *The Economist*, declared the system "wholly absurd" for a country that had found itself in the midst of a rapid industrialization process.[48] And yet, closer scrutiny reveals that the massive accumulation of wealth during the age of industrialization and beyond owes much to legal protections such as the entail that protect holders of capital from their creditors. "The use," "the trust," and later on the corporate form were employed to similar ends.

And yet, even the best coding strategies don't always hold water. The highly complex and opaque system of land relations, with individual property rights at its core but carefully guarded against the rights of creditors who might seize these property rights to cover their claims, increasingly came under stress. At a time when new technologies were becoming more widespread and mining coal and other natural resources fueled the process of industrialization, the legal constraints associated with entailing the land for future generations prevented life tenants from making much needed investments. This would have altered the family estate in violation of the life tenant's legal commitment to maintain the estate intact for the next generation.

For some time, landowners were still able to find creditors willing to lend money or roll over their debt yet another time. To offer these creditors better legal protections, lawyers advised life tenants to negotiate a partial release from the "entail" that protected the family estate from their claims; sometimes, however, the life tenant with the help of his lawyers separated out assets and placed them into a trust to the benefit of certain creditors—a reversal of fortunes, but with identical coding techniques.[49] Banks came up with their own solution; they demanded that life tenants handed over the title deed to the property to secure their loan, which made it impossible to offer the land to other creditors as security; thus the "bankers' mortgage" was born.[50]

But when free trade policies gained ground in the middle of the century, and the corn laws that had protected agriculture from foreign competition through tariffs were repealed in 1846, it was only a matter of time before the economic logic of a carefully crafted but increasingly uncompetitive system would run its course, and it came down like a house of cards: creditors refused to roll over the debt of landowners one more time, over-indebted landowners defaulted on their loans, the credit system ground to a halt, and agricultural production collapsed.

The depression that gripped agriculture in the 1870s finally brought about legal reforms that had been in the making since the 1830s, and, remarkably, had been implemented in England's North American colonies 150 years earlier.[51] Still, without concurrent political change, the project of reforming the English law of realty may well have faulted yet again. As it happened, in 1880 landowners for the first time lost control over the House of Parliament. A year later, the Conveyance and the Settled Land Acts were adopted, which declared the life tenant the rightful owner of the property and allowed creditors to enforce against the entire family estate. Only the family mansion retained a special status: its sale required family members' consent, but if withheld, a court could sanction the sale.[52]

The courts, which had long sided with landowners and protected the coding strategies their lawyers had devised to keep their family wealth intact, now turned against them.[53] A famous case that was filed a few years after the reform legislation was enacted turned the deeply indebted heir of one of the oldest estates in England, the Savernake Forest, against his uncles who sought to prevent him from selling the Tottenham Mansion to Lord Iveagh, the head of the Guinness brewing empire.[54] The case made it all the way to the House of Lords, which approved the sale of the mansion. The reform legislation, the lords ruled, "was to prevent the decay of agriculture." The court therefore had an obligation to consider not only the interests of the parties to the settlement, that is, the "spendthrift peer" and his uncles, but also the "interests of the estate itself, including in that

expression the well-being of the persons from whose industrial oc-
cupations its rents and profits are derived"—the peasants and other
workers whose livelihoods also depended on the productivity of the
land. Private property, in the eyes of the Lords, also served a public
purpose, giving courts the power to curtail private rights—here the
uncles' power to veto the sale of the mansion—when their exercise
threatened to undermine it.

The legal reform of the English law of realty went hand in hand
with the decline of rural land as the most important source of private
wealth—first in Britain, and increasingly elsewhere. It marked a dramatic change in the legal coding of land. Prior to the 1881 reforms,
landowners not only enjoyed priority rights but could mobilize complex coding strategies to ensure that the family wealth remained intact, no matter how much debt the life tenant had accumulated. The
reform legislation effectively stripped land of one of capital's critical
attributes, namely, durability. From one day to the next, the same
land that had served as the primary source of wealth for centuries
was turned into an ordinary asset, a simple commodity that could
not only be freely bought and sold but could easily end up on the
auction block. Indeed, the reform legislation triggered a reallocation
of land in England on a scale not seen since the enclosure movement.
More than 20 percent of land changed hands within the two decades
following the reforms.[55]

Coding Land in the Colonies

In Britain's North American colonies, the equivalent of the Settled
Land and Conveyance Acts of 1881 had been introduced 150 years
earlier. The "Act for the More Easy Recovery of Debts in His Majesty's Plantations and Colonies in America" (Debt Recovery Act)
of 1732 gave creditors the right to seize all land, including family
estates, and to put it on the auction block.[56] The immediate effect
of the law was to break up large agricultural estates, especially in
the southern states. It also triggered the first major slave auctions
as creditors made good on foreclosing against all "assets" they had
secured for their loans.[57]

The fact that England enacted these reforms in North America in 1732 but waited until 1881 to implement similar reforms back home demonstrates the ideology, but perhaps even more the political economy at work in the coding and uncoding of capital. English lawmakers did not lack knowledge about alternatives to the complex land conveyance regime that solicitors had pieced together for wealthy families; they lacked the political will to implement them.[58] The calculus in the colonies was different. There, the English legislature had few qualms about shifting the balance of power from owners to creditors; to state the obvious, in most cases the creditors in question were Englishmen.

The estate-busting effect of the Debt Recovery Act in the United States had the potential to set the stage for a more egalitarian distribution of wealth, one that was closer to the republican spirit of North American colonies, which soon constituted themselves as the United States of America. Yet, asset holders in the new world soon learned the art of employing law to code their private wealth as their forefathers had done in the old world; and they found lawyers who would do this for a fee and legislatures with a sympathetic ear. Indeed, in the decades *after* independence, American law adopted many features of legal coding techniques that had served English wealthy elites so well. At times, the legal transplants even displayed features of English law, which had already been overturned in the home country of the common law. In the words of the legal historian, Joshua Getzler, American law readily embraced "dynasticism, dead-hand controls, perpetuities, judgement-proofing of assets, and [the] creation of fanciful purpose trusts, all policies reined in or banned in English law."[59] Empirical data suggest that the United States remained much more egalitarian than Europe until well into twentieth century.[60] However, the seeds had long been sown for the path to riches for those not only lucky enough to own assets, but who also had access to lawyers who could code them as capital.

The less fortunate were still sometimes able to mobilize the political process to protect their assets from looming impoverishment in the face of a massive economic downturn, but even here power politics played a critical role. Many state legislatures in the United

States enacted debt moratoria during the nineteenth century to level a playing field of legal rights that protected creditors at the expense of debtors, who were often at risk of losing everything through no fault of their own given the volatility of commodities markets.[61] In the eyes of some economists, these debt moratoria were efficient, because they adapted contracts to a complex world that was (and continues to be) beset by future events that neither party could have possibly foreseen; by intervening and imposing temporary relief or subjecting the sale of assets to state scrutiny, the legislatures helped "complete" these contracts, making them, in the words of economists, "stage-contingent."[62] However, most of these debt moratoria were later struck down by the courts for violation of a provision in the Constitution that prohibits states from interfering in private contracts.[63]

The most telling part of the story of debt moratoria in US economic history, however, is the political economy behind the decision to invoke them in the first place. The states that were most likely to adopt them were the new states on the Western frontier of the country; the least likely were the "old" Southern states. There, landed elites had amassed enough wealth to weather even severe economic storms; in fact, they often benefited from the opportunity to buy up land at very low cost from peasants who were no longer able to carry the debt they owed to their creditors—who not infrequently were the landed elites.

Faced with the same predicaments of a highly volatile agricultural economy, peasants in British colonies were never given the option of a debt moratorium. In India, for example, British colonizers introduced legal reforms that strengthened creditor rights by allowing them to evict peasants who were unable to pay their loans as they came due.[64] The immediate goal of these reforms was to break the monopoly of usurious money lenders, lower the costs of debt finance, and ensure that peasants could expand production and thereby boost Britain's tax revenue. Yet, when global cotton markets collapsed at the time of the American Civil War, these powerful rights triggered a chain reaction that threatened Britain's rule. Creditors used their rights to evict peasants on a large scale; these landless masses in turn rose up against their rulers; they staged a "mutiny," as the Royal reports called their revolt against the plight of impoverishment.

A grand experiment to introduce property rights and encourage debt finance without any protections for the new debtor/owners from external shocks had come to a dramatic end. This, however, has not prevented a repeat of this experiment in developing countries around the globe, where titling programs continue today to privilege monetizing the value of land over sustenance of small peasants and other land users. If and when a debtor defaults, the creditors may take their assets, but they will ensure that they will have greater durability in their own hands by employing the right coding strategies.

Empirical studies suggest that, in former colonies, where Europeans were able to settle, property rights were created that resembled their home institutions, helping to spur economic development and the production of private wealth. In contrast, in colonies where disease factors prevented settlements on a large scale, colonial powers created institutions primarily for extracting wealth, leaving these countries far behind their peers.[65] The authors of these studies have interpreted these results to suggest that European settlement and the transplantation of their property rights to the colonies spurred economic development. They say little about how wealth was distributed between settlers and locals, although it is well established that colonization created substantial inequalities between European settlers with lasting effects even today.[66]

Decoding the Trust

The legal institution that has been used most frequently for adding durability to landowners' property rights is "the trust." It is a powerful device that has been used, time and again, to protect the assets of the wealthy. The trust is unique to Anglo-American law and arguably is one of its most ingenious modules for coding capital. The civil law, with its Roman law origins, has little patience for this legal device, because it muddles the distinction between contract and property law.[67] But this is precisely what makes the trust such a desirable tool: where the civil law requires a formal act for transferring property rights, the handover of an object, or the registration of a title, under English law, a trust can be established by a simple deed drawn up in the private offices of a lawyer. Without signaling a change in property rights to the rest of the world, the trust effectively reorders property rights to an asset, and courts have upheld this reordering.[68]

This is how it works: A trust allows an owner (called a settlor) to transfer an asset into a legal shell, which is set up only for this purpose. In a second step, the rights to the asset are divided between the trustee, who holds formal title, and the beneficiary, who receives the (future) economic interest. Once the trust deed is drawn up and the asset transferred to the trustee, the settlor no longer owns the asset; his personal creditors therefore cannot seize it to satisfy their claims. The trust property is now managed by a trustee who holds formal title to the asset; the trustee can sell it, but only for the benefit of the beneficiary, and he must replace it with like assets.

The trustee holds formal title to the assets in the trust, but he has no right to the profits or any other economic benefits and his creditors therefore have no access to the assets in the trust either. And last, the beneficiary has an expectancy in the asset, but not a fully matured property interest. It took some time for creditors of the beneficiary to convince courts that they should be able to enforce against this future interest.[69] In short, by insulating assets from various groups of creditors, the trust works magic in enhancing their durability. Not surprisingly, to this day it is a favorite legal coding device among the wealthy who wish to protect their assets from tax authorities and other creditors. It is also a standard legal module for securitizing assets, including mortgages, a practice that we will encounter in chapter 4.

The history of the trust reveals an intricate interplay between private coding strategies, legislative push-back, renewed innovation, and, eventually, vindication of private coding efforts by a court of law. The trust had a predecessor, which was called "the use," that made its appearance in the late thirteenth century. Some sources explain its origins with the prohibition of members of the Franciscan order to own any assets. To get around this restriction, land was legally transferred to another entity, a town or village, but "for the use" of the Friars.[70] Other explanations point to efforts to sidestep mandatory primogeniture rules, to transfer interests to land at a time when land was in principle unalienable, or simply to avoid taxes. The common law courts at first refused to enforce the "use," but the private practice of conveying land in private deeds continued nonetheless.

In 1484, Richard III recognized the use by statute in an effort to make visible the rights to land that had been created with its help.[71] The statute stipulated that the beneficiaries of the use should be treated as if they had the power to convey property; in short, they were to be treated as full owners—400 years before the Land Conveyance Act of 1881 made the exact same legal move in response to the practice of entailing land that had removed land from the reach of the life tenants' creditors. The increasing popularity of the use, however, undermined the Crown's tax revenue. By 1526, therefore, fees were levied on those wishing to create uses, and unlicensed uses were sanctioned. Subsequent legal enactments, in the form of the Statute of Uses and the Statute of Enrollments, both passed in 1535, attempted to regulate its application more generally.[72] The Statute of Uses sought to reinstate the king's entitlements and prerogatives over land, but the plan ultimately failed. Decades of private transactions proved impossible to undo. Moreover, lawyers quickly discovered loopholes in the statutes and filled them with a new device that bore an uncanny resemblance to the use but was different enough to fit within the gaps of the statutes' language; when the courts gave their blessing, the trust took the place of the use.

The trust is a legal device that is designed to protect assets and as such serves those who have assets, that is, the wealthy. Not surprisingly, it is a critical module for coding capital. In the early nineteenth century, when the middle class became richer, the trust became more popular and the assets that trusts shielded became more varied. In addition to rural land, trusts often held portfolios of urban land and houses, but also government bonds and corporate shares.[73] Trust law changed along the way, and the trust morphed from a safe-keeping device for individual or family wealth into a vehicle for shielding business assets. Long before the corporate form offered a standardized asset-shielding device, the trust was used by business owners in England and North America to similar ends.[74] Trustees obtained

greater powers to manage complex pools of assets; the role of trustees
was professionalized and many solicitors offered their services as
trustees. In response, new rules were fashioned for trustees, including
their ability to charge fees, and, not surprisingly, restrictions on their
liability to the beneficiaries as well. Finally, when courts sanctioned
the possibility that the beneficiary could not be only one person, but
many different investors, it became the go-to vehicle for pooling and
securitizing assets, as we will discuss in chapter 4.

Made in Law

The account of how land has been coded as capital offered here differs from conventional accounts that portray property rights as the
quintessential institution for economic prosperity.[75] For economists,
the major purpose of property rights is to align the interests of the
owner with the most cost-efficient use of the asset. Optimizing the
use of assets was what animated Ronald Coase's famous example
of two neighboring farmers, one herding cows, the other trying to
grow crops, which of course the cows eat or trample over.[76] There
are many solutions to this problem of conflicting interests; one of
the two farmers might build a fence, move the crops elsewhere,
start herding cows, or the other might pay for damages or switch
from cattle to crops himself. If property rights have been clearly allocated, that is, if the two parties know what their respective rights
are and what they are worth in monetary terms, they can calculate
the costs each would have to incur, enabling them to resolve their
dispute and reach an optimal solution through negotiation. Such
an efficient outcome is achievable at least in a world without transaction costs. However, Coase himself stressed that in the real world,
transaction costs are ubiquitous, which is why the *initial* allocation
of property rights by the law actually matters a great deal. Yet, as we
have seen, landowners did not just bargain with creditors to protect
their interests; they employed lawyers who coded their interests in
law and thereby helped tilt the playing field in their favor.

This then raises the question of where property rights and other
legal entitlements such as those associated with the trust come from

in the first place. Property rights are not given; they are "acquired rights," as Adam Smith acknowledged. "Property and civil government very much depend on one another. The preservation of property and the inequality of possession first formed it, and the state of property must always vary with the form of government."[77] Establishing formal title or recognizing certain claims as formal property rights under the law, however, is only a first step. Individual property rights are often said to give the owner the power to use, control, or alienate an asset as he chooses and exclude everyone else, but frequently the exercise of these rights conflicts with equally legitimate claims others might raise. There is no absolute property right with immutable boundaries. Even Blackstone recognized as much. Property, he said, is an "absolute right, inherent in every Englishman (. . .), which consists in the free use, enjoyment, and disposal of all his acquisitions, without any control or diminution, *save only by the laws of the land.*"[78] Property rights, in other words, find their limits in general laws; where the boundaries lie exactly is always and necessarily contested.[79]

In short, property rights and similar legal entitlements evolve in the interstices of states, power, and the law. When recognizing or denying claims to an asset as legally protected property rights, states often play into the hands of powerful parties. Vesting some with legal entitlements while denying similar treatment to others, and stripping certain protections from some assets and grafting them onto others are actions that make or destroy wealth. And yet, if the state's actions were limited to establishing priority rights, most of the wealth thus accumulated would be short-lived, subject to the ups and downs of economic cycles and technological change. This would arguably make for a much fairer but also a more volatile world. The first to realize the cost of volatility are typically the asset holders themselves. Once they have secured priority rights, they invariably seek additional protection to ensure that their wealth will endure. For this, they need not just priority, but durability, and both attributes must be made universally enforceable. This is something that private parties, on their own, cannot do; they need a powerful state and its laws to accomplish this.

3

Cloning Legal Persons

Market economies revolve around contracts and property rights. Capital, however, relies on more than just enforceable contracts and clear property rights that are enforceable against the world; it also depends on durability, which for business organizations takes the form of asset-shielding devices that lock in past gains and protect asset pools from all but the direct creditors of the firm. The previous chapter illustrated how the law of trusts has been used for centuries as a legal keep-safe of assets that are beyond the reach of the settlor and of the trustee's creditors. Corporate law can do the same, and even more. It can be employed to parcel assets and operations of an integrated economic entity in ways that reduce information costs, thereby lowering the cost of debt finance and minimizing taxes, even regulatory costs. Indeed, corporate law is increasingly used to maximize financial gains in this fashion; it is no longer primarily a legal vehicle for producing goods or offering services but has been transformed into a virtual capital mint. This is most apparent in the financial services sector, but similar practices have become mainstream for corporations in the "real" economy as well.

The corporation has been correctly heralded as a critical invention for capitalism, although, as I will suggest in this chapter, perhaps not always for the right reasons. Economists like to think of the corporate form as a legal fiction behind which lies a "nexus of contracts."[1] Legal scholars have held against this that private contracting alone cannot provide one of the most important features of the corporation: the ability to shield the firm's assets from the shareholders and their personal creditors.[2] Still, most lawyers agree with economists that the corporate form enhances the efficient use of scarce resources by encouraging risk taking, by broadening the investor base and thereby mobilizing funding for investments, and by creating the conditions for deep and liquid markets for the shares and bonds that the corporation issues. Markets in these assets in turn are thought to facilitate information sharing, monitoring, and the redeployment of funding from less to more efficiently run firms.

In this chapter, I offer a different perspective on the use of the corporate form. I will show that it can be and is used not just to optimize the allocation of risks and returns in the production of goods and services; instead, it can be turned into a capital minting operation by employing the ability to partition assets and shield them behind a chain of corporate veils to access low-cost debt finance, and to engage in tax and regulatory arbitrage. Separating the use of corporate law for organizing a business from its capital-minting function is not always easy, and one function frequently morphs into the other, but ignoring the power of corporate law as a capital mint risks missing a major source of private wealth in our age of shareholder value maximization.

To illustrate this, I will conduct an "institutional autopsy" of Lehman Brothers.[3] Its failure turned a lingering crisis in global financial markets into a full-blown heart attack; but it also offers a great opportunity to dissect the company's legal structure and understand how that may have contributed to its rise and ultimate fall.

Lehman's Fate

No other name is more closely associated with the Great Financial Crisis than Lehman Brothers. The company's filing for bankruptcy on September 15, 2008, marked the official onset of the crisis, which had been looming already for more than a year; the financial system suffered a heart attack, markets froze, and asset prices plummeted. Lehman's bankruptcy put an abrupt end to a business that three immigrants from a small town in Bavaria, Germany, had established in 1850.[4] At that time, they settled in Montgomery, Alabama and opened a small trading business in retail goods and commodities, with an emphasis on cotton. Cotton production was, of course, at the heart of an economy that was organized around and made profitable by enslaved labor and that enriched not only slave-owning cotton producers, but the intermediaries who traded in cotton, advanced credits for its production, and created options and futures to hedge their bets, as well.[5]

Henry Lehman, the oldest brother, died in 1855 of yellow fever during a trip to New Orleans, but his younger siblings grew the business and eventually moved it to New York City. There, they joined other cotton traders to set up the New York Cotton Exchange, an important step on the way to the financialization of cotton production. Subsequently, the firm joined the coffee and petroleum exchanges, attesting to the expanding scope of its activities and the lure of trading cotton and other commodities. By 1887, the firm had even acquired a seat on the New York Stock Exchange. Trading in corporate securities, in addition to trading in commodities, became a core part of Lehman's business, as did some private banking activities.

As the next generation of Lehmans came of age, the firm morphed into an investment bank, helping other companies to sell shares and bonds on financial markets and offering other client services. Many of the early underwritings were orchestrated jointly with Goldman Sachs, a firm whose founder, Michael Goldman, also hailed from Bavaria. In their joint ventures, Lehman provided the funding and Goldman Sachs the client list. Together they brought companies to the market, which were to become household names in the United States, including Sears, Roebuck and Co., Woolworth, May Department Stores, Peabody & Co., R. H. Macy & Co., and many others.

The Great Depression and World War II caused many disruptions and slowed down business, but Lehman survived relatively unscathed and when business picked up again in the 1950s, the firm continued its operations as one of the leading investment banks in the United States. In the early 1960s, the last descendant of the Lehman family left the firm. Nonetheless, Lehman Brothers continued under the same name but was eventually bogged down by leadership struggles and growing competition in investment banking. In 1983, the partners sold the firm to American Express, marking a temporary end to the company's autonomy and its legal organization as a partnership: Lehman was incorporated and became a wholly owned subsidiary of American Express. In 1994, however, the companies parted again; Lehman was spun off in a public offering that handed control rights to shareholders, who traded the company's shares publicly and widely and were also responsible for electing directors and indirectly appointing corporate management. The company's legal structure had been overhauled twice, but it still bore the same name, and trading in as well as underwriting financial assets remained its core business.

The corporate form grants an indefinite life span and a structure to raise funds in the form of equity or debt as needed from a broad investor base. Yet, Lehman's years as a corporate entity were numbered; the firm had survived in the much more vulnerable legal form of a partnership for more than 130 years (from 1850 to 1983), a period that witnessed the transformation of America from an agricultural into the leading industrial nation, as well as the Civil War, two world wars, several major financial crises, and more than one overhaul of the monetary system in the United States and globally. Indeed, over the course of Lehman's lifetime, the global monetary system changed from the gold standard to Bretton Woods and from there to fiat money, and from a financial sector that was tightly regulated to the rise of shadow banking on a global scale. Lehman's transformation into a corporate entity, a legal form that promises immortality, gave it only another 14 years.

Ironically, the promiscuous use of the corporate form contributed to Lehman's downfall. In its final stages, Lehman comprised a parent holding company with 209 registered subsidiaries in twenty-six jurisdictions around the globe:[6] sixty in the US state of Delaware alone, thirty-eight in the UK, and thirty-two in the Cayman Islands, followed by eleven in Australia, and nine each in Hong Kong and Japan.[7] This does not even include the hundreds, if not thousands, of special-purpose vehicles, or SPVs, in the form of trusts or limited liability companies it had employed as well. Most of Lehman's subsidiaries were forced into bankruptcy on the heels of their parent company at the top of this sprawling legal empire, notwithstanding the corporate legal shields that had separated them. Behind these shields, they had been tied together in a web of debt, which the parent company (LBHI) had guaranteed, using the shares it held in the highly leveraged subsidiaries as collateral. The subsidiaries, for their part, had moved most of their profits back to the parent, leaving few assets for their creditors. LBHI's bankruptcy (its economic death) meant that the guarantees at the apex disappeared; and as a result, the subsidiaries lost access to refinancing their debt and fell like dominos. The downward spiral followed the same dynamic as the UK's depression in the 1870s described in the previous chapter. Back then, the train wreck happened in slow motion; this time, it happened at breathtaking speed, reflecting the much shorter duration of debt instruments that are now in use. However, the logic of the rise and fall of assets—land back then and financial capital now—was exactly the same: too much debt piled on a legal structure that promised more than it could possibly hold, and that collapsed onto itself when this truth leaked out under less than benign economic circumstances.

A Family of Legal Persons

Incorporation literally means the creation of a new corpus, a new person. The Romans already used corporate entities, but for organizing public services, not private business. In the twelfth century, canonist scholars conceived of the church as a corporate legal entity that conferred legal powers on ecclesiastical officers, including the pope, but also on churches and monasteries independent of their relations to secular powers. In a similar vein, kings chartered towns, granting them legal personality and the right to govern their own affairs.[8] The modern business corporation possesses similar powers:

it is considered a legal person and as such owns its own assets and can contract, sue, and be sued in its own name. Neither churches, cities, nor corporations can act without humans, but humans are merely their agents; the legal entity is the principal.

To most non-lawyers, the relevant unit of analysis in the world of business is the firm, its legal form being only of marginal interest, or worse, a distraction from its economic substance. Generations of economists have preferred to look through the "legal fiction" where they find a network of contracts among investors, managers, employees, suppliers, and customers.[9] But this misses the very essence of the corporation: The directors don't contract with the suppliers, employees, or consumers, the corporate entity does; and the shareholders do not own the assets of the firm, only the shares; they have no say in the firm's management, but must delegate this task to their elected representatives. If there is a nexus of contracts, it is with the legal entity, not with the entity's stakeholders; calling this central node a fiction denies the ingenuity of this legal device, one of the most important modules of the code of capital.

For businesses that are run within a single legal entity structure, the distinction between form and function may be less than obvious. Increasingly, however, the corporate form is used to partition assets of the same firm into select asset pools, including receivables for certain types of claims that are shielded from the rest of its operations, with the result that a single firm may comprise dozens if not hundreds of legal shells. Establishing a separate corporate entity is not costless, but in most legal systems entry costs have been reduced to negligible amounts. The time for paperwork has been cut back, and while there may be registration fees or franchise taxes, other entry conditions, such as minimum capital requirements or full payment of all shareholder contributions, have been thrown into the dustbin of history by most legal systems.

Most countries today recognize a corporation with all its powers, if it follows the rules of its chosen birthplace, whether or not it ever did or intended to do any business there. In short, corporate law has become up for grabs. It has not always been this way. In the past, many countries required a firm to use its domestic corporate law, if this was where the company maintained its headquarters or core business operations. The real seat theory, as this rule has been appropriately labeled, however, was pushed out when the free movement of capital became the overriding concern of policymakers, recasting the imposition of local rules by a sovereign state into barriers to entry.[10] Under these conditions, it is difficult for states to sustain rules that impose too high a burden for incorporating a business, or even rules that are at odds with the interests of shareholders.

Lehman Brothers, along with other financial intermediaries, developed the legal partitioning of assets with the help of corporate law into an art form. The business operated as a fully integrated global financial services provider, but its operations, liabilities, and profit centers were divided among hundreds of legal entities.[11] The assets of the parent company, LBHI, consisted almost entirely of shares held in its subsidiaries, and it derived its income from dividend payments and other transfers the subsidiaries made to the parent.

On their own, the subsidiaries hardly could have raised the funds they needed at reasonable prices. They needed debt finance (the issuance of shares to outside shareholders would have diluted the parent's control) and in order to obtain the desired funding volume at reasonable cost, the parent guaranteed most of their debt. In effect, the parent traded away one of the greatest privileges that shareholders enjoy: limited liability. It allows shareholders to limit their exposure to a firm to the price they paid for their shares; they never have to throw good money after bad. By guaranteeing the subsidiaries' debt, the parent company assumed liability for the debt of its subsidiaries, not by law but by contract. The shareholders of the parent company LBHI itself, however, retained their "owner shield" in the form of limited liability and therefore remained well-protected from the liabilities of the parent company and those of its sprawling empire of subsidiaries. Of course, these shareholders were also the main beneficiaries of using maximum debt finance to squeeze out returns for themselves for as long as possible. All they would ever lose was their initial investment, and as long as the entire group generated positive returns, they were able to reap them by demanding dividends or selling their shares for a profit.

In short, the legal structure of Lehman Brothers resembled a family that sells off the family home to send the kids to college, giving each child a credit card that is drawn on the parents' account, which will be replenished only with money the children will send home someday. This does not bode well unless there are at least some superstars among the children. The corporate form can help deflect some of the risks that are inherent to this structure. It gives the parent an indefinite life span and thereby reduces the likelihood of its untimely death, which would upend the entire structure. Further, it insulates the assets and liabilities of each child from the assets and liabilities of all the others, so that if one fails, the others will not be affected. Finally, it gives the parent unlimited prowess to procreate in the event that new opportunities arise or a child that vanished has to be replaced.

The Romans did not use the corporate form for private business, but they developed a legal structure that resembled it in important respects—the slave-run company.[12] Two partners would set up a business, which was run by a slave, whom they jointly owned. They would allocate certain assets, bundled together and given the legal label of a *peculium*, to this business with the result that the partners' liability for any business loss was limited to these assets. Creditors of the firm could not enforce against the partners' personal assets and, conversely, the partners' personal creditors had no access to the peculium. The business could survive a turnover of its partners and an exchange of one slave for another as the manager of the business. As such, the slave-run firm had key attributes that characterize the modern business corporation; most important, it used asset partitioning and shielding devices to limit the reach of creditors to the assets of their immediate contractual parties and prevented them from seizing assets that were protected by a legal shield.

Coding the Modern Business Corporation

The modern business corporation was not born with legal shielding devices, limited liability, and other props that grant it the legal attributes of priority, universality, and durability firmly in place.[13] It acquired these attributes over time and through many legal battles. Over the course of the nineteenth century, most legal systems in Western Europe and North America allowed for the creation of a legal entity without governmental approval. It took another century for a corporate law to evolve that gave the company's founders so many options that legal scholars have called it an "enabling" corporate law, almost contractual in nature: the corporate law of the tiny US state of Delaware.[14] Most of the large, publicly traded US corporations are incorporated in this state, which has also become a hub for foreign business organizations in search of a benign (read manager-friendly) corporate law.[15]

Not all features of the corporation, however, can be created by contract. Legal personality, which gives the entity the right to own assets, contract, sue, and be sued in its own name, can be obtained only by a state act. Modern incorporation statutes no longer require state approval for establishing a new company, but they still need to register and comply with basic mandatory provisions of corporate law to benefit from using this legal form. Of all the features of the modern business corporation, three have arguably contributed most to its success, and all three are impossible to obtain by contract alone: entity shielding, loss shifting, and the prospect of immortality.

Entity shielding creates priority rights over distinct asset pools, each with its distinct creditors who can focus on monitoring a specific pool, but may not have access to the larger pie.[16] Loss shifting allows owners to limit their own losses by shifting the risk of doing business to others: to the company's contractual or tort creditors, or to the public at large by prompting governments to bail them out lest the company's demise threatens to bring down the entire economy. Such a "put option" has been fairly common for financial companies but is not unheard of for non-financial companies either, as the bailout of the large car manufacturing firms in the United States in the crisis of 2008 suggests.[17] Finally, immortality increases the life span of incorporated entities and thereby extends their durability. Corporations, like other firms, are not immune to failure, but they have to be put to death by their creditors in a bankruptcy proceeding, or by their shareholders in a voluntary dissolution. The following sections will take a closer look at each of these features to see how Lehman used them to the advantage of the parent company's shareholders, even as this put the firm itself at risk and precipitated its premature death.

ENTITY SHIELDING

It is easy to understand the temptation of an owner to protect assets from the reach of creditors. Hiding them is illegal, and so is any asset transfer at a time when creditors are already hot on the heels of a defaulting debtor. Preemptive asset shielding, however, is legal; indeed, it is one of the most powerful tools for coding capital. The Romans achieved asset partitioning with the help of the peculium; English landowners used the trust, and its sibling, the strict family settlement, to shield their family wealth from creditors; and during the Renaissance in northern Italy, Florence became the incubator for the partnership system, which created separate pools of assets and liabilities for business operations at home and abroad that were managed by junior partners, but were linked to the parent partnership through partnership agreements.[18] In a similar vein, today's shareholders employ the corporate form to create distinct pools of assets against which they raise debt finance, or which they place in jurisdictions where they can benefit from regulatory or tax arbitrage.

Entity shielding is not inherently an anti-creditor device. The personal creditors of the firm's owners may get stiffed; but the creditors who lend to the business benefit, because they obtain a priority right to its assets. They may have to share these benefits with the firm's other creditors, but entity shielding keeps the personal creditors of the firm's owners at bay. If the firm is organized as a partnership, these creditors typically will have to enforce against the owners' personal assets before reaching out to assets the firm owns, but they may do so if a partner's assets fall short of their claims. If, however, the business is organized as a corporation, they are excluded from the assets of the firm altogether; they can only seize the shares in the corporation their debtor owns. If they want to turn them into cash, they will either have to find a willing buyer or convince other shareholders to liquidate the firm and pay off its own creditors before they can claim the leftover assets for themselves.

New coding strategies that partition assets and shield entities have frequently spurred the expansion of credit, thereby boosting the returns for their owners. We lack reliable data for the impact of the slave-owned business in Roman times, but an examination of tax data from Florence has revealed that the partnership system (*sistema di aziende*), which emerged around 1380, triggered a major credit boom. A "whirlwind of products, bills of exchange, and credits cycling around" produced financial liquidity on an unprecedented scale.[19] To see why, consider the fate of creditors and owners in firms with and without entity-shielding devices in place.

A single owner might operate multiple lines of business under the same roof: textile manufacturing, trading, and money lending. The failure of a single operation can easily spill over to another, even to the entire enterprise. Creditors therefore will have to monitor all operations and closely watch the owner (possibly more than one) as well. If, instead, each line of business, each division, or each location can be placed behind a separate legal shield, creditors can focus on the business of their choice. Using a separate legal entity for each operation thus can offer superior protection to creditors. Creditors may not be able to reach other assets of the firm easily, but, if all goes well, they save a lot of transaction costs.[20]

A good illustration for the power of asset-shielding devices is the partnership system of the Medici, the family that ruled over Florence for almost a century, from 1434 to the 1530s.[21] The Medici business included textile manufacturing, banking, and trade, with far-flung operations that crisscrossed Europe and reached as far as Rome, Antwerp, London, Bruges, and Paris. Each line of business and each local operation was organized as a separate partnership with its own books and accounts. The senior partnership in Florence entered into separate agreements with junior partners who managed the operations, typically for a (renewable) period of five years;[22] it usually provided up to 50 percent or more of the capital of the junior partnerships and retained a firm grip over them. Every partnership had to send its profits back to the parent partnership in

Florence, minus the share that was owed to the local junior partner, and it had to close its books at least once a year and send them to Florence for auditing.

By its very nature, the partnership agreement binds only the partners; still, as the case recounted below suggests, at least some courts enforced the contractual asset shielding that these contracts created against outsiders. A purchaser of textiles from the London offshoot of the Medici empire brought a case against the partnership in Bruges for breach of contract in 1453. Perhaps he believed that the partnership in Bruges had more assets, or for other reasons the merchant found it easier to file in the Bruges court, claiming that the entire business empire of the Medici was in fact "one company and had the same master."[23] The court dismissed the argument, stating that the merchants had contracted with the junior partnership in London, which therefore was first in line to account for the merchant's losses.[24] First in line is not the same as absolute protection, which is why the Medici's partnership system has been described as only a weak form of entity shielding.[25]

No doubt the ruling must have disappointed the plaintiff. Given that the Medici empire was a partnership, not a full-blown business corporation (which did not even exist at the time), and that the entity-shielding devices were purely contractual in nature, he clearly had a point. He almost certainly had relied on the good name of the Medici, without thinking too much about the legal structure that may have been set up to protect the senior partners in Florence from the actions of their junior partners in London, Bruges, or elsewhere. The creditors of the Bruges partnership, however, were surely delighted. As far as they were concerned, the partnership system and its (weak) asset-shielding effects had been vindicated in law.

The legal structure of the Lehman group closely resembled the Medici empire, although it topped it by the strength of its asset-shielding devices and in complexity; and just as back then, the legal partitioning of assets behind a plethora of legal shields went hand in hand with a massive credit boom. There is, however, a downside to parceling the assets of a firm: a junior partnership of the Medici business or one of Lehman's subsidiaries may not have many assets to go around. Asset partitioning cuts both ways; it shields the assets of the sub-unit, but it also shields other units, including the senior or parent operation, from its creditors. Smart creditors will therefore require a personal guarantee from the senior partners or the parent company. That allows them to kill two birds with one stone; they can focus on monitoring only the unit to which they lend, yet retain a claim against the parent and its assets, including the parent's ownership stakes in the entire offspring. In the event that a subsidiary fails, they can still decide whether they wish to exercise the nuclear option and bring down the parent and all its other subsidiaries as well.

But what if the parent fails? Then the game is up and it is time for the reckoning that placing assets behind different legal shields does not expand the total assets of the firm, even as it fools creditors into lending more in the hope that the parent will stand in for the debt. If all the parent has is the assets in the sub-units, this is an empty hope. At bottom, the legal partitioning of assets of an economically fully integrated business organization only pretends to make creditors more secure, when in fact it renders a firm's *total* debt more opaque and more difficult to monitor for creditors and the parent company alike.

LOSS SHIFTING

Owners benefit when their assets increase in value, but they also feel the full brunt of declining asset value—as English landlords learned in the 1870s, and as many homeowners discovered when the real estate bubble burst in 2007.[26] When markets decline or a promising business opportunity turns sour, an entrepreneur can lose his entire family silver, even his shirt. Making bets on an unknown future is a risky business; economic downturns should therefore keep a natural check on the ability to maintain and grow wealth over long periods of time. Business owners, however, have found ways to capture the upside, while shifting the downside to others: to their various contractual creditors—including employees, tort creditors, and the public at large.

As noted earlier, in Roman times, business owners came up with the idea of limiting their exposure to a specific operation by transferring to one of their slaves a peculium.[27] It is the same idea that motivates shareholder limited liability. Shareholders may lose their original investment, the money they paid for their shares; however, they need not stand in for their corporation's own debt burden. They can simply wind down that company and start a new business. True, shareholders are the last in line to get any remaining assets should the firm end up in liquidation; but this does not mean that shareholders are left empty-handed; after all, they can take out the profits the corporation makes during its lifetime without paying much heed to the impact this might have on its debtors or even its long-term survival, provided they can get out fast enough.

Shareholder limited liability is the technical term for shielding owners from the liabilities of the business entity. It became a standard feature of corporate law statutes relatively late, because wary legislatures feared that savvy entrepreneurs would set up a corporate shell, convince the creditors to extend loans to the company, and then take the money and run. Facts on the ground proved that they were not entirely wrong about this; in the nineteenth century, legal system after legal system adopted free incorporation statutes, which made it possible to establish corporations without the need for prior approval. When these statutes were enacted, almost invariably a founders' boom would follow, then end in a crash.[28] In response, some legislatures tried to backtrack, but once the genie was out of the bottle, it was almost impossible to put it back in.

The vacillation about limited liability as a standard feature of corporate law in the UK is a good example. In 1844, the UK opened the door to free incorporation after the country had tried with only limited success to keep a tap on the sprouting of all kinds of business organizations that resembled the corporation in all but name: they used the trust and pushed the limits of partnership law, they lobbied for special charters for industries that included limited liability, and they contracted with creditors of firms to ensure that they would not raise claims against the firm's owners. These mutants may not have been as fool-proof as the corporate form, but they went a long way toward giving owners the legal protection they craved.[29]

The 1844 Joint Stock Companies Act allowed businesses to establish themselves as corporate entities without government approval but did not include shareholder limited liability. This feature was introduced only with the Act's revision in 1855 but was short-lived, as it was abused by unscrupulous shareholders; in response to a series of high-profile scandals, the Parliament reversed course and eliminated this legal feature only two years later. This reversal, however, proved to be short lived. Limited liability was finally reintroduced in 1862, and this time for good.

In the United States, limited liability became a core feature of most incorporation statutes the states enacted, starting with New York in 1811, although California introduced limited liability only as late as 1932.[30] This is evidence that investments even on the scale required during the process of industrialization are possible without granting shareholders limited liability. Still, the fact that this soon became a standard feature of corporate statutes around the globe suggests that powerful interests were behind this legal innovation.

Returning to the Lehman case, we can see that the shareholders of LBHI made extensive use of this loss-shifting mechanism. LBHI guaranteed the liabilities of its subsidiaries, but its own shareholders held on to their owner shield and were thus off the hook; they could take full advantage of the gains the company made on the backs of the subsidiaries' creditors. As long as enough subsidiaries made profits and transferred them back to LBHI, as they were required to do under internal agreements, LBHI's shareholders could realize these profits in the form of dividends, or by selling their shares either to others or back to the company in a repurchasing program.

In fact, LBHI shareholders received millions of dollars in dividends from LBHI long after housing markets had begun to decline and symptoms for stress in financial markets had become manifest. Lehman was not alone in doling out cash reserves to its shareholders after the onset of the market downturn in housing markets since 2006 and in financial markets in 2007; if anything, the company was at the lower end of the spectrum, paying "only" $631 million to its shareholders in the two final years of its existence. Over the same period, Citigroup paid close to $16 billion, followed by JP Morgan and Wells Fargo with $11 billion and $10 billion, respectively.[31] By driving down its asset cushion in this fashion, Lehman (and its competitors) deprived itself of the ability to absorb losses when asset prices declined and its own subsidiaries began to default on their loans. In the end, it fell to the government to decide whether to allow Lehman to fail, and after Lehman's fall threatened to put the entire system into a tailspin, to backstop other intermediaries so as to prevent a meltdown of the domestic and global financial systems.[32]

Most corporate laws impose restrictions on paying dividends to shareholders in an attempt to protect the company's asset base and, indirectly, its creditors, but they have been scaled back over time; Delaware's dividend rules, for example, have been called "nimble." And nimble they are indeed; under these rules, profits can be paid not only from this year's profits, but, in case there aren't any, also from last year's. This way, company management can smooth dividend payments and manage shareholder expectations. Still, the same rules encourage the transfer of returns from the corporation to its shareholders even when this may be detrimental for its long-term survival.

Many of Lehman's shareholders, of course, realized in 2008 that the game was up. The steep decline in the company's share price from $65 in January 2008 to just over $4 in September 2008, days before LBHI filed for bankruptcy, is proof of their change of heart.[33] Surely, shareholders that came late to the game, were asleep at the wheel, or were betting on a government bailout booked losses, but many, including the company's top management, had cashed in profits long before the company went down. Most of LBHI's top managers had had a significant stake in the company, in part because they were paid in stock options and in part because they re-invested their own savings, augmented, as it were, by sizeable pay packages, back into the company. According to estimates, Richard Fuld, the company's CEO, received a half billion dollars in salary and stock options during his tenure at the helm from 1993 to 2007.[34] He may not have been able to cash in all of these holdings in time, but even then, he was able to walk away with substantial wealth after the company had folded under his management.

The real losers of the Lehman debacle therefore were not the shareholders, but the creditors, some more than others. LBHI's creditors received on average 21 cents on every dollar they had loaned, but payouts varied considerably between creditor classes.[35] The counterparties to Lehman's derivatives transactions were made almost entirely whole, thanks to bankruptcy safe harbors that allowed them to net out their claims prior to all other creditors; in contrast, senior unsecured creditors received well below 20 percent of their claims. This confirms that priority rights matter, never more so than in bankruptcy, when losses are realized.

Why then did creditors play along and lend to LBHI and its numerous subsidiaries? It is fairly easy to look through Lehman's organization and realize that behind the hundreds of legal shells, the big winners would be the shareholders of the parent company LBHI; they would capture the gains and limited liability would effectively shield them from sharing in any losses; all they could lose were their initial investments. Of course, creditors are in this game for the same reason shareholders are—for profit. They may have been attracted by the higher yield for investing in risky assets; or believed that sticking to short-term loans that were rolled over at an ever-faster pace meant that they would be able to get out on time; or they may have counted on the parent company's financial prowess. Even if they understood that LBHI's assets were tied to the fortunes of its highly leveraged children, they may have believed that there were enough of them to ensure the parent's well-being.

As is well known, in poor countries without state-backed pension systems, families tend to have many children to ensure that enough of them survive to care for their parents in old age; the creditors to the various Lehman subsidiaries may have similarly believed that some of them would bring home enough to ensure that the parent would be able to at least make good on the loans it had guaranteed to them. Nonetheless, a few creditors realized that they had to do more to protect themselves and included provisions in their contracts with a subsidiary that disallowed the ploughing back of all profit to the parent.[36] Had all creditors done so, the great Lehman family gamble never would have taken off.

Last, but not least, some creditors may have bet that the government would not allow Lehman to fail. Few governments have the stomach to allow big banks or highly interdependent financial intermediaries to fail, unless they are pushed to do so by outsiders, such as the International Monetary Fund on which these governments depend for their own survival. When Long Term Capital Management, the hedge fund that boasted several Nobel Prize laureates among its founders and managers, tumbled in 1998, for example, the US Federal Reserve organized a private bailout; and in March 2008, the New York Fed provided a substantial dowry when Bear Stearns was forced into a shotgun marriage with JP Morgan Chase. As a wedding present, the Fed lent $30 billion to Chase to purchase Bear Stearns and waived the obligation to pay back these loans should Bear Stearns's own assets prove to be insufficient.[37]

In Lehman's case, the calculus that the Fed would always stand by as the rescuer of last resort for large financial intermediaries did not work out. Only after Lehman's demise triggered a near standstill of global financial markets did governments come to the rescue.[38] In the United States, investment banks were allowed to morph into holding banks, which gave them access to the Fed's discount window and thus to cash liquidity; and in October 2008, the governments in the leading market economies, including the United States, injected billions of dollars in fresh capital into the largest banks—the "too-big" and the "too-interconnected-to-fail."

The lesson future investors, shareholders, and creditors alike, might take away from this is that diversifying across multiple risky entities is important, but that in the end the only guarantee for a government bailout is the threat that, by allowing one firm to fail, the entire system might collapse; in other words, they need to create a "put-option" (rescue me or else . . .) that is big enough so that no government can possibly refuse it.

IMMORTALITY

Legal personhood promises, but does not guarantee, immortality. A corporation can survive only if it manages to balance its liabilities with its assets. Shareholders can put an end to it, but it takes at least a majority vote to liquidate a legal entity. In contrast, a simple partnership perishes when only a single partner dies or pulls out. This fate can be avoided by renewing the partnership when a partner leaves or dies, or by writing partnership contracts that allow for the replacement of individual partners.[39] Without such life-prolonging legal measures, the original Lehman Brothers partnership, which was established in 1850, would not have survived the early death of Henry Lehman, or the succession of other family members; and it most likely would have been dissolved in 1965, when the final member of the Lehman family left.

As useful as these measures are, they are a far cry from immortality; they work only if and when all other partners cooperate and as long as the firm has the resources to cash out partners that exit upon retirement or for any other reason. This makes the partnerships a less durable business form as compared to the corporation. On the upside, however, precisely because partners put their own assets at risk, they tend to be more cautious than managers of corporations who invest other people's money. It is hardly a coincidence that the enormous increase in leverage at investment banks closely tracks the conversion of these firms from partnerships into corporate entities in the 1980s and 1990s.

Legal personhood is the foundation for the corporation's immortality, but another important legal innovation, shareholder lock-in, greatly increased its survival chances. Shareholder lock-in prevents shareholders from taking out the initial contributions they make to a company.[40] As such, it is a prerequisite for effectively shielding corporate assets from the personal creditors of its shareholders. The year of this innovation was 1612, when the government of the Netherlands (the General Estates) imposed a charter change on the Dutch East India Company (also known under the acronym VOC) that denied shareholders their right to recall their investment at the

end of the ten-year commitment period, to which they had agreed
at the company's founding.

A ten-year commitment had already been a radical change when
compared to earlier business practices that wound down a business
after completing a single voyage. In the sixteenth century, merchants
often pooled their stock prior to the journey (thus the term "joint
stock company") and upon return they divided the spoils and closed
down the company. Of course, they could set up a new venture and
repeat the cycle; but early joint stock companies were meant to pool
resources and diversify risk, not to create durable asset pools that
would produce wealth over long stretches of time.

The ambitions of the Dutch East India Company, however, went
way beyond a single journey; it was a joint venture between merchants and the government, the Estates General of the Netherlands.
It had commerce written all over it, but also the sovereign's claim to
monopolize the trade route to East Asia, by force if necessary. To
achieve these conflicting goals, the company needed a sound capital
base and therefore forced shareholders to commit their contributions for a ten-year period. When the time came for the shareholders
of the VOC to redeem their shares, the political elites feared that
a massive outflow of funds would undermine the viability of the
company just when Portugal mounted a serious challenge to Dutch
dominance over the highly lucrative trade routes by sea to the Far
East.[41] A charter change forced shareholders to leave their initial
contribution with the company for good. This "shareholder lock-in"
laid the foundation for durable asset pools that could grow and produce wealth indefinitely—unless the company succumbed to external forces beyond its control, or, more likely, to bad management—a
fate to which even the VOC eventually surrendered.

Shareholders did not revolt against this legal imposition, and
those among them who doubled as members of the Dutch political
elite may have even supported it. But even those who had invested
purely for economic gain did not have much to complain about,
because shareholder lock-in did not mean that shareholders were
stuck.[42] To the contrary, a vibrant secondary market for the company's shares had developed already under the original ten-year

commitment period, as new investors did not have to fear that fellow shareholders would deplete the capital base any time and therefore could forge long-term expectations. The new indefinite lock-in provided an even firmer capital base and fueled a liquid market in the VOC's shares.

With the lock-in in place, the VOC expanded even more rapidly. It sent many more ships to Asia and was able to raise fresh finance and debt, which allowed it to make long-term investments in infrastructure. Comparing the VOC with its main competitor, the English East India Company, in this period produces striking results. As the Dutch East India Company embarked on an expansion spree and raised substantial amounts of debt to fund it, its English counterpart launched fewer ships, conducted shorter voyages, and had lower investments especially in long-term projects. It had to be nimble to ensure that it always had enough cash on hand to redeem shareholders who had the right to recall their contribution at any moment.[43]

Jointly, entity shielding, the ability to shift losses to creditors, and corporate immortality laid the groundwork for the rise of the modern business corporation and for its path to global dominance. Shareholders benefited hugely from these legal innovations; they were protected from losing more than they put in, and yet could lever the firm to boost short-term gains, which they would claim for themselves.

Shopping for Law

Economists have long tried to explain the ownership and financial structures of firms. What is the optimal relation between debt and equity for funding a business?[44] When should two or more firms merge into a single firm and when should a single firm be divided and spun off into different operations?[45] These are important questions, but they miss how much legal engineering goes into the organization of business as a routine matter. Maximizing shareholder wealth is not just a function of superior management and production or services skills, but also of optimizing legal arbitrage.[46] The options for doing so have greatly expanded as a result of changes in legal rules that allow businesses to choose the corporate law by which they wish to be governed.

Given that corporations are creatures of the law, it would seem that corporations should be bound by the laws of the state that created them, and by any legal change legislatures or court decisions might impose on them. In fact, regulatory competition has eroded the power of any single state and its laws over the corporation. Corporations can't exist without state law, but today they can pretty much freely choose from a menu of corporate laws different states have on offer, and through this choice also select their tax rate and regulatory costs. In a prophetic ruling of 1839, the US Supreme Court affirmed the dependence of the corporation on the state that created it (in the United States, states, not the federation, have jurisdiction over corporate law), but also hinted at the possibility that its life might extend well beyond the boundaries of that jurisdiction:

> It is very true that a corporation can have no legal existence out of the boundaries of the sovereignty by which it is created. It exists only in contemplation of law and by force of the law, and where that law ceases to operate and is no longer obligatory, the corporation can have no existence. It must dwell in the place of its creation and cannot migrate to another sovereignty. But although it must live and have its being in that state only, yet *it does not by any means follow that its existence there will not be recognized in other places, and its residence in one state creates no insuperable objection to its power of contracting in another.*[47]

The secret for the corporation's mobility is for other states to recognize the legal creatures that were organized under foreign law. The more states do so, the greater the reach of the law most corporations prefer, and the more options firms have to choose for their regulatory and tax regimes, and even the property law that governs the assets they issue or manage.

The name of this game of picking and choosing is called "conflict-of-law" rules or "international private law"; every state has a set of these rules, which determine what law shall apply if more than one jurisdiction is in play.[48] Conflict-of-law rules exist not only for corporate law, but for all legal relations that involve parties from more than one jurisdiction. The contracting parties may reside in two different states; the plaintiff may have been hurt on a trip to a foreign country; an asset may have been moved from one jurisdiction to another; or a corporation may have been created in one jurisdiction but does its business in another. If a case comes to court, the judge will have to consult these conflict-of-law rules to determine whether the buyer's or the seller's laws govern their contract, whether the damage award should be considered under the law of the place where the tort action was taken, or where the injured suffered its lasting impact; or whether a company that was founded under foreign law should be recognized as a corporate entity with all its legal privileges in the host state, whether or not it has ever done business at its birthplace.

CHOOSING CORPORATE LAW

Not too long ago, there were two conflict-of-law principles for corporate law competing with one another: the "incorporation theory" and the "seat theory," with some countries following the former and others the latter. The incorporation theory allows the corporation to choose its birthplace without compromising its recognition as a legal entity elsewhere; all it takes is to follow the rules of the place of incorporation and enough other states who are willing to recognize its legal entity status. In contrast, the seat theory privileges the law of the place where the corporation maintains its headquarters or major operations. Only if the company is incorporated under the laws of this jurisdiction will it be recognized as a corporate entity within this jurisdiction. Drawing a parallel to the citizenship of ordinary humans may help illustrate what is at stake here: Under the incorporation theory, every person would be able to choose his or her citizenship, regardless of whether she ever wanted to set foot in that country. This citizen would be able to carry her passport around the globe and obtain entry in all countries that grant this privilege to citizens of the country of her choice. In contrast, under the seat theory, the same person would have to make a choice where to live and become a citizen of that country lest she risked being stripped of her citizenship. If she chose to shift operations to another country, she would have to obtain a new passport first. For natural persons, the equivalent of the "seat theory" governs their mobility. They may acquire temporary access to foreign countries by requesting a visa, but if they wish to settle for longer, they need a new passport or permanent resident permit. In contrast, most legal persons can rely on the incorporation theory to roam the globe.

The United Kingdom is an old adherent of incorporation theory. In the United States, the Constitution's Commerce Clause has been interpreted to firmly implement the same principle. It prevents states from discriminating against corporations from other states, even if they were formed under laws that conflicted with the ones the host state had adopted.[49] Following this example, in the European Union (EU), the European Court of Justice has all but struck down the seat theory, which was used in Denmark and Germany, for example, to deny a corporation that had been formed under the laws of a different member state of the EU to shift its headquarters to the new host state without re-incorporating under its rules.[50] In the eyes of the court, this application of the seat theory violates the principles of the free movement of capital and persons (including legal persons) that are enshrined in EU treaty law.[51]

The argument sounds compelling, but in fact, no movement is necessary when shopping for corporate law; only the paperwork for registering the entity has to be sent to a different address. Re-incorporating an existing entity elsewhere is a bit more complicated, but lawyers in the field of transnational mergers do this all the time. Further, as the sprawling Lehman family illustrates, corporations themselves often make use of the possibility to create separate legal entities in multiple jurisdictions. If it works for them, it should also work for the sovereigns that make the law that breathes life into the corporate form.

The viability of Lehman's legal structure with its hundreds of subsidiaries that were spread across twenty-six different jurisdictions hinged on the acceptance of the incorporation theory in most jurisdictions where it did business. Lehman's business operations were conducted predominantly in New York and London; only seven of its entities were incorporated in the state of New York, but there were thirty-eight in the UK. LBHI, the parent company, was incorporated in the state of Delaware, along with fifty-nine other subsidiaries.

It is sometimes argued that the prevalence of company groups that consist of many legal entities is a sign of bad corporate law. Only a law that does a poor job of protecting shareholders against managers, it has been said, creates incentives to build complex company groups that allegedly are used to protect management from shareholders.[52] These arguments, however, cannot possibly explain Lehman's legal structure. Delaware law ranks among the most investor-friendly jurisdictions, yet Lehman chose to have sixty entities incorporated there—not because it liked the state or its corporate law so much, but because this way it could shield each entity's assets from the creditors of the others. Multiple subsidiaries were also incorporated in the UK, attesting to London's standing as a major hub for financial intermediaries. The fact that some of the most shareholder-friendly jurisdictions were used to incorporate dozens of entities that belonged to the same group suggests that using entity shielding is a highly lucrative strategy for shareholders— quite apart from the quality of the corporate law. The choice of the Cayman Islands for thirty-two of Lehman's subsidiaries is more straightforward, for it is a well-known tax haven.[53]

CHOOSING ONE'S TAX RATE

Most ordinary people cannot choose their own tax rate; they may move their holdings to foreign bank accounts, but they have to fear that even the toughest bank secrecy laws will be cracked and that they will be prosecuted for tax evasion. Corporations have a much easier task in choosing the tax rate they wish to pay. They can simply create a legal entity in a jurisdiction with a low tax rate and book taxable income to its account. This works even if a state imposes its taxes on the worldwide income of a corporate group, as long as tax payments from foreign subsidiaries are demanded only when their income is brought home. In addition, a parent corporation can acquire a different nationality and with it, a different tax regime, when they re-incorporate in a different legal system.⁵⁴ This can be done, for example, by a technique called an inversion merger. In this transaction, a large corporation from a high-tax jurisdiction acquires a smaller corporation in a low-tax jurisdiction and then folds itself into the smaller entity. It is like marrying to obtain a green card even when there is little love lost between the two parties, i.e., bride and groom; the main difference is that as long as it is structured properly, the inversion merger is legal.

As of late, there has been a clampdown on aggressive tax-sheltering strategies. In the European Union, the Commission's Directorate-General for Competition investigated tax-sheltering practices by Apple and other companies. The Commission asserted that Apple paid an effective tax rate for selling its products throughout the EU's territory, of as little as 1–5 percent, even as the tax rate across the union was closer to 20 percent.⁵⁵ Apple had created this tax shelter by establishing two subsidiaries in Ireland, which under Irish law were treated as "non-residents" for tax purposes, and as such were tax-exempt even from the country's low corporate tax rate of 12 percent. The company then booked almost all incomes from sales in all member states to these two companies.

The EU Commission condemned the tax scheme as illegal state aid by Ireland to the multinational corporation and ruled that Apple had to pay retroactively the taxes it owed to Ireland.⁵⁶ Apple appealed the decision (but ultimately paid up), but, more interesting, the Irish government did so as well, even as the country's citizens protested against this decision. The government sought to defend an economic development strategy that used tax competition as one of its core pillars. The inflow of foreign investments to Ireland has indeed boosted the country's GDP figures; however, this has not translated into substantial gains for its citizens, as most of the profits quickly left the country again.⁵⁷

Apple is only one of many examples, and Ireland is not the most egregious competitor for global business in exchange for a benign tax environment. Taking a closer look at this tax shelter, however, has shown that choosing one's corporate law is key for tax-sheltering schemes to work. OECD member states have vowed to crack down on tax havens and have blacklisted countries that offer rates below what they deem proper, but they have not yet reconsidered their willingness to recognize any corporation created anywhere, even if it maintains no operations and has no employees there, and its only purpose is to engage in tax arbitrage.[58]

REGULATORY ARBITRAGE

Within hours after LBHI had filed for bankruptcy on September 15, 2008, its major UK-based subsidiary, Lehman Brothers International Europe (LBIE), went into administration under UK law. Soon, seventy-five distinct bankruptcy proceedings were opened in various jurisdictions in an attempt to salvage assets for the various creditors of Lehman's many subsidiaries.

Bankruptcy is when the music stops and all but the most vital functions are halted by court order. Inside the Lehman empire, though, some transactions continued unabated, flipping assets back and forth between LBIE and several other Lehman subsidiaries, including a Swiss entity by the name of LBF.[59] Nobody seemed to have noticed or even was bothered by this until one employee, without asking anyone, pressed the "off" switch.[60] This put an end to an internal transfer and accounting system Lehman had created to protect the group from the reach of EU prudential regulations. The name of the game was RASCALS, a term the Merriam-Webster dictionary defines as a "mischievous person or animal," but it stood for "Regulation and Administration of Safe Custody and Local Settlement."[61]

RASCALS was Lehman's response to an EU Capital Adequacy Directive, which imposed new capital adequacy rules on financial intermediaries.[62] The purpose of capital adequacy rules is to make financial intermediaries more resilient in times of distress by forcing them to fund at least some of their operations with equity (that is, contributions paid in by shareholders), rather than allowing them to rely exclusively on debt finance. For their part, financial intermediaries complain that these rules add to their funding costs. While this argument is disputed in the literature, many financial intermediaries do indeed go to great lengths to avoid capital adequacy rules of this kind, and so did Lehman.[63] The RASCALS scheme is only an example of the lengths to which they are willing to go to fund most of their operations with debt.

Lehman's London subsidiary LBIE was set up as the major trading hub for the entire Lehman group, buying and selling, lending and borrowing securities to "the street" (other participants in London's financial marketplace) on its own account, but also on account of other Lehman subsidiaries. Under the new EU rules, every time LBIE acquired securities with its own funds on behalf of another subsidiary, the company incurred a "capital charge" requiring it to show that a certain percentage of this exposure was covered by equity. LBIE incurred this charge because it advanced its own money to buy securities on behalf of other Lehman subsidiaries and therefore faced the risk that these subsidiaries might not make good on their promises to compensate it. Trading on credit, however, *was* the company's business model. To protect the model and its profitability, which the new capital adequacy rules threatened to reduce or even eliminate, Lehman simply created a new subsidiarity in a non-EU jurisdiction, where the new EU rules did not apply, and set up a chain of transactions that shifted the credit exposure to that entity.

The new company, LBF, was incorporated in Switzerland, but operated out of Lehman's London offices with largely overlapping staff—thanks to the UK's adherence to the incorporation theory. A continuous loop of automated repurchase agreements, or repos, for the assets that LBIE had acquired on behalf of LBF was created between the two entities. No money ever changed hands between the two entities; when one transaction was completed and the two companies should have settled their accounts and cashed out any differences, another repo transaction was opened, and when this one was supposed to settle, a third opened, and so forth. Some RASCALS transactions were set up manually, but most ran automatically, keeping the machine humming and creating the illusion that at every point in time, LBIE had secured its claims against LBF and thus did not have to create the equity cushion that regulators demanded it should.

For the fifteen years of its operation, RASCALS benefited the entire Lehman family, but when bankruptcy loomed, the fight over the leftovers began and LBF's creditors sought to secure assets for themselves. For them and their receivers in bankruptcy who represented them, the $50 million question became, who owned the *rascalled* assets that had been flipped back and forth between them: LBIE or LBF? LBIE argued that it continuously owned them. LBF held against this that the assets had been purchased on LBF's behalf, and that LBIE was merely a trustee rather than the real owner.

The case was brought in a London chancery court and the chancellor who presided over the case sided with LBIE—a decision that was later confirmed by the high court.[64] In deciphering the scheme and analyzing its legal impact, he relied largely on the intent of the parties—no matter that RASCALS's purpose was blatant evasion of prudential rules. The parties, he argued, wanted LBIE to be "clothed" with formal title, even though the economic benefits and risks of the assets fell on LBF.[65] All parties had agreed to this, because by lowering regulatory costs, RASCALS boosted the group's overall profitability. When the creditors of LBF argued that the entire scheme was only a scam and should simply be set aside, the chancellor was in disbelief:

> It is, at least at first sight, counter-intuitive to think that one of the largest and most sophisticated investment banking institutions in the world, staffed by some of the foremost experts in the business and advised by the most eminent law firms, should have spent more than a decade solemnly entering into countless thousands of mutual transactions which were either completely unnecessary, completely ineffective or both. The suspension of disbelief called for by the parties' primary cases has not been easy.[66]

The chancellor was not surprised, it seems, that the same experts had spent all this time devising a scheme that had no intrinsic economic value but was devoted entirely to regulatory arbitrage. Like the chancery courts of the eighteenth century, which had sided with the landed elites, he had few qualms about parties using the law to their own private benefits, even if this put the entire system at risk.

Indeed, he explicitly sidestepped an inquiry into the legality of an endless chain of repos that never settle or the ramification for trust law that followed from this scheme. This willingness to bow to the interests of capital makes outright capture of lawmakers and law enforcers almost unnecessary.

Courts and legislatures have not always and everywhere been quite as accommodating. The first free incorporation statutes enacted by legislatures were spiked with safeguards against the abuse of the corporate form. In 1811, the state of New York enacted one of the first free incorporation statutes. It included a sunset provision, thereby limiting the life span of corporations to 20 years; it imposed a capital ceiling of $100,000; and it required that the directors of the corporation be drawn from among the corporation's shareholders.[67] None of these restrictions still exist anywhere, and they would, of course, be quite impractical; but they do reflect the wariness of lawmakers who sensed that they were about to create a legal structure over which they might lose control; and they surely did.

4

Minting Debt

If there is one asset that defines capitalism, it is debt—not any debt, but debt that can be easily transferred from one investor to another, and preferably debt that is convertible into state money at any time on the behest of its holders, the creditors. Convertibility of private debt on demand is typically assumed but is not always an enforceable claim. The logic of a private economy is that you can sell only if you find a willing buyer, that is, a private buyer. If private buyers retreat, demand declines, and asset prices fall, investors who recently thought that they had huge amounts of wealth at their fingertips might lose it in no time. To lock in past gains, investors will try to convert their private assets into state money, the only financial asset that is guaranteed to keep its nominal value.[1] The reason is that, unlike private entities, states do not have a binding survival constraint. They can print money and they have the power to unilaterally impose burdens on their citizens in the form of taxes or austerity measures, thereby ensuring their own survival.

When private parties run out of money, they may request help from their peers, but they cannot force them to deliver. If they fail to garner support, they face extinction; the only alternative is to go to the source of state money: the government or its central bank.

As noted in chapter 1, convertibility is one of the key attributes of capital; its relevance is most apparent in the case of financial assets, in particular, debt instruments. For holders of these assets, convertibility has the same importance that durability had for landowners or major lenders to corporations who sought a stable capital base against which to lend. Investors in tradable instruments are fickle; they are constantly on the move as their holders are out to find yet another profit opportunity. It therefore makes little sense to lock them up behind real or legal shields. But this does not mean that holders of financial assets do not crave certainty; their certainty comes from the ability to convert their assets into cash on demand without a serious loss. The trick is to make these assets look almost like state money, that is, to cloak them in legal modules that enhance the chances that they can be converted into cash on demand.

The history of debt finance can therefore be retold as a story about how claims to future pay have been coded in law to ensure their convertibility into state money on demand, without suffering serious loss. This chapter traces the coding techniques for the most basic forms of debt, the notes and later the bills of exchange that emerged between the twelfth and the seventeenth centuries, all the way to modern-day securitized assets and credit derivatives. The story also illustrates the shift away from landowners, the privileged holders of property rights who often figured as debtors in the past, to creditors as the asset holders who enjoy the strongest legal protection. Signs for this shift have long been evident, but only after land had been thoroughly dethroned in the late nineteenth century did financial assets come to the fore as a leading source of private wealth. As we shift focus from owners to creditors, and from land to debt, we will encounter the same legal modules that we have seen at play before: contract, property and collateral law, trust, corporate, and bankruptcy law. These legal modules mitigate the risk associated with debt and in doing so have fueled its expansion from one unprecedented height to another—to be followed only too often by equally steep downturns, safe only for the successful intervention of states and their central banks. Huge gains could be made along the way, and losses were often shifted to others.

These losses tend to fall primarily on two groups: The unsecured debtors, that is, creditors who by operation of general bankruptcy rules are last in line to share in the leftovers; and states, or rather their citizens, whose future productivity they commit when bailing out failing entities. In the absence of state backing, debt cycles would draw their natural circles, making and destroying wealth along the way. Many states have smoothed out these cycles by standing by to protect holders of these assets from the abyss, time and again; others that were either unwilling or unable to do so have seen their economies ravaged by debt crises that destroyed wealth and brought economic decline. In addition, they had to cede sovereignty to their creditors, to the International Monetary Fund (IMF), or "the Troika," comprised of the IMF, the ECB, and the European Commission.

When stepping into the void by offering new credit to borrowers that were shunned by private creditors, or when buying assets from creditors that no longer found any private takers, states have tended to protect assets and asset holders that were critical for the survival of the system and have left the rest to fend for themselves. In so doing, they have helped stabilize finance, but they have also contributed to the massive concentration of wealth in the hands of those at the top of a financial system that is not flat, but deeply hierarchical.[2]

NC2—A Post-Mortem

To see how deeply the legal code of capital is involved in structuring debt, meet NC2. It is one of the more complex debt instruments that lawyers have designed for their clients, but also one that allows us a glimpse into the organization of the parallel or "shadow" banking system that has emerged over the past few decades. NC2 is a securitization structure that was created in 2006, just at the time when US real estate markets began to flatten out and stress began to build in the financial system. The story of NC2 and the Kleros clones has been told before—by the US Federal Crisis Inquiry Commission (FCIC), which the US Congress had set up to analyze the root causes of the great financial crisis.[3] The FCIC had surprisingly little to say about the legal structures involved, but it made publicly available the relevant legal documents, ready to be dissected for our purposes.[4]

NC2's real name is "CMLTI 2006-NC2," which stands for "Citigroup Mortgage Loan Trust 2006-New Century 2." The name indicates NC2's genesis and parenthood. It is a trust, established under the laws of the state of New York, born in 2006 and sponsored by a member of the Citigroup family, a financial holding company whose parent company is also incorporated in the state of New York. NC2's ancestry can be further traced to New Century (NC), a mortgage originator based in California that filed for bankruptcy already in the spring of 2007, long before Lehman's demise triggered a full-blown crisis that brought global finance almost to a standstill. New Century did not have the most stellar reputation in the market, and its aggressive strategies in originating mortgages by pushing homeowners into financial arrangements they could hardly afford, were well known. Nonetheless, this did not prevent some of the more reputable banks from dealing with it.

New Century originated the mortgages that were later funneled into NC2, warehoused them, and sold them wholesale to Citigroup's Mortgage Realty Corporation (CMRC), the sponsor of the NC2 trust. New Century received a premium of 2.5 percent, or $24 million, on the transaction. The purchase price of the mortgages that were transferred to NC2 was about $750 million, comprising 4,507 residential mortgages with an average principal balance of $210,478. There was some variation in the contractual structure of the mortgages and in the interest rates and the principal amount homeowners had agreed to pay, and this was dutifully disclosed to the investors who cared to read it.[5] However, few did or were interested in doing so, primarily for two reasons: they relied on the ratings of these assets by officially recognized rating agencies, and they believed they were well protected in law.[6] Investors would receive fixed payments from the cash flow that made it back into the pool according to a plan that stratified claims according to different risk profiles and payout schedules. The remainder of the often 200-plus-pages-long prospectus that was carefully drafted by lawyers to ensure that all risks were adequately disclosed was legalese to them. The relevance of many provisions buried in the document, particularly the list of risk factors that grew longer from year to year, became apparent only when it was too late for those who had not been able to sell their assets fast enough.

Recall that to establish a trust we need a settlor, a trustee, and a beneficiary.[7] In the old days when land and mansions were placed in trusts, all three tended to be individuals, most likely personal acquaintances if not family members: a friend, neighbor, or relative of the settlor would be the trustee and the beneficiary would be the settlor's later born son, daughter, or other relative. In the eighteenth century, solicitors increasingly took on the role of trustees in business trusts, and in the nineteenth century they were joined by banks. Along the way, trusts morphed from safekeeping land for family members into vehicles that segregated assets on a much larger scale and protected them from the credit risks associated with the bank that served as the trust-sponsor and eventually into off-balance structures for securitized assets and their derivatives.

Whereas previously, beneficiaries had to await the death of the settlor or similar event to take control over the asset, investors of securitized assets have been less patient. They care not for mortgages but for fixed payments from cash flows that these mortgages generate and their ability to convert their interests into cash to lock in their gains. The mortgages themselves only serve as collateral to be realized by some agent should a borrower default; given that investors were well diversified (or at least they thought they were), it did not concern them if some homeowners defaulted, as long as, according to the models used, not all did so at the same time, and as long as the houses of the ones who did default kept their value.

Similarly, in the modern securitization business, trustees are not friends or family members of the trust's settlor, but financial intermediaries. They don't offer their services as fiduciaries for free but are paid a fee based on a small percentage of the asset value. Their new mandate to manage a portfolio of assets created new questions about trustee liability. Most of these issues were addressed in relevant contracts that specified the scope of their rights and responsibilities, including limitations on their liabilities. As always, new legal coding strategies such as these were developed in private practice by transactional lawyers; they made their way into case law only if and when challenged, but during boom times, litigation was a rare occurrence, and so the practice spread and became a new way of how business was done.

NC2's trust sponsor, or settlor, was the Citigroup affiliate, CMRC, which had acquired the mortgages from New Century. The US Bank National Association, a Cincinnati-based private bank, was appointed trustee. In addition to the trustee, there was a "trust administrator," a depositor, a custodian, and a credit risk manager. These various functions were filled in part by other Citigroup affiliates and in part by outsiders, and those on the inside at NC2 would often offer services as outsiders for similar trusts set up by their competitors. This way, financial intermediaries could be earning fees left and right, while protecting themselves from conflicts of interest by employing their competitors for services they could not provide themselves without running afoul of the law.

The NC2 prospectus circulated to attract investors discloses the volumes of mortgage-backed securities of the kind that were assembled in NC2 handled by the key players. According to the prospectus, CMRC (the sponsor) had already securitized assets worth $50 billion, and US Bank N.A. disclosed that it acted as trustee for "667 issuances of MBS/Prime securities with an outstanding aggregate principal balance of approximately $292,570,800,000.00." The trust administrator, another affiliate of Citigroup by the name of Citibank N.A., was reported to manage "in excess of $3.5 trillion in fixed income and equity investments on behalf of approximately 2,500 corporations worldwide."[8]

Securitization became a fee-based business. The servicer of the NC2 trust, for example, was paid 0.5 percent multiplied by the principal balance of the mortgage loans on the day it was established, and the credit risk manager, 0.015 percent.[9] This may not sound like much, but even small percentages add up, provided, of course, that the business is humming. The logic of private-label securitization was mass production, and new mortgages had to be fed into this machine constantly to sustain it. In addition, investors came to rely on the ready availability of assets with high ratings. Indeed, the post-crisis autopsy conducted by the FCIC reported that New Century and other mortgage originators received requests for more mortgages from banks in the securitization business, often before they had originated them.[10] Prior to the onset of securitization, only the US government and a few blue-chip corporations had bonds consistently rated in the triple-A range. This new coding technique, however, would create safe assets on demand by picking the assets that went into the pool and by tranching the claims against the pool such that there were always some that would receive top rating and therefore attract money market and pensions funds, which are proscribed from investing in high-risk assets.[11]

The number of homeowners with a decent credit record, however, is not unlimited; invariably the quality standards for the assets that were securitized declined. This was not a secret. Anyone who cared to read the prospectus of NC2 or other SPVs could find out.[12] Citi's affiliate CMRC reported in the NC2 prospectus that over the course of only three years, it had shifted its portfolio from mostly prime MBS, that is, assets with a low-default risk, to an equal share of prime and subprime, or high-default risk, products. During the same period, it increased its entire portfolio from $2.9 billion to $18.4 billion, or by a factor of six, indicating that the expansion of its portfolio was caused mostly by embracing subprime products, which, of course, were more likely to default.[13]

This change in Citi's portfolio coincided with a shift in the overall market; in 2003, subprime mortgages accounted for 22 percent in dollar volume of all securitized mortgages. By 2004, this number had increased to 46 percent.[14] The risk that these practices created for the chain of intermediaries that participated in the minting of debt is reflected in the fate of the intermediaries that were involved in the NC2 deal. Almost everyone suffered severe financial distress in the financial crisis, not caused by NC2 alone, but by the business practices for which NC2 was emblematic. New Century filed for bankruptcy already in the spring of 2007. Bear Stearns was forced into a shotgun marriage with JP Morgan Chase in the spring of 2008, as discussed in chapter 3. And Citigroup received several capital injections, first from the sovereign wealth funds of foreign nations (Qatar and Singapore in particular) and eventually from the US government.[15]

So much for the basic structure of NC2, which is more complex than the trusts we encountered earlier, but the basic structure is still the same. But what about the assets in the pool? Here too we can see remarkable advances in the coding strategies that were meant to enhance the marketability of these assets. A basic securitization structure is rather simple and resembles the pooling of risks and resources of the early joint stock companies discussed in chapter 3. The claims to future payments on many home loans, all backed by mortgages, are placed behind a legal shield, like a trust. The trust then issues certificates to investors. They now hold a claim, not against an individual homeowner, but against a pool of loans to many homeowners that are backed by mortgages on their homes; what is more, by moving the assets to a trust, they become "bankruptcy remote" from their sponsor, in the case of NC2 from the Citi affiliate CMRC. This means that investors need not worry about what happens at Citi and its affiliates, all they need to worry about is the quality of the loans backed by the mortgages in the pool, although even this proved to be more than many investors could handle, especially once the claims against the pool had been rearranged into tranches, each of which carried a different pay-off structure and risk profile.

Following this model, assets inside NC2's mortgage pool were tranched and each tranche was rated separately. Tailoring claims to cash flows from the pool made it possible to attract different groups of investors, each according to its ability and each according to its needs: The safest super-senior tranche in NC2 went to Fannie Mae, one of the government-sponsored entities (GSEs), for $155 million.[16] Buying senior tranches seemed to be a safe bet and generated profits for this GSE. Note that Fannie Mae appears here as the buyer of securitized assets, not as the securitizer, a role that it had played earlier and would assume again after the crisis.

NC2's second most senior tranche found interest among leading financial intermediaries from the United States and elsewhere, including a subsidiary of JP Morgan Chase (Chase Security Lendings Asset

Management), China's sovereign wealth fund (the China Investment Corporation, or CIC), and six other investment funds. The third and fourth most senior tranches were acquired by a mix of domestic and foreign banks and investment funds that included, among others, Federal Home Loan Bank of Chicago (US), Fidelity (US), Société Générale (France), and Bayerische Landesbank (a German bank owned by the state of Bavaria). All of these entities were seeking higher returns than Fannie but were not willing to risk too much. As it turned out later, however, they all did, including Fannie, because when the markets turned, no tranche escaped the run on the market.

Of the investors in the lower ranked, mezzanine tranches, the French entity Parvest ABS Euribor acquired the largest stake for a total of $20 million. Launched only in 2005 by the French bank BNP Paribas, Parvest was supposed to conquer the market for securitized assets and produce above-average returns. That, of course, meant that it had to invest in risky assets. In 2005, when the real estate market was still booming, this may have looked like a good bet. Unfortunately, Parvest entered the market at its very peak; in August 2007, BNP Paribas froze assets in Parvest and two other funds, effectively barring investors from redeeming their assets and converting them into cash.[17] This marked one of the first warning shots for the crisis to come, just over a year before Lehman went down.

Finally, Citigroup Global Markets (CGGM), which served as an underwriter for the NC2 deal, acquired the junior tranche at the very bottom of the claims against the pool to be sold subsequently in private placement. The tranche just above was given to the sponsor of the NC2 trust, the Citi affiliate CMRC, as "partial consideration for the sale of the mortgage loans."[18] It is interesting to note that the trust's sponsor acquired the tranches that bore close to the highest risk. It flies in the face of a business model that has been characterized as a "pass-through model," which means that the originators or buyers of mortgages do not hold risky mortgages on their own balance sheet but repackage them and sell them off as securitized assets to other investors. This practice also came as a surprise to regulators and market observers, who found to their astonishment that when the crisis broke out, many banks were sitting on a lot of high-risk assets that were now toxic. There are many reasons for this, but two stand out: to close a deal, all tranches had to be sold off, and it may have been easier and cheaper to warehouse the riskiest assets for a while than to locate a buyer for them. Moreover, high risk promises high yield and some banks that sponsored securitization vehicles may have been sufficiently enthralled by the prospects of high returns to take on that risk. This still left securities just one step above the junior tranches in NC2, and they went to a peculiar type of investor, the Kleros clones, which we will encounter below.

NC2 is a fairly complex debt instrument. It is the product of asset holders' imagination and their lawyers' coding skills. Yet, the legal modules for coding these assets should be familiar by now. They rely on property rights to land and collateral law (mortgages) that can be used to secure land for a personal loan. They use trusts and corporate law to protect the loans backed by mortgages, i.e., their assets, behind a legal shield and thereby separate them from other operations of the trust's sponsor. Finally, they use contract law to subdivide and rank the claims against the pool, creating tranches that can be tailored to the needs of different investors and thereby ensure that all or at least most of them will find buyers. By combining these legal modules in new ways, new debt assets were minted in the trillions of dollars. Once the private sector had discovered securitization, it securitized any claim imaginable, from residential mortgages to receivables for products and services from cars to credit cards and student loans; the original policy goal of lowering the costs of credit for homeowners gave way to minting as much private money (or debt) as investors demanded. In this pursuit they were greatly aided by the rating agencies.

As we have seen, NC2's tranches ran the gamut from "AAA" all the way down to lower B ratings.[19] Rating agencies used the same nomenclature they had used for decades to rate government or corporate bonds to rate MBS and their derivatives.[20] This created the appearance to investors that the credit risk they were assuming was indeed comparable with these familiar assets, but in fact disguised the most important difference between these different assets. Whereas for government and most corporate bonds, historical data exist for many years, even decades, similar long-term data did not and could not exist for asset-backed securities (ABS) or collateralized debt obligations (CDOs), which had only recently seen the light of day. Any comparison was therefore misleading.

Yet, rating agencies have largely escaped liability for the use of misleading labels, for their willingness to work closely with the sponsoring entity to ensure that the right mix of safe versus risky assets would emerge once they were done with their ratings, or for their failure to downgrade their ratings when markets began to turn. The reason for this can be found once more in law: rating agencies have successfully defended themselves in the United States with the argument that they are in the business of offering opinions, and that their utterances should therefore enjoy the protection of free speech under the US Constitution's First Amendment.[21] The fact that they received remunerations for their "opinions" from banks and other clients that by far exceeded the returns made by other opinion providers, such as ordinary news outlets, did not prevent courts from granting them this constitutional protection. Post-crisis, some US courts have moved away from this position and have labeled ratings that do not reach the public at large as "commercial speak," a shift that should increase the vulnerability of these agencies to liability in the future.

Minting Convertible Assets

As previously noted, NC2 is a complex and complicated product, which made use of the basic legal modules of the code, but in their adulterated forms. Had it been coded in earlier centuries, even decades, it may have been struck down by the courts, because the assets inside NC2 would not have been eligible for trusts, or because the structure was too obvious a maneuver around mandatory bankruptcy rules.[22] Moreover, without additional tax privileges that were created specifically to ensure that the trusts that harbored tranched assets remained tax-exempt, it may never have been economically viable. In other words, NC2 like other residential mortgage-backed securities (RMBS) is the quintessential legal steroid: it is made in law and lives off extra-legal boosts that are not available to other assets.

To see more clearly how much legal coding has been added to debt instruments over time in the quest for turning claims to future pay into tradable assets that can be turned into state money on demand, it is useful to begin in the twelfth century, when debt obligations first became transferable. A *note* is a written statement that "I owe you" (IOU) the amount stipulated. It is a simple debt contract between two parties. Anybody can issue an IOU, but not all will find takers, and even those who do at first, may lose them down the road.[23] In the twelfth century, promissory notes made a regular appearance in Genoa, a major trading hub and port on the eastern coast of Italy. The buyer of goods would write a promise to pay the seller or "your messenger." These additional two words added to a simple note allowed the parties to get around the legal prohibition against transferring their contractual obligations to someone else.

Today, such a prohibition may strike many as strange. Global debt markets have reached trillions of dollars, which are moved in fractions of seconds by the stroke of a key. But even now, not all contractual obligations can be freely passed on to others. A contract is a relation between two persons who may have spent considerable time selecting with whom they wished to contract. Creditors' claims are fully transferable as a default in most legal systems today, even without explicit consent by the debtor; but the reverse is not true. A homeowner, for example, can't just transfer her mortgage to the buyer of her house; this buyer will need to find his own lender.

Bills of exchange are notes on legal steroids. They are transferred from merchant to merchant, each accepting it as a means of payment and then using them to pay their own bills. By signing them, they assume the full liability of the amount stated on the bill. Whoever acquires a bill of exchange can approach anyone who had signed or endorsed it previously and demand payment of the full amount stated on the bill. The holder of the bill does not have to seek enforcement from the original debtor first; and neither does he have to listen to the defense that the contract for which the bill had been accepted and signed was never carried out. The persons from whom payment is demanded may not even counter that the bill was stolen.[24] By signing the bill, the endorser accepts a liability that is independent of the contractual relation for which he accepted it.

The famous English judge, Lord Mansfield, explained the difference between a note and a bill in 1794 as follows:

> While a promissory note continues in its original shape of a promise from one man to pay another, it bears no similitude to a bill of exchange. When it is indorsed, the resemblance begins: for, then *it is an order, by the indorser, upon the maker of the note, (his debtor, by the note) to pay the indorsee.* This is the very definition of a bill of exchange.[25]

This special quality, in legal jargon "negotiability," makes bills fungible and akin to state money. True, any one of the previous endorsers might default, but the likelihood that the creditor will be able to convert the bill into cash is much higher when he can enforce against multiple endorsees than if he had to rely on the original debtor alone. And by eliminating the requirement to turn to the original debtor first, the transaction costs for enforcing bills of exchange were greatly reduced.

Bills were widely used to transfer funds, outstanding balances, or advances, and to extend credit among buyers and sellers, producers, and merchants without having to carry piles of gold or silver coins from one place to another. They further evolved into a full-blown payment system for long-distance trade across Europe. Local merchants operated through agents in distant trading centers, sending them orders to pay others for charges they had incurred. Bills were passed from hand to hand and endorsed along the way in ever longer chains of payment commitments. They formed the basis of the first domestic and international payment systems long before banks and central banks took charge.

By the late seventeenth century, it had become common practice to draw bills for goods that would be sold (or produced) only at some future date. This form of "acceptance finance" soon became one of the most popular applications of the bill. It transformed the bill from a means of payment to a debt instrument, illustrating the semblance between (private) money and debt.[26] Merchant banks played a pivotal role in accepting bills against cash, thereby facilitating the conversion of credit claims into cash on demand. They assumed the risk of collecting the outstanding debt and protected themselves by buying bills not at face value, but at a discount. In finance jargon, they assumed the role of dealers, providing liquidity to others and assuming the liquidity risk.

Bills were also a convenient vehicle for getting around anti-usury rules, which prohibited or at least capped interest rates. Sellers who accepted a bill in lieu of payment typically required an amount exceeding the price of the good, and merchant banks discounted them as well. This may look like an interest rate, but it withstood usury policing, because it was deemed a risk premium rather than a charge for the time value of money. Charging money for time, which was of God's making according to church doctrine, was prohibited as immoral.[27] Not every regulatory arbitrage around usury rules, however, passed muster in the courts, both canon and secular, that policed them. Transactions that flipped bills between two parties without exchanging goods, merely to make profits of exchange rate differentials, for example, were condemned as "dry exchanges" and struck down.[28] These and similar restrictions have since fallen by the wayside and turned carry trades from outlawed transactions into hugely lucrative deals.[29]

The emergence and widespread use of bills of exchange are often cited as evidence of the *law merchant*—a set of purely private practices that sustained long-distance trade without relying on the state, its laws, or its coercive powers. The scale and scope of the *law merchant*, however, seems to have been exaggerated and romanticized by writers in the nineteenth century who used it to argue that commerce is best left to its own devices and the state should refrain from regulating finance.[30] There is little doubt that the origins of bills lie in private practice. Merchant bankers made money by accepting and discounting notes and bills; they set the standards for what they would accept and how much they would discount such claims. Still, absent the legal support structure that city governments and courts extended to them, this payment system most likely would have faced early extinction. The bill's endorsers could have simply refused to pay, hoping that a local court would treat the bill as an ordinary note that had to be enforced against the original debtor. In fact, the proliferation of bills throughout Europe went hand in hand with statutory protections of bills in the major trading towns, marking the expansion of trade and trade finance.[31] City councils in these towns were packed with merchants who, not surprisingly, supported legal protection for this instrument on which their business depended. The early statutes were eventually incorporated into domestic law and ultimately found their way into an international convention, adopted in 1930 under the auspices of the League of Nations.[32] By that time, however, a new payment system was on the rise and the bill started its slow decline as the first debt instrument with trans-national reach; other private assets soon took its place, among them asset-backed securities and their derivatives.[33]

From Bills to Securitized Assets

Notes and bills were designed to facilitate trade and commerce. They could also be flipped into assets that were used purely for financial speculation, as the example of the "dry exchange" given above suggests. When banks made their first appearance, they did not offer deposits, but rather notes, to willing takers, using the proceeds to make their own investment, even as they promised noteholders prompt payment in species (i.e., gold or silver) upon demand. Once states created monopolies for issuing notes, private banks that were now prohibited from issuing notes found a solution in creating deposit accounts for their customers. Although functionally the equivalent of issuing a note that promises redemption in species on demand, deposit accounts passed legal muster and have since become the standard for raising funds from the broader public—another example of effective regulatory arbitrage.[34]

Competition in finance will always push some to find new ways of making money. State money is boring, as every banker would tell you; it can be used as a means of exchange and to *store* value, but it does not *create* much of a return. While every textbook about banking describes financial intermediation as the process by which household savings will be channeled to productive investments, more gains have always been made by minting debt. This private money, however, carries a risk that state money does not, and that is liquidity risk. Only state money comes potentially in unlimited quantities; private money is limited by the willingness of other private actors to accept it and that depends on its prospects to generate future returns. By dressing private debt in the modules of the legal code of capital, it is possible to mask the liquidity risk for a while, but not forever. Whenever investors realize that, contrary to their expectations, they may not be able to convert their debt assets into cash, they head for the exit; and if many do so simultaneously, this will precipitate a financial crisis.

Bills of exchange were more liquid than notes, because their legal coding precludes anyone who endorsed it from exercising the rights against a creditor that would be available to the holder of a simple note. Limiting the rights of debtors and forcing them to pay cash upon demand is one way to enhance, though not guarantee, an asset's liquidity. Individual debtors may, of course, default, but if enough debtors are lined up, this risk can be mitigated to some extent. For some assets, however, more had to be done to turn them into readily tradable assets. Land is a case in point; it is the most stable and least liquid asset imaginable. It stays put; most legal systems require that changes in land ownership are registered, typically in local land registries, and any collateral or similar right to the land must be registered as well. And yet, it has long been tempting to try to monetize the value of land, turning rights to land into tradable financial assets. We are already familiar with the legal technique to accomplish this feat, namely securitization. The securitization of mortgages transforms a claim for repayment of a loan that is backed by the value of the house into a claim against future cash flows made by the debtor in fulfillment of her obligations under the loan, and this claim can be traded and thus converted into cash as long as there are willing buyers.

The claim to fame as the inventor of securitizing land does not belong to Ginnie Mae, which kicked off the securitization of mortgages in the United States in the early 1970s; rather, it belongs, of all places, to Prussia under Frederick the Great—not exactly a hotbed for financial innovation and entrepreneurship. In the late eighteenth century, the country emerged victoriously from the Seven Years' War it had fought against all the major European powers, including France, Austria, Saxony, Sweden, and Russia in 1763. But victory came at a huge cost. The warring troops had turned arable land into battlegrounds and, as a result, the members of the East Prussian aristocracy, the bedrock of the Prussian monarchy, found themselves not only deep in debt, but unable to serve their creditors. Many were forced into selling parts of their assets at fire sale prices, which, if brought to its logical conclusion, threatened to bring down the landed aristocracy— and possibly the Prussian monarchy along with it.

In this precarious situation, a Berlin merchant by the name of Büring devised a plan to monetize the value of the nobility's land.[35] His calculation was simple: Prussia had two core assets—cash (state money) and land, but the value of land was about ten times that of cash. If it was possible to monetize the value of land, the country's problems could easily be solved and the future of the monarchy secured. He managed to persuade a skeptical Frederick the Great, who later acknowledged that the scheme had saved four hundred of Silesia's "best families" from ruin.[36]

The basic idea behind it was similar to securitizing mortgages today: Assets are pooled and placed into a legal vessel that can issue tradable interests, the value of which is backed by the assets in the pool. In Prussia, a "credit association" (called a *Landschaft*, or land association) was formed, which the indebted landlords joined as members; indeed, membership was made compulsory. They assumed joint liability for the payment of principal and interest for the debt instruments the association issued. Each member could apply to receive debt instruments amounting to between one-third and one-half of the estimated value of the member's estate and use these certificates to pay off its "annoying creditors."[37] The king backed the scheme with a guarantee to the tune of 200,000 Thalers.

The credit cooperative became a huge success and sparked an entire movement of cooperative banking in Germany. Within a year, the certificates were trading at a premium in a liquid market, and similar associations were soon established by cities and local governments throughout Germany. Some helped bonded laborers to pay off the money they owed their former lords when they were set free; others operated as mortgage banks that helped fund the construction boom in commercial centers. An article published in the *Quarterly Journal of Economics* in 1894 urged American policymakers to take a closer look at this scheme, but this had to wait another few decades.[38]

In 1968, an amendment to the US Federal Housing Act empowered the GSEs to securitize loans backed by mortgages they bought from private banks. The policy rationale was that securitization would diversify risk and thereby reduce the costs of credit for homeowners. For low-income families, the GSEs also guaranteed the performance of the securitized assets for a fee. However, when private players took over the market for residential mortgage backed securities (RBMS), the GSEs also assumed the role of buyers of tranches in securitization structures private parties had created, typically the more senior tranches.

By buying tranches in NC2 and similar entities, the GSEs helped fuel private-label securitization. As government-sponsored entities, they could raise debt on international lending markets at a lower rate than the private intermediaries, because investors assumed that the US government would stand behind these entities. They also added their stamp of approval, because they bought only assets that complied with their standards (which, however, were considerably relaxed over time) and this furthered their marketability. Somewhat ironically, post-crisis, the securitization business has fallen back into the lap of the GSEs. Fannie Mae and Freddie Mac were put into government conservatorship, the legal equivalent of life support, in the summer of 2008, where they still linger.[39] In the first two months of 2018, ten years after the onset of the crisis and with the GSEs still in government conservatorship, they accounted for almost 97 percent of all issuances of mortgage-backed securities.[40]

The Prussian and American securitization schemes varied along several dimensions. In the case of Prussia, the SPV was organized as a cooperative that counted the debtors as members, not a brainless creature owned by no one, like NC2. Moreover, the certificates the Prussian co-op issued were used to pay off existing creditors rather than attract new investors. But the basic idea of pooling risk to reduce the costs of credit is the same. There is also something else these two securitization schemes share: backstopping by the state. As mentioned, the Prussian monarch backed the scheme with 200,000 Reichsthalers, even if only reluctantly. In the United States, the securitization of mortgages was backed by government-owned or government-sponsored entities and some carried an explicit government guarantee. Moreover, private-label securitizers in the United States were handed tax-exempt status for the vehicles they had set up, a subsidy called REMIC, or "real estate mortgage investment conduits."[41]

The scale of securitizing land in Prussia of the late eighteenth century, of course, pales in comparison to the securitization business in the United States prior to the crash of 2008. Indeed, the fact that the securitization of mortgages took off, notwithstanding legal obstacles that stood in the way, is remarkable. In truth, it took not only legal ingenuity but also shrewdness on the part of the financial industry to overcome these legal obstacles, foremost among them the good old law of realty.

In the United States, land law is governed by states, not the federation, and land registries are local, not national. Land law was designed to leave little doubt about who owns a given piece of land at any moment in time, or who might hold a quasi-property right, such as a mortgage, against it. These rules were not made for a mass market in tradable MBS. The private sector used stopgap measures to get around these obstacles, but some intermediaries found themselves trapped in the legal entanglement of the law of realty—most of them, however, only after the crisis had hit.[42]

On July 5, 2007, U.S. Bank, the trustee of a securitization vehicle, foreclosed against the home of Mr. Antonio Ibanez. Mr. Ibanez, a veteran who had served in the US military, had bought the home in late 2005, taken out a loan, and given a mortgage to his lender, Rose Mortgage. Rose Mortgage then pooled the loan and mortgage together with others and sold them off, leaving a blank for the acquirer's name in the relevant documents. The documents eventually passed to Option One Mortgage Corporation (Option One), which was recorded as mortgagor of Mr. Ibanez's home in the land registry. Even before its title was officially recorded, however, Option One assigned the same pool "in blank" to yet another intermediary.

According to papers later filed in court, "Option One assigned the Ibanez mortgage to Lehman Brothers Bank, FSB, which assigned it to Lehman Brothers Holdings Inc., which then assigned it to the Structured Asset Securities Corporation, which then assigned the mortgage, pooled with approximately 1,220 other mortgage loans, to U.S. Bank, as trustee for the Structured Asset Securities Corporation Mortgage Pass-Through Certificates, Series 2006-Z."[43]

Not a single one of these entities' names could be found in the documents that U.S. Bank presented to the court to prove its own rights and obtain clean title over the property. When Mr. Ibanez defaulted, U.S. Bank foreclosed the property under Massachusetts law: it took out a notice of foreclosure sale in the *Boston Globe* and seized it.[44] Subsequently, U.S. Bank brought action in the local court to receive title documents free of any claims by the previous owner or third parties.[45] What might have looked like an afterthought—the paperwork needed to document title—became a major legal headache when a judge refused to sanction the above practices and refused to grant clean title.

A clean title is critical for demonstrating to the rest of the world that the land has been cleansed from competing legal claims. Only then can a future buyer be assured that she will acquire full title, that is, a priority claim that is enforceable against the world. However, in the Ibanez case, the judge refused to provide the requested legal cleansing post foreclosure, and the Supreme Court of Massachusetts upheld his decision in 2011. The court's reasoning was fairly straightforward. Existing law makes possible the assignment of title in land, including mortgages, but requires the specification of the assignee. A blank assignment is insufficient, indeed is void under applicable law. Moreover, an assignment must list the specific mortgage to be assigned; pooling mortgages is fine but claiming that a mortgage is within the pool without listing it specifically is not enough, given the power to foreclose against a homeowner the mortgage bestows on its holder. The only legally valid assignment in this case therefore was the first one—from Rose to Option One.[46] According to the court, Option One now held the mortgage in trust for other investors; consequently, it alone had the right to foreclose. In contrast, U.S. Bank did not hold a valid priority right in Mr. Ibanez's property; it should never have foreclosed and was now barred from receiving clean title.

The case pitched the finance industry and its hunger for safe assets against (some) courts as the guardians of legal rules and of legal certainty. The finance industry accused the courts of being overly formalistic and of failing to understand that modern markets for debt finance require different rules. The courts in turn pointed to age-old principles of the law and put the burden of complying with them on the financial industry. Perhaps the parties in this deal were particularly sloppy, although it became quite well-known after the fact that the back offices of financial intermediaries were often unable to keep up with the deals that were made in the front offices.[47]

In effect, the conflict boils down to the fundamental question: Who should guard the credibility of legal priority rights? As much as the financial industry needs "clear property rights" to sustain a market in MBS, this can hardly mean that it gets to set the rules for who might claim a collateral or title to the land. There may be few reasons to shed tears for Mr. Ibanez, who, after all, defaulted on his mortgage, but clearly, homeowners must be protected from just any intermediary foreclosing on their home and in the absence of clear documentation, possibly more than one.

Had the ruling in the Ibanez case come down in 2004 rather than in 2011, it likely would have made a major dent in the MBS market. Luckily for the finance industry, it happened only post-crisis. There had been the odd foreclosure action earlier, but few judges or debtors challenged the practices of the industry. Courts allowed banks who lacked proper documents to plead that they had lost the note, even when they had never obtained one that properly recorded their name to begin with.

To address some of the legal concerns, the finance industry devised its own solution: it created a dummy company to pose as the mortgage holder from beginning to end, even as the loans themselves switched hands.[48] This way, there was no need to maintain a proper paper chain or to re-register every new mortgage holder. The name of the dummy was Mortgage Electronic Registration Systems, or MERS, a corporate entity, wholly owned by a parent company that had been established by the key players in the securitization market. MERS had no employees and delegated the task to register mortgages in its name to the banks that originated the mortgage.[49] It served simply as a legal shell that outsourced its operation to the finance industry. Some doubts remained as to whether a true legal agency relation had, in fact, been created with each acquirer of the loan along the chain. In the quest to pave the way for mass-mortgage markets, the industry sidestepped this question and instead set in motion a massive scheme that was questioned only after the number of lawsuits shot up in the midst of the crisis.[50] If, as some have claimed, the sell side of the financial industry had bet that foreclosed homeowners would not dare to bark and that courts would not challenge the all-powerful industry, allowing financial intermediaries to sell their products before the law caught up with them, this bet clearly paid off.[51]

The Kleros Clones

Turning illiquid assets, like land, into liquid assets is not just a matter of supply and demand; it is a matter of the right legal coding. Assets must be transferable to begin with, something the early notes accomplished; and they must be transferable without too many legal obstacles. And once all of this had been accomplished, these assets had to be made convertible into cash, preferably on demand. Yet, not all assets find willing takers, and complex products tend to be more difficult to place even if rating agencies can help dumb down the informational content that investors need to digest. Some tranches in securitization structures, such as NC2, were especially difficult to place. Not the super-safe tranches on the top, which found buyers easily, and not even the tranches at the bottom, which were frequently warehoused by the sponsor or sold to risk-loving, yield-hunting investors. The real problem was the lower mezzanine tranches. They were too risky for most investors and not risky enough for some. However, in order to keep the securitization machine humming, all tranches in every securitization structure had to be sold. The finance industry came up with another ingenious solution: it cloned the missing buyers, another vehicle that would buy tranches in securitization vehicles, which had been shunned by most investors, and repackaged them to make them more attractive. This marked the birth of collateral debt obligations, or CDOs.

The now largely defunct CDOs were financial assets that were issued by yet another SPV, which was created for the sole purpose of buying lower ranked tranches from NC2 and its likes.[52] This new vehicle funded the purchases of these tranches by issuing fixed-income interests to investors who were seeking high returns and who were willing to believe that by repackaging mezzanine tranches in MBS structures, some tranches could be designated as safe enough to obtain a AAA or AA rating. Of course, this left lower rated tranches, but if they could not be placed either, the scheme of cloning the missing buyers could be repeated by setting up yet another trust or corporate entity that would repackage the leftover CDOs, tranche them again, and sell tranches off to investors; and so forth. This daisy chain of trusts, corporate entities, and the assets they issued gave us not only CDOs, but also their "squared" and "cubed" versions. To see how this works, let's take a look at the Kleros clones.

Kleros Real Estate CDO III Ltd. was established in 2006 as a limited liability company in the Cayman Islands (hereinafter "Kleros-C"), a well-known tax haven. Moreover, the country's laws shield companies registered there from judgments disgruntled investors might obtain in other jurisdictions; it simply does not recognize or enforce judgments obtained abroad. The only shareholder Kleros-C had was Kleros Real Estate CDO III Common Holdings, LLC (or "Kleros-D"), a limited liability company that was incorporated in Delaware (United States). The Delaware clone's sole purpose in life was to operate as a Kleros-C shareholder and to appear as the co-issuer of the assets it would issue. Most of the time, financial assets are issued by a single entity; but cloning Kleros served the purpose of enabling certain US investors that had a regulatory cap on investing in foreign assets, such as insurance companies, to placate their regulators by being able to name a US-based co-issuer.

Kleros-D was capitalized with only $1,000 and had no other assets except the shares in Kleros-C. It invested the sum total of $2,500 to buy these shares, giving Kleros-C the opening to issue $1 *billion* in CDOs that promised fixed returns to its investors, to be paid from the securitized assets Kleros-C was yet to buy. Rating agencies assessed the possibility that all of the claims against homeowners that had been lumped together in the mezzanine tranches of the structures that had securitized them would default simultaneously as sufficiently low to give the most senior tranches of the CDOs in Kleros-C a AAA rating. The whole structure looked like a stroke of genius, made possible by yet another promiscuous use of the corporate form combined with probability calculus based on some bold assumptions. The assets inside Kleros-C had been shunned by investors when they were first offered in the disguise of mezzanine tranches in NC2; but in combination with similar tranches from other securitization structures, they looked much more appealing. After all, not all mezzanine tranches would necessarily default, and as long as enough cash flow was coming in to keep most investors happy most of the time, there was little to worry about, or so it seemed.

With the credit risk associated with the homeowners at the end of this chain of legal entities and structured assets seemingly diversified away, CDOs mushroomed. $700 billion worth of CDOs were issued between 2003 and 2007, the height of the market, often underwritten by reputable intermediaries.[53] Taken together, Merrill Lynch, Goldman Sachs, and Citigroup's securities arms "accounted for more than 30 percent of CDOs structured from 2004 to 2007"; and Deutsche Bank and UBS, which underwrote the Kleros deal, belonged to the top group of global banks in this market segment.[54]

Still, the investors who did buy CDOs in their basic, squared, or cubed forms, soon found themselves in a bind. When real estate markets declined, homeowners defaulted, and investor demand dried up, CDOs became toxic. Nobody wanted to hold them any longer, because nobody could be sure what was inside them—the extensive disclosures in the prospectuses that marketed them to potential investors notwithstanding; and they certainly had to scrap the idea that they could be easily converted into cash on demand. Investors who did not exit fast enough had to watch their fortunes tumble. Worse, securitization deals no longer had a reliable acquirer of tranches nobody else wanted; with the fall from grace of the CDOs, the securitization market came to a grinding halt. This in turn precipitated the fall of the financial intermediaries that had created this market, the Bear Stearns and Lehman Brothers of this world along with their peers.

The financial system, which had been based on assumptions about future returns that were dressed up by the modules of the code of capital, fell apart like a house of cards. It is possible to dress up any claims by placing them into trusts or corporate entities and garnish them with alphabet soup labels, such as SPVs, MBS, CDOs and their squared, cubed, or even synthetic variants. However, at the other end of the deal, there are still the same little old houses, which their owners can barely afford and that may not hold their value once the funding machine that helps fuel prices in real estate dries up.

The Alchemy of Private Money

The dream to create something from nothing is as old as mankind. Alchemists have long searched for recipes to make their own gold; and governments have time and again diluted the gold contents of the coins produced in their mints by mixing it with lesser metals to enhance their spending power.[55] When governments abandoned the gold standard, many could not resist the temptation to print as much money as they needed for ambitious war efforts or social welfare reforms—not infrequently imposing huge inflation "taxes" on their citizens, and in worst-case scenarios triggering episodes of hyperinflation that destroyed private savings and fueled social and political instability. Germany in the 1920s is the textbook case, but hyperinflation, conventionally defined as monthly inflation of 50 percent or more, has not been eradicated. Consider, for example, Venezuela, where inflation was projected to reach 1 million percent in 2018.[56]

Governments typically hold out the promise of future growth to back the money they (or their central banks) issue or the debt they use instead to fill their state coffers. States at least have the power to impose obligations on their citizens to make good on these promises; even if this means that they have to impose draconian austerity measures on them.[57] Private parties do not possess such powers; they have to make good with what they have or with what others are willing to give them voluntarily. Nonetheless, private intermediaries have not been able to resist the temptation of minting money as if there was no tomorrow. They imagine fantastic returns in the future, but in fact will have to obtain new loans to cover old debts, and when this no longer works, as is increasingly likely once default rates increase and lenders become wary, they will have to beg for a lifeline from the state.

In nineteenth-century France, the Péreire brothers created a new type of financial intermediary, the Crédit Mobilier. They hoped to realize their dream of "banking without money."[58] More than a century later, Robert Merton, co-recipient of the 1997 Nobel Memorial Prize in Economic Science for his contribution to Option Pricing Theory, lived out a similar dream about "returns without investments," by co-founding the hedge fund Long-Term Capital Management (LTCM).[59] It is not without irony that the Péreire brothers, who were followers of the socialist spiritual movement known as Saint-Simonianism, and a contemporary economist who is deeply versed in the art of mathematic modeling financial assets, sought to realize the same dream. Sadly, for them and for the rest of us, not many dreams come true.

The Péreire brothers' claim to fame is their invention of banking based on continuous refinancing of outstanding debt.[60] The Crédit Mobilier was established in 1852 after intense lobbying to obtain the necessary banking license.[61] The bank was organized as a joint stock company. It raised 60 million French francs backed by personal guarantees of the founders, only 50 percent of which was actually paid up. Crédit Mobilier then took in 120 million francs in deposits (i.e., debt) and also issued debt instruments to the tune of 600 million francs. For the most part, these corporate bonds were short-term interest-bearing fixed obligations—the kind of assets that investors in RMBS preferred as well. The bank used the money it had received from its creditors to invest in railroad, canal, road, and mining companies as well as banks in France and across Europe, from Spain to Russia. The shares Crédit Mobilier owned in these companies were used as collateral to back the bonds CM issued in its own name—a structure that anticipated Lehman's game of debt.

In effect, the Péreire brothers levered a bank to fund investments in infrastructure companies throughout Europe. The company paid high dividends to boost the value of Crédit Mobilier's share price, thereby keeping existing shareholders happy and attracting new ones; but to sustain the scheme over time, it was not enough to attract new shareholders or bondholders and take their contributions to pay out dividends or fixed returns to old shareholders and old bondholders. This resembles a Ponzi scheme, named after an Italo-American of the early twentieth century who attracted investors by promising them extraordinary returns, when in fact he simply used the money that new investors paid in to pay out dividends to the previous ones.[62] This works as long as enough investors show up every day; indeed, it can work for decades even under the eyes of powerful financial market regulators, such as the SEC, as Bernard Madoff's secretive Ponzi scheme, which blew up only after the 2008 crisis, has demonstrated.[63] Still, at some point some investments must produce some real returns for the company to survive—a tall order in the case of Crédit Mobilier, given that most investments were made in infrastructure projects that, by nature, are long-term investments.

Eventually, investors in Crédit Mobilier grew weary and once too many did, others followed. When the price of the bank's shares began to tumble, the whole scheme went into reverse and a stampede ensued. New creditors stopped coming, old creditors demanded pay, and when that was not forthcoming, they sought to recover against their collateral. Unfortunately for them, the assets that backed their investments—the shares in the companies Crédit Mobilier had acquired—failed to deliver actual returns in time. Indeed, many were underperforming and as their value declined, so did the creditors' hope of ever recovering their losses, even when they went to court.

Few observers had looked through the structure of Crédit Mobilier and seen it for what it was at a time when Crédit Mobilier was still thriving, with one notable exception. In 1856, ten years before the bank collapsed under its debt burden, Karl Marx wrote a scathing review in the *New York Tribune*. "The holders of these debentures," he observed with reference to Crédit Mobilier's creditors, "accordingly, share in all the risks of the shareholders, without participating in their profits."[64] The same point could have been made about Lehman Brothers and its peers. As Marx saw it, Crédit Mobilier's financial structure meant that it was bound to fail, making a government bailout all but inevitable, but he warned that the success of such an intervention could not be taken for granted. "Will he [Louis Bonaparte] prove more solvent than the Crédit Mobilier? That is the question."[65]

It turned out that Louis Bonaparte *was* more solvent than the bank and he, or rather the French central bank, the Banque de France, did rescue Crédit Mobilier in the end. Many other governments, however, have gone broke attempting to bail out private financial intermediaries that had overplayed their hands and pushed the financial system to the brink. Examples in the context of the 2008 global crisis alone include at least the governments of Iceland, Ireland, as well as Spain.[66]

The business model of LTCM may have been more sophisticated than that of Crédit Mobilier, but the basic intuition behind the business strategy was similar: lever up on bets that the future will evolve as predicted, and if it all fails, hope for a liquidity boost from the government. LTCM was established in 1994 to put into action the Option Pricing Theory that would earn Merton and his collaborators the Nobel Memorial Prize in Economic Sciences in 1997—just a year before their fund experienced a near-death event. The theory holds the promise that with the right hedging strategies, risk can be eliminated by dividing it in all its subcomponents and placing them with a diversified group of investors.[67] As long as markets operate continuously (which real markets, unfortunately, rarely do), investors can always re-hedge their position in response to a changing environment, accepting certain risks while shifting some to others, and in this way cover their backs against future downturns.

LTCM was established by the theorists to turn the option price theory into private gain for themselves. The hedge fund levered its assets to invest in sovereign debt, basing its exposure to emerging and developed markets on the prediction that the price gap between these different instruments would converge over time. LTCM went "long" on the sovereign debt of many emerging markets and "short" on US treasuries. At first, everything went according to plan; in its first three years of operation, LTCM returned between 19 percent and 42 percent to its investors; and by late 1997 it had generated $7 billion in equity. After the peak came the fall; by early 1998, investors had taken out $2.7 billion and, in the fall of 1998, LTCM faced imminent collapse.

Something had happened that was not supposed to: The East Asian Financial Crisis erupted in the summer of 1997 and cast a spell over emerging market debt; and in August 1998, Russia defaulted on its sovereign debt.[68] In response, the price for debt of *all* emerging markets tumbled almost simultaneously as if orchestrated and the yields between US treasuries and emerging market debt widened rather than narrowed, as the model had predicted. In theory, LTCM should have been protected even against this calamity, because it had invested in emerging markets all over the world, assuming that they would not all move in the same direction, and yet, they did.

Far from designing a perfect hedge, LTCM had made just a single bet: that the yields of sovereign debt issued by emerging markets and advanced economies would converge over time, and that each country's debt was distinct.[69] That bet was upended by a highly contagious sovereign debt crisis. The question now was whether Mr. Greenspan, then chairman of the US Federal Reserve, or rather the Fed itself, would be solvent, to paraphrase Karl Marx. It was, but Greenspan favored a private bailout and put enough pressure on the LTCM's creditors, major US-based regulated banks, to swap their debt, the loans and bonds they had extended, for equity, or shares, thereby replacing the fund's Nobel Prize–winning owners.[70] In doing so, they created a bigger equity cushion, which allowed the fund to raise new debt finance and continue operation.

The banks were reluctant at first to convert their claims into equity, but they did turn a profit eventually. This outcome has been much touted as proof that LTCM had been right all along. In truth, time is money, and when trading in short-term debt, timing is everything as option traders should readily appreciate; running out of time means losing a bet, and the stringent rules of a competitive market economy will push you to the exit. This happens to delinquent homeowners or pensioners who cannot pay their medical bills; there is no reason that it should not also happen to a hedge fund run by Nobel Prize awardees.[71]

The lure of money, and the temptation to create more of it, can fuel growth and wealth, but if pushed too far, it can have corrosive effects on the economy. Bouts of hyperinflation in some, and entrenched inflation in other countries, have convinced many states to place the supply of state money, and monetary policy more broadly, firmly in the hands of independent central banks.[72] The excessive supply of private money, the booms and busts of credit cycles that accompany business models like Crédit Mobilier, LTCM, or Lehman and their cohorts, can be just as devastating as lax controls over the public money supply. On this front, however, reform efforts have been timid at best. Only the devastation of an uncushioned, full-blown crisis, like the Great Depression in the 1930s, has been met with rigorous and long-lasting regulatory reforms. Reforms after the 2008 crisis in the United States, the United Kingdom, and the European Union have tackled the safety of banks, but they have put few if any brakes on the basic drive to mint private money.[73] Surely, new debt instruments will take a new form next time around, as they always have to get around the new regulatory constraints that were put in place against their now outlawed predecessors. And as soon as memories of the past crisis have faded, advocates of free markets will raise their heads again and demand the dismantling of regulatory structures that stand in the way of the private sectors' unconstrained debt minting.

Yet, as the story of NC2 and its sibling that has been recounted in this chapter illustrates, when it comes to debt markets, the mantra of free markets is flatly wrong. The question is not even about regulation or de-regulation. NC2 and the Kleros clones and their many predecessors are all coded in law and exist only in claims that are carefully crafted in private, not public law, but private law too rests ultimately on state power; without the modules of the code of capital, these instruments would not even exist.

At heart, all these assets are simple IOUs—promises to pay a certain amount at some future date. Such promises can be based on personal relations, or they can be framed as binding legal commitments. Cloaking them in the modules of the code of capital turns them into financial assets that are attractive for investors. Property and collateral law establish priority rights; trust and corporate law partition assets and shield them from too many creditors; and bankruptcy law can be designed to give some debt minters a head start over others, even if they never contracted or paid a premium for it. Debt, the private money that has fueled capitalism since its inception, is coded in law and ultimately relies on the state to back it up. States should realize this and keep the inflation of private money under control, because the more they bend to the will of private debt minters in boom times, the more they will be on the hook when it turns out that the economy cannot sustain the debt burden they created.

5

Enclosing Nature's Code

The previous chapters have shown how a handful of legal modules have been used creatively over centuries to code various assets as capital, starting with land, a resource that exists outside the law, but quickly moving on to assets that owe their very existence entirely to the law: the corporate shares and bonds that were discussed in chapter 3, and the notes, bills of exchange, RMBSs, and CDOs we encountered in chapter 4. In this chapter, we will discover that the legal code can also be used to code knowledge, including of nature's own code, by legally enclosing it to the exclusion of others. Most intellectual property rights are of only limited duration so that the fountain of wealth they create will dry out eventually. Still, there are ways to prolong their life span by altering some features of the original invention, or by recoding them with legal modules that do not have an expiration date, such as trade secrecy law.

The genetic foundation of life was discovered only in the nineteenth century by the friar and botanist Gregor Mendel. By 1944, scientists had discovered that DNA (deoxyribonucleic acid) was the carrier for genetic information, and in 1953, James Watson and Francis Crick published a paper in which they depicted the double helix structure of the DNA.[1] Their work marked a major breakthrough that revolutionized our understanding of biology, inheritance, and evolution and earned the two scientists, together with Maurice Wilkins, the Nobel Prize in Medicine in 1962. Genetic research has made huge strides ever since. Fifty years after the publication of the double helix, the Human Genome Project completed a map of the entire gene sequence for *homo sapiens*, giving us "the ability, for the first time, to read nature's complete genetic blueprint for building a human being."[2]

The race to convert this knowledge into wealth-producing assets did not wait until the full sequence was known. It kicked off decades earlier, as patents were filed to protect biotechnological inventions. The US government, which funded the Human Genome Project at the National Institutes of Health (NIH), is responsible for keeping the human genome in the public domain rather than being monopolized by patent holders. Still, bits and pieces of human genetic code have been patented, most of them in the United States, whose patent regime boasts that it will create an intellectual property right for "anything under the sun that is made by man."[3] This expansive perspective on intellectual property rights is the backdrop for the aggressive enclosure not only of our discovery of nature's code, but of skills and knowledge in other areas as well.

In 1918, Justice Brandeis could still claim that "[t]he general rule of law is, that the noblest of human productions—knowledge, truths ascertained, conceptions, and ideas—become, after voluntary communication to others, free as the air to common use."[4] Indeed, why should anyone have exclusive rights, even if only temporarily, over goods that remain undiminished even after some have made use of them? Knowledge, after all is a "non-rivalrous good," for which there cannot be a "tragedy of the commons"; instead, everyone should be able to share the knowledge that has been accumulated over centuries. Nonetheless, less than a century after Justice Brandeis wrote these wise words, legal enclosure has reduced the "knowledge commons" much further than he could have imagined.[5]

Legal enclosure battles have always pushed the limits of existing boundaries as we have seen with respect to the enclosure battles over land in England and its colonies. Once the genetic code had been discovered, it did not take long for the Supreme Court to confront the question of where to draw the line when nature's own legal code was slated for legal enclosure.[6] The first major case involved the synthetic creation of bacteria with the capacity to break down crude oil. These bacteria do occur in nature, but not in this genetically engineered specific form; the court affirmed the patent.

Finally, in 2013, 60 years after Watson and Crick had published their paper about the structure of DNA and 10 years after the completion of the human genome project, the US Supreme Court had to decide whether unaltered human genes were patentable—i.e., whether nature's raw code could be legally enclosed with the effect of granting a patent holder priority rights over the rest of humanity.[7] The Court's answer was a unanimous no, but only a qualified one. It did not raise the fundamental normative question of the patentability of genes. Instead, it took a black letter approach to interpreting the Patent Act, which had first been enacted in 1790, and which in its current version states that "whoever invents or discovers *any new and useful* process, machine, manufacture, or composition of matter, or any new and useful *improvement* thereof, may obtain a patent therefor, subject to the conditions and requirements of this title."[8]

The statute emphasizes novelty and usefulness and includes not only original inventions but also "improvements," a concept we have also encountered in the context of land enclosure in the colonies. Its language is broad, leaving it to the judiciary to police the outer boundaries of patentability, which the Supreme Court has stipulated as "laws of nature, natural phenomena, and abstract ideas."[9] These exceptions may seem self-evident, but their boundaries are anything but. A whole gene sequence may be part of nature, but what if humans isolated only parts thereof; would this be patentable? And what if lab technicians replicated nature's ingenuity, altering it just a little bit, for example, by cutting off a sequence where nature typically would not do this?

This is where the line was drawn by the US Supreme Court in 2013: The mere isolation of a DNA sequence without any man-made change or alteration falls into the law of nature exception and is therefore not patentable. In contrast, the *synthetic* creation of cDNA, which does not occur exactly in this form in nature, was deemed to be patentable. The justices were unmoved by scientists arguing that the distinction they drew in law made little sense in science. "The nucleotide sequence of cDNA," they argued, "is dictated by nature, not by the lab technician."[10] Instead, the Supreme Court was satisfied that humans had generated an intron-less DNA and thereby had created an exon-only molecule. It did not even matter that such intron-less molecules occur in mature messenger RNA (mRNA), of which the cDNA is an exact copy, only written in DNA.

The Court also took pains in its decision to point out that the ruling in this case had no bearing on the patentability of scientific alterations of human genes.[11] This could be read as an invitation to private parties to test the boundaries of gene patenting in future cases. The Court has drawn another line, but it has not closed the door to further challenges.

Whose Choice?

In an op-ed entitled "My Medical Choice," the actress Angelina Jolie disclosed in May 2013 that she had undergone a double mastectomy.[12] She had made this difficult decision after a genetic test confirmed that she was carrying BRCA (the breast cancer susceptibility gene) type 1, which greatly increases the likelihood that she might develop breast cancer. Whereas the average woman has a 10–15 percent risk, her own was estimated at 87 percent, paired with a higher risk of developing ovarian cancer as well. The op-ed was very personal; it was about her mother, who had died of breast cancer at age fifty-six, her children, her husband, and her own surgery and recovery from it. Only at the end of the op-ed did Jolie hint at a bigger battle that was being waged in the background: the battle over privatizing genetic testing. The costs of genetic testing for BRCA, about $3,000, she suggested, were well beyond the means of many women, who were therefore denied the choice she had.

What she did not say was that the $3,000 fee for the genetic test went to a company that held multiple patents for the BRCA sequence and which had monopolized the market for genetic testing in the United States, even as unpatented tests that were available before BRCA was patented cost as little as $100.[13] It was this patent that gave the US Supreme Court the opportunity to determine the patentability of human genes in the case mentioned earlier. Oral hearings had already been held in April 2013, and the decision was announced in June 2013.

The background story of this legal dispute is intriguing, because it showcases yet another enclosure struggle, this time not over land, not just over human know-how or skills, but over nature's own code.[14] Myriad Genetics poses in this story as the landlords who banned the commoners from the land they had shared in the past.[15] It is a publicly traded for-profit corporation located in Salt Lake City.[16] The company was established in 1991 by Dr. Mark Skolnick, a member of the faculty at the University of Utah, jointly with a local capital venture group. The founding of the company came on the heels of the publication of a path-breaking scientific paper that demonstrated that breast cancer was linked to a gene and identified its location, though not its sequence.[17] This breakthrough had been made possible by a major collaborative scientific undertaking, the International Breast Cancer Linkage Consortium, in which hundreds of scientists, supported mostly by government grants, had participated.

Identifying the precise sequence would be next, and the NIH had already funded a major research undertaking to do just that. Dr. Skolnick spotted an opportunity and urged private investors to add money behind his own efforts to out-compete that consortium. Academic scientists, of course, compete head-on all the time, that is, as long as patents or similar restrictions don't prevent them from doing so. Their prize is a publication in a leading journal, such as *Nature* or *Science*, recognition among peers, and better access to future funding cycles as well as promotions. Dr. Skolnick and the venture capitalists he mobilized, however, were after a different prize: the revenue that would flow from owning the patent for the breast cancer gene.

In September 1994, Myriad and its collaborators announced that they had the sequence, and Myriad quickly proceeded to patent it. A few years later, they also received a patent for BRCA2. On the other side of the battle over access to human genes were the mostly academic scientists who invested time and effort that was paid for by universities, research labs, and government and private grants, to research the underlying genetic defects of major diseases.

Several clinics had already offered tests for BRCA to women with a family history of breast cancer. These were the commoners of knowledge, if you will. Before long, however, they confronted the legal equivalent of the hedges and fences the English landlords erected against the commoners in the past. After friendly overtures to sign collaborative license agreements, but with limited scope for research and information sharing with patients, did not bear any fruit, Myriad hired a law firm that sent "cease and desist" orders to clinics at Pennsylvania University, New York University, and the Cancer Genetics Network Project, among others, threatening lawsuits if they failed to comply with the company's newly registered patent.

For patents, there is no equivalent for hedge-breaking and ploughing fields the landlords had claimed as their own; patents are creatures of law and the only battlefield therefore is a court of law. And so, the commoners joined forces and brought suit to invalidate Myriad's patents. The lead plaintiff was the Association for Molecular Pathology; others included the American College of Medical Genetics, and the American Society for Clinical Pathology, as well as several doctors and scientists who had received Myriad's cease and desist orders and had been forced to stop offering tests to patients and to discontinue related research. It was not an easy battle. The district court held for the scientists, but the appeals court sided with Myriad. The plaintiffs had to push the battle all the way to the US Supreme Court, where they finally scored a win.

The ruling surprised many patent experts who had relied on the fact that the US Patent Office had patented gene sequences quite liberally for more than two decades. Myriad even argued that the court owed some deference to the US Patent Office, but to no avail. The Supreme Court asserted its prerogative over determining the meaning of the US Patent Act and applying it to new technological developments. Nonetheless, the positive outcome for the plaintiffs has little effect on all the other patents that had been granted earlier and now potentially conflicted with the new ruling. Unless private contenders mobilize the resources to attack them in court, one by one, these monopolies will continue to enclose nature's code to enrich the patent holders and their shareholders.[18] And they will continue to invoke the time-tested argument that in the absence of financial rewards, innovations of this kind won't happen. The background story to the BRCA case, however, proves the contrary: there are a lot of scientists, governments, as well as private foundations, who are willing to invest their resources to discover the root causes of devastating diseases and to understand the laws of nature. Indeed, basic science tends to be funded by governments, not private companies, as the returns on this investment are highly unpredictable. Private entrepreneurs wait patiently for discoveries that can be made profitable and, with the help of the legal code, can be turned into capital.[19]

Given the monetary value of patents, one would have expected that the loss of its patents should have been a severe blow to Myriad. In fact, the company suffered less of a blow financially than one might have expected. The reason is that between 1994, when the first patent was registered, and 2013, when the DNA-only patents were invalidated, Myriad had built a monopoly over BRCA breast cancer testing. The company claimed its test as the new "gold standard," but others have been less sanguine, arguing that the monopoly had prevented superior tests from gaining prominence. Either way, between 1997 and 2013, Myriad "sold around one million tests and generated $2 billion in revenue, 80 percent of it coming from its RCA Analysis product."[20] Revenues in 2017, four years since the BRCA gene had been invalidated, stood at $771 million, 74 percent of which the company's financial statements attributed to "hereditary cancer testing."[21]

The US Constitution granted Congress the power to "promote the progress of science and useful arts, by securing for a limited timed to authors and inventors the exclusive right to their respective writings and discoveries."[22] It thereby acknowledges that intellectual property rights are creatures of law and allocates the power to define them to Congress. The justification for creating these temporary monopolies is to incentivize the inventor or artist by allowing them to fully capture the monetary value of their creativity for fear that they would otherwise seize activities that might be of tremendous social value. Yet, human creativity has been driven over the millennia by motives other than monetary gains. Even with a comprehensive system of intellectual property rights in place, most authors, composers, and inventors receive only a tiny return for their creativity. The ultimate beneficiaries of the legal monopolies that intellectual property rights create are corporations that extract returns from patents for the financial benefits of their shareholders.[23] Indeed, most patents in the United States today are filed not by individuals, but by corporate entities, creatures of law that have neither intellectual power nor creativity of their own. Between 2002 and 2015, more than 4.6 million patents were granted by the US Patent Office to US and foreign patent holders. About 12 percent went to individuals, less than 1 percent to governments, but 43.5 percent to foreign and 44.1 percent to US corporations.[24] These numbers highlight that the power of patents is more closely associated with commercial use than gratification for creativity.

Granting monopolies is always about creating gains for some (the monopolists) and costs for the rest; it may be justified in exceptional circumstances but requires a careful balancing act between the costs and benefits on both sides of the equation. The social costs of enclosing knowledge can be huge, because control over knowledge is monopolized even though it could benefit everyone without taking anything away from the inventor. And yet, states have supported the enclosure of knowledge and left it to the code's masters and official agents in patent offices to police its borders, with only sporadic court oversight.

Intangible Capital

At long last, economists have discovered that capital is not a thing, but a quality, although most don't know it yet. In a recent book entitled *Capitalism without Capital*, Haskel and Westlake argue that the market value of leading corporations today is not determined by the physical assets they own and use to produce goods, but by intangibles: the patents, copyrights, and trademarks they own, and the branding and business processes they have developed.[25] However, the authors limit the definition of capital to physical things that you can see and touch, and therefore conclude that we live in a wondrous new world of capitalism *without* capital.

This happens when one relies on the outward appearance of things and ignores the code that determines their look, for appearances can be deceiving. Haskel and Westlake are not oblivious to law; in their book, they even compile a table that lists variants of intangibles and map them into their treatment in law on one hand, and in national accounts on the other.[26] As they show, about half of the intangible investments are not recognized in national accounts; but law has a label for all of them, called patents, trademarks, property rights, and a catchall category of "other," which can be deciphered as trade secrets as well as business processes. Still, the authors hesitate to draw the obvious conclusion that there is a powerful link between law and intangibles, indeed, that the law is the source code for transforming ideas, skills, know-how, even processes, into capital.

The reluctance of these accounting experts to cut through their own belief structure resonates with the late US Supreme Court Justice Scalia's personal struggle over the scientific basis of the BRCA case against Myriad. In a concurring statement, he distanced himself from the first part of the Court's ruling that detailed the scientific knowledge about genetics as the source of life. "I am unable to affirm those details on my own knowledge or even my own belief," the devout Catholic wrote.[27] And as accounting experts, Haskel and Westlake seem unable to recognize law for its central role in coding capital, and, as a result, leave it outside the equation.

More generally, economists and accountants have clung to the notion that capital is a physical input, one of the two factors of production, when in fact, capital has never been about a thing, but always about its legal coding; never just about output and input, but always about the ability to capture and monetize expected returns.[28] Marxists at least hold that capital is a relational concept, emphasizing the exploitative relation between capital and labor. Yet they too underestimate the role of law in the process of wealth creation.[29] By grafting the modules of the legal code of capital onto an asset, its holder obtains a right over and above others; her claims enjoy greater durability and face fewer obstacles to lock in past gains by converting them into state money. Last, these special rights are universal and can therefore be enforced against the world.

Exceptions prove the rule; some economists have recognized that restricting the world to things one can see and touch can be highly misleading. The eminent scholar Robert Solow, for example, remarked in 1987 that "you see the computer revolution everywhere except in the productivity data."[30] Since then, efforts have been made to measure intangibles for national accounts, firm productivity, and shareholder wealth. As the saying goes, "that which is measured, improves," but in this case, the reverse seems to hold: because there seems to be something of value here, we must be able to measure it.[31]

Measuring and valuing intangibles has become more important since the more conventional "bricks and mortar" capital in the form of land, factories, machines, and other tangibles has been in decline. Available evidence suggests that traditional capital investments have accounted for only 8 percent of economic growth in the United States between 1995 and 2003, whereas investments in intangibles have increased from only 4 percent in the late 1970s to more than 10 percent by 2006.[32] In the United States and the United Kingdom, though less so in other leading economies, investments in intangibles now exceed investments in tangibles.[33]

The powerful arguments in favor of enclosure of assets for the promotion of private investments and creativity notwithstanding, monopolizing knowledge has not been an unmitigated success for economic development; to the contrary, the shares of intangibles in the market value of major corporations has gone hand in hand with a *decline* in investments. Several economists have called the current state of affairs, in which firms are sitting on stockpiles of cash but with few investment projects on hand, a "secular stagnation." Some argue that once investments in intangibles are fully accounted for, this phenomenon will disappear.[34] Others, however, have suggested that the enclosure of knowledge is responsible for the decline in viable investment opportunities and has led to an "investment famine."[35] Even though patents are only temporary monopolies, their longer-term effects go well beyond the duration of the patent itself. They preclude others from using, perfecting, and investing in knowledge and thereby contribute to the skewed distribution of wealth. As Pagano writes,

> there seems to be an evident paradox in the institutional tendencies of modern capitalism: the knowledge-intensive characteristics of its technologies should favour a democratic economy made up of small firms employing non-rival knowledge; by contrast, however, thanks to knowledge private ownership, big global firms, whose shares are traded on global financial markets, are increasingly predominant in the world economy.[36]

From the perspective of this book, this is not a paradox at all; it's the logic of capital coded in law, which rests on the principle that some assets, and by implication, their holders, enjoy legal privileges over others. They obtain stronger rights against the world and even get to make them durable in order to withstand not only unexpected events, the "exogenous shocks" that create imbalances in standard economic models, but the forces of competition. Competition is essential for the operation of markets; it fuels the forces of creative destruction, which, according to Joseph Schumpeter, are the drivers of economic progress.[37] But the legal code of capital does not follow the rules of competition; instead, it operates according to the logic of power and privilege.

Property Rights as Industrial Policy

The rulers over cities, regions, and countries discovered long ago how by offering special legal protection they could retain local and attract foreign craftsmen and artisans. And those professing superior knowledge and skills have pleaded with rulers for centuries to protect them from competitors by cloaking their skills in legal privileges. Historical records of these protective privileges date back to the fourteenth century. In 1331, for example, King Edward III assured John Kempe protection for his company, Flemish Weavers on the English isle.[38] And in 1440, John Shiedame received a patent for a new technique for processing salt.[39] In England, patenting foreign artisans became particularly prevalent during the Tudor dynasty, when artisans from all over Continental Europe were brought into the service of the Crown. It was a form of industrial policy that allowed England to compete with rulers on the continent who displayed their power in beautiful architecture, textiles, ceramics, and the arts.

The earliest example of a general legal statute that assured all craftsmen full legal protection was a decree the Senate of the city of Venice passed in 1474.[40] It required artisans to register "new and ingenious devices, not previously made in our jurisdiction" with the local authorities. Once registered, everyone else was prohibited from using the same device. Its holder could file a case against the violator "before every office of this city, by which office the aforesaid infringer would be compelled to pay one hundred ducats and his artifice would be immediately destroyed." The city itself, however, was free to use it "for its own use and needs."[41] The Senate, it seems, was unwilling to extend legal privileges without reserving the right for the city to access it, making sure that private privileges would not crowd out their public use and benefits.

There is an important difference between ad hoc conferrals of legal privileges on one hand, and a general statute, like the Venetian Statute of 1474, on the other. Ad hoc privileges are discretionary; they can be used to grant favors, increase revenue, attract foreign artisans, or promote local craft and industry. The highly discretionary use of such monopoly rights especially by Queen Elizabeth I eventually gave birth to England's first statutory law on patents, the 1624 "Statute of Monopolies." The statute was meant to restrict the promiscuous granting of patent and similar monopoly rights by the Crown, including letters, grants, commissions, licenses, or patents.[42] Aggrieved parties were empowered to challenge such privileges under general principles of the common law. Notably, "new" manufacturing in the realm of the "trust and first inventor" or "first manufacturer" was exempted from such challenges, and so were patents and other privileges granted by Parliament.[43] Apparently, Parliament thought itself to be above the fray of fashioning special privileges for a few.

By regularizing the granting of privileges, Parliament curtailed the Crown's discretionary powers, but regularization produced its own costs. Patents used to be a narrowly construed exception to a general prohibition of monopolies; now they became a valuable capital asset to be fought over in court or lobbied for in legislatures. The patent hunters invoked natural rights and the Lockean freedom to enjoy the fruits of one's labor, while opponents of patents emphasized monopolies' anti-competitive effects. In many states, the regularization of intellectual property rights was hotly debated and fiercely opposed. The Netherlands went as far as abolishing patents in 1869; other countries changed course several times in response to both internal and external pressures.

When the Austro-Hungarian Empire sought to attract companies from all over Europe to an international exhibition held in Vienna in 1873, prospective attendees insisted on legal protection for their intangibles before committing to attend. To ensure the success of the exhibition, the Austro-Hungarian Empire adopted a temporary law that protected the intellectual property rights of these foreigners.[44] In the end, the exhibition turned out to be a colossal disaster, but because of two unrelated events—a major financial crisis and a cholera outbreak. Still, it had put the question of transnational property rights on the agenda of domestic and international lawmakers, and it provided the impetus for the first international treaty, the 1883 Paris Convention for the Protection of Industrial Property.[45]

By signing up for international treaties such as the Paris Convention, sovereign states committed to recognize the legal protections of intellectual property rights that were created under foreign law, but they did so strictly in a reciprocal fashion: they would recognize the rights granted by foreign states provided these states did the same for the rights they created under their own laws. The internationalization of property rights in intangibles created a powerful argument in favor of domestic protections and it is easy to see why. Countries that did not follow the trend now faced the unpalatable choice of staying outside the club, thereby undermining their ability to attract foreigners while also exposing their own companies to intellectual property "theft" abroad.

The battle between free traders and advocates for temporal monopolies also waged in the United States. For much of the nineteenth and early twentieth centuries, the balance tilted against comprehensive protections for intellectual property rights. With an economy that was still relatively backward and seeking to catch up with the industrializing powerhouses of Europe, especially the UK, the country had little reason to take a strong position on protecting intangibles and thereby potentially closing off critical sources of knowledge that could be used for economic advancement. As the country matured into a leading industrialized nation, however, attitudes changed, and the United States morphed into the foremost champion for intellectual property rights in the globe.

US-based private industry took the lead in the elevation of US intellectual property rights to global legal standards; it pleaded not only for strengthening intellectual property rights at home, but for extending these protections globally. This was easier said than done, because principles of comity among sovereign states limit the reach of each country's domestic laws beyond their own territory. The solution was to characterize as unfair competition infringements of property rights that were protected under US law, whether or not this was also the case under the laws of the country where this infringement occurred. Moreover, private industry urged the US government to use trade sanctions against countries that failed to adhere to US norms.[46] Under the new Trade Act of 1974, companies even obtained the right to petition the US government to bring trade sanctions against other countries.[47] Such a petition was nonbinding, but gave industry a powerful tool to twist the arm of its government. The 1974 Trade Act also introduced a system of advisory committees that embedded the private industry's interests deeply in US global trade policies. The Act speaks of "citizens," who shall inform the government about their needs; yet most, if not all of the individuals who have sat on these committees over the years were chief executives (CEOs) or presidents of major corporations, not ordinary citizens.[48]

One person in particular left a deep mark on the globalization of US patent protection: Ed Pratt, the CEO of Pfizer Pharmaceuticals, who assumed the chair of the Advisory Committee for Trade

Negotiations (ACTN) in 1981 and shaped the committee's direction for years to come.[49] The company was a major supplier of penicillin to the Allied Forces during the Second World War and operated under a government-imposed compulsory license system. When, after the end of the war, these restrictions were lifted, the rush by each company to patent its own drug resulted in a highly inefficient fragmentation of property rights.[50] For the US market, companies soon agreed to swap patents to consolidate their respective gains—a practice that eventually gave rise to an anti-trust investigation. There were, however, markets beyond the United States and the reach of its patents where wound infections needed treatment, and Ed Pratt directed Pfizer to build a significant global market share in developing countries. At first, Pfizer did not bother much about patents for its overseas operations; as long as these countries lacked the technical skills to compete, the company could reap profits simply by relying on the know-how gap as its major comparative advantage. Increasingly, however, Pfizer faced two obstacles: some developing countries, India foremost among them, enacted laws that encouraged the production of cheap drugs for their people while also imposing restrictions on the scope of private rights.[51] In addition, more and more developing countries acquired the know-how that put them within reach of competition with companies from the West.

The answer to this conundrum was to globalize patents on the standards that US law had developed, and the ACTN, the committee Pfizer's CEO Ed Pratt chaired, became a critical tool to advance this agenda. Strengthening the US trade sanctions systems was part of this strategy. The United States pushed for better protection of intellectual property rights elsewhere by making this a condition for signing new bilateral or multilateral trade deals, without which countries lacked access to the US market.[52] Ultimately, though, the goal was to incorporate the standards US companies had secured in the United States into a single multilateral agreement.

Forcing Other States' Hands

On January 1, 1995, the World Trade Organization was established, an organizational umbrella for governing international trade that had been long in the making. The idea for it dates back to the end of World War II, but the International Trade Organization faltered when the US Congress did not ratify its founding treaty. Multilateral trade negotiations under the auspices of a much looser General Agreement on Tariffs and Trade (GATT) took its place; the GATT was used as a platform that was controlled by the most developed economies to liberalize international trade step by step, in a series of negotiation rounds. As the scope of the agreements expanded and more countries participated, a renewed push was made to create an international trade regime, the WTO. Just as global free trade was finally institutionalized, The Agreement on Trade-Related Aspects of Intellectual Property Rights, or TRIPS, created major carve-outs from the free trade regime for monopolies under the label of intellectual property rights. TRIPS gave the technologically more advanced companies of the global North the option to enclose their know-how and thereby remove free access to it by potential competitors in less advanced countries.

The TRIPS agreement does not fully harmonize intellectual property rights, but instead establishes minimum standards for the scope and duration of these rights. Following the US model, it mandates that not only processes, but products are also patentable—an increase in scope relative to patent rights that existed in many countries. Further, the duration of patents was standardized at 20 years. The most remarkable aspect of TRIPS, however, was that it was adopted at all. Preliminary inquiries by the US trade representative had found little resonance in other advanced economies and had been met with stern opposition from the developing world.

The fate of international agreements and norms is not always determined by states and their representatives. Closer inspection of how global rules emerge suggests that the capacity of key private players to organize themselves domestically is crucial.[53] Indeed, the making of global intellectual property rights can be traced directly to the organization of private businesses in the United States and their ability to mobilize their fellow businesses in other advanced economies as well. In the United States, business took the lead by establishing the Intellectual Property Committee (IPC) in 1986. It was modeled on the ACTN, which had paved the way for using trade sanctions to protect US intellectual property rights abroad, and its explicit goal was to extend the US intellectual property rights regime to the rest of the world. Membership of the IPC included a cross-section of industry leaders in sectors from pharmaceuticals to computer technology and communications, including Bristol-Myers, DuPont, FMC Corporation, General Electric, General Motors, Hewlett-Packard, IBM, Johnson & Johnson, Merck, Monsanto, Pfizer, Rockwell International, and Warner Communications.[54]

These companies reached out to their counterparts in Europe and Japan and jointly with them formed a global business alliance that demanded stronger intellectual property rights protection.[55] The US trade sanction regime helped win over developing countries and emerging markets after several of these countries had learned the hard way that the United States would be willing to employ trade sanctions to protect US intellectual property rights in foreign countries. In 1989, for example, the United States levied tariffs worth $59 million against Brazil, which were removed only after Brazil pledged to update its IP regime. Fearing similar repercussions, Mexico agreed to extensive IP protections in the North American Free Trade Agreement (NAFTA) of 1994, prompting an industry representative to remark that "Mexico gave us all we wanted."[56] Other countries agreed to TRIPS for fear that they would be squeezed out from major markets should they fail to do so. Yet others counted on better access to markets for their agricultural products if they agreed; this proved to be a bad bet, as the agricultural trade negotiations have faltered, largely because of resistance in the global North.

Despite the powerful voice of industry, TRIPS had many critics, including most leading trade economists in the United States and elsewhere.[57] They classified intellectual property rights as monopolies that would create new obstacles to global trade, mirroring the arguments free-trade advocates had made back in the nineteenth century. Nevertheless, TRIPS was adopted. One observer put his finger on the underlying mechanisms. "States coerce other states," Drahos opined, often with military, but in this case with economic, power.[58] But states were not the main drivers behind legal reforms in this case; rather, some states, foremost among them the United States, were doing the bidding of powerful industry interests.

States may make a lot of commitments in international agreements, but whether they will implement them is usually a different matter; and there is little that other states can do to ensure compliance. Even if they bring a case before the International Court of Justice and the court rules in their favor, they cannot rely on bailiffs or other enforcement agents to execute a judgment should a sovereign state ignore it. Unlike most international agreements, the WTO incorporates a full-blown dispute settlement mechanism, even an appellate body. It does not have sheriffs or bailiffs and as such lacks the insignia of coercive law enforcement that characterizes sovereign states. Instead, WTO law empowers a state that won a dispute to retaliate against the losing state if it fails to comply with the ruling.[59] Importantly, only the disputing state can take retaliatory measures, rendering this an empty weapon for countries with little economic prowess, but making it an even more powerful tool for states with big economies. It still takes a state to bring a case, but certainly in the United States, private parties have secured powerful levers over the US government to ensure that this enforcement mechanism will be used.

The story of TRIPS has interesting parallels to the legal conquest of land in foreign territories discussed in chapter 2. When the settlers arrived in the "new world," they claimed that no one before them could possibly claim prior title, because only the settlers had discovered the land and improved it. No matter that the indigenous peoples had been there first; they were expelled from their land without due process or just compensation, because their claims were not recognized in law. Discovery and improvement were deemed sufficient to override the principle of seniority for ranking competing claims to the same resource.

In a similar vein, early attempts to ensure that TRIPS would mediate between different approaches to defining intellectual property rights were rejected by private business from the global North. Their telling argument was that such alternative legal treatment offered "inadequate treatment of IP rights."[60] In their minds, there was only one way to configure intellectual property rights—the American way. In truth, there is no such thing as a generic property right, whether intellectual or otherwise. The Privy Council and the Supreme Court of Belize understood as much when they recognized indigenous land use practices as property rights—and the same principles could and arguably should apply to intellectual property rights. By endorsing a singular approach based on the business interests in the most advanced economy, the world missed a critical opportunity to create an intellectual property rights regime of meaningful diversity and, critically, to preserve at least parts of the global commons in knowledge. Then and now, the quest to monetize assets won over, requiring their coding as capital.

Trade Secrets in the Age of Big Data

Property rights are state-endorsed legal privileges that extend an owner's priority rights against the world. States don't offer their coercive powers to protect just any claim; property rights tend to be enumerated and subject to formalities and disclosure requirements. This is true also for patents; they have to conform to the standard the law establishes for patenting an invention, such as its novelty and utility. As a quid pro quo for obtaining a patent the patentee must disclose the core features of the invention, which implies that some information about the product will be leaked to others. If, however, the inventor needs a state to recognize and protect her rights against the world, others must be put on notice about their contents and scope. How else would others know when they trespass them?

Disclosing the details of the invention, is, of course, rarely in the interest of an aspiring monopolist. Of course, nobody is forced to seek a patent for an invention or discovery. Prospective patent holders who fear that too much secrecy might compromise their discovery or invention may therefore decide to forgo patenting altogether and to rely on the law of trade secrets instead.[61] Even better, they might combine the two. In the age of big data and technological advances, patents and trade secrets are no longer sought in the alternative, but they have become complements, and with powerful, exclusionary, effects.[62]

Myriad's ability to turn the BRCA patent into profits years after the patent had been struck down illustrates how this works. Myriad obtained the patent for BRCA type 1 in 1994 and it was struck down by the US Supreme Court in 2013. Nonetheless, as late as 2017, Myriad was still living off the BRCA patent. The secret for the ongoing success is that the company had used the BRCA patent to generate data, building a database that had no match among its competitors. Myriad used its BRCA patent to compel doctors and patients to use their process to test for the gene and to share data with the company, and the company now protects its unmatched data with the help of trade secrecy law. The BRCA patent has been aptly described as a "data-generating patent" and the data, not the patent as such, proved to be the lasting fountain of wealth for Myriad. From a social welfare perspective, these data would be even more valuable in the public domain to advance public health concerns, but public and private welfare don't always correlate, and neither do private and public wealth.[63]

Myriad's founder, Dr. Skolnick, spotted the potential of marrying genetics with genealogy early on in his career, when he pursued his doctoral research for a degree in genetics (he already had a degree in economics) in Italy and came across three Mormons who were collecting parish records to identify the ancestors of their communities in Utah. A few years later, he suggested linking the Utah Mormon Genealogy to the Utah Cancer Registry to facilitate the process of identifying genes.[64] After Myriad had identified the BRCA sequence and patented it, the company did not just offer the test, but it collected detailed data from every patient, including her specific variation of the defective gene, the manifestation or phenotype of the cancer, her family history, and the gene pool to which she belonged. This database became Myriad's greatest asset. In 2005, the company stopped contributing information to public databases and stopped sharing its own data with others.[65] As Simon and Sichelman observed, "[w]hat began with patent protection over genetic information now includes trade secret protection for Myriad's databases of patients' full genetic sequences and phenotypic information, as well as correlations and algorithms resulting from access to that wealth of data."[66]

In essence, "data-generating patents" give the patentee a head start over others in building a huge, private database that will be enforced through trade secrecy law long after the patent itself has expired. In contrast to conventional intellectual property rights, trade secrets have no time limit.[67] It is, of course, not without irony that the companies at the cutting edge of technological progress in the twenty-first century are employing one of the oldest tricks in the trade, one that is more closely associated with the protectionism of guilds than with free markets. But this is nothing new either; recall that the newly minted landowners of early modern times took refuge in the feudal law of the entail to protect their property rights against creditors.[68]

The guilds of the Middle Ages revolved around clubs of artisans and craftsmen who protected their interests against outside competitors. Members of each guild were sworn to protect the skills of the trade and apprentices who joined a master to learn a trade had to take an oath that they would not divulge their master's secret to outsiders. They would learn it, master it, and pass it on to the next generation of apprentices, who bowed to the same principles of secrecy. It is unlikely that all guild members or apprentices always lived up to these promises, but there has been astonishingly little litigation in courts.[69] One can only speculate that these norms were enforced informally through reputational bonds and, as a last resort, expulsion.[70]

The barriers to competition that guilds created were eventually dismantled in the name of free and competitive markets. In Polanyi's account, "deliberate action of the state in the fifteenth and sixteenth centuries foisted the mercantile system on the fiercely protectionist towns and principalities."[71] In so doing, the state cleared the path for the rise of the market principle, subordinating society to it.[72] Equally important, the changing organization of the workplace, from small shops that were individually owned to big factories with thousands of employees, fundamentally changed the old master-servant relationship.[73] Freeing labor from bondage and destroying anticompetitive practices of the guilds set the stage for the emergence of large business operations with thousands of employees. Yet, these new businesses soon began to resort to guild-style practices, which they often defended successfully in court, in order to keep their employees from freely trading their knowledge on the labor market. Freedom, it seems, is a double-edged sword, and the winners of the last battle to free assets and their holders from the shackles of previous rules soon find themselves adapting these very rules to protect their own gains.

The gist of the trade secrecy doctrine, as it evolved in the United States, is that certain information and know-how can be shielded from use by others, even if it does not reach the level of a patentable innovation. In the nineteenth century, this body of law was put to use to prevent employees from using the skills they had acquired in one company to freely employ them elsewhere. The US company DuPont spearheaded the use of contractual covenants to this end.[74] US courts readily enforced these restrictions, thereby bringing the feudal calculus of Middle Age labor relations into the modern age. The result is a deep contradiction at the very heart of US labor relations. On the one hand, US labor law endorses "employment at will," which gives employers great flexibility in firing workers, on the other, it allows employers to restrain employees' ability to re-deploy their skills.

In the past, patents and trade secrets rarely crossed paths; inventors chose between patenting and relying on trade secrecy law depending on the nature of the invention, the costs, and the likelihood of obtaining a patent. The advent of big data, however, has created conditions for a new and powerful mix of patents plus trade secrets— and this is not limited to the pharmaceutical industry. Google's success story, for example, parallels that of Myriad in interesting ways. It is often said that Google and other big tech companies don't use patents. They seem to be able to do without the coercive powers of the state when it comes to protecting their most valuable asset: data about us. That story, however, is at best incomplete. The search technology Google has deployed to build its data empire *was* patented. Stanford University owned, but Google held the exclusive license to PageRank (which has since expired). Google's own patent lawyer called PageRank "one of the most famous and valuable of all modern software patents."[75]

This may be dismissed as the typical hyperbole of a lawyer, but it fits squarely the worldview of patent lawyers who have claimed that patents, not humans, were responsible for the Industrial Revolution.[76] Yet, we often celebrate the new discoveries and technical breakthroughs, but ignore the legal work behind the scenes that gives these breakthroughs lasting wealth effects. The notion that patents propelled the Industrial Revolution aligns well with the argument advanced in this book that capital is coded in law; and that includes the coding of human intellectual "property." Patents have been equally central in producing the private wealth associated with the two post–industrial revolutions: biotech and software. Making the case that BRCA was patentable was already quite an achievement in legal engineering, even if it ultimately failed, but Google's PageRank is a close match. Google's lawyers were able to obtain a patent for something that is best described as a filing system, something so ordinary that it is difficult to see why it would qualify as an invention at all. What set it apart from ordinary filing systems was not its substance but its digital form: an algorithm for organizing and ranking digital documents based on the quantity and quality of links between them. This pushes the envelope of requirements for process-patents, which require some output or "transformation," not just a change in form, to be patentable.[77]

The patent allowed Google to build an enormous database of ordinary Internet users that is matched only by close rivals such as Facebook or Amazon. And Google has not shied away from using trade secrecy law to restrain former employees, thereby undermining one of the greatest comparative advantages of Silicon Valley's legal landscape: the non-enforceability of non-compete clauses.[78] When information technology first came of age, other technology companies, such as IBM along Route 128 in Massachusetts, were invoking these rules to keep know-how in house but were soon outcompeted by Silicon Valley with its free-wheeling start-up culture. It did not stay this way. Google recently sued Uber after one of its prized employees switched sides, claiming that he had appropriated trade secrets for self-driving cars of one or more of the company's subsidiaries.[79] The civil case was settled, but criminal proceedings continued and Google cooperated with the authorities.[80] The pattern should be familiar by now: The former disrupters of existing law or technology learn quickly that only by invoking legal protection of their own (often the same protection they only recently fought) can they protect their own gains. Remarkably, they often get a court, even the legislatures, to side with their new worldview.[81]

The second enclosure (this time of knowledge rather than land) is occurring more quietly than the first and without physical violence, but its repercussions may well go further. It was traumatic for the commoners to lose the basis for their sustenance, or the First Peoples to be pushed from the lands they had occupied and used for centuries. We are now in danger of losing access to our own data and to nature's code for the sole purpose of giving select asset holders yet another opportunity to expand their wealth at the expense of the rest.

6

A Code for the Globe

Capital has become mobile and seems to know no borders; goods cross oceans and corporations roam the globe in search of new investment opportunities, or simply a more benign tax or regulatory environment; financial assets worth trillions of dollars are traded daily at the stroke of a key and settled in digital clouds with no land in sight. Yet, there is no single global legal system to support global capitalism; nor is there a global state to back it with its coercive powers. We thus confront a puzzle: If capital is coded in law, how can global capitalism exist in the absence of a global state and a global legal system?

The solution to this puzzle is surprisingly simple: global capitalism can be sustained, at least in theory, by a single domestic legal system, provided that other states recognize and enforce its legal code. Global capitalism as we know it comes remarkably close to this theoretical possibility: it is built around two domestic legal systems, the laws of England and those of New York State, complemented by a few international treaties, and an extensive network of *bilateral* trade and investment regimes, which themselves are centered around a handful of advanced economies.

Extending law in space to people and territories in faraway places is reminiscent of empire. In ancient Rome, Roman law was available mostly for the elites, but was "out of the reach of most of the population"; to them it was more a "threat to be feared" than a "possible protection."[1] For most people in most countries, the law that sustains global capitalism is also beyond reach, because these countries only recognize and enforce laws that were made by others. Even the citizens of England and New York State, the jurisdictions where the legal code for global capital is forged, have little say, because most of the activities take place in private law offices, not public legislatures and no longer even in courts, which have been sidelined as potentially too disruptive for private coding strategies.

Exporting law has a long history. English settlers and colonizers applied the common law throughout the growing empire and sent judges to far-off places to implement it. Napoleon Bonaparte's troops brought the French legal codes with them wherever they went, extending the reach of French law to Poland in the East, and to Spain, Portugal, and Egypt in the South. Imperialism was not only about military conquest, but also about spreading the legal system of the European states to the colonies they created in Africa, Asia, and the Americas. This is why the legal systems of most countries around the globe belong to one of the three leading "legal families": the English common law, the French civil law, and the German civil law.[2] Even countries that escaped colonialization were pressured to adopt Western law, Japan being the most prominent example. The Meiji Restoration triggered an extensive legal modernization project that first focused on French law, but the country ended up transplanting mostly German law.[3]

The diffusion of European legal systems throughout the world has greatly reduced legal variance, but it has not produced uniformity. To begin with, not only do the dominant legal families vary from one another, but even legal systems that belong to the same family are quite different. Law is not static but evolves over time as new cases are litigated and statutory law is amended in response to changing norms or political preferences. The same legal family lineage therefore does not produce identical or even similar laws on the books, much less the convergence of these laws in practice. Societies have copied laws from one another for millennia, but to be effective they have to be adapted to local conditions.[4] Static laws that fail to reflect preferences of social norms, or do not respond to a changing environment, remain black letters on the books with little impact on social ordering.[5]

But what is good for effective law and democratic self-governance is not necessarily good for capital. The same qualities that make law vibrant and relevant for a polity make it volatile and uncertain in the eyes of foreign traders and investors. They are unfamiliar with local practices and political processes, which render local institutions unpredictable in their eyes. Recall that in Adam Smith's account, the lack of institutional certainty in foreign places *was* the invisible hand that drove merchants back home, where they would invariably share some of their spoils with their community. For the merchants, this presented itself as a massive institutional failure, which greatly increased their costs of doing business and reduced their private gains. If institutions could be streamlined around the globe, business would become more predictable and the merchants could simply dispense with the invisible hand and keep their spoils for themselves.

Building the legal infrastructure for global commerce has taken, for the most part, one of two forms: the harmonization of laws in different states, and the recognition and enforcement of foreign law. The latter has been much more successful in protecting capital globally, but it did require that countries adapted their own conflict-of-law rules to ensure that private choice and autonomy would prevail over public concerns.

Expanding Private Choice

The trend to outsource law to private agents by offering the option to choose domestic or foreign law as they please has been a response to the difficulty of harmonizing the law by political means. Extensive legal harmonization was tried at first—especially in the period following the Second World War, with the goal of reinvigorating global trade and investment. The European Union (EU) is the poster child for countries coming together to forge common rules for a common market. Negotiating a common set of rules that are agreeable to all, however, proved to be slow and cumbersome—even for countries with a long history of mutual borrowing and common roots going all the way back to Roman law.

The alternative to the deliberate harmonization of laws through the political process is legal and regulatory competition among states combined with private autonomy for the law's end-users, who get to pick and choose what is best for them. For this to work, countries do not need to engage in laborious legal harmonization projects regarding the contents of, say, contract or corporate law; they only need to put in place conflict-of-law rules that endorse the choices that private parties make. These rules have the additional advantage that they are so arcane, their passage ruffles few feathers in the day-to-day political process.

There are specific conflict-of-law rules for every area of the law, such as contracts, torts, property rights, corporate law, and so forth. For contract and corporate law, conflict-of-law rules have converged to a remarkable extent on the principle that the parties to a contract or the founding shareholders are free to choose the law by which they wish to be governed. Without this legal support structure, Lehman could not have built an empire of hundreds of subsidiaries that were incorporated in different jurisdictions and often ones where none of them ever did any business, nor intended to do so; neither would the certificates that NC2 or the Kleros clones issued to investors have found many buyers, had they not been assured that the legal rights they embodied would be recognized beyond the Cayman Islands or the tiny US state of Delaware. The willingness of states to allow private parties (and their lawyers) to pick and choose the law that best suits their interests explains the remarkable dominance of English and New York laws for the coding of global capital.

When it comes to property rights, however, most states still insist on their legal sovereignty and impose domestic law on assets that are located within their territory. But territorial control is of little use for assets that lack physical form or location; for tradeable financial assets, other criteria had to be found to determine whose law should govern them—and ideally criteria that would point to one and the same legal system when invoked in different countries. To this end, legal practitioners and some academics gathered under the auspices of a prominent forum, the Hague Conference on Private International Law, and hammered out an international treaty that standardized conflict-of-law rules for financial assets.[6] The result was a rule with the catchy acronym PRIMA, which stands for the "place of the relevant intermediary approach."[7] Under this rule, the legal system in which the entity that is issuing the assets is incorporated also determines the property law for the assets it issues. Since under the now dominant incorporation theory, the place of incorporation is for private parties (the founders) to decide, so is the property law for the financial assets this new entity will issue. Some jurisdictions offer even greater flexibility to private parties by allowing them to choose, in the contract between account holder and account manager, the law that shall govern them.[8]

In contrast, most intellectual property rights have remained a sticking point, because they can't be minted in private contract; patents don't exist but for an *official* act, as discussed in chapter 5. While patent lawyers may convince a patent office of a novel interpretation of what counts as an invention, the final decision lies in the hands of the courts. States have harmonized some aspects of intellectual property rights in international treaty law, TRIPS for example, but many details still remain in the hands of individual sovereign states.

Despite their resistance to divest control over property rights, states ended up giving away more than they may have intended. They have done so not through legal harmonization of substantive law or even of conflict-of-law rules, but by signing on to regional or bilateral investment treaties. These treaties rarely talk about property rights and instead focus on the *investments* made by foreign investors and their protection in the host state. Investments can take any form, from entering into contracts, licenses, concessions, all the way to ownership of shares or real property. The Trojan horse in these treaties is a dispute settlement mechanism that goes by the acronym ISDS (investor-state dispute settlement). It allows a foreign investor to bring a case for damages against the host state in an arbitral tribunal outside its territory. The language of the treaties is sufficiently open-ended to give arbitrators the power to grant damages for "unfair and inequitable treatment" that are on par with damages for expropriation.[9] In doing so, they effectively confer property rights status on contractual commitments and curtail the powers of states to determine the claims they wish to recognize as property rights.

Next to property rights, bankruptcy law as well has remained stubbornly local. The reason is that bankruptcy law is the place where losses are realized and allocated, which is inherently a political task. Moreover, bankruptcy is the acid test for the rights and privileges the parties negotiated or that state law granted them long before default loomed on the horizon. If these rights cannot be enforced in bankruptcy, they are not worth much, which is why bankruptcy law is said to exert substantial ex ante effects.[10]

One would think, therefore, that standardizing bankruptcy rules should not be a problem for global trade and finance, but this could not be further from the truth. Politicians are reluctant to assume losses or devise rules that would force them to commit to a loss allocation mechanism. Ever since the fall of the German Herstatt Bank in 1974, the need for a common resolution mechanism for banks that live globally has been apparent. The bank was relatively small but internationally active, with extensive foreign exchange operations in New York that had racked up substantial losses. German regulators closed down the bank in the middle of the trading session at the New York Stock Exchange, leaving everyone there to run for cover.[11] Yet, to this day there are still no rules to govern the resolution of globally active banks; only the Eurozone has put in place a common resolution regime for banks that are regulated at the EU level.[12] For the remaining banks there is still no transnational resolution regime in place.[13]

Given how politically sensitive property and bankruptcy laws are, it should not come as a surprise that this is where the battles over the global code of capital are being waged. The following sections will discuss separately the battles for property and bankruptcy law.

Private Property versus Sovereignty

Property and sovereignty are distinct but related concepts. Morris Cohen drew attention to the mirror image of "Property *and* Sovereignty" in a paper published in 1927, just a few years before a massive financial crisis revealed the fragility of the system he analyzed.

Property, he suggested, is private and signifies *dominium*; sovereignty is public and stands for *imperium*.[14] Yet, as he explained, "[t]here can be no doubt that our property laws do confer sovereign power on our captains of industry and even more so on our captains of finance."[15] Property rights are derivative of sovereignty, but they also confer on private parties certain sovereign powers. Indeed, the battle over the global code of capital is all about who should determine the contents and meaning of property rights: states or private parties; the democratic public or the captains of industry and finance.

The disputes that mark these battles often look like classic expropriation cases, in which a powerful state confiscates an asset in violation of private property rights. In most cases that concern the protection of property rights in global relations, however, the dispute is not at all over the object itself or the violation of specific rights but rather is over who gets to determine what *is a property right*: the Sovereign or private parties. When private parties claim this prerogative for themselves, Sovereignty is "under siege."[16]

Intellectual property rights have been harmonized by international treaty law, but even the much-maligned TRIPS Agreement of 1994, established only minimum standards, which leave plenty of room for divergent national rules. Recently, however, a case brought under the ISDS regime of the (former) North American Free Trade Agreement (NAFTA) has sought to dislodge a sovereign state's power to set the terms for recognizing intellectual property rights. This quest was ultimately unsuccessful, but it took the tribunal two years to reach this conclusion, while taking the opportunity to review the case law of a sovereign state for compliance with the interests of a foreign investor. The US pharmaceutical company, Eli Lilly, brought the case and has led the way for turning ISDS into an appellate body for domestic courts, and surely others will follow.

Eli Lilly was founded in 1876 by a veteran of the US Civil War, Mr. Eli Lilly. The company is headquartered in Indiana but operates on a global scale. The company secured patents in Canada for its drugs Strattera and Zyprexa used for patients who suffer from schizophrenia, depression, and other psychiatric disorders, in 1979 and 1980, respectively. Years later, the company filed for separate patents for a new set of components that were used in these drugs, thereby seeking to prolong the duration of the original patent (a practice that is not uncommon). These patents were granted as well, but later became embroiled in a legal dispute in which Eli Lilly sued another company in Canada for infringing its patents, and it was in this context that a Canadian judge revoked Eli Lilly's second patents for Strattera and Zyprexa.

Under Canadian law, a patent must be "new, useful and non-obvious" at the time the patent is filed.[17] After reviewing the patent, a lower court held that replacing a few components did not make the drug any more useful than it had been before. The second patent for Strattera and Zyprexa therefore did not meet Canada's legal requirements for granting a patent and the patents were therefore revoked. The case went on appeal and was remanded to the lower court, but on a second appeal Canada's Federal Court upheld the lower court's ruling. Eli Lilly was still not ready to give up and appealed to Canada's constitutional court, which did not take the case.[18] Having run out of legal options under Canadian law, the company notified the Canadian government in 2015 that it would file an investor-state dispute under NAFTA, demanding $500 million in compensation.[19] The company argued that the revocation of the patent amounted to an infringement of the company's "investments" in Canada.

NAFTA was an international treaty between Canada, Mexico, and the United States with the goal of fostering trade and investment among these three countries, which has since been replaced by USMCA, the "United States-Mexico-Canada Agreement."[20] As one would expect in a treaty among sovereign states, most of the rights and obligations it spells out, such as opening their borders to goods and services from the contracting parties, bind these three countries as the treaty's signatories. However, NAFTA also created rights for private parties, specifically for foreign investors, and these rights are armed with a powerful enforcement mechanism. If a foreign investor believes that his "investments" have been infringed by a host state, it can lodge a complaint with an arbitral tribunal and seek compensation for damages. Unlike victims of human rights violations, investors do not have to seek remedies in a domestic court first; they can go straight to a tribunal outside the territory of the host state they are suing.[21]

Similar enforcement mechanisms by private parties against host states have been built into more than three thousand bilateral investment treaties (BITs). More than eight hundred cases alleging infringements of investments have been filed over the past three decades, with a total of $522 million in damages paid out, or about 40 percent of the sums demanded.[22] Investors don't always win; states do so in at least one-third of the cases, with the remaining cases being either settled (typically without disclosure about the terms of the settlements) or decided in favor of the investor.

As noted, Eli Lilly did not seek dispute settlement under NAFTA right away. It first battled in the Canadian courts for recognition of its (second) patents. This makes sense, because the company needed an act of state: the recognition of a property right in the form of a patent.[23] After having lost its case, Eli Lilly now argued that the patent's revocation by the Canadian courts amounted to "unfair and inequitable treatment" and "indirect expropriation" under the NAFTA treaty. The reason given was that the Canadian court's interpretation of the Canadian Patent Act deviated from its earlier case law in a "dramatic" fashion.

In effect, the claim challenged the prerogative of Canada to create its own intellectual property rights; it also sought to subject the country's judiciary to review by an ad hoc arbitral tribunal. Both claims stretched the limits of investor protection under NAFTA. The treaty had not harmonized patent law among the three countries; their power to stipulate their own property regimes was therefore not affected. And while courts are not beyond the reach of review of ISDS tribunals, the threshold for holding states liable for a wrongful court decision is pretty high: under existing legal standards, only the *denial of justice* would be reviewed, not just any court ruling that seemed legally doubtful or even faulty—and Eli Lilly had already spent ample time in the halls of Canada's courts. At bottom, the company challenged the interpretation of Canadian law by Canadian courts, but it managed to spin it into a violation of investor protection rules under NAFTA and found a tribunal that was ready to hear the case.

Anyone can make audacious claims, but to win a case one needs a legal authority—a statute, a case, or a treaty on which a claim can be grounded. NAFTA's open-ended language gave investors ample ammunition. Article 1105 of the agreement stated that foreign investors have a right to "fair and equitable treatment" in the host state where they invest, and Article 1110 further stipulated that "[n]o Party may directly or indirectly nationalize or expropriate an investment of an investor of another Party in its territory or take a measure tantamount to nationalization or expropriation of such an investment."

A state is, of course, not a unitary actor; state power is usually divided among three branches of government—the executive, the legislature, and the judiciary; and in the federal system, municipalities and states exercise authority quite independent from the central government. However, for the rights and obligations states have under international law, the internal division of power is secondary; the sovereign state is the subject of international law and actions other official actors take, such as regulators, administrators, even judges, that are deemed to violate international law will be attributed to that state. In fact, it is not uncommon for states to be held liable under international law for actions taken by sub-units of a federation, whether or not the federal state had jurisdiction over the issue in dispute. A good example is the Metalclad case, which imposed $16 million in damages on the federal state of Mexico for the refusal of a municipality to grant an American investor a license for a waste management facility in its community, notwithstanding the fact that under Mexican law the town had the exclusive power over granting or denying the license in question.[24]

Extending a state's liability for acts of its judiciary, however, is more contentious, and for good reasons. In countries that are committed to the rule of law, the judiciary is designed to be independent of both the executive and the legislature; judges are accountable only to the constitution and the laws of a given country. If a foreign investor was able to easily challenge a ruling by an independent court and obtain a huge damage award from the country in which the court is located, this could easily sway courts in future cases and undermine their impartiality. In fact, the Canadian government insisted that only the complete denial of justice might possibly give rise to liability. After some more probing by the tribunal, however, the government's lawyers conceded that failure to grant due process might count as well. The tribunal quickly turned this into a new standard for its review powers over domestic courts: an allegation of "manifest arbitrariness or blatant unfairness" of a country's case law opens the door to investor-state disputes.[25]

The tribunal then proceeded to examine the history of Canadian patent case law to see whether the legal treatment of Eli Lilly received by the Canadian courts met this standard. But the tribunal did more than this; it heard an expert witness who presented statistics comparing the Canadian court's patent rulings with similar rulings in the United States and in Mexico, pointing out that patent holders have a much lower probability of seeing their patents revoked in the United States than in either Canada or Mexico.[26] This argument was obviously off target, because NAFTA did not harmonize patent law, or any other area of the law for that matter; nor does the treaty require court practices in the three countries to converge. The only relevant question was whether, in the Eli Lilly case, *Canadian* courts had strayed from their own established record in a manifestly arbitrary fashion. The tribunal's willingness to entertain the comparison between Canadian, Mexican, and US courts suggests a bias in favor of investor interests over state sovereignty.

In the end, the tribunal concluded that the courts' rulings in the Eli Lilly case fell well within the scope of existing case law; it took two years to reach this decision, during which the arbitrators who presided over the case earned hundreds of thousands and the fees for the lawyers who represented the two parties reached millions of US dollars.[27] Eli Lilly had clearly tried to pull off an aggressive litigation strategy, which may have persuaded governments with fewer resources to settle the case early in order to avoid additional costs. Dealing with aggressive litigants is, of course, nothing unusual. Domestic courts do so on a daily basis and they have few qualms over dismissing a case when all the plaintiff has to offer are wordy allegations that are not well supported by the facts. Their incentive structure is, of course, a different one. Judges on state courts are not paid by the cases they resolve but work on a fixed (and much lower) salary than do most professional private arbitrators. In contrast, private arbitrators earn their fees one case at the time.

Attorneys who aggressively seek cases for litigation have appropriately been termed "bounty hunters"; but this term also fits private arbitrators who pursue dispute resolution as a for-profit business. Worse, by accepting the case and then expanding the tribunals' scope of review into judicial conduct beyond the threshold of denial of justice, the tribunal in the Eli Lilly case turned itself into another appeals court, its own assertions to the contrary. In the end, Canada won the battle; but it is not yet clear who will win the war and have the final say in *making* property rights: sovereign states or private agents.

Paving the Way for Global Derivatives

Patents and financial assets are both commonly described as *intangibles*; these are not objects that can be touched, but are creatures of the law. If anything, financial assets may be even more footloose than intellectual property rights, because they do not need an official act of state to come into existence. They are coded in the modules of the code of capital, over which lawyers have much sway subject only to the odd challenge in a court of law. Granted, they still need some domestic legal system to sanction the coding strategy, but lawyers can pick and choose from among a menu of legal systems on offer.

This may sound as though financial assets might be coded in a garden variety of legal systems, but this would defy the purpose of creating assets that have global reach. In practice, most financial assets that are traded globally are coded in only two legal systems—the laws of England or New York State. Finance may be global, but the legal code that carries the core features of financial assets is remarkably parochial. Other states may impose regulations on financial intermediaries or assets within their borders, but even mandatory rules are rarely airtight, and the art of coding capital is all about identifying gaps and fitting coding strategies, including those permitted under foreign law, within them.

The big stumbling block for seamless global markets based on domestic law, however, is bankruptcy law. As suggested earlier, bankruptcy is where life and death decisions are made and where losses must be accounted for. Not surprisingly, sovereign states have been reluctant to relinquish control over this sensitive legal domain.

England was one of the first states to adopt a modern bankruptcy statute in 1705, which enabled traders to escape their old debt and start a new life in commerce after bankruptcy. To take advantage of the new law, one had to prove one's status as a trader.[28] Over time, bankruptcy law became a battle field for big vs. small creditors. Big creditors lobbied hard in England to retain their stronghold over the bankruptcy process; eventually, they had to cede control to judges.[29] However, the big banks among them have managed to reassert their own control over debtors by using a special kind of collateral, a floating lien, which gives the bank a powerful position vis-à-vis other creditors and ensures that insolvency cases involving their debtors are settled for the most part outside the bankruptcy court.[30]

The contemporary equivalents to big banks that seek to control the bankruptcy process are counterparties in derivatives transactions. As discussed in chapter 4, derivatives markets were built on the assumption that all assets will trade continuously and that therefore positions can be bought, sold, or re-hedged at any moment to find the optimal hedge for a new exposure. But if and when only one of the counterparties files for bankruptcy, the music stops. Bankruptcy law is geared toward protecting the debtor's remaining assets in order to make whole as many creditors as possible; and sometimes to give the debtor a new chance in life.

To achieve this end, creditors of the insolvent debtor are typically barred temporarily from enforcing their individual claims. They have to wait long enough to ensure that all claims are gathered and ranked according to their priority status pre-bankruptcy. Yet, representatives of derivatives traders, the modern captains of finance, successfully lobbied the legislatures in more than fifty countries to amend their bankruptcy codes and create a "safe harbor" for derivatives and repos, thereby exempting these financial assets from rules that are binding for everybody else. The main selling point was that making domestic laws compatible with private contracts was key for countries to participate in global derivatives markets.

The tribute for accomplishing this feat belongs largely to the International Swaps and Derivatives Association (ISDA).[31] Organized as a nonprofit corporation in the state of New York, its operation now spans the globe, with offices in New York, London, Tokyo, and several other global financial centers. It is not the only private organization in the business of coding law for global finance but is arguably the most influential.[32]

ISDA was formed in 1985 at a critical moment in the development of the market for credit derivatives. At the time, the issuers of these innovative instruments each fashioned their own derivatives contracts with the help of lawyers, who mapped out the legal terrain, ensured that innovative products would fit within the constraints created by existing laws and regulations, or devised ways to mitigate their impact. These contracts were tailored to the specific needs of their clients, but this limited their potential to be scaled and eventually be traded in global financial markets.[33] Standardization greatly enhances the scalability of assets, and ISDA was formed to create the foundation for scalable markets in products that were standardized, yet offered enough room for tailoring them to meet the needs of specific clients and for lawyers to charge the fee premiums that come with bespoke products.

The success of ISDA has been beyond anyone's imagination. Today, the association has more than 850 primary members in sixty-seven countries—the who's who in global finance and, as associate members, the who's who in global law.[34] ISDA's contracts are used primarily for derivatives that are traded over the counter (OTC) to the tune of hundreds of trillions of dollars.[35] These markets were hit by the financial crisis, but statistics for 2016 suggest that, in aggregate, they have rebounded almost to their pre-crisis level.[36]

ISDA's key contribution to the emergence of a global derivatives market was a contractual platform for swaps and other derivatives—the "Master Agreement," or MA for short.[37] It is a framework contract, fondly referred to by ISDA insiders as a piece of private legislation, which specifies the rights and obligations of counterparties wishing to engage in derivatives transactions with one another. Once the basic MA has been signed, a special schedule is drawn up that contains the details for each specific transaction between the two parties to the MA. Still, the MA is not intended as a substitute for domestic law but uses it as a gap filler. It prompts the parties of the MA to choose a default law and to elect the courts from that legal system for resolving any disputes. Notably, the MA advises the parties to limit their choice to one of two legal systems, English law or the law of New York State. The parties may choose otherwise, but they are advised that they risk increasing legal uncertainty if they do so.

Until the global crisis of 2008, ISDA favored dispute resolution in courts over private arbitration. During the benign market environment that preceded the crisis, only few disputes ever made it to court.[38] In the crisis, however, litigation spiked and ISDA had its hands full trying to explain to judges who had never before encountered the MA or the transactions it governed, how it should be interpreted, and to do its best to ensure that individual judges would not stray too far from interpretations that most market participants had taken for granted. In order to contain the risk of legal uncertainty, a new arbitral tribunal has now been established: the "Panel of Recognized International Market Experts in Finance," or its somewhat contorted shorthand PRIME, which sounds more like a steak house than a private court for high finance.[39] The location is as noteworthy as the name: The panel does not reside in just any town, not even in one of the global financial centers, but in The Hague, where the International Court of Justice, the Permanent Court of Arbitration (which houses PRIME), and the International Criminal Court, among others, reside. The priests of high finance, who issue their own "private legislation," still like to bask in the aura of legal authority, or so it seems.

Well-crafted contracts offer guidance not only for good but also for bad times and ISDA's MA is highly attentive to questions of default and termination, which loom large in finance. The counter-parties to derivatives are in the business of minting private money, assets that are cloaked in law to give them the appearance of state money, only at higher rates of return; and invariably they will find themselves from time to time unable to convert their private money into state money at the speed and for the price they desire. Typically, this occurs at the most inopportune time, that is, when their own creditors are knocking on the door and insolvency looms.

According to ISDA's MA, bankruptcy is a triggering event that allows the non-defaulting party to clear out all outstanding claims against the party that finds itself in bankruptcy proceedings, and to pay what it owes, or take out what the debtor owes to it.[40] There is no waiting, no concern for the other creditors, and no consider-ation for reorganizing the defaulting debtor. With these contractual provisions, the MA sought to create a special default regime for derivatives traders that allows them to reposition their bets even as one of their counterparties finds itself in bankruptcy. In fact, the close-out netting provisions of the MA were in direct tension to most countries' bankruptcy laws. These laws typically prohibit the use of bankruptcy as an event that triggers contractual default; they also impose a wait period, or automatic stay, on any enforcement actions by any creditor;[41] and they give the receiver in bankruptcy the right to cherry pick contracts that the other party must fulfill, even though it may not recover its own obligation in full from the insolvent debtor.[42]

Bankruptcy is mandatory law, therefore private actors cannot just contract around it; they can't even strategize about where to file for bankruptcy, because it is almost impossible to know in advance which of the parties might default at some future date, and because of bankruptcy's mandatory nature, it will typically be the debtor's home laws that will govern bankruptcy. The only remaining option was to get legislatures to change their bankruptcy laws so that they would accommodate the provisions of ISDA's MA, that is, to make state law consistent with private contracts. ISDA did just that; in total, the association successfully lobbied more than fifty legislatures to change their bankruptcy laws.[43]

The United States is where it all began. The federal bankruptcy code of 1978 included safe harbors for derivatives of *government* securities, presumably to protect the market for sovereign debt from the default of a financial intermediary; this small opening was used to lobby for similar carve-outs for derivatives on private assets.[44] The argument in favor of bankruptcy safe harbors was that the default of a single counterparty could rapidly spread throughout the entire market and threaten to bring it down. These markets therefore had to be insulated from the ordinary working of bankruptcy statutes. After the battle was won for swaps and other derivatives, repurchase agreements, or repos, followed, although the case for them was much weaker than for derivatives.[45] Step by step, the list of assets that were exempted from core features of bankruptcy proceedings was expanded; in 2005, even the veneer of judicial scrutiny of assets that the private sector slated for special treatment under bankruptcy safe harbors came off, when the US Congress required judges to refrain from using their own legal judgment to classify them. According to the law as amended, it was enough that an agreement "is of a type that has been, is presently, or in the future becomes, the subject of recurrent dealings in the swap or other derivatives markets."[46] The market, not the judge, defines the meaning of derivatives—a remarkable outsourcing of judicial competence.

With the groundwork laid in the United States, ISDA knocked on the door of regulators in Brussels with an in-house report in hand that highlighted "inefficiencies" in the laws of many EU member states for derivatives, in particular in their bankruptcy and collateral laws.[47] Unless it mended its ways, the report suggested, Europe would miss out on the wonders of the global derivatives markets. With hindsight, Europe may have been better off had it taken a pass on this opportunity. The European Commission and its staffers, however, were receptive students of ISDA; a new directive was passed that required all EU members to create safe harbors for derivatives in their domestic laws.[48]

These legal changes hardly ever raised objections or caught the attention of the broader public. Exemptions from the ordinary operation of bankruptcy law were sold to legislatures as technical fixes that were necessary to ensure that their country would be able to integrate with the global marketplace. The fact that bankruptcy safe harbors altered the priority rights of creditors and subordinated trade creditors, as well as claims of employees and other ordinary creditors to the counterparties of derivatives transactions, was swept under the carpet. So was the fact that the privileging of these assets prompted others to organize their loan contracts as derivatives as well. Who would not want a priority right that is enforceable against the rest of the world, if all it takes is tweaking a contract? Lawmakers tilted the playing field in favor of the top tier of financial intermediaries, who were deeply vested in derivatives markets without giving it much thought. They realized only after the crisis that in doing so, they had also put their own governments on the hook.

When financial markets collapsed, the close-out netting rules allowed derivatives traders to get out faster than everybody else, and their exit poured oil on the fire.[49] When Lehman's UK subsidiary LBIE filed for insolvency, 1,693 of its over 2,000 outstanding derivatives transactions were closed out immediately.[50] Far from insulating counterparties from the downfall of one of their fellow market participants, close-out netting helped deepen the crisis, because derivatives traders ran for the exit as soon as they saw the writing on the wall, closed out their outstanding claims, and took the cash the debtor owed them, thereby reducing the assets available for others or for a possible reorganization. The possible contagious effects of close-out netting rules had been identified already in the late 1990s by a prominent policy forum, the Bank for International Settlements (BIS).[51] However, nobody dared to openly oppose these rules; they only politely drew attention to their potentially adverse effects. This was not enough to prevent far-reaching legal changes from taking hold that an organization as powerful as ISDA was lobbying for at the time.

When these warnings finally materialized, states had the option of allowing the debtors to fall or injecting fresh capital into the failing debtor, only to watch counterparties of derivatives transactions walk away with the cash. Of course, if close-out netting showed that they owed something to the debtor, the counterparties had to pay up themselves; but this still put them into a better position than most other creditors: They could draw a line and move on with their business and reposition their bets, while other creditors had to wait until all claims had been filed and a full assessment of the debtor's leftovers had been made.

The great financial crisis served as a wake-up call that the concessions lawmakers had made to finance not only did not produce the desired effects but were even counterproductive. Contrary to the advocates of these new financial instruments, they were not safe, and neither did bankruptcy safe harbors protect the market for derivatives, much less anybody else. Many legislatures now had second thoughts about bankruptcy safe harbors and decided to roll them back.

One would think that what a legislature has given it can also take back. But this proved more difficult, not the least because of the size of global derivatives markets. Millions of MAs governed by English or New York law were in use that contained close-out netting rules. Even if one state decided to change its domestic bankruptcy law and to roll the clock back to the state of the world prior to ISDA's global lobbying campaign, that state would not necessarily be able to prevent a foreign private party from making use of its contractual close-out netting rights in time to preserve the debtor's assets. Because ISDA's MA is governed by English or New York State law, the court that presided over a bankruptcy case in a different country would have to ask a court in one of these two jurisdictions for assistance. Even if they accommodated the request, this takes time, and time is in short supply whenever a major financial intermediary has to be put on life support.

Because the MA was used in millions of *transnational* derivatives transactions, no single state had the power to effectively roll back the bankruptcy safe harbors; states had no option but to coordinate, and they needed to impose on ISDA and its primary members that they had to play along. States used the "Financial Stability Board" (FSB), a relatively new policy body, which is housed at the Bank for International Settlements (BIS) in Basel, Switzerland, to coordinate and act as a spokesperson for their demands.[52] They agreed not to dismantle close-out netting entirely, but to impose a 48-hour waiting period before any netting rights could be exercised. Nevertheless, they struggled to find a viable strategy for enforcing this mandate, as modest as it was, because states cannot simply rewrite the contracts that private parties use for their own transactions.

In the end, the FSB negotiated a deal with ISDA to create a new protocol to the MA that would include the new waiting periods. Of course, there was no guarantee that the financial intermediaries that use the MA would sign up for that. After all, contracts are voluntary in nature. So, the states that the major players in global derivatives markets call their home, namely the United States, United Kingdom, France, and Germany, pressured "their" banks to sign, or else face major regulatory repercussions.

Under the protocol, the parties to a derivatives contract agree that they will respect the bankruptcy law of the defaulting party and abstain from close-out netting for up to 48 hours or two business days (whichever was longer).[53] In November 2014, ISDA announced that the new "resolution stay protocol" had been signed by eighteen banks, bringing 90 percent of the outstanding derivatives (in notional amounts) into the fold.[54] The big banks had been caught in the regulatory net, which was tightened in the aftermath of the financial crisis. In contrast, the players on the other side of the derivative deals, mostly hedge funds, are only lightly regulated and therefore did not face similar pressure. They balked and refused to sign the protocol, thereby largely muting its effect. The conundrum was solved only when the US Federal Reserve stepped in and issued a rule that prohibited banks that fall under its regulatory supervision, including subsidiaries of foreign banks—a substantial share of globally active banks—from entering into derivatives trades with any counterparty that refuses to sign up for ISDA's protocol.[55]

The hedge funds had, of course, the option to look for counterparties other than the big, regulated banks; but in truth, this is easier said than done. They knew very well that the big banks had something no other financial intermediaries do: a lifeline to their central bank in the form of liquidity backstopping (through reserves and access to the discount window), and, in the worst-case scenario, perhaps even bailouts. Like other financial markets, derivatives markets too operate in the shadow of the state and its financial prowess.

After a long battle, governments scored a goal, even though a 48-hour waiting period may not seem all that remarkable. Of interest, however, is not only what they did, but *how* they accomplished it. Governments took a page from the script of ISDA's own screenplay. ISDA had used contracts to forge a piece of private legislation; the government now used a protocol to the same contract as a regulatory tool. The fact that sovereign states had to co-opt a private business association, namely ISDA, to achieve their regulatory goals, indicates the extent to which states have lost control over the governance of global finance. The silver lining is that ISDA participated in the deal and positioned itself not just as industry advocate, but as co-regulator. The key actors representing the association may have realized that only by playing along would it be able to fend off more aggressive regulatory strategies and thus retain much of its stronghold over global finance.

In the Service of Capital

The Eli Lilly case and the story about bankruptcy safe harbors for derivatives illustrate how traditional law enforcement agencies, such as courts and regulators, have been put in the service of capital. The holders of capital do not always win their first battle; rather, they chip away at existing legal barriers slowly but stubbornly until little stands in the way for principles that, not too long ago, appeared— to use Justice Cardozo's words—as "unbending and inveterate," to erode into sand.[56]

Eli Lilly mobilized private arbitration tribunals to scrutinize state courts in their role as lawmakers and law enforcers. The company sought to portray its treatment by the courts as akin to denial of justice. It argued that it had a right to a patent, however flimsy the evidence that the new compounds it added for the second patent over the same drugs actually made a difference, and that the Canadian courts denied Eli Lilly justice by revoking it. Denial of justice is by no means beyond what some courts in some countries might do; but even according to the complaint the company had filed, there was not much "there" to build such a case. Instead, Eli Lilly must have hoped that the prospect of a $500 million liability verdict would force the Canadian government to cave in and settle, if only for some smaller amount. Eli Lilly fought a lonely battle, but the strategy of shedding doubts on the impartiality of courts and intimidating governments has been effectively tried and tested to discredit the legal system of foreign countries; this time it was used even against a country that scores high on indicators that measure the rule of law and non-corruptibility; and consistent with these data, the Canadian government was unwilling to budge.[57]

The story about ISDA and its lobbying of legislatures and regulators in dozens of countries takes the relation between private actors and law enforcers to another level entirely. ISDA created facts on the ground by developing the MA, a contractual device that was soon used for millions of transactions involving derivatives, many of which were used in cross-border deals. After having demonstrated that a private contract can sustain a global market in financial instruments, ISDA began to lobby legislatures to adapt their laws to make them consistent with ISDA's contractual instrument—turning the principle that contracts have to be consistent with the law on its head. Within a couple of years, it had persuaded all the leading economies, as legislatures feared to harm their domestic financial industry if they did not play along.

In the end, though, ISDA had to concede that it could not rule global derivatives markets alone. The network of contracts, which resembles a bowl of spaghetti that is almost impossible to disentangle, needs not only default rules, which some countries will always happily provide, but it also must reckon with default and bankruptcy of key participants—this is where private contracting finds its limits. When states pushed back in a concerted action, ISDA had little choice for fear that they might regulate it out of existence. However, in assuming regulatory functions over industry members, ISDA crossed the line between private and state regulator.[58] It may not have coercive powers on par with states (yet), but its MA is the foundation for global derivatives trades, and players in these markets have little choice but to adhere to ISDA's rule book. And now, the association has demonstrated that it is willing not only to cross swords with states, but to cooperate with them in order to bring about regulatory change, however modest it might seem to advocates of even stricter rules.

The two stories highlight the transformation of law enforcement that has taken place over the past several decades. Powerful holders of global capital with the help of their lawyers have not only found ways to utilize the law for their own interests; they have turned the legislatures, regulators, even courts in most countries, into agents that serve their interests, rather than those of the citizens to whom they are formally accountable. Contrary to standard Marxist accounts, they have done this without occupying directly positions of state power; instead, they have perfected the art of utilizing the powers of the state indirectly. They have concocted their own world of law, stitched together from different domestic legal systems with international or bilateral treaty law thrown into the mix.

Looking back, there was no grand strategy that set out how private parties would conquer the state's coercive powers without submitting to its rules. Instead, private lawyers have pieced together different portions of legal rules that were adopted in different eras, and their combined effect became apparent only after all the pieces had been put into place.

The first piece of the puzzle was the 1958 New York Arbitration Convention.[59] It offers coercive law enforcement to parties who prefer to resolve their disputes in private arbitration by assuring them that they can use the courts of any state that has ratified this convention to execute these awards against assets found on their territory. State courts may not review the case on its merits before executing the award; they may only check that basic principles of due process have been observed. Alternatively, they may raise the specter of a violation of "public interests," but although this principle sounds like a catchall phrase, it is narrowly construed and only rarely used to justify setting aside an arbitral award.[60]

The second piece of the puzzle is a convention adopted in 1966, which established the International Centre for Settlement of Investment Disputes (ICSID).[61] It is housed at the World Bank and facilitates investor-state disputes by maintaining a roster of arbitrators for parties to choose from, for filing cases, and, laudably, nowadays making most of them available online. Countries that sign up to the ICSID Convention accept that state-investor disputes will be heard by a private tribunal under the auspices of ICSID and that they must accept the verdict. There is no appeal, only a request for interpretation and revision, and as a last resort, an annulment process, which requires a pretty high threshold of proof.[62] In recent years, several countries have cancelled their membership in ICSID in protest of rulings that they found unjust. However, the convention still counts 154 states as its members.[63]

The third piece of the puzzle is the 1969 Vienna Convention on the Law of Treaties.[64] It incorporates the ground rules of international law, building on centuries of international practice, and stipulates what an international convention or treaty is, how it is adopted, when it enters into force, and what rights and obligations states assume once they have ratified such an instrument.[65] The provision of greatest interest for investors that find themselves engulfed in disputes with sovereign states is Article 27; it holds that a state cannot invoke its own "internal law as justification for its failure to perform a treaty." In plain English, the rights that arbitral tribunals fashion from the thin language of bilateral investment treaties supersede domestic law, including a country's constitution. Again, it seems puzzling that sovereign states would sign up for this, but until the introduction of ISDS in bilateral investment treaties, international law was enforced by international courts or by arbitration between two sovereign states; disputes at this level are rare, as most conflicts are resolved through diplomacy, but private parties have proven much less constrained.

Fast forward 40 years, with more than three thousand bilateral investment treaties in place and more than eight hundred state-investor disputes brought, and we can see how the puzzle comes together into a powerful picture. The treaty language of most BITs requires that investors are given "fair and equitable treatment" (this is similar to the language of NAFTA discussed in the Eli Lilly case above) and should be protected from direct or indirect expropriation, but what this means is nowhere defined. It is left for arbitrators, who are drawn primarily from private practice. They are less interested in public policy and have insisted that state law, including constitutional law, is irrelevant for interpreting treaty law.[66] Article 27 of the Vienna Convention gives them effective cover to raise their own interpretation over and above domestic law of the host state in a dispute.

The interpretation of law is always an act of lawmaking; this lies in the nature of trying to make sense of words in light of the complex reality of facts to which the law is applied. Still, the open-ended language of the treaties and the absence of a higher court that would unify its interpretation gives arbitrators enormous interpretative powers. Moreover, arbitration is a one-off affair; there is no appeal, there are only annulment proceedings, which, as mentioned, are difficult to win.

Determining what kinds of tribunals should have the power to determine when foreign investors may claim priority rights over public interests in their host states has come to a head in the public debate over TTIP—the Transatlantic Trade and Investment Partnership between the United States and the European Union. This bilateral agreement was meant to further break down barriers to trade and investment between these two economic powerhouses, giving companies unfettered access to markets on either side of the Atlantic. A cornerstone for deepening international economic relations for the Obama administration, it suffered a serious backlash when civil society organizations mobilized against it across Europe. The inclusion of ISDS was a major bone of contention, because it sidelined domestic courts in the member states of the EU as well as the European Court of Justice for matters that often cut to the core of domestic constitutional and EU treaty law.[67]

In the end, the adoption of TTIP (and its trans-Pacific counterpart) was thwarted for domestic reasons in the United States, where the election of Donald Trump as the forty-fifth president has ushered in a period of greater unilateralism and the primacy of national interests.[68] However, there has been progress on a different front. Canada and the EU have entered into a "modern" treaty (CETA), as the two parties call it, which acknowledges the right of states to change their laws "regardless of whether this may negatively affect an investment or investor's expectations of profits."[69] This might sound harsh to investors who have come to rely on using investment treaties as an insurance device against future legal change; but it only confirms the basic principles of democratic self-governance. Legal change is part and parcel of political and social change, and foreign investors should not be given a veto right over such change by threatening with a multi-million dollar liability claim.

Moreover, in a clear break from the practice of using ad hoc tribunals staffed with private arbitrators, CETA will establish a new standing tribunal for resolving disputes between foreign investors and their host states—Canada or one of the EU member states. The tribunal shall have a panel of fifteen members who will be appointed for a renewable 5-year term by a joint committee of the two parties to the treaty (i.e., the EU and Canada) rather than be selected by the parties to the dispute; and the tribunal's president in turn chooses three members of the panel for resolving a specific dispute.[70] What difference this new tribunal might make in practice remains to be seen; however, its design suggests that there is more than one way to constitute tribunals that resolve disputes between foreign investors and traders and their host states. In the best of all worlds, the new tribunal will show how to solve disputes between sovereign states and foreign investors in a balanced fashion, giving due course to the private as well as the public interests that are at stake.

7

The Masters of the Code

"There is an estate in the realm more powerful than either your Lordship or the other House of Parliament, and that [is] the country solicitors."[1] Lord Campbell uttered these words of warning to his fellow members of the House of Lords years before a major depression hit England's agriculture in the 1870s. He had just tried and failed, like many others before him, to introduce a bill that would have reformed England's land law and abolished the legal protections the landed elites enjoyed over their creditors. At the time he spoke those words, most landowners had already conceded the need for legal reform; the only holdouts, Lord Campbell suggested, were the country solicitors.

These lawyers made their living by conveying, or transferring, land for the clients; they had mixed modern notions of individual property rights with feudalist restrictions on alienability; they had employed trusts to protect family estates, but then turned around and used the trust again to set aside assets for creditors so that they would roll over the debt of the life tenant one more time. Last but not least, they were the ones who would settle the rights to the estate among family members upon the death of the life tenant. Their legal coding techniques assured landowners of priority rights, while protecting them from unwanted creditors, thereby affording their and their families' assets greater durability.

The web of legal relations they had created was complex: an empire of claims and counterclaims, rights and restrictions on these rights, all fashioned in the modules of capital's legal code, which was beyond the grasp of most, including the landowners themselves. They had built this empire not according to a master plan, but one deal at a time, like a quilt that is stitched together from many patches of different colors and patterns. And they were the only ones who knew how this quilt had been put together and what it would take to add or cut out a patch of fabric to satisfy the needs of their next client. The lawyer's services were therefore in high demand, and, as a result, they had little interest in reforms that would have streamlined the law of realty and in doing so would have taken away an important source of their income.

Fast forward a century, and we can see the makings of an even more impressive empire of law, which stretches far beyond the territory of a single state and encompasses the globe: the legal empire that sustains global trade, commerce, and finance, the most lucrative of them all for lawyers as well as for their clients. This chapter will take a closer look at the lawyers, the rise of the legal profession, and its impact on the coding of capital in different legal systems. It should be clear by now that law is much less static than often assumed. There is not a fixed set of property rights, for example, neither a clear line between contracts and property, nor only one way to set up a trust or a corporate entity. While the options that lawyers have may not be limitless, they have a lot of room to be creative (more so, as we will see, in some legal systems than in others) and to recombine the modules of the code in ways that few legislatures and courts, and even many lawyers themselves, might have ever imagined.

Mastering the Code

Lawyers are commonly described as legal service providers. This description, however, greatly understates the contribution that lawyers make in the coding of capital, and through it, to the creation and distribution of wealth in society. It may well be the case that the majority of practicing attorneys continue to offer mostly basic legal advice for a fee; but the true masters of the code use their legal know-how, which they built over years of practice in exchanges with clients and their professional kin, to craft new capital and in this process often *make* new law from existing legal material.

Their toolkit consists of the modules of the code: the rules of property and collateral law, the principles of trust, corporate, and bankruptcy law; and contract law; the most malleable of them all. These modules have been around for centuries. Today these modules are mostly available off the shelf; they have been vindicated by courts and they no longer require pre-approval. As such, they are ready to be molded and grafted onto an ever-changing roster of assets. It has not always been that easy. In the past, states watched their legal sovereignty more closely and imposed their own property law on any assets located within their borders; property law was standardized and a *numerus clausus* limited the number and types of property rights.[2] Further, many states insisted that a corporation that wishes to conduct most of its business on their territory should be incorporated under their laws.

Most of these restrictions have since fallen by the wayside, and this has greatly expanded the playing field for lawyers. If certain financial assets face regulatory hurdles in one country, the intermediary that issues these assets or manages the account in which they are held can be moved to a more accommodating jurisdiction; ditto with tax liabilities, and environmental or labor laws. The flip side of this greatly expanded choice set for lawyers is that no single state controls the limits of what or how lawyers code capital in law. Lawyers still depend on the aura of authority and legitimacy that states give to their work, but for many (not all) of their coding strategies, they can pick and choose the state that is willing to do so.

Asset holders for their part greatly value the lawyers' coding efforts; why else would they pay them hourly rates that nowadays run into in the upper three or four digits, and even go along with demands by some lawyers at the top of the profession to receive remuneration on a par with investment bankers?[3] It is hard to think of a better indicator for showing that, when lawyers are called into the room, more is often at stake than routine legal advice or ordinary transaction-cost engineering. Clients crave something that only the best lawyers can deliver: strong priority rights for the assets of their choice, durability over and above the life expectancy of competing assets, the option to convert financial assets into cash at will, and all of the above with legal force against the world.

The lawyers who design new assets or intermediaries are deeply familiar with laws, rules, and regulations, often from multiple jurisdictions: the rules that are meant to constrain certain actions; the scope, limits, and possible exceptions to these rules; and, of course, the tax law, given that taxes form the single largest liability for many businesses. It goes without saying that they also must have mastered the modules of the code, and ideally in more than one legal system. These legal modules comprise the toolkit lawyers use to cloak assets in the attributes of capital; to arbitrage around legal constraints; and, last but not least, to hand to their clients the powerful defense, "but it is legal."

To avoid future liability for themselves and their clients, lawyers must anticipate every possible risk and guard against it by employing asset-shielding devices, shifting risk and possible losses to others, and by disclosing enough so that investors are put on notice and cannot claim later that they were misled—although many will try nonetheless with their own lawyers by their side. Indeed, one of the great ironies of the litigation frenzy that followed the 2008 crisis is that some of the big players in the market sued each other, each claiming that they had been misled—even though many of them had engaged in similar conduct themselves, were sophisticated players in financial markets, and had been advised by equally sophisticated lawyers.[4] In other words, lawyers are managing risk, no less than do financial intermediaries, but their focus is on legal risks. This helps explain why so few lawyers are ever held accountable for their work; it is their job to protect their clients from liability; but they also keep a safe distance from their clients and their preferred assets. Clients may come and go and so too may the assets for which they seek coding as capital; but the lawyers remain and can quickly turn their legal skills to new assets and new clients.

This is not to say that lawyers have never been caught commit-ting illegal acts or indicted for them.[5] But such cases are few and far between, not just because lawyers know "how to use law in two crucial ways: to seize an opportunity for quick gain and, having done so, to cover their tracks," as critics of the legal profession put it in the context of the railway manias of the nineteenth century.[6] Rather, coding capital is a work that requires expert legal knowledge in order to identify opportunities for legal innovation while also guarding against legal risk. The masters of the code don't just use and apply existing law; they actively fashion new law—subject only to ex post scrutiny by a court, or, if they so choose, by private arbitrators, many of whom, of course, are their peers.

The code's true masters are often trained at elite law schools, in-cluding my own; they are recruited by top law firms and, after years of learning the tools of the trade and logging long hours, advance to become partners.[7] They are incredibly smart and hardworking and are more likely to view themselves as servants of their clients than as masters in their own right. They see their job as making sure that clients can achieve their business goals without getting into conflict with the law.[8] But as lawyers know only too well, what matters is not so much what individuals think they are doing, but the impact their actions may have on others; and as the materials discussed in this book suggest, there is little doubt that lawyers are central to the cod-ing of capital and the distribution of wealth in society. The masters' close alliance with capital is reflected in their portfolio of clients and in the sources, as well as the level, of their income.

The trend over the last few decades in the United States and else-where has favored larger firms concentrated in major commercial and financial centers with a high degree of specialization by lawyers inside these firms who can bring their selective knowledge to bear for the benefit of their firms' clients.[9] As late as 1984, the top fifty firms in the United States had on average only 259 attorneys and an average rev-enue of $3.4 million. By 2006, the average law firm employed 974 at-torneys and was bringing in revenue just short of $40 million, a more than tenfold increase;[10] and the head count at the top ten largest firms in the United States ranges from 1,100 to 1,800 attorneys per firm.[11]

While in 1984 the average partner was making just over $300,000 annually, by 2006 this had increased to just short of $1.5 million.[12] Many top firms also maintain substantial pro bono operations, where they bring their legal talent to bear for the benefit of clients who cannot possibly afford their fees, but the scale and scope of these operations pales against their for-profit business. This only makes sense, because law firms are for-profit operations and their fees reflect the value they help create for their clients. Conversely, given that the greatest value is created by coding capital, most law school graduates flock to the firms that hire them in large numbers to do just that.

The account of transactional lawyers as the code's masters offered here differs from two other accounts that can be found in the literature, one portraying lawyers as transaction cost engineers, the other as rent seekers. Ronald Gilson has characterized lawyers as "transaction cost engineers"; according to him, they navigate complex regulations, structure transactions so as to avoid unnecessary costs, and from time to time negotiate with regulators to obtain clearance for more adventurous transactions.[13] In doing so, they are said to reduce the tension between "transaction form and regulatory purpose."[14] There are obvious parallels to their role as master coders, but there is also an important difference. The engineering account subordinates the work lawyers do to the entrepreneurs, who are viewed as the architects of new business strategies. Lawyers merely cloak grand ideas in legal garb, even when it comes to complex transactions, such as mergers and acquisitions. No doubt, these are important services, and no doubt, this is what most lawyers, including highly paid corporate lawyers, do most of the time. Some lawyers, however, do much more, and it is for them that I reserve the title "master."

By way of illustration, compare a plain vanilla merger transaction with the invention of the "poison pill," an ingenious defensive device that protects firms from hostile takeovers, or the acquisition of control by another company contrary to the plans and wishes of the target company's management team.[15] Hidden behind the poison pill's catchy label is a complex legal arrangement that forces a company that wishes to acquire control over another to seek approval from the board of directors of that company, rather than simply buying shares from existing shareholders on the market. If they proceed without negotiating with the board and buy more than the threshold amount that is stipulated in the legal documents that comprise the poison pill, the block of shares they just acquired at the prevailing market price will be seriously diluted, thus inflicting massive economic loss on the acquirer. This is done by giving special rights to existing shareholders long before a hostile bid is on the table, which enables them to acquire new shares in the target company at a fraction of their market price if and when a hostile bidder buys more than, say, 10 or 20 percent of the company's shares. The hostile bidder itself is of course excluded from this bonanza.

Poison pills are complex legal documents that stretch over many pages; to be effective, they must carefully navigate corporate law, securities law, and tax and accounting rules. Once they had been invented, they were quickly copied across the industry and became standard for most publicly traded corporations until shareholders pushed back against them; but only one lawyer, Martin Lipton, is credited as the brain behind this new legal device.[16]

As an aside, the effect of the poison pill bears eerie resemblance to the strict family settlement that protected land in the hands of wealthy families: both were designed to protect asset pools from the auction block—even when it had become clear that they were no longer economically viable. In the case of land, the beneficiaries were the family members of the landowning elites; in the case of the poison pill, they were corporate managers. This did not end well for the landed elites, as we have seen. In comparison, the poison pill is a more flexible device than strict family settlement has been, mostly because courts have protected shareholders against its excesses, such as the dead-hand pill (a pill that can be redeemed only by the same directors who adopted it), and shareholders have forced the directors of their companies to drop the pill in recent years.[17]

More examples of truly innovative coding strategies abound. Consider only the major legal innovations that we have discussed in this book: the elevation of use rights to land to absolute property rights; the invention of the peculium, the use, the trust, and finally the modern business corporation for shielding assets of the firm from various groups of claimants, including even their own owners, thereby creating durable pools of assets; the transformation of simple securitization schemes into financial assets with the payoff structure as well as the risk profile that investors desire; and, last but not least, the construction of complex credit derivatives, such as CDOs (remember the Kleros clones), including their squared, cubed, and synthetic variants. All this has been the work of lawyers who honed their skills over centuries and have unparalleled access to information about how to code different assets as capital for different clients.

This is how one (former) practitioner characterized the contributions lawyers make in the top law firms today:

> Yet, in practice, clients are paying for law firms' ability to pool information across clients and to make use of that information in transaction negotiations. (...) Such clients do not seek bespoke, professional service based on a long-term, confidential relationship. They are, in effect merely purchasing information from law firms, which in turn are merely engaged in the increasingly ubiquitous practice of knowledge management.[18]

Plainly stated, clients are hiring lawyers to have access to the empire of law, which these lawyers have stitched together over centuries and that reaches far beyond the territorial boundaries of any nation-state. Still, lawyers are not "merely" engaged in the management of knowledge; not only is knowledge power in our "knowledge society," but lawyers don't manage just any knowledge: they manage knowledge about the law and about how to use the modules of the code to create private wealth. Lawyers have been in the business of coding capital for centuries, but the value of their coding efforts has increased over time with the changes in the nature of the assets they code as capital. They started with land, an asset that exists outside the law, and transformed it into capital; they have ended up creating the very assets in law that shower their holders with huge returns.

A considerably less sympathetic depiction of lawyers and their contribution to society than the transaction cost engineering account can be found in the writings of Stephen Magee, a financial economist. He published an op-ed in the *Wall Street Journal* in 1992 with a graph that plotted the number of lawyers in the US economy against GDP growth rates. The result was an inverted U-shaped curve, with the clear implication that lawyers contribute to economic growth, but only up to a point; too many lawyers have a negative effect on growth.[19] These data and their interpretation triggered a fierce debate between Magee and legal scholars, who challenged his calculations, methodology, and his assumptions about the coherence and organizational capacity of the legal profession.[20]

Resolving this debate at a statistical level may well be impossible, because a simple head count of lawyers says little about what lawyers do and how different parts of the profession contribute to economic and social well-being. Still, Magee may have had a point in that the contributions lawyers make to society may not always be welfare enhancing. The masters of the code are in the business of coding private, not public wealth, and the two don't always go together.[21] Critically, however, the lawyers I have described, from the English country solicitors all the way to the partners of the global law firms, are not rent seekers, as Magee would have it; they don't skim the cream off of business activities that could just as well operate without them; rather, they make the cream. Yet, the over-production of assets that promise legal certainty but ultimately fail to deliver economically can bring down the financial system and stall the economy or force it into reverse. It also makes for a highly skewed distribution of wealth in society. Lawyers tend to ignore these external effects of their coding efforts. They put their clients' interest first and are paid well for doing so. Few therefore consider the broader effects of their doing, and the ones who do hope for the invisible hand to correct the structural biases they create for their clients. They don't realize that the success of their coding strategies has turned the invisible hand into a fairy tale.

As we have seen, the legal protection of family wealth from the competitive market forces in the nineteenth century resulted in a major depression that affected not only the landowners, but also their tenants: the peasants that had worked their land. When the depression hit, they lost everything and, in contrast to many landowners, they lacked accumulated wealth to buffer the impact of the crisis. Similarly, the toxic assets that brought down the financial system in 2008 were legal products that fueled the expansion of debt in the economy for years, before a massive correction of their value turned into a death spiral for many financial intermediaries. The effects of the crisis were not limited to the financial sector, however; the crisis cut deep into the economy and left millions of people without jobs. It has taken a decade and massive government investments to bring down unemployment and to stimulate stock markets and the revival of credit; but even though the numbers are back up, this does not fully reflect the hardship and wealth destruction that many households, especially at the lower end of the income spectrum, have experienced. While the crisis dampened the rise of inequality for a while, the steep rise of asset prices following the crisis, in part thanks to the policies of major central banks, suggests that holders of assets that benefited from government largess were the winners, once again.[22]

Whether the master coders contribute to national wealth or help destroy it depends on where we find ourselves in the revolving cycle of the production of private wealth: on the upside, when new legal coding strategies promise greater legal certainty for new assets and fuel the expansion of credit that is used for investments or consumption; or on the downside, when even the best legal steroids can no longer disguise the discrepancy between expected and actual returns and the entire scheme goes into reverse. In fact, these trends are two sides of the same coin: The same legal strategies that help create private wealth will bring down the entire financial and economic system, when the legal rights they created are enforced against assets that are no longer in demand or against asset holders that are no longer able to balance their liabilities. Like Magee's curve, this dynamic also resembles an inverse U-curve, but with a proxy for ever more complex coding strategies, not the number of lawyers, on the X-axis of the graph.

The Masters' Legal Origin

Global capital exists and thrives without a global state or a global law. The explanation for this is that law has become portable; it is possible to code assets in the modules of one legal system and still have them respected and enforced by courts and regulators of another country. In this way, a single domestic system could sustain global capitalism; in practice there are two that dominate it, as mentioned above: English and New York State law. Most of the true masters of the code harken from one of these common law systems, or have received additional legal training there, as reflected in the large number of master students from abroad who are trained at law schools in the United Kingdom and the United States.[23] What gives the common law this edge over civil law systems? And, is it the common law itself, the organization of the legal profession in common law systems, or a combination of the two?

There has been a lively debate about the differences between and the pros and cons of the common law and the civil law families for quite some time. Comparative lawyers had long concluded that the difference lies less in the contents of legal rules and more in features broadly labeled as legal culture. Nonetheless economists called for a re-assessment of the virtues of common law versus civil law, a field they called "new comparative economics."[24] They brought statistical tools to the table and coded what they believed were key provisions in corporate and bankruptcy law to demonstrate that the level of shareholder and creditor protection varies among the major legal families in statistically significant ways. The common law comes out on top for shareholders' rights; on creditor rights, the German civil law family is a close second, but the French civil law system trails on both fronts.[25] Critically, these legal differences have been identified as important determinants for financial outcomes: common law systems tend to have bigger and more liquid financial markets than do civil law countries, especially those of the French type.[26]

These findings have spurred a cottage industry that used these data to test the impact of legal origin (common law vs. civil law) on the size of government, levels of investments, corruption, the pace of law enforcement by the courts, and so forth; but they also gave rise to critical reviews of the quality of the data and questions about the robustness of the findings.[27] This is not the place to review this debate, except to say that it has omitted a key variable—the lawyers and their role in the different legal systems. If the argument advanced in this book is correct, that capital is coded in law and that lawyers are the masters of the code, and most master coders originate from one legal system—the common law—then it is time to revisit the legal origin debate.

The English jurist, Simeon E. Baldwin, described the role of lawyers in the common law as follows: "The development of law . . . is primarily the work of the lawyer. It is the adoption by the judge of what is proposed at the bar."[28] Baldwin correctly emphasizes the development of law, not the contents of specific rules. Indeed, what distinguishes the common law from the civil law is the latitude it gives private lawyers in fashioning the law. They don't just advise on existing law, they constantly make new legal rights from old cloth. They need no one's approval as they embark on coding assets as capital; all they need to do is to mimic the argumentative strategies that have convinced courts in the past to uphold the coding of new assets, adapting the argument to the new assets and to the specific needs of their clients. At times, they will have to defend their work in a court of law, but there they will confront a judge, who only recently was one of them, because in common law systems, judges are recruited from the practicing bar.

In England, traces of legal professionals can be found as early as the twelfth century in documents that speak of a "sizeable group of men who were recognized as having specific, professional skills in the representation of litigants."[29] This was a new breed of lawyers, who did not serve the Crown or in state courts, but pursued the interests of private clients in private practice. Over time, and as a result of happenstance more than major events or well-reasoned policy rationale, the legal profession in England branched out into litigants and transactional lawyers. The litigants, or barristers, train at the Inns of Court and, for the most part, don't have direct client contact, while the solicitors perform the transactional work and interact with the client in preparation for litigation; and this division of labor has been largely retained to this day.[30] Coding capital has been for the most part the work of the solicitors, but in earlier times, when new coding strategies were more frequently reviewed by a court of law, barristers played a key role in convincing courts of the validity of innovative coding efforts. The barristers have long enjoyed greater prestige and were viewed as politically more powerful than the solicitors.[31] However, as the coding of capital has shifted from the courtroom into private law offices, not only the number of solicitors, but their power, has greatly increased—as indicated also by Lord Campbell's quote at the outset of this chapter.

English solicitors established themselves as trusted advisors to clients with whom they initially formed long-term relations. Aspiring lawyers were trained by other solicitors in a one-on-one relation, a setting that resembles the master-apprentice relation found in guilds, where apprentices spent years under their masters' guidance and supervision. Many lawyers held university degrees, but in the past more likely in history or the classics, not in law. This changed only over the course of the twentieth century, when the demand for lawyers increased dramatically and the traditional apprenticeship model proved unable to meet that demand. It was only then that the university's law departments came to play a central role in the training of the English legal profession.

In contrast, in Continental Europe, law was next to theology and medicine, one of the founding disciplines at Europe's oldest universities, such as Bologna, Toulouse, Orléans, or Palermo, some of which date back to the thirteenth century. During these early days, students of law studied mostly Roman law—based on the digests that had been compiled by the later Roman emperor Justinian, and that had been re-discovered around 1135.[32] This was not only an academic exercise of interpreting ancient law texts, but had real world applications, because Roman law came to be used as a default in cases where the rules of cities, regions, or states did not offer an answer, or conflicted with one another.[33]

On the Continent, the study of law became a path to higher state office, or at most, in-house counsel in commercial undertakings. Freelance lawyers who advised fee-paying clients about the law were frowned upon. This is evident already in the early formation of the legal profession. In France, a royal ordinance dated 1345 set the conditions for admission to the legal profession, including the obligations and liberties of its members. Only persons that met the conditions set forth in state law were allowed to call themselves lawyers, and only they could represent defendants in a court of law. The French legal profession "was part of the formation and development of the State and of the justice system, and it was governed by a regulatory body" at least for the first several centuries after it was established, and not by its own rules as with the legal profession in England or the United States.[34] The respect for the legal profession in France suffered greatly as more and more high offices they occupied were converted into venal offices that were up for sale to the highest bidder.[35] It reorganized itself in the seventeenth century, and at that time also began to set its own rules; finally, in the late eighteenth century, many lawyers fought for greater autonomy from the state and openly opposed the absolute monarchy before its fall, although others collaborated with the monarchy in an attempt to reform it before it was too late.[36]

Lawyers also worked for private clients; indeed, the demand for lawyers who work as in-house counsel or attorneys for companies has greatly increased since the 1970s. However, the lines between public and private office are more clearly drawn in the French legal system than has been the case in England, or, as we will see, in the United States. Lawyers pursue different postgraduate training in law depending on whether they wish to become judges, prosecutors, or private attorneys. There is no straight path from the bar to the bench. This also implies that judges are less open to innovative coding strategies that lawyers who advise private clients may create.

Baldwin's notion that lawyers make the law and the courts only recognize it does not hold in France. Indeed, the judges' lawmaking powers were explicitly curtailed in the grand codifications of the early nineteenth century, and Article 5 of the French civil code explicitly prohibits judges from making law.[37] One might dismiss this as pure legal formalism, for even in France judges have to interpret the law and in doing so will inevitably adapt if not alter its meaning over time. Still, there is an important difference in emphasis, which narrows the scope for lawmaking by lawyers and judges as compared to the English common law. In France and other civil law systems, the statute guides the legal analysis, not the facts, and changes on the ground are more likely retrofit to the statute than the statute adapted to them.

While less rigid than outsiders might think, the civil codes pigeonhole legal relations, and a court would always start with the classifications of legal relations in statutory law when reviewing new coding strategies. Just like the common law, civil law systems endorse the freedom to contract, but the types of contract, and even more so, the types of property rights, are formed by statutory law, not the private masters of the code of capital, who therefore face more of an uphill battle when trying to change them.

Germany was a late developer, both economically and politically, and one might add, even legally.[38] Whereas in France, social forces propelled the legal profession to become a powerful political actor in the eighteenth century, during the same period, the state of Prussia (the rump state in the unified Germany after 1871) conducted a purge of the private legal profession that halved its numbers.[39]

The state assumed the regulation of entry to the profession and the fees attorneys could charge and announced severe punishments for anyone who dared practice law without proper authorization. Prior to this, the legal profession in Prussia was relatively dense (about one attorney per 2,000 inhabitants), well educated, and largely unregulated. The only entry ticket to the legal profession was a university degree, but making a living by practicing law was a different matter even before the government's crackdown. Lawyers adapted to the prevailing political and economic pillars of power and many represented aristocratic interests "as legal advisors, agents, or administrators," prompting one commentator to suggest that the legal profession was "in a certain sense bought."[40]

After the crackdown, private lawyers were closely guarded by the state. A 1781 rule went as far as prohibiting lawyers from appearing in court and replaced them with state appointees. While this arrangement was only short-lived, it documents the deep distrust that the state harbored for lawyers who worked for private rather than state interests. Indeed, the Prussian state retained control over the number of lawyers that could be admitted to the bar. As late as the

1850s, Prussia had about one attorney for every 12,000 people, as compared to one per 1,240 in England and one per 1,970 in France. Attorney fees skyrocketed in response and many a judge chose to leave the bench and become an attorney—exactly the opposite of the practice in England, where lawyers would be appointed to the bench after a long and successful career.

Only in the later part of the nineteenth century did the legal profession in Germany acquire a greater degree of autonomy; it started to self-organize and to resemble the legal profession in France and England in terms of numbers and (relative) independence from the state.[41] Still, remnants of Prussia's attempt to put private lawyers in the service of and under the control of state interests remain. Even today, all law students in Germany are trained to become judges, not private attorneys; only after they qualify as a judge may they take up the private legal profession.[42] Further, university training in law does not end with a university diploma, but with a *state* exam, and admission to the bar requires passing a second state exam after spending time clerking with judges or prosecutors in addition to apprenticing with a private firm. Critically, judges are recruited to the bench directly after having passed this second state exam without first working as private attorneys as is required of judges in common law countries.

To summarize, in civil law countries, private attorneys emerged later than in England, and they have never gained the kind of autonomy from the state that characterizes the private legal profession in England. This autonomy, combined with the fact that, in the common law, they have the opportunity to fashion new law subject only to occasional vetting by a court, has given the common law the comparative edge in the coding of capital. Civil lawyers have caught up with their Anglo-Saxon peers in recent decades, but their own legal system affords them a less accommodating playing field, which is why they often avail themselves of the common law system and seek access to its world of law by merging with firms from this legal origin.

The American legal profession may best be described as a more freewheeling, that is, a less regulated and more competitive, version of the English model. It is, of course, much younger, but not only because the country was formed relatively late; formal legal training was almost completely absent in most of the United States until the late nineteenth century, even as there were plenty of lawyers around. Estimates put their number at 40,000 by 1870, which translates into roughly 970 attorneys per person for a population of about 38 million people, with only 3 percent having attended law school. There was little need to invest in education at a time when only fifteen states imposed any formal requirements for entering the legal profession.[43] And yet, the United States had been called a "legal economy" already in the early 1800s, and for good reason.[44] Lawyers were not only numerous, they were in high demand. In a vast country that, prior to the Civil War, was without a powerful central state, lawyers played a critical role in surveying and conveying land on the Western frontier, in coding credit instruments, setting up firms, locating assets of defaulting debtors, or salvaging defunct firms for value, and offering other services for clients who craved legal certainty under conditions of otherwise great uncertainty.[45]

In the United States, the impetus for formalizing legal training and the organization of a professional bar came from a mix of protectionism and a yearning for greater professionalism. In commercial centers, competition among lawyers was often fierce, given the constant influx of new entrants to the legal job market by way of migration. Established lawyers sought to differentiate themselves from them, and what better way to do this than to increase entry barriers to the profession? Another reason was that the best lawyers could not take full advantage of their skills, because judges on the bench often lacked formal legal training, which affected the quality of legal disputes and lawmaking.[46] As a welcome side effect, formal legal training, it was hoped, would make these judges less beholden to the political "machines," the close alliance of politicians and corporate wealth that had a stronghold over political and economic life.

The solution proposed to both problems, competition and quality, were bar associations and law schools. Bar associations were first established in the major commercial hubs. They started off as social clubs for the "best men" (women were denied admission to the bar and to law schools well into the twentieth century), but evolved into associations for the regulation of the profession.[47] The blue-chip law firms committed to hiring only associates that had been formally trained at an accredited law school; and, under the deanship of Christopher Columbus Langdell, Harvard Law School took the lead in training lawyers for the elite legal profession. The organized bar also put pressure on the appointment process for judges and re-quired that access to judgeships should be limited to lawyers with at least some legal training. The bar also committed practicing lawyers to certain ethical rules; they had to work diligently for the clients' interests and avoid putting themselves in conflict with them, but also to uphold the rule of law. In a perhaps slightly idealized picture of the traditional American lawyer, Anthony Kronman describes the "outstanding lawyer" as someone who is "not simply an accomplished technician but a person of prudence or practical wisdom as well"—only to add that in the late twentieth century, lawyers have lost their way mostly by succumbing to the lure of private money.[48]

Soon, law schools began to flourish nationwide—and they have trained an increasing number of lawyers ever since.[49] By 1950, most practicing lawyers in the United States could boast some legal education, including evening training programs that were frequented especially by new immigrants.[50] By 1964, there were 135 law schools in the country with more than 22,000 students enrolled in the first year; and by 2013, the number of law schools had increased to more than 200 and the number of enrolled first-year students had doubled.[51] By 2018, there were 1.3 million lawyers in the country, the highest number yet, but the rate of growth had decreased from 1.8 to only 0.2 percent over the previous year.[52]

These changes in legal education had a noticeable impact on legal practice. The elite law firms in the late nineteenth century had ad-vised a combination of large corporations and leading financial inter-mediaries, such as Lehman Brothers or Goldman Sachs. They relied on long-term clients and were cautious not to ruffle their feathers by engaging in legal practices that might put them in conflict with the interests of any one of them. This helps explain why partners in these firms were reluctant to employ overtly aggressive legal strategies, such as hostile corporate takeovers, which might have put them into conflict with one of their clients, as they could easily find themselves on opposite ends of such transactions.[53]

The expansion of legal education meant that more lawyers and new firms populated the market, particularly after World War II. With growing competition among well-trained lawyers, the network of relational ties between blue-chip firms and the top tier of US manufacturing and financial firms came under pressure. The old elite firms had been thoroughly white, Anglo-Saxon, and protestant (WASP), but law schools graduated an ever-greater number of well-trained lawyers who were of Jewish descent or were female.[54] If these candidates were lucky enough to land a job as an associate in a blue-chip firm after graduating from law school, they were almost certainly shunned from partnership, because they did not fit into the established partnership mold.[55] These new entrants to the market for lawyers formed their own firms; they built their own client base and created new markets by disrupting the old relational networks and taking on the "biggies," as they called the blue-chip firms.[56] They were not reluctant to take on aggressive legal strategies, and they brought legal innovation in the United States to an entirely new level, only to transpose their skills soon to other jurisdictions.

A Global Legal Profession

The different legal traditions sketched out in the previous section set the stage for the globalization of law. In the absence of a global state and a global law, the key was to extend the reach of domestic law to the transnational realm. Lawyers who had honed their skills in the past by coding capital for their clients and finding innovative solutions for new problems and, of course, new assets, were in a much better position to do so than their peers in countries with a history of greater state oversight over the legal profession.

English firms also benefited from the country's colonial past. Great Britain had long supplied its former colonies and members of the Commonwealth with lawyers steeped not only in colonial administration but also in the common law; and it had trained members of the local elites throughout its empire in its own law. They had to master the modules of the code of capital, but they were exempt from the English law of realty, and were instead examined in Hindu, Islamic, and Roman law. As one commentator put it, England's land law was beyond the grasp of anyone who had not been born and raised in the UK.[57] For the English legal profession, the colonial backdrop provided a natural setting to expand legal networks that supported the globalization of business by clients from England and elsewhere.

American lawyers had something else to offer. The country was not a major colonizer, but its own legal system offered plenty of opportunities for lawyers to develop their skills in more than one legal order and exploit differences among them to advance their clients' interests. The United States has a highly fragmented legal system, more so than most other federate states. The areas of the law that make up the code's modules, including contract, property, collateral, trust, and corporate law, are governed not by federal (central) but by state law.[58] The field is even more crowded in financial regulation, where states not only compete with each other, they compete with federal law, and at the federal level, multiple regulatory agencies compete with one another.[59]

Lawyers quickly learned to exploit this plurality of laws for competitive purposes; if they did not like the laws of one state, they would code their clients' assets in the laws of a different state. This did not cost them the legal validity of their coding strategy or the ability to invoke a state's coercive powers to enforce them, because courts interpreted the Constitution's "Commerce Clause" as prohibiting states from denying legal recognition to transactions or business organizations that had been coded under the laws of another state in the federal system.[60] This made for an ideal incubator for developing highly competitive legal coding strategies; and when American firms began branching out internationally, American lawyers simply transposed these coding skills to the globe.

Lawyers from these two common law systems took advantage of their superior starting position. Indeed, the rise of the global legal profession is best described as the globalization of Anglo-Saxon legal practice, a claim that is borne out by available data about the rise of global law firms, that is firms that maintain offices in more than one country. Most global law firms are located in the United States and the United Kingdom, although their number in China is on the rise.[61] Among the top global law firms, there are only a few from France and Germany; firms from these civil law countries only made it into the top one hundred list if they had merged with either an English or US firm.[62]

The concentration of global law firms in the United States and the United Kingdom is also reflected in revenue figures. Of the top global one hundred firms by revenue, eighty-one are based in the United States and twelve in the UK. Global legal fee revenue totaled $618 billion in 2014–2015, 10 percent of which was generated in the UK, where legal services contributed 1.6 percent of Gross Value Added (GVA) in 2015.[63] This is considerably less than the combined contribution of the financial and insurance service sectors, which reached 7.2 percent of GVA in the UK over the same period.[64] It should, however, be kept in mind that legal service is a fee-based business, meaning that lawyers don't get a share in the profits their clients generate with the help of their advice. Still, the largest fees come from the most profitable clients, and in recent decades this has been the financial services sector, which accounts for more than 40 percent of the deal value conducted by UK firms.[65]

The UK has not only produced its own global lawyers, it has become a leading hub for global firms. More than two hundred foreign firms (one hundred from the United States alone) have a presence in the UK, most of them in London.[66] Many foreign firms have hired local lawyers in addition to the partners they brought in from their home base. This allows them to advise clients on all matters of UK law in addition to any cross-jurisdictional legal issues. Locating themselves in London gave foreign law firms access to one of the two leading global financial centers, but also to English common law, which is still the most sought-after law for transnational commerce. A survey of the most popular law that is used in arbitration shows that 40 percent of all contractual disputes were governed by English law, with another 17 percent by the laws of the state of New York.[67]

And, finally, London has been a convenient base to branch into Continental Europe (at least prior to Brexit), as well as to Africa and Asia. In fact, US and UK firms seem to be crowding out domestic firms in leading European economies in areas of the law that are key for coding capital, such as corporate law, mergers and acquisitions, and capital market law.[68] In France, domestic firms still control most corporate and merger deals (nine out of ten) but only less than a quarter of all capital market transactions; the remainder is now firmly in the hands of global law firms. And only five of the top German firms are among the top twenty firms that practice corporate law and mergers and acquisition in the country, and only one ranks among the top ten by market share; all others are Anglo-Saxon firms.[69]

To be sure, not all firms in the United Kingdom and the United States have become global or compete head-on with foreign lawyers. Even in these countries, the majority of lawyers still practice law in small- or medium-sized firms, advise clients on buying homes or commercial real estate, or help local entrepreneurs choose the right legal form for their business. For them, the world of law has not changed much from what it was several decades ago; they are experts in the law of their respective home jurisdiction, and they rarely peek across its border. But this is not where lawyers are at their most creative, and neither is it where most of the money in legal services is made.

Master Coders versus States

Capitalism owes its vibrancy to the ability of lawyers to fashion new capital and organizations from existing materials; this is how they code capital on behalf of their clients. Lawyers first used the domestic law they were trained in, but in the age of globalization they have been able to pick and choose from among many different states' laws. Globalization works because the masters of the code have been able to stitch together from their favorite legal system and a handful of international treaties a patchwork that sustains global markets for goods and services. They did not wait for states to harmonize the law, a process that would have been much slower and, of course, more politicized. Instead, they used the malleable modules of the code to structure transnational deals, opting into a legal system of their choice as a default and selecting its courts or private arbitration to settle any disputes.[70]

From this analysis, an image of law and of lawyering emerges that places the code's masters at the crossroads between the clients they serve and the states that furnish the cloth from which capital is coded. They are second to none in navigating the complex interdependencies of multiple legal systems from which they pick and choose the rules for coding their clients' capital. They would have been unable to do this without states or their law, but now they are no longer beholden to a single state, not even the one whose laws they have learned to master or selected for their coding strategy. This distinguishes today's masters of the code from their predecessors. They have never had as much latitude and their services have never been as valuable as they are today.[71] As a result, the relation between lawyers on one hand and states and their laws on the other been transformed.

Yet, despite all the latitude they have gained in crafting new capital by grafting the modules of the legal code onto an ever-changing roster of assets, lawyers still need to make sure that their coding efforts will be recognized and enforced by *some* state. After all, it is the shadow of coercive law enforcement that makes the commitments they craft credible and scalable. And yet, many lawyers will go to great lengths to avoid giving a court an opportunity to render a negative ruling on the legal coding they have employed for the benefit of hundreds, if not thousands, of clients. This is why they have increasingly insisted on settling disputes out of court or selecting arbitration over litigation. But this also puts lawyers in a strange and potentially quite vulnerable position. They depend on the authority of state law, but they avoid the courts, the law's traditional guardians, for fear that they might interfere with their coding work.

Something is lost, however, when cases are resolved not in a courtroom where they can be seen, dissected, and critiqued by others, but in its shadows. Disputes are the oxygen that keeps law alive and ensures that it is continuously adapted to a changing world.

When cases are no longer vetted in the open, the law becomes stale and judges lose expertise, thereby giving lawyers and their clients even more reasons to avoid them. More generally, dispute settlement has private and social costs as well as benefits, as Steven Shavell has pointed out; private benefits, however, do not always translate into social benefits.[72] When entire areas of the law are carved out from the public space that courts provide, the private benefits of out-of-court dispute settlement may well exceed the social benefits. In fact, the main beneficiaries of private settlements may not even be the parties to the dispute, but their attorneys. Perhaps they have to forego a larger fee in a case they settle; but they benefit overall, because in the absence of cases that clarify the law, their advice will be sought more frequently. Moreover, as time goes by, private attorneys become the only repeat players in solving disputes over contracts, which they themselves have fashioned, and can therefore position themselves as the only authoritative spokespersons for the law.

Courts have also ceded space to private arbitrators, as we have seen in the previous chapter. Arbitrators are often practicing attorneys in their own right, with some law professors thrown into the mix.[73] Hard numbers about the volume of arbitration are difficult to come by; this lies in the nature of a dispute settlement practice that is private and more secretive than its public counterpart. Still, available data suggest that disputes over major global transactions are increasingly resolved through arbitration, not litigation. And these are big cases. Data from 2013 based on surveys of law firms with substantial arbitral practices showed that of 109 cases these firms reported on, most had more than $500 million at stake, and close to half exceeded the $1 billion threshold.[74]

Arbitration started off as a welcome alternative to a slow-moving court system and attracted disputes because it was faster, cheaper, and offered arbitrators with expertise in the business, not generalist judges. Each party to the dispute typically selects one arbitrator, and these two appoint the third.[75] Despite the fact that arbitration today is no longer as fast or as cheap as it once was, its market share is still expanding. Mandatory arbitration clauses are now regularly found in contracts with consumers and employees, who lack the bargaining power to insist on disputing their case in court where they might avail themselves of class action procedures and other procedural benefits. To protect consumers' interests, the US Consumer Financial Protection Bureau, which was established after the Great Financial Crisis, issued a rule in the summer of 2017 that banned arbitration clauses in consumer loan contracts with banks and credit card companies on the other side; yet in a joint resolution passed by Congress and signed by President Trump, this provision was quickly overturned—another example of how closely the interests of states and capital are often aligned.[76]

As a result of these court avoidance strategies, the distance between presumed and actual recognition of the validity of the work that private attorneys perform is increasing, and the assertions lawyers make to soothe their clients that their legal opinions are grounded in law is becoming more tenuous. Rather than building their legal opinions on existing case law, they have to guess how a court might decide if a case ever came before it. Their own clients will play along and continue to rely on the "legal opinions" private lawyers write as a substitute, because they are the primary beneficiaries of their lawyers' coding strategies. Others, who find themselves on the other side of a dispute with these clients, might, however, refuse to yield to priority or durability privileges that lack the actual backing by courts. To attain legal certainty, asset holders and their lawyers have instead lobbied for legislative or regulatory change and have been remarkably successful to get what they needed. After all, who would not understand the need for legal certainty? The political winds, however, may be changing. If and when this happens, the empire of law that sustains global capitalism, which has been stitched together by private coding strategies, may begin to falter.

8

A New Code?

Law is code; it turns a simple asset into a capital asset by bestowing the attributes of priority, durability, universality, and convertibility on it. But it is also true that "code is law," as Lawrence Lessig suggested almost two decades ago.[1] Since his book was published, digitization has expanded at a rapid pace; indeed, we are witnessing the rapid digital enclosure of social, political, and economic life. This raises the specter that the law may soon be replaced by the digital code as the dominant mode of ordering complex social and economic relations. And the lawyers, who have taken center stage as master coders in the minting of capital, may have to cede most of their terrain to the "digital coders" who are already busily digitizing contracts, firms, money, and knowledge. The masters of the legal code of capital may, of course, acquire the skills for digital coding as well, and some are already well on the way toward doing this. Large fractions of the digital coders, however, wish to use this new technology to quite different ends.

It remains to be seen whether the digital code has the capacity to replace law, whether it can operate without legal crutches as many digital coders believe it can, and whether the masters of the legal code will retreat and surrender the task of coding capital to the digital coders. It is equally possible that the legal code will keep the upper hand and, with the help of the lawyers and of "legacy" state institutions, impose constraints on digital coders that will stop them in their tracks. This chapter outlines the battlefield between the digital and the legal code as it currently stands by briefly surveying the state of the art for the digital versions of the code's legal modules for smart contracts, digital property rights, digital firms, and of course, digital money.

Like the real world, the digital one too is populated by utopists and realists. In the eyes of the social utopists, one of the greatest attractions of the digital code is that it can be designed as a decentralized governance system that will place control over all aspects of life in the hands of individuals. Using digits rather than law to code commitments and social relations is not synonymous with decentralization. To the contrary, the scalability of digital codes allows a few super-coders to establish the rules of the game for everyone else. Some advances in digital technology, however, have created the possibility of decentralized governance, most prominently among them, blockchain technology.

A blockchain is a tamper-proof ledger that contains a complete history of all state changes in transactions that take place on it.[2] Smart contracts are pieces of code set to execute on the blockchain. Since every action on the blockchain is recorded automatically, blockchain-based smart contracts create an unprecedented level of granularity, completeness, and trustworthiness in the data gathered. A blockchain typically can only be written onto; it cannot be modified. Because they do not allow parties to back out from existing commitments, smart contracts that are written on blockchain create even more binding commitments than do legal contracts. By transacting through blockchain-based smart contracts, participants agree to a set of coded rules that are enforced by deterministic computers.

As a result, there will no longer be any need for state power or state law and the world may at long last become as flat as many economists have long imagined it to be. When the digital code replaces the legal code, the commitments we make to one another become hardwired, and even the powerful cannot simply wiggle out of them.

We may have reached the stage of the withering away of the state and its laws, just not exactly in the manner Engels more so than Marx, and their followers, may have imagined.[3]

In fact, even most social utopists among the digital coders are not anti-market; far from it.[4] They believe that the digital code will create the conditions for a perfect market, just as standard textbooks in Economics 101 depict them: A world with close to zero transaction and information costs and little if any need for institutions, such as contract, property, or corporate law, for humans to govern themselves and others, even as they might abuse their powers for their own personal benefit from time to time.

Despite their goal to radically change the way social relations are structured, the digital utopists see little point in challenging existing power structures in the open. The state and its regulatory apparatus as well as the big financial intermediaries, along with other highly visible representatives of the current order, are almost dismissively described as "incumbents," whose end, they prophesize, is near. There is no need to overthrow them; once the digital code has gained prominence, they will simply be thrown into the dustbin of history. This will happen without the violence that characterizes revolutions, because, unlike the legal code, the digital code does not depend on power and knows no territorial or jurisdictional borders; instead, it links willing users from around the globe, on whichever platforms they wish to join and for whichever purpose they care to pursue. Once they have agreed to join, they are bound by the rules of the digital code, which can be made self-enforcing.

Whether the digital code can escape from hierarchy and power is, of course, an open question, and there are reasons to be skeptical about this. Someone has to write the code, watch it, and fix its bugs; and someone must find an answer to the question of whose interests the code serves, or perhaps ought to serve. Indeed, some coders have already conceded that the digital space needs institutions akin to property rights and have made proposals for how to create them. But the greatest source of hierarchy may well be the coders themselves. They make the rules for the digital platforms they create, for the digital contracts, property rights, and coins they produce. The digital code may be a meritocracy, but meritocracies are, by definition, hierarchical, as those with superior skills make the rules that others must follow. Even if more than one person participates in the creation of a digital code, this rarely means that all coders have equal rights. Rather, collaborative coding projects usually get started by a lead coder with a team of followers; some may later break away from the original code, but typically this happens only after someone takes the lead and others follow, and only with enough followers can a new digital adventure become a true success.

It is not just the relation among the coders that has traces of hierarchy; the relation between the coders and the consumers of their coding efforts does as well. After all, the coders create the code and in doing so, establish the rules of the game; moreover, they often reserve the power to go offline when the code needs a fix, which is akin to the exercise of emergency powers in a legal system. Indeed, the digital coders can be said to command greater power over the digital code than the lawyers did historically over the code of capital. The latter assumed their role as masters of the code only gradually and have always had to walk a fine line between the demands of their clients and the need to have their coding strategies vindicated by the state. In contrast, the digital coders create digital codes without much, if any, regard for existing laws and regulations. They ignore not only state law, but states themselves, as their codes easily crisscross territorial and jurisdictional boundaries. What better way to prove that the digital code needs neither states nor their laws?

Nonetheless, the digital code is not immune to the powers that have come to control the legal code. The first steps for legally encoding the digital code are already under way; and the realists among the digital coders seem to have placed their bets on this outcome already. They are negotiating with state regulators and they are employing intellectual property law to enclose the digital space to their advantage. The race has not been decided yet; but if I had to place a bet, I would put it on an elite group among the "incumbents"; they will do everything to enclose the digital code in law and leave little space to the digital utopists.

Smart Contracts

A smart contract is a contract written in digits; in its simplest form it is a generic computer program that codes legal contracts in digits. Blockchain technology, however, makes it possible to go a step further yet and bears the promise that we can do without the apparatus of law and law enforcement. A contract that is placed on a blockchain, that is, a tamper-proof digital ledger, is not just a commitment device; it *is* the commitment.[5] The digital code will execute the commitment without either party being able to interfere. This requires, of course, that the code can control the delivery of goods, services, or pay, but assuming it does, we can dispense with courts to interpret and enforce the law as we know it.

These contracts are a dream come true for economists who have long bemoaned the fact that contracts are incomplete and parties often fail to live up to the commitments they made in the past.[6] Unlike legal contracts, smart contracts are self-executing; once the bargain has been struck, the digital code executes it without leaving room for interruption, deviation, or breach. The old Roman principle of *pacta sunt servanda* (contracts are to be honored) seems to be, at long last, within reach—and not as a normative aspiration, but as fact, as how things are done in digits.

In the real world, only the simultaneous exchange of goods and money (spot transactions) comes close to this ideal. Whenever either delivery or payment is postponed to a future date, one party is at risk that the other might flout her obligations. As discussed earlier, the legal coding of a claim enhances the probability that the other party will get what it bargained for. Collateral law does this by giving the exposed party a claim against another asset as hostage—a piece of land, a valuable object, or a bank account—that can be seized and sold to recover any losses from a defaulting debtor. And, as a last resort, the duped party can take recourse to the state's coercive law enforcement apparatus. The legal coding enhances *legal* certainty but is no substitute for economic performance. If the debtor has no assets left at the time the creditor seeks to enforce her claim, or if her assets have become worthless, there is nothing the law can do to make the creditor whole again.

For all their appeal, smart contracts have found their critics, some of whom have called them a really "dumb idea."[7] An obvious weakness of self-executing digital contracts is that even an immutable code is not immune to change.[8] Change may come from the outside, that is, the proverbial "exogenous shock" that populates economic models. If the world changes in ways that neither party has anticipated, they may well wish to renegotiate or reach out to a mediator to divide the losses among them. In the alternative, the changes may come from within in the form of mistakes (bugs) in the original code, or incompleteness, that is, the failure of the coders to anticipate all the ways in which the code might be used or abused in the future. Theorists of legal contracts conceded long ago that there is no such thing as a complete contract; contracts are inherently incomplete, because the contracting parties are simply unable to anticipate all future contingencies and trying to do so would be too costly to justify the effort.[9]

Most digital coders who have placed their fate in decentralized blockchain systems seem to be unfazed by these problems. To them, a malfunctioning code or even a crash is a sign of a "bug" that needs to be fixed next time around, not a fundamental problem that besets all efforts to create binding commitments in the face of an uncertain future.[10] Indeed, the orthodox among the digital coders treat the digital code as sacrosanct, as more binding than most lawyers would treat the legal code. Tampering with it is considered an ethical violation that is justified only if done by consensus. To be sure, there is well-functioning code and there is malfunctioning code. Fundamental uncertainty, however, is a different thing altogether; it means that there is no escape from "unknown unknowns"; the best one can do is to approximate a range of possible outcomes. Some contracts may be easier to code on immutable ledgers, but others must be amenable to future change.

As always, context matters, and much will depend on the specifics of the contracts in question. Many contracts are simple enough to be automated or put on an immutable ledger. Vending machines automate a simple sales contract. You pay your money and the machine delivers the snack or the drink. There is not much to negotiate here. Today, mathematical algorithms control the trading of corporate shares on stock exchanges, and a number of financial transactions, such as swaps, have been put on a blockchain. When the digital code has access to the account from which payment will be made as it becomes due (and provided that there will be enough money on the account), these contracts will be fully self-executing.

Other contracts that are coded in law are open-ended and the parties simply agree to cooperate at a future date, when the outcome of joint efforts in research and development are better known.[11] For them, digital coding may be used for certain aspects, but in large part they will most likely continue to rely on legal code. Indeed, some law firms are already experimenting with libraries that contain digital contracts that can be combined with legally coded agreements.[12] Incidentally, this suggests that the masters of the legal code of capital are not sitting on their hands; they are aware of the challenge the digital code poses to their profession and are meeting that challenge head-on.

The legal code, as we have seen, is highly malleable. Contracts are meant to be kept, but they are incomplete, and parties will renegotiate them when confronted with radically altered circumstances. Most legal systems have even formalized such opt-outs, by creating doctrinal or even statutory opt-outs from binding contracts.[13] For smart contracts to match legal contracts on this front, they would have to acquire the capacity to adapt to future change. Some digital coders are already on the task, including for blockchain-based smart contracts. In an attempt to square the circle between immutability and the need to respond to unforeseeable change, they have re-invented a problem solver from our archaic past, the oracle. Before humans mastered medicine and science, they would address an oracle—often depicted as an agent of a god—to find answers to which they themselves had none. Similarly, some digital codes include references to an external agent, an oracle, whose input is needed for the code to run its course for the remainder of a transaction. Oracles can feed a smart contract with benchmark prices, such as interest or exchange rates and price developments, but they can also request a decision from an external arbiter. Choosing the right oracle will, of course, be critical, because a bad choice that is hardwired on an immutable blockchain will be difficult to reverse.

The legal code has not been completely without oracles, either. Take the London Interbank Offered Rate (LIBOR), a benchmark interest rate that serves as a reference point for trillions of debt contracts around the world. A handful of trusted banks set LIBOR by reporting the borrowing costs they face. The trouble is that they may not always report the entire truth. Evidence emerged after the crisis of 2008 that LIBOR was manipulated to artificially keep borrowing costs at lower than actual rates.[14] Regulators have tried hard to push financial intermediaries to phase it out and replace it with a tamper-proof reference point, which is scheduled to replace LIBOR in 2021—although the fine details have yet to be worked out.[15] The costs of switching from one outside anchor to another are high and there are likely to be losers who will resist any change. But even the winners currently face enormous legal uncertainty.

Changing a digital oracle may be even harder, because of the digital code's immutability. While this feature has many advantages, its rigidity is likely to privilege the status quo.[16] This will always clash with changes in the real world, and the more so in areas where change is a constant, as it is in finance, for example. The experience with writing legal contracts for financial assets holds important lessons. The relentless enforcement of legal rights, such as margin or collateral calls, that allow one party to extract cash payments from its counterparty when asset prices were falling across the board, brought the financial system close to the abyss already in 2007, a year before Lehman would trigger a near-fatal heart attack.

A good example is the fate of credit default swaps (CDS), a kind of insurance contract that enables a party to acquire protection on the value of financial assets it does not own.[17] According to a CDS contract, the insurer must make cash payments to the insured parties ("collateral calls"), if and when the value of the assets he is protecting declines beyond a certain threshold.[18] Nobody had expected that these thresholds would ever be crossed, or if so, that this would happen only for select assets. When, against all the odds, asset prices declined across the board, the main seller of CDS insurance, a subsidiary of the multinational insurance company "American International Group" (AIG), found itself inundated by collateral calls. It disputed the size of the calls only to find out that there was no contractual solution to the predicament in which it and the counterparty it had insured, found themselves. The contract they had concluded provided that the party demanding the payment had the right to calculate the loss based on observable market prices. Yet, when the parties to these contracts needed markets most, they no longer existed. Few dealers were making deals and therefore had no prices to quote; all they could do now is estimate, and, not surprisingly, estimates varied widely.[19] Only by going "offline" and negotiating on a case-by-case basis the amounts counterparties to CDS contracts owed each other was the onset of the crisis postponed, and its blow softened.[20] Smart contracts may not be as smart.

Digital Property Rights

For most digital coders, contracts are everything and property rights are at most a second thought. This resembles economists' understanding of property rights, who consider them as *residual* rights, as whatever is left over after all specific contractual obligations are accounted for. From a legal perspective this leaves open the question as to what gave a contracting party the right to contract over the other obligations in the first place? In other words, using residual rights to explain property rights assumes what ought to be explained. In the digital world, the right to contract shall be determined by examining the history of asset transfers. If the transacting party has acquired the asset in a verified transaction, it is assumed to have the right to further transact over it. Without such proof, a new transaction will not be executed. Because the digital code itself verifies every transaction, there may be no residual rights left in search of an owner. At least if we ignore how the right of the first person entering into the transaction shall be verified, smart contracts may mark the end of property rights.

Some digital coders have realized, however, that the notion of property as residual rights captures at most part of the work that legal property rights do. As discussed in chapter 1, a key feature of property rights is that they create priority claims that are enforceable against the world. Nick Szabo, a prominent voice in the world of cryptocurrency, who may be best known for his work on digital contracts, explored how to create property rights in the digital space.[21] He explained that property rights are "a defined space, whether a namespace or physical space," that marks the scope of control rights an owner can exercise. Once the initial allocation is coded in digits, there will no longer be any doubt as to who owns what, because all claims will be recorded on tamper-proof digital code. This demonstrates how important the initial allocation of property rights is, a point Ronald Coase made half a century ago.[22] Szabo restates Coase's insight by emphasizing that it is critical to "agree on simple attributes of or rights to control subdivisions of that space."[23] Only after this initial allocation has been made can transactions occur and blockchain (or similar) technology be used to verify each subsequent transaction.

This then once again poses the "genesis question": How should the initial allocation of property rights in the digital world be achieved, and who is in charge? For this task, Szabo proposed three strategies. The first strategy is the digital equivalent to a social contract. Existing communities shall collectively agree on the boundaries of their respective property rights.[24] For this to work, it must be clear who belongs to the community and has a right to participate in the negotiation. Collective decision-making requires its own process governance, such as voting rules and rules governing the settlement of disputes. Finally, property rights need not only be protected for the parties to the social contracts, but against outsiders who might have their own, and different, property rights arrangements and make claims to the same space. In short, someone will have to resolve the question of what assets are free to be claimed as property rights, and what assets have been taken already. These are the same questions the commoners disputed with the landlords and the settler challenged the First Peoples about, as discussed in chapter 2.

Ultimately, these issues were resolved by establishing legal priority rights, backed by the coercive powers of a state.

The second strategy Szabo proposed was to leave the delineation of property rights to the digital marketplace. Any participant on a digital platform may stake out a claim to a digital space. The strength of the claim will be determined by the number of followers, and if there are none, the "root" will die. The trick then is to amass followers. "Roots who give away more property to more people, or who actually deploy mechanisms to protect their property, will gain more respect for the tree they started," and as a result, "convergence on a particular tree" will be achieved.[25] This race is likely to be won by a first mover with sufficient resources to pay off potential followers, and it raises the question of where her resources come from. More important, it is not clear that this market-driven process will render any meaningful allocation of rights. Suppose there are many claimants and only few followers; this would defeat the attempt to delimit the digital space.

Finally, Szabo suggests that the task of defining the scope of property rights and their initial allocation might be delegated to "property clubs." Lest anyone thought that this would mark a return to state power and state law even in a digital world, Szabo insists that a "property club" performs only "one narrow function normally associated with government."[26] But this is a serious understatement of the significance of property rights in all their different manifestations in today's legal systems. Creating, enforcing, verifying, and vindicating priority claims against the world is arguably the most important function of states—next to maintaining peace externally and internally. By conceding the need for property clubs, Szabo effectively recognizes the need for some authority to say what claims deserve to be elevated to priority rights and who should hold such rights. If this decision is left to property clubs among the coders, they are our de facto government.

Creating property rights from scratch is, of course, a difficult task. However, even if we were to limit the role of the digital code to translating the legal attributes of priority, durability, and convertibility with universal effects from legal into digital code, there is the non-trivial question of how to get from here to there—from legal claims that are often fuzzy around the edges to their digitization as binary variables. Experience suggests that *any* formalization of pre-existing claims alters the boundaries of existing rights, even if only inadvertently. This is why the zoning and titling of land has always been and continues to be a deeply contested undertaking. De Soto has proposed to simply listen "to the barking dogs," which means in practice that the most powerful members of a community will obtain formal title at the exclusion of everyone else.[27] Other members of the community may have relied for decades, if not centuries, on practices that gave them access or use rights, if only temporarily, but their claims may not easily fit the new code, or they may lack proof that their practices were part of the normative fabric of their communities, and they will almost certainly have the smaller dogs.

In summary, the process of formalizing preexisting rights gives whoever is literate in words, script, or digits the upper hand, leaving the less resourceful ones behind. It is well-documented, for example, that in titling programs, male members of the household often receive title when land relations are formalized at the expense of females; and collective use rights are regularly sidelined in favor of individualized property rights, which give the select few the opportunity to monetize the assets in question for personal gain.[28] There is no reason to believe that the digitization of claims will be any different—and these digital rights will now be eternalized in immutable code.

It should be clear by now that the digital space is not flat. For every new digital platform that is created, access and control rights over a "defined space" need to be allocated. The challenges that the digital coders face are therefore no different from those that societies governed by the legal code have been wrestling with for centuries.

Digital Autonomous Organizations

Digital firms, also referred to as digital autonomous organizations (DAO), represent the latest advance in digital coding on immutable code.[29] In 2016, the first digital financial intermediary, "The DAO," was launched to much fanfare. Its coders wished to re-invent a financial intermediary in code alone, but The DAO did not operate in a legal vacuum. In the wake of a frenzy in the offerings of tokens or coins in digital ventures to the public, also dubbed "initial coin offerings," or ICOs after the legacy practice of "initial public offerings" of shares or bonds, the US Securities and Exchange Commission (SEC) intervened. It affirmed that ICOs qualify as "securities" that are subject to standard registration requirements, a decision that reached The DAO only posthumously.[30]

The DAO was a venture capital fund that was built on the Ethereum blockchain. The DAO was designed to operate without a board of directors or any human officers. Instead, the firms' investors received voting rights that allowed them to participate directly in developing investment strategies by proposing new investment opportunities to the firm. If agreed by the majority of investors, they would be implemented by the code, an open-source software that was available for everyone to see, but not for everyone to change.

The DAO was touted as more democratic and transparent than its legal counterpart, the business corporation. As a legal entity that requires humans to act on its behalf, the corporation is beset by agency problems. Managers often have more de facto power than de jure rights, and shareholders lack the willpower or resources to constrain them effectively.[31] This results in substantial waste; the idea to put the operation of a company on a digital platform that can run without agents therefore seems to make sense.

The DAO's founders even went a step further, and insisted that this firm had no owners, but only contractors, curators, and token holders. The token holders used the Ethereum blockchain (ether) to buy tokens in the ICO. As token holders, they may propose investments, which are selected by majority vote and are carried out by contractors, which in turn are selected by the curators. This setup comes close to the idea that firms are nothing but a nexus of contracts.[32] Direct participation replaces the representative governance structure of the modern business corporation. Token holders were given the right to split from the original firm and divert their investments elsewhere if they were outvoted.[33] The split entails a return of the tokens for Ether, the cryptocurrency, which may then be re-invested in a new company. Had it lived longer, this would have made The DAO vulnerable to the problem of capital withdrawal, a problem that corporate law overcame half a millennium ago, when the Dutch East India Company invented shareholder lock-in.[34] Instead, the company had (inadvertently) its own undoing literally written into its digital code.

The idea of using an immutable code to create and run a financial intermediary without fear of managerial slack or abuse quickly attracted interest among investors. They paid $168 million of ether, which they used to acquire tokens in The DAO, turning its ICO into the most successful crowdfunding venture ever at that point in time.[35] Unfortunately, The DAO crashed only weeks after it had been launched: Someone found a loophole in the code and exploited it to drain $50 million, almost a third of the firm's capital contribution, into a separate account that was inaccessible to the firm.[36] The trick the intruder used was to establish a digital subsidiary (or child) and to direct payments from the intruder's account to that entity. "By repeatedly requesting splits before the attacker's balance sheet was adjusted, the attacker was able to fool The DAO into giving out more funds than the attacker's original balance."[37] Happily, not even the intruder himself had immediate access to his stolen goods, but neither did The DAO.

The intruder did not have to break any windows or seals; the code itself had left the gap he exploited. The Ethereum community debated for days how to respond. To some, this was a clear breach, if not of the digital code itself, of its spirit. They advocated to reset the code to its state prior to this incident and to return to investors their original contribution, thereby effectively liquidating The DAO. Others wanted to hold on to the principle that "code is law" and binding as written. If the code had bugs that could be exploited, this was a mistake that should be fixed by writing better code in the future; changing the code retroactively went against the fundamentals of the digital code as immutable and threatened to undermine its standing as an alternative to the discretionary power that is associated with states and state law.

The decision rules of The DAO required a majority vote, and the pragmatists won the day; they altered the code, unwound The DAO, and returned the ether to the majority of the token holders. The minority, however, held on to the original code, which they now labeled "Ethereum Classic" (ETC), a new digital asset, which competes with the adulterated original Ethereum (ETH).[38]

The DAO is a cautionary tale of coded determinism operating in an unpredictable world. It also is a good illustration of how codes evolve, whether they are legal or digital. The pragmatists among The DAO's token holders decided to leave the final say about its fate in the hands of humans. This was wise if one considers that the code itself is of human creation and if one values human autonomy over an abstract principle of immutability. Nonetheless, by altering the code, the pragmatists entered into a Faustian bargain; they conceded that the digital code is malleable and that there is room for human intervention and discretion, after all. It remains to be seen how this opening will be used in the future. Drawing from the history of the legal code of capital, it might be good advice for the social utopists among the digital coders to watch out for the lead coders and monitor their relationships with the most resourceful among the legacy investors.

Cryptocurrencies

The alchemy of money has bedeviled fortune hunters forever, and the coders of cryptocurrencies are no exception. Bitcoin, a digital cryptocurrency based on blockchain technology, was one of the hottest assets in 2017. When it was launched in 2009, it was lauded as a new form of money without a state, and its most fervent advocates were crypto-anarchists who wished to create a new world beyond big finance and the corruptibility of state power. Soon, however, the gold rush set in and drew characters from every walk of life into the fold, including money launderers, gamblers, fortune hunters, and even high finance. Bitcoin traded at only $900 at the beginning of 2017, but was quoted at $20,000 per coin in December of the same year. Since then, the trend has been downward, and by the fall of 2018, it stood at roughly $6,000, having shed more than two-thirds of its value in dollar terms—and other cryptocurrencies did not fare much better.[39]

Nobody knows exactly who invented Bitcoin. Satoshi Nakamoto, the official creator, is an alias for one, or perhaps several, digital coders. Some have proposed that Nick Szabo, the brain behind smart contracts and digital property rights, is the man behind Bitcoin, but he has denied this. Another contender is Craig Wright, a professed gambler from Australia who outed himself as the person behind the pseudonym, but not everyone is convinced.[40] Be this as it may, Bitcoin embodies the hope of crypto-anarchists of a state-less future, but also the fears of conventional law enforcers about losing control over the financial flows that fund illicit businesses.

Bitcoin is often referred to as digital money.[41] Bitcoin may, however, be more adequately described as yet another form of private money: a privately coded asset that can shower its holders with enormous wealth in the short to medium term, but that will crash sooner or later absent effective state backing. Some have sensed the retrograde nature of Bitcoin's design. "Much of 'Blockchain Finance' is really a political programme to bring back *bearer assets* in cryptographic form," as explained by a financial analyst.[42] These bearer assets include the paper certificates of bonds, notes, or bills of exchange that were discussed earlier in this book. The paper (or wooden sticks, which represented sovereign debt of the Crown) not only served as proof of, but it embodied, the claim. Transferring the piece of paper transfers the right it carries; and without the paper in hand, one cannot claim a right to payment. Just like Bitcoin, bills of exchange were used as substitutes for real money, gold and silver coins, because these were difficult and risky to transport over long distances. But notes and bills of exchange also did something else: they created new money in the form of credit; when a buyer issues a note or endorses a bill, she does so because she does not have the money on hand but expects to have it in the future. Sometimes, a debtor may have assets but not liquid ones that can be easily exchanged into state money and therefore must defer payment to a future date. Recall the dilemma of Antonio in Shakespeare's *Merchant of Venice* discussed in chapter 4, whose ship had not reached shore yet. As it happened, it never did, but it might have; and indeed, most ships do at least most of the time.

There is, however, one aspect in which Bitcoin departs from these other forms of private money. Bitcoin is designed as money without credit: nobody can spend Bitcoin without proof of ownership.[43] The "Bitcoin Manifesto," published by the ominous Satoshi Nakamoto, explains that a key motivation for creating Bitcoin was to solve the "double-spending problem."[44] Yet, the ability to spend money one does not have is—for better or worse—the very essence of capitalism. Other forms of private money, the notes, bills of exchange, asset-backed securities, etc., are IOUs that are all assigned and traded with the expectation that they are convertible into state money whenever needed, and hopefully at a profit; convertibility may not be guaranteed, but the promise of convertibility makes these assets attractive and finds them buyers.

Spotting opportunities to make money on the hope of others is what intermediaries do, and their business is levering up in the expectation of future returns. The old merchant banks made money by accepting bills of exchange at a discount, hoping to recover the full amount in species from the original debtor or any other person who had endorsed the bill. Obviously, they took a risk, which is why they discounted the bill, but as long as they were able to fully recover the outstanding debt in most cases, this was a profitable business. Today's dealer banks take a similar position as intermediaries for all kinds of assets; they buy in the expectation of selling at a higher price; and by accepting all kinds of assets, they provide liquidity in the form of hard currency to the market. Critically, the most privileged among the old merchant banks and today's major dealer banks always have access to state money. Without it, they would be doomed whenever private demand for these assets dries up.

Cryptocurrencies promise greater purity than either state or private money in theory, but in reality, they are deeply infected by the same features that afflict the real world of money, namely, credit, instability, and power. As noted, proof of sufficient funds is required before a Bitcoin transaction closes and the complete chain of verified transaction is recorded on an immutable digital ledger. Yet, nobody prevents investors from buying Bitcoin on credit, which will have to be paid back in state money, whatever the future price of Bitcoin might be when the debt becomes due. The purity of Bitcoin was also compromised when the cryptocurrency was admitted to futures trading on the Chicago Mercantile Exchange.[45] In a futures trade, parties are betting on the ability to predict future price movements, but they will have to deliver, even if they lose. In short, trading in futures is just another way of spending money you don't have.

Using debt to buy speculative assets is, of course, a tried and tested strategy for the lucky few who will make huge gains in the short term, and for the rest another lesson in how to get burned when markets turn, leaving behind those who failed to exit before it was too late. It is only a matter of time for holders of Bitcoin and similar cryptocurrencies to find out whether they will find themselves on the side of winners or losers in this game. The only alternative is dispensing with private credit entirely, a decision that is tantamount to abandoning capitalism. It would give us the choice between leaving the task of investing largely to the state; or, alternatively, of insisting that investments can be made only in equity, i.e., with resources one has, not with debt.[46] This is the radical utopia of Bitcoin, but we better understand its hard reality: this would be a world with much diminished prospects for accumulating wealth, both public and private.

Another feature of the decentralized utopia of Bitcoin is that its holders, not some higher authority, are tasked with verifying transactions through a process that is referred to as "mining."[47] The miners can earn additional Bitcoins by offering computing space and providing the electricity required for the algorithm to run its course. Indeed, this decentralized mining process consumes inordinate amounts of energy. This also means that, contrary to the ideational posture of the "cryptos," not all miners are equal; those with high-powered computers and real money to burn for electricity bills are more equal than others.[48] This is borne out by available data. As of December 2017, only "four mining pools controlled over 50 percent of the Bitcoin network, and two mining pools controlled more than

50 percent of Ethereum."[49] Even the most decentralized of the digital platforms is succumbing to the forces of hierarchy.

Last, unlike fiat money that can be issued in unlimited amounts, the number of Bitcoin was limited to 21 million. Creating scarcity was meant to boost its value and to avoid the temptation of inflating the currency to please powerful players. Yet, this limit on the money supply also seems to be fraying around the edges. New variants of the original cryptocurrencies can be coined by creating a hard fork in the original protocol; they may not be identical with the original Bitcoin, but they still create new money. It has even become possible to buy fractions of Bitcoin, which creates the illusion of an expanding pie, even when the only change is the size of each slice.

Returning to the question whether Bitcoin is money, it is certainly true that the cryptocurrency has shown that artificial scarcity combined with a dearth of alternative assets that promise superlative returns (if only temporarily) can create huge demand. That alone, however, does not turn it into money in the true sense of the word. Classic theories of money hold that money must perform three functions: it should be a store of value, a means of exchange, and a unit of account.[50] Bitcoin has at best traces of the first two features: Its value has been pushed temporarily to unprecedented heights—but the high volatility of its price suggests that it is a lousy storage of value. And while many banks, retailers, and private parties now accept Bitcoins as a means of exchange, their reference price remains the US dollar and, like all holders of private assets, most investors expect to be able to convert Bitcoin into dollars (or another hard currency) at the time of their choosing. The brains behind Bitcoin, whoever they might be, had envisioned that this new private currency would become independent of, indeed an alternative to, state money. For others, Bitcoin was an asset to invest, if not speculate in, and since nobody prevented them from buying Bitcoin with state money of their own or with borrowed sums, so they did.

For Bitcoin to evolve into money on par with state money, a leap of a different magnitude and quality will be necessary: Someone must be willing and able to protect its value. Without such a backstopping mechanism, Bitcoin and its digital siblings will crash sooner or later. This is the logic of all private moneys, the debt instruments from notes to bills to asset-backed securities and their derivatives. There is no reason to believe that the same logic does not hold for digital currencies. Of course, we may dispense with the sort of money that enjoys the protection of its par value by a powerful authority, but we also know from history what this entails: frequent financial upheavals of the kind that accompanied the era of free banking in the United States in the nineteenth century, only on a much larger scale.

There is a silver lining, however. With the help of the digital coding technology, it may well be possible to gain a better check over the hierarchy of money. I have argued throughout this book that only states can effectively back money, because only states have the power to unilaterally impose burdens on others. The digital code, however, offers an alternative. The future costs of a financial crisis may be built into the code in such a way that all who benefited from the asset in question (Bitcoin, for example), will have to chip in when its survival is at stake. Losses, in short, would be mutualized through a collective backstopping mechanism that is baked into the immutable, digital code.

A similar idea has informed "contingent convertibles" (CoCos), that is, corporate bonds that automatically convert into equity when a certain event is triggered. CoCos were invented in the aftermath of the 2008 crisis and are meant to stabilize the financial system in times of crisis by forcing creditors to absorb some of the losses of a downturn by turning them into shareholders at the sign of trouble.[51] Whereas creditors can drain resources from a company by enforcing their legal claims, shareholders get paid only if the company is profitable. CoCos are typically freely tradable, and the obligations they entail can be transferred by selling them. Early experience with these new instruments suggests that investors have strong incentives to get rid of them as soon as they see the prospect for loss-sharing on the wall, which was to be expected.[52]

Only the last ones have to carry the can, as the saying goes. It remains to be seen whether digital coders can tighten the screws and more effectively impose losses on *all* holders of a digital currency—perhaps adjusted for the benefits they derived from them. If they succeed, they will have offered the world a truly innovative solution to the curse of private debt finance, and that is its tendency in crises to protect the gains of the few and leave it to the rest to socialize the losses—not by an invisible hand, but by the guiding hand of a state.

The Digital versus the Legal Code

We are in the midst of encoding the world, this time not in law, but in digits. The digital code carries enormous promises; it may well improve the plight of millions of people who lack access to reliable payment systems, minimize fraud, and lower the costs of contracting and contract enforcement; and it might do all of the above at relatively low cost. However, there is also the possibility that the digital code will be used to entrench the interests of only a few; and the most serious threat comes from the combination of the digital with the legal code to serve the incumbents of legally coded capital.[53]

There are unmistakable signs already that, like nature's code before it, the digital code too has been slated for legal enclosure, and the legal module of choice is intellectual property rights. The number of patent applications for digital currencies has increased dramatically in recent years. In July 2016, Coindesk, a website for cryptocurrencies, reported that patent filings amounted to between 70 and 160 applications per year.[54] By the end of July 2018, the US Patent Office had more than a thousand patents pending that contained the words "blockchain," and that does not count all the other patents that seek to protect other digital advances in finance.[55] Further, whereas earlier, individuals and small firms dominated the filing of patents, large, publicly traded corporations have since taken over the field.[56] The biggest players in finance are making a major push to legally enclose this digital gold mine. Goldman Sachs, for example, secured a patent for a new coin used to settle securities that are denominated in different currencies in 2017; Mastercard won a patent for a faster crypto payment system in 2018, and Barclays filed a patent application for blockchain-based banking services at the same time.[57]

In addition, major incumbent banks have joined forces with tech firms to create consortia that exploit the powers of the digital code, including blockchain technology for the members of these clubs. They use open-source digital codes, but don't necessarily offer open access.[58] The incumbent "captains of finance" have discovered the power of the digital code and are using it to advance their interests. Moreover, they are using the legal code to protect the digital work that their hired technologists have crafted for them.[59] How far their advances will go in enclosing the digital commons will depend in significant part on the future of patent and trade secrecy laws. As discussed in chapter 5, the long-term trend in intellectual property rights has been an expansive one that tended to bend to the desire of private industry to enclose the commons and capture its monetary rewards.

The battle between the two codes, the digital and the legal, is on. Each has its own advantages and disadvantages. The legal code has proven to be highly malleable and adaptive to change, but mostly for the benefits of those with access to good lawyers. In contrast, the digital code has the potential to be more inclusive, provided that this still new technology is used to provide low-cost access to both assets and coding devices. While we cannot affirm yet which one will come out on top, all indicators suggest that the arbiter over this battle will be the "legacy" institutions: the courts and legislatures that are themselves products of law. This seems to be a strong predictor for which of the two codes will emerge from this battle victoriously.

9

Capital Rules by Law

Capital rules, and it rules by law.[1] It owes its capacity to create wealth to the modules of a legal code that is backed by state power; and its resilience in times of crisis can be attributed to a combination of legal asset-shielding devices and the state's willingness to extend a helping hand to capital to preserve not only capitalism but social stability, and by implication, the state itself. In short, capital is inextricably linked to law and state power, because in its absence, the legal privileges capital enjoys would not be respected by others.

Privileges were at one time tied to social and political status, which was affirmed by law. Under feudalism, the nobility enjoyed greater prerogatives than peasants; foreign merchants were able to negotiate trading privileges with the authorities of cities where they convened for trade fairs, which were often overseen if not controlled by local merchants; men enjoyed superior rights to, even rights over, women; and so did white people over people of color during colonialism and under slavery. While prejudices still surface today, most legal systems no longer differentiate by status or personal attributes in such an unabashed fashion. Most subscribe to the principle that all are equal before the law; and yet, law often deals a better hand to some than to others.

Nobody saw this more clearly than the lawyer and sociologist Max Weber, an astute observer of power structures. Max Weber is often cited for his claim that capitalism requires a "rational" and "predictable" legal system to thrive.[2] Replacing fiat with predictable laws, Weber argued, would allow entrepreneurs to make plans and invest in an unknown future. But Weber also noted that soon after nation-states had forged general laws to be applied consistently throughout their territory, a new "modern particularism" was born.[3] The term recalls the particularistic legal orders that were characteristic of the Middle Ages, when every fiefdom, guild, or city had its own laws and courts. Weber singled out commerce as the leading force behind modern particularism. Having their own, special, rules or obtaining exemptions from general laws that applied to the rest was a question of "expediency," as the advocates of commerce would explain. The term "efficiency" may be more fashionable today; it signals greater theoretical depth, but it is used to similar ends. If business interests benefit from special treatment, this, their proponents argue, should suffice for granting it. After all, what is good for business is good for everybody; it will expand the pie and the invisible hand will ensure that at least some crumbs will be shared with the rest, or so the argument goes.

Asset holders, however, are not interested in sharing their spoils; they will take legal protection where they can find it, and if they find it on foreign shores, they have little reason for returning home, where, as Smith suggested, they would invariably share some of their gains with their home base. They are not even interested in the rule of law as such, only to the extent that it advances their own interests. Often, the same asset holders who only recently waged a battle to have their private rights fully protected by law will then seek exemptions from those very rules, when they realize that these rules might also be used against them.

Examples abound; recall that English landlords first fought for priority rights over the commoners. After they had effectively excluded the commoners, they used their title to raise debt finance and mortgaged their land to creditors. However, when creditors tried to seize their property to recover the value of the loans they had extended to them, they cried foul and turned to lawyers and to courts for help. The lawyers helped them to protect their family wealth behind the legal veil of the trust and thereby to immunize it from their personal creditors; and the courts recognized and enforced these new boundaries, keeping creditors at bay. In doing so, they prolonged land's status for a few decades as the most important source of wealth.[4] It took a major economic depression to redraw these boundaries in law and to empower creditors to fully enforce the mortgages they had obtained.

Creditors soon learned to play the same game. They lobbied hard for bankruptcy rules that would uphold their rights and give secured creditors priority rights over unsecured creditors, although they faced considerable push-back from entrepreneurs who convinced the English parliament that insolvency was not necessarily evidence of their immorality, but just as likely, of bad luck. Indeed, persons that qualified as "traders" received special treatment in bankruptcy. Unlike the paupers, who were imprisoned for failing to pay their debt, bankruptcy offered a cleansing process for them, whereby they could rid themselves of past obligations.[5]

The latest champions of debt finance, the derivative traders of our own time, similarly demanded and obtained exemptions from general bankruptcy rules to ensure that they could re-position their portfolio at any time, even if this put other creditors at risk. The last thing any creditor wants is a run on the debtor's assets—unless of course she gets there first, which is what bankruptcy safe harbors are all about. They allow creditors of privileged assets to net out their claims before any other, including secured, creditors get their share, while everybody else has to yield to the automatic stay.[6]

It is not difficult to understand why asset holders might want these legal privileges; after all, it gives them an edge over competitors in amassing and protecting their wealth. Less clear is why states fall for this and often create additional carve-outs for holders of capital assets over and above the privileges they already enjoy by virtue of the code's basic modules. To some, the answer to this question will seem only too obvious. To Marxists, the question of power and rule is inextricably linked to class struggle and rule by one class over others. Once the bourgeoisie gains control over the state and its lawmaking apparatus, it will, of course, use it to entrench its power. On the other end of the spectrum, we find rational choice theorists who shift the analysis from social classes to individuals and from class struggle to bargaining. To them, scarcity is key and power is never absolute, because no one controls everything needed to retain it. This, they argue, is why the power wielders will inevitably enter into bargains with their likes.[7] Whereas Marxists see law primarily as an instrument for exercising power, for rational choice theorists, law operates both as a constraint on and as an expression of power, and the balance between the two is struck through bargaining.

Both camps have marshalled a lot of evidence to buttress their respective claims. My goal here is not to dispute them, but to suggest that both theories suffer from a similar blind spot. They ignore the central role of law in the making of capital and its protection as private wealth. Using the analytical lens developed in this book, it is possible to explain the political economy of capitalism without having to construct class identities, as Marxists feel compelled to do, or to make heroic assumptions about the rationality of human beings, as rational choice theorists would have it. The key to understanding the basis of power and the resulting distribution of wealth lies instead in the process of bestowing legal protection on select assets and to do so as a matter of private, not public, choice. There will, of course, be times when the state strikes a bargain with the wealthy, or state agents succumb to side payments that are meant to grease those wheels of the bureaucracy that directly benefit them. There are also times when we can observe powerful private interests obtaining direct control over the state, but these sporadic events are better described as epiphenomena. Of course, the choice of assets is not random; the point is that powerful interests need not bargain with the state; all they need are good lawyers who master the code of capital.

The roots of capital's ability to rule by law run deep and lie in the emergence of modern rights as private rights that are dependent on state power yet have become dislodged from the social preferences of the citizens of the states that make them. The essence of these modern rights is not their content, but their form as individual, or subjective, rights, as the German philosopher Christoph Menke has shown in his recent *Critique of Rights*.[8] Autonomous law has become "the law of rights," whatever its contents might be. This does not mean that no attempts are made to justify why certain interests, but not others, are cloaked in the authority of law. In the Western legal tradition, a natural state of the world that preceded the legal order typically serves as a justification. The imagined natural state was legalized and what was once natural has been turned into a subjective right that is enforceable irrespective of the social effects it might have.

They became the foundation for a new economic and political order. "Without the legal form of the subjective right capitalism would not exist," according to Menke;[9] and neither would the political order that sustains capitalism, an order in which subjective rights are enshrined in the constitution and state power is directed to protect them.

Put differently, the modules of the code may be part of the private legal order, but private law is imbricated with a constitutional order that has elevated subjective private rights to foundational principles.[10] Public and private law are intertwined and jointly constitute the system we call capitalism. To see this more clearly, the following section discusses how the process of coding and recoding capital in private law relates to its public law foundations.

A Private Code

Law is the cloth from which capital is cut; it gives holders of capital assets the right to exclusive use and to the future returns on their assets; it allows capital to rule not by force, but by law. The cloth is woven of private law, of contracts, property rights, trust, corporate, and bankruptcy law, the modules of the code of capital. Capital owes its vibrancy and frequent transmutations (from land, to firms, to debt, to ideas, etc.) to the fact that private and not state actors code capital in law. Asset holders in search of higher returns and greater wealth have been the main driver for adapting the modules of the code to ever newer types of assets, but they needed lawyers to, quite literally, perform the deed. The asset holders and their lawyers did not steal the code, and neither was it handed to them on a silver platter. Rather, they benefited from the indeterminacy and malleability of private law on one hand, and on the other, a first mover advantage enshrined in the procedural law that governs the enforcement of claims.

Economists have long realized that contracts are incomplete.[11] The parties to a contract simply cannot foresee all possibilities the future might hold; trying to address every possible event that might affect their relation and providing for it in the contract would be far too costly, indeed hopeless, because the future can't be known at the time of contracting. If contracting parties are unable to write complete contracts, clearly lawmakers cannot write complete laws. The legislature's task is arguably even more difficult, because law is meant to apply not just to a single case, but to many like cases in the indefinite future. For this reason, statutory laws are often purposefully couched in general, open-ended language, which necessarily renders them highly incomplete.[12]

This does not mean that legislatures don't try to limit the scope of indeterminacy. They often include examples or illustrations to make statutes more specific and to turn general "standards" into specific "rules."[13] Yet, examples can always beget more examples and finite lists of contingencies encourage new differentiation around the edges. If A and B are prohibited, maybe one can structure a transaction as D. And if only X and Y are expressly allowed, surely a case can be made that Z is close enough to still fall within the ambit of the law.[14] Differentiating fact patterns or rules to carve out space for new coding strategies or, alternatively, using analogy to extend the reach of a given rule to a new fact pattern, are part of the ordinary toolkit that judges and lawyers employ day in and day out when interpreting and applying "the law." There is nothing pernicious about this, because a changing world will always leave even the most carefully crafted statutory or case law incomplete.

Law's inherent incompleteness therefore makes for fertile ground for legal creativity and imagination in every possible direction. It allows lawyers to graft the modules of the code onto new assets for which they were never designed, or to reconfigure existing assets to ensure that they can sidestep new regulations designed to limit the excesses of past coding strategies. These strategies employ the modules of the code to avoid restrictive rules and regulations, but without losing the endorsement by state law. The latter point is critical, because absent this endorsement, the legal attributes of priority, durability, universality, and convertibility that help turn a simple into a capital asset would not stick and the entire exercise would be in vain.

Most of the time, the boundaries of the code's modules are pushed slowly, step by step. If a legal module, such as the trust, can be used to harbor land and thereby protect it from creditors, perhaps it can protect other assets as well, such as government bonds or corporate shares, and eventually mortgage pools or their derivatives, such as CDOs. This gives you the history of trust law in a nutshell, from its feudal origins to modern-day shadow banking. Similarly, if swaps of government bonds are safe harbored in bankruptcy, why not extend this privilege to swaps and other derivatives of private assets, and not only to derivatives in the strict sense but also to repos; and why do this not only in one country, but why not lobby legislatures around the globe to create the conditions for global derivatives markets, no matter that it pushes the claims of other creditors further down, making it less likely that they will fully recover their own claims. This legal metamorphosis occurred from 1978 to 2005. In addition, if any man-made discovery or invention can be protected by patent, why not push patent authorities to recognize even the smallest alteration of nature's code as such an innovation? Once the US Supreme Court asserted that *parts* of nature's code might patentable in 1980,[15] the floodgates opened for biotech companies to renegotiate the boundaries of legally coding the code of nature with the patent office and the lower courts. Three decades later, the court had to find an answer to the question, whether nature's own genetic code could be enclosed by the legal code.

When new assets are coded as capital or established coding practices are extended beyond existing boundaries, every little step is carefully argued by the asset holders and their lawyers, the code's masters. They tend to be blind to the social implications of their actions, if only because the rights they claim can be traced to a legal order that has separated content from form—not the substance of a right, its purpose, but the form itself is what matters, as well as the legal coding techniques that can extend the legal attributes of capital to yet another claim that promises monetary returns. The autonomy of individual subjective rights as the foundation of the capitalist legal order creates the conditions for pushing the outer bounds of private entitlements.

Two features of private law have greatly facilitated a pattern of development that has bestowed legal privileges on some at the expense of others: its incompleteness, or indeterminacy, and its malleability. Indeterminacy makes law gameable; private law being not only indeterminate, but also highly malleable, makes gaming even easier.

Contract law is often viewed as the embodiment of private autonomy. It is up to the parties to the contract to further their own interests, and the law enforces contracts without paying attention to differences in actual bargaining power. In contrast, property rights are more carefully guarded by state law, because states effectively pre-commit to protect property rights against any contender, and most states assert their national law over assets that are located on their territory. However, states have lost control over assets that do not have a location, such as financial assets—but they have also been complicit in outsourcing law. They have changed their conflict-of-law rules to accommodate private autonomy, and private actors have seized the opportunity to mint assets in jurisdictions that give them the most options. It may still be the case that some intangibles, such as patents, require an act of state power, but carefully crafted coding strategies have pushed back against the restrictions that statute and case law may have erected in the past. One teacher of intellectual property rights reminisced about this erosion:

> The annual process of updating my syllabus for a basic Intellectual Property course provides a nice snapshot of what is going on. I can wax nostalgic looking back to a five-year-old text, with its

confident list of subject matter that intellectual property rights *couldn't* cover, the privileges that circumscribed the rights that did exist, and the length of time before a work falls into the public domain. In each case, the limits have been eaten away.[16]

Private law's incompleteness and malleability make the code's modules highly adaptive devices that can be used to respond to new legal and regulatory challenges as well as changes in the economic or social environment. The innovations take place in deals and transactions in which lawyers seek to ensure that their clients can accomplish their goals *legally*. They push the boundaries of existing law, using the power of legal reasoning to defend the likeness of the new devices to what courts have already approved, or to differentiate them from transactions that have been struck down. They don't always succeed, but they don't have to for the basic argument to hold. By constantly contesting the existing boundaries of legal rules in general, and by expanding the remit of the code's modules to make them fit for ever newer asset classes, lawyers turn any of their clients' assets into capital. At times, they might be violating the spirit of the law, but formal compliance is often deemed sufficient in legal systems that equate freedom with the respect for subjective rights and private autonomy.

The power of private law in coding capital is further evidenced in how infringements of this law are policed: it lies in the hands of private parties, not the state. There is no public agency that monitors ordinary breaches of contracts, infringements of property rights, or shareholder rights. The state, through its police force, prosecutors, or regulators, intervenes only when breaches reach the threshold of theft, fraud, or embezzlement—and even these boundaries are constantly under attack. Victims of lesser transgressions have to take the law into their own hands; and they will often have to bear the costs for doing so.[17] This is both a source of freedom for resourceful parties and the reason weaker parties—in terms of economic and legal prowess—so often have to seize their rights to them.

We have seen examples of how superior access to legal coding advantages the claims of some over others throughout this book. After the landlords fenced in the land that used to be held in common, the commoners first fought back in the field by breaking hedges and ploughing the fields that were now set aside for large sheep herds or cash crops. But they soon realized that in the long term, they could win their battle only in the courtroom and filed lawsuits—many of which they ultimately lost. Similarly, the plaintiffs that challenged Myriad's claim to exclusive property rights over the BRCA gene (see chapter 5) fought an uphill battle to protect nature's code as "a commons" to which all have access. They had to battle all the way to the US Supreme Court to make their case. They won, but that does not mean that the issue has been settled for similar patents. Whoever wishes to contest these other patents will have to fight similar battles, patent by patent.

Would-be plaintiffs face additional hurdles. For good reason, the law does not give access to courts to just anybody. As a general rule, only someone who was a party to the contract that was breached, is the owner of the property that was damaged, or was the victim of a harmful tortious action, has "standing" in court. If this were not the case, anybody with a grievance might file a suit, impose costs on others, and clog the court system. But for the legitimate plaintiffs, the costs of private policing often exceed its benefits, and many victims will discover a loss that empowers them to bring an action only too late to recover anything; they may be formally barred by statutes of limitation, which bar litigation after the lapse of time, or may find it difficult to obtain the evidence needed to make their case. Taken together, these hurdles give the coders of capital a first-mover advantage. A practice that may have been deemed a transgression of the rights of others when first introduced can therefore spread and evolve into a new standard of behavior before it is legally challenged; after all, if everybody does it, it can hardly be wrong. Courts might even sanction it as the new standard of behavior.

The first-mover advantage, which structurally disadvantages plaintiffs, can be overcome, at least in theory, by giving would-be plaintiffs powerful tools, such as class action suits; by affording them a multiple of the damages they have suffered; or by shifting the burden of proof to the defendant—all well-known strategies for rebalancing the legal powers between private opponents. It may not come as a surprise, however, that holders of capital have pushed back against such rebalancing; they have lobbied to roll back class action suits in countries where they were once common and have blocked them where they were not.[18] They have used their bargaining power to force their contracting parties, including consumers, to accept arbitration over courts for settling disputes and disavowing class actions in arbitration along the way. For the most part, they have gotten away with this, as courts seek answers in legal orders that favor private autonomy even when its use exerts costs on the rest,[19] and as legislatures bend over backwards to expand the scope of private autonomy in the hope of keeping the motor of the economy humming. The representatives of the people fail to see or do not want to see that the additional benefits they shower on capital serves primarily their individual holders, not society at large.

Policing the boundaries of private law is a constant battle, and a costly one. The players with the best access to the code's masters push existing boundaries of the code's modules to bestow yet another claim of know-how with durable priority rights that are shielded against the world. They are betting that they will not be challenged, at least not too soon. Time works in their favor, because even if they fail to convince a future court that their specific coding strategy should be upheld, they have likely reaped a lot of wealth in the meantime. A first mover can stake out a claim and simply wait to see what happens. The pattern is a little different when the creation of a legal right requires explicit state action, as in the case of patents or trademarks, for example. Here, the asset holder does not have the luxury of waiting; instead, she must battle her case first with the patent office and, if the legal privilege is denied, with the courts. Once granted, however, the burden to question this new property right falls on the challenger.

In sum, the code of capital benefits from law's indeterminacy, from private autonomy that makes the modules of the code highly malleable devices in the hands of sophisticated lawyers, and from the fact that aggressive coders can play offense and exploit first-mover advantages. Under these conditions, there is little reason for asset holders to bargain with the state as rational choice theorists would have it; all they need is a good lawyer who commands the skills to code their assets as capital. And, contrary to Marxists, they don't need to storm the Bastille to exercise power; they only need to position their lawyers at the major intersections of the nation's capital to manage the traffic lights so that they can ride a green wave.

Private Code and Public Power

Public power is essential for ensuring that the code's attributes are respected and enforced. Two parties can agree to a contract and live up to its terms, but if they want to prevent others from interfering with their agreement, they need more. Anyone can assert physical control over physical assets and claim that it has always been hers; but it takes vigilance and resources to protect assets in this fashion. If these costs can be socialized by delegating the protection of legal rights to a state, asset holders save huge costs. More important, they can use their assets in ways that simply would not be available otherwise. They can own assets without exercising physical control over them. They can even own intangibles, assets that cannot be touched and exist only in legal code, and move assets into legal shells where they are protected from their own creditors, pledge and even repledge them without leaving more than a paper trail. They can do all of this only with the help of law that is backed by state power.

Private and public power are often juxtaposed and depicted as engaged in ongoing bargaining with each other for favors. This, at least, is how public choice theories depict the relation between public and private, states and markets.[20] For Marxists, this separation between public and private makes little sense, because they view the ruling class as utilizing the state and its law for its own purposes. They own the state and therefore need not bargain with it. Neither perspective fully explains the materials presented in this book. Explicit bargains between public and private power are the exception rather than the rule. Most of the coding of capital occurs in small, incremental steps, in the context of private transactions and deals, by regulatory forbearance, and only in the occasional court case.

There is a palpable preference to move coding decisions outside the public eye; to leave them to private attorneys, not public legislatures, and to private arbitrators, not state courts; and to lobby for explicit legislative change only if there is no other option for advancing a new coding strategy or extending it to a new asset type.

The state and its agents, the courts and regulators, often play a passive role. There are times when they actively break down barriers to new coding strategies or extend additional legal subsidies to holders of capital—typically in the form of exemptions from existing rules or tax benefits. For the most part, however, the state needs to do little more than recognize and enforce the rights that private parties have coded in order to protect, and even expand, the interests of the holders of capital. This does not mean that the state always sides with capital. Efforts have been made in the past to balance powerful private property rights with public interests, which can take the form of seizing private property, although only for adequate compensation. Several legal systems have created powerful labor rights or have bestowed "new property rights" in the form of entitlements to social protection and other claims against the state on citizens that found themselves on the short end of a system that tends to create enormous wealth for some, while leaving the rest to fend for themselves.[21] Not only capital is coded in law, but so too are other entitlements; it is a matter of social choice to whom to leave the final say about which assets deserve special status in law. On balance, privately coded capital has won the day, time and again, although not with periodic convulsions that have forced the hand of legislatures to rebalance the playing field or at least to mitigate the losses that less well protected individuals face.

Indeed, Menke argues that the conflict between a liberal legal order that is single-mindedly focused on protecting private rights on one hand, and the use of law to advance social goals on the other, is built into the very fabric of the capitalist legal order. A legal order that has de-politicized the social sphere by fortifying private rights without regard to the effects the exercise of these rights might have on others, is prone to crises. It brings about "radically different positions of power," which endanger the system from within.[22] Therefore, the state has no choice but to counter, at least in times of crisis, the excesses of private rights coded in law.

This begs the question, how did this specific relation between private and public power, private code and public law, come about? No doubt, it manifested itself from time to time in revolutionary moments, most notably during the French Revolution and its (seemingly) radical shift from feudal privilege to private property. Property became a private right that enjoyed protection not only by, but from, the state. It marks the separation of the public and the private spheres, or so the argument goes.[23] It is certainly true that in the wake of the French Revolution, many old forms of property were formally abolished.[24] Many privileges of the past, however, crept into the new legal order. The new lawmakers initiated a massive property rights reform but took it upon themselves to classify assets into those that were stripped of legal recognition, and others that were still valid and therefore could be acquired by the new elites. The way they classified these different assets displayed a keen awareness for their respective economic potential.[25] The revolutionary moment notwithstanding, the transformation of property rights in France was more gradual and displayed more continuities than the bold political proclamations of the revolutionaries might suggest.

We have seen similar dynamics up close in England, where the absolute right of the king to all the land in the country conflicted with rising claims to absolute property rights of private parties, a struggle that played itself out over centuries in case law and legal treaties. It could not possibly be the case that both the king and private owners had absolute rights; private owners eventually prevailed in the case of freeholds, but only by chipping away at the superior rights of the king one case at a time. The new constitutional order that gradually emerged from the struggles in the fields and the courtroom was no longer governed by ad hoc privileges the Crown would bestow on its subjects, but by law.[26] Yet, as should be clear by now, there are plenty of ways to create a privilege in law if one can obtain control over the legal coding process.

The national legal orders that emerged in the late eighteenth century endorsed the sanctity of private autonomy, of contracts and property rights, and elevated these individual rights over others, over the rights of the commoners who were driven off the land, the indebted paupers who had to serve prison time for failing to pay their debt well into the nineteenth century—even as the better off merchants escaped this fate, and the workers whose attempts to organize themselves to enhance their bargaining powers were crushed, in the United States, for example, by invoking anti-trust law against labor unions.

Measures taken by states to strengthen the rights of the under-privileged were always viewed with suspicion and depicted as a potential infringement of private rights; as entitlements, not legal rights. Rights were deemed not only superior, but qualitatively different, because they were of God, of nature, or could be rationalized by efficiency claims. Globalization has further strengthened the powers of capital, which now has the option to choose from a menu of legal systems the one that best serves its interest; it has little reason to return home and therefore also no reason to strike a balance between its own claims for legal support and similar claims others may raise. Once the claims of capital holders have been vindicated in law, they assure a trickling-up effect, or perhaps horizontally to other aspiring asset holders around the globe, but with no guarantee of any trickling down.

Roving Capital

It has become quite fashionable to compare rulers and states with bandits. Charles Tilly compared the process of state-making in early modern Europe with organized crime.[27] The thugs first battled over territory until a winner emerged who secured the border of the conquered territory against external enemies. To stabilize his rule, the winner needed to secure internal peace as well, and to this end he built coalitions, paid off the clients of his collaborators, and with their help extracted resources from others to fund external and internal peacekeeping operations. Similarly, Mancur Olson has depicted alternative political systems as rule by either roving or stationary bandits.[28] Roving bandits pursue a scorched earth strategy; they move from place to place, extracting from each location as much as they need, and once they have exhausted the resources of one, they move on to loot another. Stationary bandits, in contrast, learn to leave enough to the people they conquered so they can extract resources from them in the long haul. They take all of the cream and most of the milk, but they leave enough behind to replenish the resources on which they depend. Stationary rulers are also bandits, but they are more benign for economic growth and development than their roving brethren.

Transposing Olson's imagery from states to capital, we might say that at the time when Adam Smith drew the image of the invisible hand, capital was mostly stationary. It ventured out to foreign shores but invariably returned home to take advantage of local institutions, and in doing so, asset holders necessarily shared some of their gains with their home base. In contrast, today's capital is of the roving kind; it has and needs no (physical) home and instead moves from place to place in search of new opportunities. Because capital depends on law to thrive, it cannot become completely footloose; it always needs a state's helping hand—but, and this is critical, not necessarily its home state. Any state that recognizes and enforces the legal coding of capital will do.

States have actively participated in turning stationary capital into roving capital by breaking down legal barriers and expanding its holders' private autonomy. They have allowed private actors to choose the law that governs their assets without losing access to coercive law enforcement, they have offered their own laws to foreign capital for business on shore or off shore, and they have agreed with other states to recognize and even to reciprocate the deals each offers to capital within its own borders. Writing in the 1940s and trying to make sense of the collapse of legal and social orders at the heart of Europe, Polanyi asserted that long-distance trade subordinated societies to the market principle with the states' helping hand. Globalization, one might add, has completed this process. The advocates of globalization have ignored his warning that this radical transformation is one of the root causes for the rise of communism and fascism in the early twentieth century.[29]

In fact, globalization is the product of a greatly expanded choice set for the coders of capital. Competition, including legal and regulatory competition, can promote innovation and change and should therefore be embraced.[30] The presence of a plurality of legal orders from which at least some stakeholders could choose in the Middle Ages, for example, has been singled out as a key factor in fostering the rule of law by using legal competition as a check on state power.[31] It gave persons who sought legal protection more than one legal system or court system to choose from and thereby helped reign in overt corruption and capture. Legal competition, however, is different from competition over goods and services, because the object of this competition is law, the means by which societies are governed or govern themselves.

In addition, legal and regulatory competition are not equally available to all. Albert Hirschman illuminated the power dynamics in organizations, a firm, an association, or a state, by suggesting that any member of such an organization has essentially three options: exit, voice, and loyalty.[32] Members can vote with their hands or with their feet; if neither works, they have no option but to be loyal. In large organizations with many members, only few have an effective voice. This is why exit is such an important option to have. Not everybody, however, has the same exit options. It takes resources to move physically, and it takes law and good lawyers to move legally. Moreover, the current legally constructed global order allows asset holders to fully exploit the benefits of legal and regulatory competition, while confining natural persons to the country of their citizenship. Legal persons can easily roam the globe and enrich their owners, and the holders of capital can search for the legal order that gives it the best protections. In contrast, natural persons are held up at borders and can cross only, if at all, with visas. If only some have a viable exit option, they can turn this into a bargaining chip, even into a business strategy. If they do not get what they want from one state, they threaten to leave, either physically or, cheaper yet, by adopting another country's laws for their coding purposes. For roving capital, the law of a given state is just an option, which its holders and their master coders will exercise only if it promises greater wealth than the laws of another state.

Governing the Code

Every society faces the fundamental question about how to govern itself. This is a choice not only between democracy and autocracy, parliamentarian and presidential systems, constitutional powers or the voting system; it is also a choice about creating and allocating wealth, and this includes the legal tools for coding capital.

If the capacity to create or secure private wealth is coded in law, as I have argued throughout this book, then the power to control the coding of capital is key for the distribution of wealth in society. It is easy to agree that the state should protect property rights and enforce contracts. More important, but less often asked, is the question, who determines what assets or claims deserve to be coded as property or receive legal protection on par with property rights. This has become largely a matter of private choice, a choice that is exercised more often than not by the current or prospective holders of capital themselves.

There is nothing wrong with private choice—as long as it does not impose a burden on others or piggyback on state power to enforce that burden, as this smacks of moral hazard and inefficiencies.[33] Yet, the practice of coding capital is largely exempt from the level of scrutiny that is applied to other forms of privileges or subsidies that are granted by the state. Law is taken as a given, as exogenous to the assets that are the harbingers of wealth; and enormous deference is given to the claim that one's actions are "legal," that they are based on rights. The aura of authority immunizes the legal production of wealth in society from political scrutiny. The legalization of private interests has depoliticized critical questions of self-governance.

Subsidies and other "entitlements" are typically viewed with great suspicion, because they are regarded as distortive of markets and lead to inefficiencies, even corruption. Yet, the legal protections capital enjoys are arguably the mother of all subsidies. Without the code's modules and the possibility to fashion them to one's liking, neither capital nor capitalism would exist. The code's modules are available off the shelf, but their power depends on the widely held expectation that they will be enforced, if necessary, by state power.

The masters of the code know how to code capital without losing the guarantee of enforceability. They don't require state approval beforehand and they can opt into private arbitration or negotiate settlements to insulate their private coding strategies from courts as the guardians of the law, not just the private interests in a given dispute. Yet, capital needs the state and its powers in more than one way. Its holders also rely on state power in times of crisis, when only state intervention can prevent the collapse of the value of their assets for fear that failing to do so might bring down the entire system. In these ad hoc rescue actions, the "feudal calculus" reigns overtly;[34] but it is equally present in every exemption and special treatment that capital and its holders enjoy.[35]

The feudal calculus stands in direct tension to the aspiration of democratic polities for which law is the primary tool of collective self-governance. In the current configuration of rights and law, this tool is bent toward capital. Rising inequality is the logical conclusion of a legal order that systematically privileges some holders' assets, but not others. This is the case especially in a globalized world, in which intervention on the side of the less advantaged can be so easily punished by capital taking to the exit. The logical result of such a system is rising inequality and the disenfranchisement of the democratic constituents, of "we, the people" in determining if and how law should be employed to protect some at the expense of others.

Even the *Financial Times*, which can hardly be accused of socialist leanings, has recently called for a new social contract between capital and society.[36] This proposal presumes that there is still a well-organized society that could possibly be a match for capital and, in addition, that roving capital has an interest in cutting a deal with society from which it has safely escaped with law's help. The truth is that in a world in which well-coded roving capital faces a diffuse and unorganized public scattered over multiple polities, a social contract is beyond reach, even if capital wanted it for the sake of its own survival.

In response, disgruntled voters have turned against their own leaders, forcing them to take seriously the ones who have been left behind by decades of policies that dismantled most protections for jobs and lowered expectations of ordinary people without any assets or assets that enjoy special legal protection. These voters sense that they have lost control over shaping their own destiny with the tool they had taken for granted: the laws their legislatures pass and the cases their courts decide. Blaming other states, supranational organizations, such as the European Union and, most conveniently, natural persons with no or only a foreign passport, is hardly a solution when in fact the real winners are hiding in plain sight in their own midst and use the law to fashion their capital.

For democracy to prevail in capitalist systems, polities must regain control over law, the only tool they have to govern themselves, and this must include the modules of the code of capital. At the very least, they must roll back the many legal privileges that capital has come to enjoy over and above the modules of the code of capital. Short of another massive financial crisis and its unpredictable aftermath, a fundamental restructuring of the legal systems that support capitalism may be impossible. Too much is at stake and the defense "it is legal" is a powerful and potentially expensive one. After all, holders of assets that currently enjoy the status of property rights or similar entitlements will demand compensation for expropriation should the scope of their legal rights be curtailed. Given the amount of wealth that is tied up in property rights, collateral, trust, and corporate law, a peaceful or affordable reconfiguration of rights may well be beyond reach.

Yet, the fact that capital depends on state law and state enforcement of private contracts and deeds gives agency to lawmakers, legislatures, courts, and regulators. If they can free themselves from the cognitive (and in some cases) financial grip of capital, they may help advance the project of democratic self-governance. The basic task would be to roll back control by current asset holders and their lawyers over the code of capital by limiting the choices lawyers have at their disposal when coding capital, but also by granting special legal protections to assets (and their holders) that have been neglected in the past.

A first step in this direction would be a bright-line rule to refrain from offering capital legal privileges over and above the basic modules of the code. The default answer to requests for new exemptions, special regulation, or preferential tax treatments should simply be "no." Claims that this would deny some actors the opportunity to increase the pie to the benefit of all should be eyed with suspicion, as past experience shows that even big pies are usually devoured in solitude or only by invited guests. Whoever claims that individual private gains will translate into social welfare improvement should bear the burden of proof for showing the mechanisms by which this feat will be accomplished. Enough of waving the invisible hand; as this book has shown, the legal infrastructure has long been put in place to allow savvy asset holders to reap the full returns of their selfish action. We need real arguments and proof, not fairy tales, to show that the societies that sponsor the legal code will get their share.

Next, choosing the law that is most convenient for your own interest should be made more difficult. Some might denounce this as protectionism; in fact, it follows from basic principles of democratic self-governance. Democratic polities govern themselves by law; the more loopholes there are for some to escape the reach of these laws, the less effective self-governance will be. There should be room for mutual recognition between states to avoid duplication of regulatory efforts and burdens, but there should be far fewer opportunities for asset holders to go on a legal shopping spree. To achieve this end, coordinated action by states is desirable, but not absolutely necessary. The conflict-of-law rules that facilitate the legal mobility of capital are part of domestic legal orders and for the most part are not enshrined in international treaty law and may therefore be rolled back by one state at a time.[37] Doing so may incur the wrath of foreign investors, and domestic capital holders may threaten to exit, but realizing these threats would be quite costly for many. Even if real, the effects the exit by some might have on the economy should be balanced against social and political benefit of retaining the option to self-govern. Incidentally, rolling back the choice of the place of incorporation might also be a more potent weapon against tax sheltering than blacklisting countries that offer competitive tax rates. If a corporation exists only as a legal shell for the sole purpose of avoiding taxes or engaging in regulatory arbitrage, why recognize it as a legal person?[38]

Third, arbitration or the private settlement of disputes may be great ways to resolve disputes among parties with roughly equal bargaining power and for matters that do not affect others. It is one thing for private arbitrators to resolve a contractual dispute; it is quite a different story when private arbitrators preside over issues of social concern, as they do in investor-state disputes, when they trespass into major policy issues, such as anti-trust law or other regulatory domains, or when they resolve cases between parties with highly unequal bargaining powers as they do in disputes involving consumers.

Fourth, capital often imposes costly externalities on others, especially when asset holders mistake the legal certainty that well-designed coding strategies offer them for guaranteed future returns. Building one's fortunes on such mistaken assumptions typically ends not only in tears but in a crisis that imposes costs on many others, not just the privileged asset holders. Like any negative externality, this one must be proactively guarded against. There is no evidence that asset holders will ever fully internalize the social costs of exploring every loophole or ambiguity in the law to avoid regulatory costs without losing the legal protections they need. Rather, they will take what they can get and, when a crisis looms, will head for the exit, or, in the alternative, will present states with a put option to protect them or else risk the implosion of the entire system—an option that states usually find hard to refuse. Waiting until the crisis strikes rather than seeking to preempt it is therefore an invitation for bailouts, because states will always do "whatever it takes" to ensure stability, as their own rule depends on it.

Fifth, laws and regulations that curtail the ability to freely choose the legal modules necessary for converting simple into capital assets and any other regulatory constraints meant to limit the externalities that capital holders impose on the rest, will, of course, be attacked the minute capital has been pulled from the abyss—typically with a helping hand from a state, though not necessarily its home state. To counter capital's tendency to regain its hold over lawmakers and regulators, new mechanisms are needed that give voice to the ones who have the most to lose in a crisis. This may include empowering affected parties to seek compensation for damages ex post, and in amounts that may exert effective deterrence.[39] There is no need to re-invent the wheel, as treble and punitive damages, class action suits, or injunctive relief have long been part of the legal toolkit legislatures and courts have developed to level the playing field. Not every mechanism will suit every legal system and careful tailoring will be required, but clearly, leaving the monitoring and supervision of capital to state regulators is not sufficient. The history of capital suggests that the asset holders themselves, including their lawyers, tend to do too little too late and pass the costs of their past coding strategies to the rest of society.

Sixth, age-old limitations on coding capital that have been dismantled over time should be resurrected. A good start would be the principle that purely speculative contracts, or wagers, are not enforceable in a court of law. The elimination of this time-tested doctrine with the argument that it may no longer be impossible to distinguish between good capital and bad speculation speaks volumes. As others have argued, the US Commodities Futures Modernization Act of 2000 has contributed substantially to the rise of derivatives, many of which were used purely for speculative purposes.[40] It may be possible to use credit derivatives for hedging purposes instead, but the burden of proof should be on their users, not the public at large, and there is little reason to add additional privileges to such assets, by, for example, safe-harboring them from bankruptcy. This follows already from the first principle: no additional legal privileges for assets that enjoy the privileges of the legal code.[41]

Seventh, there is much to be said for democracies to join forces and pursue these strategies in tandem to avoid subjecting themselves to regulatory competition. This does not necessarily require a concerted act of legal harmonization, which is too slow and too ridden with influence by special interests. As long as a significant number of countries make some changes along the lines suggested above, this would make a difference. Ideally, the polities that sponsor the legal systems at the heart of global finance—the United States (or

New York State for a start) and the United Kingdom—should take the lead, but currently this is still not very likely, notwithstanding the severe political backlash both countries are currently dealing with at home. The UK electorate has forced its government to take leave from Europe—mistakenly believing that Brussels rather than "the city" are the cause of their predicament. In the United States, President Trump tapped into the sentiment of part of the electorate, which feels that it has lost control over its own future. Unfortunately, he is using the support of his base not to right wrongs, but to wage ad hoc battles with all institutions, domestic and international, that stand in the way of his vision of a strong America. In the best of all worlds, the internal struggles of these two countries will make for a new opening, in which even roving capital concedes that without a more reliable state at the center of the global capitalist system, it may lose too, and thereby make way for a rebalancing of the interests of capital with other social goals. The hope is that this will happen without a crisis on the scale that prompted Polanyi to warn against the subversion of society to the market principle against which society will eventually revolt.

And, finally, there are the lawyers, the masters of the code of capital. Not all lawyers are in the business of coding capital, and even the ones that end up doing it rarely went to law school with this goal in mind. Yet, the market for young lawyers, the pay structure at law firms, and the relentless push to recruit clients in order to make it to partnership hardly incentivize lawyers to employ their skills creatively for purposes other than capital. Moreover, given the high costs they must pay for law schools, especially in the United States, and the debts they incur in the process, many do not have a realistic alternative but to spend at least the first part of their career in its service. Some law schools renounce their fees retroactively for the select alumni who practice in underpaid jobs after leaving law school, such as nongovernmental or human rights organizations. But clearly, few law schools would survive if most of their students chose this career path.[42] If lawyers wish to become truly independent from capital, we need to deeply rethink how to fund legal education, and how to structure pay at leading law firms. Without these structural changes, proposals to subject lawyers to more training in ethics are unlikely to bear much fruit.

These roll-back strategies may be less than some readers might have hoped for. And yet, one of the major lessons of coding capital is that persistent incrementalism has advanced the interests of capital holders; persistent incrementalism, I suggest, may also be a viable strategy to push back and ensure that democratic polities may rule themselves by law.

Law without Capital?

There is no capital without law, because only law can bestow priority, durability, convertibility, and universality on assets, and thereby privileges its holders. Capitalism exists because modern legal systems are built on and around individual subjective rights and put the state in the service of protecting these rights. Even though these rights are couched as negative rights against the state, they have been turned into a claim for positive protection by the state against intrusion by others, including fellow citizens.[43] As negative rights, they are effectively used to prevent the state from crafting similar legal protection for other interests, not just the assets capital holders select themselves. In legal systems that are configured in this way, capital will continue to rule, and law will remain its primary tool. Rolling back the legal privileges on certain assets as suggested above will therefore not alter the game; it will only balance the one-sided empowerment of capital and thereby make capitalism more sustainable.

The fact that capital cannot rule without law does not imply the reverse, namely that law could not be used to protect other interests on par with capital. One could, for example, harness the code and its modules to empower others who have experienced the empire of law mostly from below: as losers in the battles over enclosure of land, knowledge, or nature, as mostly involuntary risk bearers of a financial system that primarily benefits the one percent at the top, or as workers in firms whose expectations to future income are denied the same protection that shareholders' expectations to future profit have readily received.

Several examples for such a strategy have already been discussed. Recall the quest of the Maya in Belize to have their indigenous use rights recognized as property rights under their country's constitution; or the ability of advocacy groups representing scientists and patients to marshal a successful challenge against patenting genes, or the movements to protect open sources in the digital world.[44] Oftentimes, these creative strategies of employing the powers of the legal code to different ends are met with only temporary success. In the case of the Maya, discussed in chapter 2 of this book, the highest court of Belize recognized centuries-old use practices as property, yet its own government decided instead to side with capital. There is no better proof that property rights without state backing are not worth much; and property rights that do not promise returns, including tax revenue for the state, apparently are less likely to get a helping hand from the state.

More generally stated, elevating new claims by bestowing on them legal protection of the kind that capital has enjoyed for centuries does not change the system; it reproduces it. In the absence of better solutions, this may not be a bad outcome. But it may still be worth pondering what a truly different solution might look like. Currently, there are two radically different options on the table.

One option is to do away with the legal privileges of capital and turn our economic and political system into "radical markets."[45] According to Posner and Weyl, radical markets are meant to dismantle the last vestiges of politics by subordinating all decisions and, one might add, all values, to the price mechanism. The two authors claim that the efficient allocation of resources based on a fully competitive market is the path to a "just society."[46] It follows that property rights shall be replaced with contingent use rights.

Rather than hoarding wealth over time and protecting it against competing challenges, in this new world, the law protects only temporal use rights. These use rights can be challenged by anybody who offers a price over and above the value we have assigned to these assets. Our own asset valuations will be recorded in a public register and will also be used as the basis for taxing our wealth. Attempts to protect your wealth by increasing its value will therefore be punished by taxes, and doing the reverse, that is, undervaluing your assets to avoid taxes, will likely trigger offers by others who wish to buy them at the lower price. In stark contrast to existing law, which requires that both parties to a contract agree to the exchange, unilateral offers shall become binding. Consensus is eradicated and substituted with a social rule that price trumps everything else. Refusing a bid for one's assets will be sanctioned as theft. This is consistent with the premise of *radical markets*, because if the law protects only temporal use rights, then refusal to relinquish control after a bid effectively ends the term is a violation of the law. Implementing this radical proposal is likely to trigger a serious backlash once individuals and entities with enormous resources are set loose to claim any asset for which they can pay a higher price, unless a massive redistribution of resources precedes these reforms—but on this, the two authors are silent.

Establishing radical markets may sound radical, but it is only the logical conclusion of attempts to eliminate political deliberation from economic life and to privatize the governance of society in the hands of the most resourceful. Or, as Menke put it, "The individual pays for its political empowerment by subjective rights the price of disempowering politics."[47]

The alternative to marketizing society is the re-politicization of social and economic life through a transformation of rights, this time not as enduring privileges for the self-select few, but as temporal empowerment for change. In his *Critique of Rights*, Christoph Menke maps out a vision of a system in which there will still be rights and there will still be law, but neither will be available primarily to defend the status quo. His starting point is a fundamental critique of the philosophical base of our rights-based legal system. Their natural law foundation, he suggests, is not just myth, it is a lie. The modern system of rights, which has officially abandoned god and other extra-legal powers, still selects some claims as worthy of rights protection on principles that stand outside the legal system. This legalization of extra-legal claims undermines the claim that our system is one of rights, of the rule of law rather than the rule of man. After all, someone must identify claims as rights and fortify them with legal protection.

Turning this critique into a vision of a new legal order, Menke argues that no civil rights should be sacrosanct forever; instead, all rights and all claims to rights need be assessed in their relation to the rights of others—they must be reflexive.[48] The state's coercive power that protects rights and law should no longer be used to protect the status quo, but to empower the future. Just as in Posner and Weyl's account, rights become more transitory than they currently are, but there are important differences. Whereas the radical market model prophesizes that change lies in the sum of all transactions that individuals will trigger through their unilateral actions, in Menke's sketch of a new order, change results from an open political process in which all may, but nobody has to, participate. In this new order, rights are purposefully forged to achieve change and lose at least some of their power once a given purpose has been achieved to make way for new rights and new purposes.

Which of these alternatives one prefers will depend largely on one's view of humans as either self-interested, profit-maximizing individuals, or as social beings capable of self-reflection and collective self-governance. It also depends on one's idea of freedom—economic freedom devoted to a sole cause, that of efficient resource allocation with the help of the pricing mechanism, or only as a means to an end, the end being individual freedom within a just society.[49] These big philosophical debates cannot be resolved here. But contrasting these two models helps illuminate two core messages of this book.

First, law is central for the organization of modern society, including for the organization of markets and the assets that are created for and traded on them. Law creates the conditions for realizing our individual and social aspirations either as preference aggregating machines in a system in which efficiency is idolized, or as autonomous individuals in a deliberative polity, where reason, not just money, rules. Through law, societies commit to preserve formal rights, insulate them from political contestation, subordinate them to the market, but might also turn transitory rights into instruments of change.

Second, without power, law is at best fleeting and at worse ineffective. As different as the two visions of Posner and Weyl on one hand, and Menke on the other, are, both will need to be implemented, and both will require at least the threat of coercion to do so. Just imagine the amount of resources that would have to be devoted to evict reluctant home owners from their houses, not because they defaulted, but because someone else came along and offered a price higher than their estimate and beyond their own means. Back in the sixteenth century, the commoners who were excluded from their land were threatened with capital punishment. Even without going that far, radical markets will have to rely on equally radical state law.

Similarly, attempts to transform our current system of subjective rights, as Menke advises, will undoubtedly trigger massive claims for compensation, because altering existing rights will likely be declared an expropriation that requires adequate compensation, lest they will be deemed unconstitutional.

The situation we confront is like the joke about the two farmers in Ireland who met somewhere in the hills of Donegal and one asked the other for the best way to Dublin. "Don't start from here," was the answer.[50] This suggests that there may not be a viable alternative to the pragmatic, gradual approach sketched out in the previous section, to rolling back the legal privileges that give capital its edge over competing claims, but also to legally empowering stakeholders other than capital holders, one step at a time. If done with the same care and stubbornness with which capital has been coded over the centuries, capital's and its holders' stronghold over our laws may be weakened. After all, the attributes of capital, its priority, durability, convertibility, and universality are relative, not absolute, rights. They privilege some assets relative to others, or their holders over others who lack access to assets or to the code's masters. This also means that as more assets receive comparable treatment, capital's relative value will be diminished.

Coding new rights in law may be another path out of the dilemma we currently face, caught between capital holders that claim the law for themselves and a democratic public that is desperately trying to regain control over its own destiny by electing whoever promises to do so. It will make visible the critical role of law in determining an asset's worth but also demonstrate that the power to determine the contents of law lies ultimately with the people as the sovereign of democratic, constitutional systems;[51] not with asset holders, and neither with the lawyers, their master coders. Only from such a deliberate effort can come a true transformation, not an elimination, of rights and of law. This does not exclude the possibility to delegate some coding to private actors, but would subject private coding efforts to more careful scrutiny to ensure their compliance with social goals that societies set for themselves through law.

The only other trajectories are a violent disruption of the current order, that is, a true revolution, or, short of it, the further erosion of law's legitimacy as a means of social ordering. The first outcome cannot be excluded entirely, but revolutions to overcome capitalism have been far less common than Marx and his followers have predicted. The second trajectory may, sadly, already be under way, as illustrated by the rampant attacks on independent judiciaries and the free press, not only in relatively young democracies, such as Poland or Hungary, but in countries with a long tradition of democracy and the rule of law, such the United Kingdom and the United States. If these trends continue, naked power will once more gain sway over legal ordering, as it has done over most of human history—and we will all be worse off for it.

NOTES

Chapter 1. Empire of Law

1. Facundo Alvaredo et al., *World Inequality Report 2018* (Creative Commons Licence 4.0-CC-BY-NC-SA 4.0: World Inequality Lab, 2017), fig. E4 at p. 13. The data measure the sum of all national income at the global level, where national income includes public and private income as well as income from existing resources, labor, and the expected value of future gains.

2. Note that in terms of global income, they still fall squarely in the center of the income curve, accounting for the range from 50th to 90th percentiles.

3. Fukuyama's provocative thesis about the "end of history" has become emblematic for this period. See Francis Fukuyama, *The End of History and the Last Man* (New York: Free Press, 1992).

4. See, for example, Ellen Meiksins Wood, *The Origin of Capitalism: A Longer View* (London, New York: Verso, 1999).

5. Joseph E. Stiglitz, *Globalization and Its Discontents* (New York, London: Norton, 2002); Dani Rodrik, *The Globalization Paradox* (New York: Norton, 2011).

6. Thomas Piketty, *Capital in the 21st Century* (Cambridge, MA: Harvard University Press, 2014).

7. This is, according to Padgett, the key question in the evolution of institutions. See the introduction to John F. Padgett and W. W. Powell, eds., *The Emergence of Organizations and Markets* (Princeton, NJ: Princeton University Press, 2010).

8. Morgan Ricks, *The Money Problem* (Chicago: University of Chicago Press, 2016).

9. Piketty, *Capital*, suggested a global capital gains tax, that is, a tax on assets owned by an individual, to address the problem of inequality he had documented in this book. Yet, the coordination of such a tax at the global level might be impossible for political reasons, and for many countries may not even be desirable, as Tsilly Dagan has shown in her recent book. See Tsilly Dagan, *International Tax Policy: Between Competition and Cooperation* (Cambridge: Cambridge University Press, 2018).

10. For a heroic effort to quantify GDP growth over the centuries, see Angus Maddison, *The World Economy—Historical Statistics* (Paris: OECD, 2003).

11. See Douglass C. North and Barry R. Weingast, "Constitutions and Commitment: The Evolution of Institutions Governing Public Choice in

Seventeenth-Century England," *Journal of Economic History* 49, no. 4 (1989):803–832; and David S. Landes, *The Wealth and Poverty of Nations* (New York, London: Norton, 1998).

12. See also Jonathan Nitzan and Shimshon Bichler, "New Imperialism or New Capitalism?," *Review (Fernand Braudel Center)* 29, no. 1 (2006):1–86, esp. p. 26.

13. Piketty, *Capital*.

14. The title of chap. 3 of his book.

15. Bernard Rudden, "Things as Things and Things as Wealth," *Oxford Journal of Legal Studies* 14, no. 1 (1994):81–97, pp. 82–83.

16. Adam Smith, *The Wealth of Nations* (Chicago: University of Chicago Press, 1776), book IV, chapter 2, p. 477.

17. Ibid., p. 475.

18. Ibid. Emphasis added. The second force behind the invisible hand is more familiar. Individuals in pursuit of their self-interest, Smith argues, will choose from many projects the one with the greatest value "either of money or of other goods" and will do so more effectively than a king, council, or senator.

19. For details, see chapter 7.

20. See the entry "empire" in William Darity Jr., ed., *International Encyclopedia of the Social Sciences*, 2nd ed., vol. 2 (Detroit, MI: Macmillan, 2008), where the concept is defined as "a large political body that rules over territories outside its original borders."

21. The preamble of the US Constitution famously opens with these words: "*We, the People* of the United States, in Order to form a more perfect Union, establish Justice, insure domestic Tranquility, provide for the common defence, promote the general Welfare, and secure the Blessings of Liberty to ourselves and our Posterity, do ordain and establish this Constitution for the United States of America" (emphasis added). Text available at http://constitutionus.com/.

22. This will be explained at great length in chapter 6.

23. See also Avi J. Cohen and G. C. Harcourt, "Whatever Happened to the Cambridge Capital Theory Controversies?," *Journal of Economic Perspectives* 17, no. 1 (2003):199–214, p. 200, calling the meaning of capital one of the "unresolved controversies over deep issues."

24. Karl Marx, *Das Kapital* (London: Lawrence and Wishart, 1974).

25. Fernand Braudel, *Sozialgeschichte des 15.—18. Jahrhunderts: Der Handel (Social History of the 15th—18th centuries: Trade)* (München: Kindler, 1991), p. 248.

26. Anti-usury rules were common in the West until well into the nineteenth century; at first, they were restricted only to transactions with members of the same faith, and over time became rather toothless, as lawyers learned how to transact around them. For a succinct history of the religious origins of usury rules, see Mark Koyama, "Evading the 'Taint of Usury': The Usury Prohibition as a Barrier to Entry," *Explorations in Economic History* 47, no. 4 (2010):420–442.

27. Geoffrey M. Hodgson, *Conceptualizing Capitalism: Institutions, Evolution, Future* (Chicago: University of Chicago Press, 2015), chap. 7 at p. 173.

28. Ibid., p. 176, with reference to Adam Smith's conception of capital.

29. Jonathan Haskel and Stian Westlake, *Capitalism without Capital: The Rise of the Intangible Economy* (Princeton, NJ: Princeton University Press, 2018).

30. See only Stiglitz, in a review of Piketty's book. Joseph Stiglitz, "New Theoretical Perspectives on the Distribution of Income and Wealth Among Individuals," *NBER Working Paper* (2014).

31. Eric Hobsbawm, *The Age of Capital: 1848–1875* (New York: Vintage, 1996). See also Meiksins Wood, *Origin of Capitalism.* Robert Brenner, *Merchants and Revolution: Commercial Change, Political Conflict, and London's Overseas Traders, 1550–1653* (Princeton, NJ: Princeton University Press, 1993).

32. David Harvey, *The Enigma of Capital and the Crisis of Capitalism* (Oxford: Oxford University Press, 2010), p. 40.

33. Karl Polanyi, *The Great Transformation: The Political and Economic Origins of Our Time* (Boston: Beacon Press, 1944), p. 72.

34. See, however, Bruce Carruthers, "Financialization and the Institutional Foundations of the New Capitalism," *Socio-Economic Review* 13, no. 2 (2015):379–398, who seems to conflate commodities with capital and markets with capitalism.

35. See Cohen and Harcourt, "Whatever Happened," at p. 201 for a good summary of the theory and the assumptions that go into this equation. For definitions that exclude human resources from capital, see Piketty, *Capital*, p. 46, and Hodgson, *Conceptualizing Capitalism*, p. 186, arguing that humans cannot collateralize themselves.

36. See Ludovic Hunter-Tilney, "Ludo Ltd: What I've Learnt as a One-Man Corporation," *Financial Times*, April 7, 2017, available at www.ft.com (last accessed November 16, 2017).

37. Hodgson, *Conceptualizing Capitalism*, p. 188, emphasizing that wage labor cannot collateralize itself.

38. Priest suggests that in colonial America, about 35.6 percent of the wealth in Southern states were slaves and 48.6 percent held in the form of land. See Claire Priest, "Creating an American Property Law: Alienability and Its Limits in American History," *Harvard Law Review* 120, no. 2 (2006):385–459.

39. Stephanie McCurry, "The Plunder of Black Life," *Times Literary Supplement*, May 17, 2017.

40. Katherine Franke, *Repair: Redeeming the Promise of Abolition* (Chicago: Haymarket Books, forthcoming). On the financial and commercial entanglement of the Northern states in the United States with the slave-owning Southern states, see Maeve Glass, "Citizens of the State," *University of Chicago Law Review* 85 no. 4 (2018):865–934, p. 865.

41. Geoffrey M. Hodgson, *How Economics Forgot History: The Problem of Historical Specificity in Social Science* (London and New York: Routledge, 2001). Hodgson has kept much of their work alive. For an excellent summary of their contribution to the concept of capital, see chap. 7 of his book *Conceptualizing Capitalism*.

42. Thorstein Veblen, "On the Nature of Capital," *Quarterly Journal of Economics* 22, no. 4 (1908):517–542.

43. John R. Commons, *The Legal Foundations of Capitalism* (New York: Mac-Millan, 1924), p. 28.

44. Commons based this analysis on the famous slaughterhouse cases. See ibid., pp. 13 and 21, where he argues that the "substance" of capitalism is "production for the use of others and acquisition for the use of self, such that the meaning of property and liberty spreads out from the expected uses of production and consumption to the expected transactions on the markets."

45. Jonathan Levy, "Capital as Process and the History of Capitalism," *Business History Review* 91 (Autumn 2017):483–510, p. 487.

46. On the "new capitalism" see Nitzen and Bichler, "New Imperialism or New Capitalism?," and Carruthers, "Financialization."

47. The term "financialization" is widely attributed to Greta A. Krippner, "The Financialization of the American Economy," *Socio-Economic Review* 3, no. 2 (2005):173–208; see also Krippner, *Capitalizing on Crisis* (Cambridge, MA: Harvard University Press, 2011).

48. The traditional civil codes include contract, property, family law, and inheritance law, while the commercial codes govern contracts among merchants, including agency relations, and the law of business organizations. The French "Code Civil" was enacted in 1804 followed by the commercial code in 1807. The German civil code followed only in 1900, almost three decades after Germany's unification in 1871.

49. Note that the terms "collateral" and "security" or "secured interests" are often used interchangeably. For an analysis of the legal techniques and practices of collateral in global capital markets, see Annelise Riles, *Collateral Knowledge: Legal Reasoning in the Global Financial Markets* (Chicago: University of Chicago Press, 2011).

50. See also Hernando De Soto, *The Mystery of Capital: Why Capitalism Triumphs in the West and Fails Everywhere Else* (New York: Basic Books, 2003), p. 46, arguing that property rights can turn "dead" land into "life" capital.

51. This feature of legal personality has been dubbed "asset shielding" or "asset partitioning." See Henry Hansmann and Reinier Kraakman, "The Essential Role of Organizational Law," *Yale Law Journal* 110, no. 3 (2000):387–475, and Henry Hansmann, Reinier Kraakman, and Richard Squire, "Law and the Rise of the Firm," *Harvard Law Review* 119, no. 5 (2006):1333–1403. For details, see chapter 3.

52. The ability to maintain its nominal value distinguishes state money from private money. See Ricks, *The Money Problem*, and the discussion in chapter 4.

53. The notion of private money will be explained in chapter 4; for a discussion of cryptocurrencies, see chapter 8.

54. See, for example, Bernard S. Black, "Is Corporate Law Trivial?: A Political and Economic Analysis," *Northwestern University Law Review* 84 (1990):542–597. While Black limited his argument to corporate law, its gist, namely the power of markets to discipline and incentivize market participants, has been transferred to other aspects of economic life. Indeed, a cottage industry in law and economics has sought to demonstrate the irrelevance of law for economics.

See only Robert C. Ellickson, *Order Without Law—How Neighbors Settle Disputes* (Cambridge, MA: Harvard University Press, 1991) and Lisa Bernstein, "Opting Out of the Legal System: Extralegal Contractual Relations in the Diamond Industry," *Journal of Legal Studies* 21, no. 1 (1992):115–157. The arguments of these authors have strong Hayekian flavor. Hayek famously argued that law is older than states and that people are capable of governing themselves in a bottom-up process. Friedrich A. Hayek, *Law, Legislation and Liberty—Rules and Order*, vol. 1 (Chicago: University of Chicago Press, 1973).

55. See Douglas G. Baird, *The Elements of Bankruptcy* (New York: Westbury, 1993) for a functional account of bankruptcy law (focused on the United States).

56. Arruñada calls this "sequential exchange" and argues that it relies on a property regime that is enforced by impartial authorities. See Benito Arruñada, "Property as sequential exchange: the forgotten limits of private contract," *Journal of Institutional Economics* 13, no. 4 (2017):753–783; for a qualified endorsement of this thesis, see Henry Smith, "Property as Complex Interaction," *Journal of Institutional Economics* 13, no. 4 (2017):809–814.

57. See Avner Greif, *Institutions and the Path to the Modern Economy: Lessons from Medieval Trade (Political Economy of Institutions and Decisions)* (Cambridge: Cambridge University Press, 2006), who contrasts the experience of the Maghribi traders with the rise of Genova as a powerful hub for trade and the law that governs it.

58. Dan Berkowitz, Katharina Pistor, and Jean-Francois Richard, "Economic Development, Legality, and the Transplant Effect," *European Economic Review* 47, no. 1 (2003):165–195.

59. There is empirical evidence that in countries with weak legal institutions, relatively few people deposit their money in banks. See Christopher Clague et al., "Property and Contract Rights in Autocracies and Democracies," *Journal of Economic Growth* 1, no. 2 (1996):243–276.

60. For a good overview of competing theories in the social sciences and a powerful argument that the coercive powers of the state are critical, see Geoffrey M. Hodgson, "On the Institutional Foundations of Law: The Insufficiency of Custom and Private Ordering," *Journal of Economic Issues* 43, no. 1 (2009):143–166. In contrast, Hadfield and Weingast advance a behavioral account of the decentralized enforcement of norms that are announced by an authority. See Gillian Hadfield and Barry R. Weingast, "What Is Law? A Coordination Model of the Characteristics of Legal Order," *Journal of Legal Analysis* 4, no. 2 (2012):471–515.

61. Max Weber, *Economy and Society*, ed. Guenther Roth and Claus Wittich (Berkeley: University of California Press, 1978), Vol. I, ch. 1, p. 314. See also Hodgson, "On the Institutional Foundations of Law."

62. The key mechanism is deterrence, as explained by Gary S. Becker, "Crime and Punishment: An Economic Approach," *Journal of Political Economy* 76, no. 2 (1968):169–217.

63. Hayek, *Law, Legislation, and Liberty* as well as Hadfield and Weingast, "What Is Law?"

64. This phrase has been coined by French president Giscard D'Estaing in reference to the status of the US dollar as the global reserve currency and has since been used as the title of a book by Barry Eichengreen, but seems apt in this context.

65. This is the assumption of the efficient capital market hypothesis. See Eugene Fama, "Efficient Capital Markets: A Review of Theory and Empirical Work," *Journal of Finance* 25, no. 2 (1970):383–417.

66. Ronald Gilson and Reinier Kraakman, "The Mechanisms of Market Efficiency," *Virginia Law Review* 70, no. 4 (1984):549–644.

67. Polanyi, *Great Transformation*, especially chapters 7 and 8.

68. Adam Smith recognized as much with respect to property rights. See Smith, *Wealth of Nations*, p. 232, where he states that "[t]he acquisitions of valuable and extensive property, therefore, necessarily requires the establishment of civil government."

69. On the rise of inequality at the individual level, see Alvaredo et al., *World Inequality Report 2018*.

70. For a powerful argument about the link between law and inequality, see also Robert Hale, *Freedom Through Law: Public Control of Private Governing Power* (New York: Columbia University Press, 1952), especially chap. 2 entitled "The Legal Bases of Economic Inequality," p. 13, where he discusses in particular the role of property rights as sources of inequality.

Chapter 2. Coding Land

1. Claim Nos. 171 and 172 (Consolidated) *Aurelio Cal et al. v. the Attorney General of Belize and the Minister of Natural Resources and Environment*, October 8, 2007. Available online at http://www.belizejudiciary.org/ (last accessed November 19, 2017). Hereinafter *Maya v. Belize*.

2. On the importance of the state and its power to enforce property rights universally, see also Arrunada, "Property as Sequential Exchange."

3. Olivier De Schutter, "The Green Rush: The Global Race for Farmland and the Rights of Land Users," *Harvard International Law Journal* 52, no. 2 (2011):504–559.

4. Piketty, calling this the "metamorphoses of capital"; see *Capital*, chap. 3, p. 113.

5. Andro Linklater, *Owning the Earth: The Transforming History of Land Ownership* (New York and London: Bloomsbury, 2013) gives a comprehensive account of humans' relations to land.

6. Many law schools in the United States run "clinics," where law students learn basic skills of legal advocacy and litigation by taking cases usually of clients who cannot afford a lawyer. In this case, the "Indigenous Law and Policy Program" of the James E. Rogers College of Law, University of Arizona, provided legal advice. See https://law.arizona.edu/indigenous-peoples-law-policy-program (last accessed November 22, 2017).

7. Article 3(d) of the Constitution of Belize (1981), available online at http:// www.constitution.org/cons/belize.htm (last accessed November 19, 2017).

8. Ibid., Article 17(1)a and b(ii).

9. Amendment 5 to the US Constitution, which was ratified as part of the Bill of Rights in 1791. The text of the Constitution and its amendments is available online at http://constitutionus.com/.

10. A partial exception is a provision in the US Constitution that grants Congress the power to enact a law about intellectual property rights, as will be further discussed in chapter 5 below. Note also that the German Constitution assigns the legislature the power to define the "meaning and scope" of property rights. See Article 14 of the country's constitution, its Basic Law. English translation is available online at https://www.btg-bestellservice.de/pdf/80201000.pdf.

11. *Maya v. Belize*, recital 22.

12. *Maya v. Belize*, recitals 69ff., especially recital 71.

13. For a recent account of the history and political economy of international law with a focus on investment law and transnational property rights, see Kate Miles, *The Origins of International Investment Law: Empire, Environment and the Safeguarding of Capital* (Cambridge: Cambridge University Press, 2013). See also Lorenzo Cotula, "Land, Property and Sovereignty in International Law," *Cardozo Journal of International & Comparative Law* 25, no. 2 (2017):219–286.

14. For an insightful juxtaposition of these two concepts and their historical pedigree, see Morris R. Cohen, "Property and Sovereignty," *Cornell Law Quarterly* 13, no. 1 (1927):8–30. For a more recent reassessment of the two concepts, see the special issue in the *Journal on Theoretical Inquiries in Law* 18, no. 2 (2017), available online at http://www7.tau.ac.il/ojs/index.php/til/index (last accessed November 22, 2017).

15. *Amodu Tijani v. Secretary of the Southern Provinces*, The Judicial Council of his Majesty's Privy Council, July 11, 1921, available online at http://www.nigeria -law.org (last accessed November 19, 2017).

16. *Maya v. Belize*, recital 67.

17. Section 2 of the Belize Law of Property Act (2000) as cited in ibid., recital 9 (emphasis added).

18. This point has been made with exceptional clarity by Hanoch Dagan, "Lawmaking for Legal Realists," *Theory and Practice of Legislation* 1, no. 1 (2013):187–204.

19. The literature is voluminous; see Felix Cohen, "The Problem of a Functional Jurisprudence," *Modern Law Review* 1, no. 1 (1937):5–26 for a realist's perspective, and Duncan Kennedy, "Form and Substance in Private Law Adjudication," *Harvard Law Review* 89, no. 8 (1976):1685–1778, for a critical legal studies perspective.

20. The Indigenous and Tribal Peoples Convention is available online at https://www.ilo.org/dyn/normlex/en/f?p=NORMLEXPUB:12100:0::NO:: P12100_ILO_CODE:C169.

21. C. Ford Runge and Edi Defrancesco, "Exclusion, Inclusion, and Enclosure: Historical Commons and Modern Intellectual Property," *World Development* 34, no. 10 (2006):1713–1727.

22. That is almost the exact amount of land (22 percent) that was converted by the later Parliamentary Enclosure Acts. Gregory Clark and Anthony Clark, "Common Rights to Land in England, 1475–1839," *Journal of Economic History* 61, no. 04 (2002):1009–1036.

23. J. Stuart Anderson, "Changing the Nature of Real Property Law," in *The Oxford History of the Laws of England: 1820–1914 Private Law*, ed. William Cornish et al. (Oxford: Oxford University Press, 2010), p. 86; and Claire Priest, "Creating an American Property Law: Alienability and Its Limits in American History." *Harvard Law Review* 120, no. 2 (2006):385–459, p. 402.

24. David J. Seipp, "The Concept of Property in Early Common Law," *Law and History Review* 12, no. 1 (1994):29–60, p. 36.

25. Ibid., p. 84 (emphasis added).

26. Briony McDonagh, "Making and Breaking Property: Negotiating Enclosure and Common Rights in Sixteenth-Century England," *History Workshop Journal* 2013, no. 76 (2013):32–56, p. 36.

27. See Anderson "Changing Nature," pp. 208 and 213. On the continent, Prussia introduced a public registry for land to verify property rights in 1783 and France followed suit under Napoleon Bonaparte. They built on earlier registries that can be traced back to Roman law, which were used primarily for tax purposes. For a brief overview (in German), see Walter Böhringer, "Geschichte des Grundbuchs," in *Grundbuchrecht*, ed. Georg Meikel and Bestelmeyer (Köln, München: Heymann, 2004).

28. McDonagh, "Making and Breaking Property," p. 38.

29. See Lawrence Stone, "Social Mobility in England, 1500–1700," *Past and Present* 33, no. 1 (1966):16–55. Ibid., reporting that three-quarters of the lawyers who were trained at the Inns of Court were of gentry or clergy stock.

30. Ibid., p. 33.

31. G. E. Aylmer, "The Meaning and Definition of "Property" in Seventeenth-Century England," *Past and Present* 86, no. 1 (1980):87–97.

32. Ibid., p. 95, quoting from John Lilly who drew on cases dating back to 1641.

33. For an excellent and highly critical review of the World Bank's approach to property rights, see Jeremy Waldron, *The Rule of Law and the Measure of Property* (Cambridge: Cambridge University Press, 2012).

34. John C. Weaver, "Frontiers into Assets: The Social Construction of Property in New Zealand, 1840–65," *Journal of Imperial and Commonwealth History* 27, no. 3 (1999):17–54.

35. Lindsay G. Robertson, *Conquest by Law: How the Discovery of America Dispossessed Indigenous Peoples of Their Lands* (Oxford: Oxford University Press, 2005).

36. John C. Weaver, "Concepts of Economic Improvement and the Social Construction of Property Rights: Highlights from the English-Speaking World," in *Despotic Dominion*, ed. John McLaren, A. R. Buck, and Nancy E. Wright (Vancouver: UBC Press, 2003), chap. 4. These arguments may have been inspired by Locke's famous argument that property rights should be bestowed on those who

labored for its improvement as a matter of natural law. For a critique of the Lockean approach to property, see Jeremy Waldron, *The Right to Private Property* (Oxford: Oxford University Press, 1988).

37. *US S.Ct. Johnson v. M'Intosh*, 21 U.S. (8 Wheat.) 543 (1823), p. 111/2.

38. 21st Congress, Sess. I, Ch. 148 (1830), p. 411.

39. Robertson, *Conquest by Law*. See chapter 5.

40. Hannah Arendt famously pointed out that only the citizens of a state have "rights to have rights"; the stateless don't, putting them in the most precarious position. Hannah Arendt, *The Origins of Totalitarianism* (New York: Harcourt, Brace and World, 1966).

41. For a succinct statement of this property theory, see Harold Demsetz, "Toward a Theory of Property Rights."

42. The so-called Black Act 9 Geo. 1. c. 22 was motivated by complaints that "ill-designed and disorderly persons" that have "of late associated themselves under the name of Blacks" had resorted to violent actions on a large scale in order to gain access to the land that had once belonged to them as well.

43. The reference, in doctor of laws, to "laws" (in plural) suggests training in the two major legal traditions: The English common law and the Roman law. To this day, law schools in England and the United States confer a "master of laws," or LLM, even as Roman law is rarely taught anymore.

44. Stanley Wells and Gary Taylor, eds., *The Oxford Shakespeare: The Complete Works* (Oxford: Oxford University Press, 1998), *The Merchant of Venice*, pp. 425, Act IV Scene 1, p. 446.

45. Ibid.

46. Eileen Spring, "Landowners, Lawyers, and Land Reform in Nineteenth-Century England," *American Journal of Legal History* 21, no. 1 (1977):40–59.

47. B. L. Anderson, "Law, Finance and Economic Growth in England: Some Long-Term Influences," in *Great Britain and Her World 1750–1914: Essays in Honour of W.O. Henderson*, ed. Barrie M. Ratcliffe (Manchester, UK: Manchester University Press, 1975), p. 101.

48. *The Economist*, July 7, 1866, as cited in Spring, "Landowners, Lawyers," p. 42.

49. J. Stuart Anderson, "Property Rights in Land: Reforming the Heritage," in *The Oxford History of the Laws of England: Volume XII: 1820–1914 Private Law*, ed. William Cornish et al. (Oxford: Oxford University Press, 2010), p. 47.

50. Anderson, "Changing the Nature of Real Property Law," p. 32.

51. Ibid., p. 49.

52. Section 10, subsection 2 of the Settled Land Act of 1890 states that "[n]otwithstanding anything contained in the Act of 1882, the principal mansion-house (if any) on any settled land, and the pleasure grounds and park and lands (if any) usually occupied therewith, shall not be sold, exchanged, or leased by the tenant for life without the consent of the trustees of the settlement or an order of the Court."

53. See Spring, "Landowners, Lawyers," and M. R. Chesterman, "Family Settlements on Trust: Landowners and the Rising Bourgeoisie," in *Law, Economy*

and Society, 1750–1914: Essays in the History of English Law, ed. Gerry R. Rubin and David Sugarman (Oxford: Oxford University Press, 1984).

54. H. L.(E) in *Lord Henry Bruce et al. v. The Marquess of Ailesbury et al.* [1892] 1, ch. 506.

55. Spring, "Landowners, Lawyers," p. 40.

56. Priest, "Creating an American Property Law," p. 421.

57. Ibid., p. 431.

58. Anderson, "Property Rights in Land," offers a detailed history of the many failed attempts to reform land law in England since the 1820s.

59. Joshua Getzler, "Transplantation and Mutation in Anglo-American Trust Law," *Theoretical Inquiries in Law* 10, no. 2 (2009):355–387, p. 359.

60. Piketty, *Capital*, p. 292.

61. Lee J. Alston, "Farm Foreclosure Moratorium Legislation: A Lesson from the Past," *American Economic Review* 74, no. 3 (1984):445–457; see also Murray Newton Rothbard, *The Panic of 1819* (New York: Columbia University Press, 1962).

62. Patrick Bolton and Howard Rosenthal, "Political Intervention in Debt Contracts," *Journal of Political Economy* 110, no. 5 (2002):1103–1134.

63. For a review of how courts have interpreted this "contract impairment clause," see David Crump, "The Economic Purpose of the Contract Clause," *SMU Law Review* 66, no. 4 (2013):687–709.

64. Rachel Kranton and Anand V. Swamy, "The Hazards of Piecemeal Reform: British Civil Courts and the Credit Market in Colonial India," *Journal of Development Economics* 58 (1999):1–24 offer a succinct summary of these reforms and their economic and political effects. For an analysis of the long-term effects of land reforms undertaken by British colonizers on the productivity of the land, see also Abhijit Banerjee and Lakshmi Iyer, "History, Institutions, and Economic Performance: The Legacy of Colonial Land Tenure Systems in India," *American Economic Review* 95, no. 4 (2005):1190–1213, showing that land that was given to landlords continued to have lower productivity rates even in post-independence India.

65. Daron Acemoglu, Simon Johson, and James A. Robinson, "The Colonial Origins of Comparative Development: An Empirical Investigation," *American Economic Review* 91, no. 5 (2001):1369–1401.

66. Luis Angeles, "Income Inequality and Colonialism," *European Economic Review* 51 (2007):1155–1176.

67. Some legal systems developed legal constructs that resemble the trust; others introduced the trust by way of an international convention. For a recent account of the dissemination of trusts, see Lionel Smith, "Stateless Trusts," in *The Worlds of the Trust*, ed. Lionel Smith (Cambridge: Cambridge University Press, 2013) and other contributions of that volume.

68. H. Hansmann and U. Mattei, "The Functions of Trust Law: A Comparative Legal and Economic Analysis," *New York University Law Review* 73, no. 2 (1998):434–479.

69. For a detailed account of the historical evolution of the trust, see J. Stuart Anderson, "Trusts and Trustees," chap. 6 in *The Oxford History of the Laws of*

England: Volume XII: 1820–1914 Private Law, edited by William Cornish et al. (Oxford: Oxford University Press, 2010), 232–295.

70. William Fratcher, "Uses of Uses," *Missouri Law Review* 34, no. 1 (1969):39–68, p. 39.

71. 1 Rich. 3 cl (23 January 1483/4). For details see Fratcher, "Uses of Uses," p. 55.

72. A.W.B. Simpson, *An Introduction to the History of the Land Law* (Oxford: Oxford University Press, 1961), p. 179.

73. Anderson, "Trusts and Trustees," p. 234.

74. John Morley, "The Common Law Corporation: The Power of the Trust in Anglo-American Business History," *Columbia Law Review* 116, no. 8 (2015):2145–2197.

75. See Douglass C. North, *Structure and Change in Economic History*, 1st ed. (New York: Norton, 1981), highlighting the role of property rights allocation in America's Wild West; and Robert Cooter and Hans-Bernd Schäfer, *Solomon's Knot: How Law Can End the Poverty of Nations* (Princeton, NJ: Princeton University Press, 2011) suggesting that property rights help resolve the "double trust" problem by offering legal protection to the party most exposed to this problem.

76. Ronald H. Coase, "The Problem of Social Cost," *Journal of Law and Economics* 3 (1960):1–44.

77. Adam Smith et al., *Lectures on Jurisprudence*, The Glasgow Edition of the Works and Correspondence of Adam Smith; 5 (Indianapolis: Liberty Classics, 1982); Part I: Of Justice, p. 8.

78. William Blackstone, *Commentaries on the Laws of England*, vol. 1 (Oxford: Clarendon Press, 1765), Facsimile Vol. 1, Chapter 1, "Of the Absolute Rights of Individuals" (emphasis added); available online at https://lonang.com/library/reference/blackstone-commentaries-law-england/.

79. For the parallel notion that the "rule of law" is an essentially contested concept, see Jeremy Waldron, "Is the Rule of Law Essentially a Contested Concept (in Florida)?," *Law and Philosophy* 21 (2002):137–164.

Chapter 3. Cloning Legal Persons

1. Michael C. Jensen and William H. Meckling, "Theory of the Firm: Managerial Behavior, Agency Costs and Ownership Structure," *Journal of Financial Economics* 3, no. 4 (1976):305–360.

2. Henry Hansmann and Reinier Kraakman, "The Essential Role of Organizational Law," *Yale Law Journal* 110, no. 3 (2000):387–475.

3. On institutional autopsies as a method for comparative institutional and legal analysis, see Curtis J. Milhaupt and Katharina Pistor, *Law and Capitalism: What Corporate Crises Reveal about Legal Systems and Economic Development Around the World* (Chicago: University of Chicago Press, 2008), p. 45.

4. The history of Lehman's first 100 years is documented in a self-published booklet, *Lehman Brothers 1850—1950* (New York: Lehman Brothers, 1950). The summary of the history that follows draws from this booklet.

5. Recent research has brought the nexus between slavery, cotton, and early American capitalism to the fore. See Kathryn Boodry, "August Belmont and the World the Slaves Made," in *Slavery's Capitalism: A New History of American Economic Development*, ed. Sven Beckert and Seth Rockman (Philadelphia: University of Pennsylvania Press, 2016), p. 163.

6. For a careful autopsy of the Lehman bankruptcy, see Michael J. Fleming and Asani Sarkar, "The Failure Resolution of Lehman Brothers," *FRBNY Economic Policy Review* 20, no. 2 (2014):175–206.

7. A detailed list of all holdings is available in a Registration Document filed on August 28, 2008, with the German financial authority BAFIN in compliance with the EU Prospectus Directive (2003/71/EC). *dl_Formular28082008.pdf*, available at www.bafin.de (last accessed June 23, 2017). Hereinafter "Lehman's BAFIN Registration."

8. Harold J. Berman, *Law and Revolution* (Cambridge, MA: Harvard University Press, 1983), p. 215. See also Harold J. Laski, "The Early History of the Corporation in England," *Harvard Law Review* 30, no. 6 (1917):561–588.

9. Michael C. Jensen and William H. Meckling, "Theory of the Firm."

10. For a discussion of the seat vs. the incorporation theory, see Yitzhak Hadari, "The Choice of National Law Applicable to the Multinational Enterprise and the Nationality of Such Enterprises," *Duke Law Journal* 1974, no. 1 (1974):1–57; on the specifics of EU law, see Eva-Maria Kieninger, "The Law Applicable to Corporations in the EC," *Rabels Zeitschrift für Ausländisches und Internationales Privatrecht / The Rabel Journal of Comparative and International Private Law* 73, no. 3 (2009):607–628.

11. See "Lehman's BAFIN Registration," p. 4.

12. Barbara Abatino, Giuseppe Dari-Mattiacci, and Enrico C. Perotti, "Depersonalization of Business in Ancient Rome," *Oxford Journal of Legal Studies* 31, no. 2 (2011):365–389.

13. A shareholder may not force the corporation to convert his share into cash unless the share is "redeemable." However, a corporation may buy back shares from its shareholders, for example, to support its own share price.

14. On the merits of the contractual approach to corporate law, see Roberta Romano, "Answering the Wrong Question: The Tenuous Case for Mandatory Corporate Law," *Columbia Law Review* 89, no. 7 (1989):1599–1617; for a more nuanced assessment, see John C. Coffee, Jr., "The Mandatory/Enabling Balance in Corporate Law: An Essay on the Judicial Role," *Columbia Law Review* 89, no. 7 (1989):1618–1691.

15. As of 2017, more than 66 percent of all Fortune 500 firms were incorporated in Delaware and 80 percent of all initial public offerings were made by Delaware firms. See https://www.delawareinc.com/blog/new-delaware-companies-2017/.

16. Hansmann and Kraakman used this term in "The Essential Role of Organizational Law." They later adopted the terms "entity" and "owner shielding," where the former stands for using the corporate veil to protect the firm from its

owners and their personal creditors and the latter for protecting the shareholders from the creditors of the firm.

17. They included Ford, General Motors, and Chrysler. It is hardly a coincidence that all of these companies had subsidiaries in the financial services sector, which had cross-subsidized the manufacturing entities of their group on the upside of the market but posed a threat to their survival on the downside. A summary of the bailout net costs is available online at https://www.treasury.gov/initiatives/financial -stability/TARP-Programs/automotive-programs/pages/default.aspx.

18. See the elaborate study on the emergence of the partnership system in John F. Padgett and Paul D. McLean, "Organizational Invention and Elite Trans-formation: The Birth of Partnership Systems in Renaissance Florence," *American Journal of Sociology* 112, no. 5 (2006):1463–1568.

19. John F. Padgett and Paul D. McLean, "Economic Credit in Renaissance Florence," *Journal of Modern History* 83, no. 1 (2011):1–47, p. 10.

20. See also Anthony J. Casey, "The New Corporate Web: Tailored Entity Partitions and Creditors' Selective Enforcement," *Yale Law Journal* 124, no. 8 (2015):2680–3203, showing how entity-shielding devices are used extensively to expand access to credit in major corporations today.

21. The Medici's rule was interrupted several times. For a detailed history of their business and political rule, see Nicolai Rubinstein, *The Government of Florence under the Medici (1434 to 1494)* (Oxford: Clarendon Press, 1997), and Raymond De Roover, *The Rise and Decline of the Medici Bank, 1397–1494* (New York: Norton, 1966).

22. Raymond De Roover, "The Medici Bank Organization and Management," *Journal of Economic History* 6, no. 1 (1946):24–52.

23. Ibid., p. 31.

24. Note that this comes close to the "jingle rule," which courts in the United Kingdom and the United States developed for their own partnership law. It says that the creditors of the partnership and of the partners first have to enforce against the assets of their contractual partner before partnership creditors can seize the assets of the partners, or partners' creditors can seize the assets of the partnership.

25. Hansmann, Kraakman, and Squire, "Law and the Rise of the Firm," p. 1371.

26. Those who bought close to the peak of the bubble, say in 2006, saw the value of their houses decline by as much as 36 percent, on average. See Edward Glaeser, "A Nation of Gamblers: Real Estate Speculation and American History," *American Economic Review* 103, no. 3 (2013):1–42, who offers a long-term historical review of real estate speculation in the United States.

27. See Abatino et al., "Depersonalization."

28. Katharina Pistor et al., "The Evolution of Corporate Law: A Cross-Country Comparison," *University of Pennsylvania Journal of International Economic Law* 23, no. 4 (2002):791–871.

29. For an insightful account of the proliferation of different forms of business organizations in the UK during the eighteenth and nineteenth centuries,

see Ron Harris, *Industrializing English Law: Entrepreneurship and Business Organization, 1720–1844* (Cambridge: Cambridge University Press, 2000); see also Joshua Getzler and Mike Macnair, "The Firm as an Entity Before the Companies Act," in *Adventures of the Law; Proceedings of the Sixteenth British Legal History Conference*, ed. P. Brand, K. Costello, and W. N. Osborough (Dublin: Four Courts Press, 2006).

30. For details of the evolution of core features of corporate law in major jurisdictions since the early nineteenth century, see Pistor et al., "The Evolution of Corporate Law."

31. Viral V. Acharya et al., "Dividends and Bank Capital in the Financial Crisis of 2007–2009," *NBER Working Paper Series* 16896 (2011), tables 4a and 4b.

32. This was part of the Capital Purchase Program, which was implemented under TARP. Citigroup, JP Morgan Chase, and Wells Fargo each received US$25 billion. The details are available in the Government Accountability Office's Report on the Troubled Asset Relief Program of December 2008, available online at http://www.gao.gov/new.items/d09161.pdf.

33. Lehman's stock chart for the last 12 months of its existence is available online at http://www.ino.com/blog/2008/09/looking-back-3-key-signs-to-sell-lehman/#.WWZad9PytBw (last accessed July 12, 2017).

34. Nicholas Kristof, "Need a Job? $17,000 an Hour. No Success Required," *New York Times*, September 18, 2008, available online at http://www.nytimes.com/2008/09/18/opinion/18kristof.html (last accessed July 12, 2017).

35. Fleming and Sarkar, "The Failure Resolution," p. 178.

36. See "Lehman's BAFIN Registration."

37. Steven M. Davidoff and David Zaring, "Regulation by Deal: The Government's Response to the Financial Crisis," *Administrative Law Review* 61, no. 3 (2009):463–541, p. 476.

38. The details of the crisis and the thoughts that went into the rescue actions governments took have been detailed elsewhere. For an authoritative account by the former chairman of the Fed's Board of Governors, see Ben S. Bernanke, *The Courage to Act: A Memoir of a Crisis and Its Aftermath* (New York: Norton, 2015).

39. Renewing the partnership was the strategy of choice at Goldman Sachs as well as other investment banks prior to their incorporation. See Lisa Endlich, *Goldman Sachs: The Culture of Success* (New York: Knopf, 1999).

40. Margaret M. Blair, "Locking in Capital: What Corporate Law Achieved for Business Organizers in the Nineteenth Century," *UCLA Law Review* 51, no. 2 (2003):387–455, and Guiseppe Dari-Matiacci et al., "The Emergence of the Corporate Form," *Journal of Law, Economics and Organization* 33, no. 2 (2016):193–236.

41. Dari Matiacci et al., "The Emergence of the Corporate Form," p. 211.

42. Hirschman famously argued that members in organization have three options: exit, voice, and loyalty, where loyalty is equivalent to being stuck. See Albert O. Hirschman, *Exit, Voice, and Loyalty: Responses to Decline in Firms, Organizations, and States* (Cambridge, MA: Harvard University Press, 1970).

43. See Dari-Matiacci et al., "The Emergence of the Corporate Form," p. 221 with figures 10 and 11, p. 223.

44. Modigliani and Miller addressed this question in a seminal paper published in 1958. See Franco Modigliani and Merton H. Miller, "The Cost of Capital, Corporation Finance and the Theory of Investment," *American Economic Review* 48, no. 3 (1958):261–297.

45. See Oliver Williamson, "Transaction-Cost Economics: The Governance of Contractual Relations," *Journal of Law and Economics* 22, no. 2 (1979):233–261; Sanford J. Grossman and Oliver D. Hart, "The Costs and Benefits of Ownership: A Theory of Vertical and Lateral Integration," *Journal of Political Economy* 94, no. 4 (1986):691–719.

46. Economists have long recognized the relevance of tax law. Modigliani and Miller even went as far as restating their theorem about the costs of capital in light of tax law. They have also recognized differences in the quality of shareholder protection. However, Rafael La Porta et al., "Law and Finance," *Journal of Political Economy* 106, no. 6 (1998):1113–1155 have little to say about tax or other features of the law that might determine the place of incorporation or the number of legal entities a single business might operate.

47. *Bank of Augusto v. Earle*, 38 US 519 (1839).

48. The latter is the technical term used mostly in civil law countries. I will use the term "conflict-of-law rules" throughout the book.

49. Case law dates back to the nineteenth century. For a recent restatement of the principle, see *CTS Corp. v. Dynamics Corp. of Am.*, 481 U.S. 69, 89.

50. For a summary of these cases, see Eddy Wymeersch, "Centros: A Landmark Decision in European Company Law," in *Corporations, Capital Markets and Business in the Law*, ed. Theodor Baums, Klaus J. Hopt, and Norbert Horn (London, The Hague, New York: Kluwer Law International, 2000), and Kieninger, "The Law Applicable to Corporations in the EC."

51. The free movement of goods, services and persons (including natural and legal persons) was established in the Treaty of Rome, which created the European common market, which later morphed into the European Communities. In 1992, the Maastricht Treaty created the European Union and extended the free movements to the free movement of capital.

52. Rafael La Porta, Florencio Lopez-de-Silanes, and Andrei Shleifer, "Corporate Ownership Around the World," *Journal of Finance* 54, no. 2 (1999):471–517.

53. See also the discussion in chapter 2 about Kleros I, which was incorporated in the Cayman Islands.

54. See Michael Graetz, "Taxing International Income: Inadequate Principles, Outdated Concepts, and Unsatisfactory Policies," in *Follow the Money*, ed. Michael Graetz (New Haven, CT: Lillian Goldman Law Library at Yale Law School, 2016).

55. See https://ec.europa.eu/taxation_customs/business/economic-analysis -taxation/taxation-trends-eu-union_en (last accessed November 26, 2017).

56. For details, see EU Commission Decision of August 30, 2016, "On State Aid SA.38373" (2014/NN) (ex 2014/CP), p. 27.

57. According to the OECD Observer, Ireland moved to rank 5 on the GDP scale, but dropped to rank 17 on a different scale, which measures gross national income (GNI). The findings indicate that "outflows of profits and income, largely from global business giants located there, often exceed income flows back into the country." See Observer No. 246/247, December 2004–January 2005.

58. These countries seek to protect their own tax base, but have little interest in protecting the interests of lower income countries that wish to attract corporations. On this bias in the efforts to harmonize tax law, see Tsilly Dagan, *International Tax Policy*.

59. LBIE was an indirect subsidiary of LBHI; a holding company incorporated in the UK, Lehman Holdings Plc (UK), was sandwiched between the two.

60. *In the Matter of Lehman Brothers, [2010] EWHC* 2914 (Ch), Recital 215. Hereinafter "*In the Matter of Lehman.*"

61. https://www.merriam-webster.com/dictionary/rascal.

62. The directive entered into force only in 1996, but had been widely anticipated. Note also that LBF and LBIE entered into a master agreement, which set up the RASCAL scheme between these two entities in 1996. See *In the Matter of Lehman* at recital 113ff.

63. Anat Admati and Martin Hellwig, *The Bankers' New Clothes* (Princeton, NJ: Princeton University Press, 2013) argue for raising capital adequacy requirements to 30 percent to ensure greater resilience of banks in times of crises. Ricks, in contrast, suggests that money claims have "instrumental value" to their holders that are different from their "intrinsic" value, namely, their "extraordinary low pecuniary yields," a quality that equity lacks. This, he argues, translates into sizeable differences in funding costs. See Ricks, *The Money Problem*, Kindle version at Loc. 1914.

64. *Pearson & Ors v. Lehman Brothers Finance S.A.* [2011] EWCA Civ 1544 (December 21, 2011).

65. *In the Matter of Lehman* recitals 295ff., esp. 307, and for LBF in particular, recitals 320ff.

66. Ibid., recital 35.

67. Laws of New York, 34th Session, Chapter LXVIII, p. 151; especially Articles II, III, V.

Chapter 4. Minting Debt

1. Morgan Ricks, *The Money Problem* (Chicago: University of Chicago Press, 2016). See also chapter 1 on this point.

2. On the hierarchy of moneys, see Perry Mehrling, "The Inherent Hierarchy of Money," in *Social Fairness and Economics: Economic Essays in the Spirit of Duncan Foley*, ed. Thomas Michl, Armon Rezai, and Lance Taylor (New York: Routledge, 2013), chap. 21.

3. FCIC, *The Financial Crisis Inquiry Report* (Washington, DC: US Public Affairs, 2011), especially chapters 7 and 8.

4. These documents, including the prospectus of NC2 (hereinafter "NC2 Prospectus") can be found online at http://fcic.law.stanford.edu/ (last accessed January 30, 2017).

5. The hedge fund manager, Michael Burry, in Michael Lewis's book, *The Big Short* (and the film of the same name) famously read all of them. Michael Lewis, *The Big Short* (New York, London: Norton, 2010).

6. Note that rating agencies are private businesses; however, the US government officially recognized several rating agencies and stipulated in financial regulations that their credit risk rating was critical for regulatory purposes. For a history and function of rating agencies, see John Coffee Jr., *Gatekeepers: The Professions and Corporate Governance* (Oxford: Oxford University Press, 2006), and Frank Partnoy, "How and Why Credit Rating Agencies Are Not Like Other Gatekeepers," *Legal Studies Research Paper Series: Research Paper No. 07–46* (2006):59–102.

7. See chapter 2.

8. NC2 Prospectus p. S-60.

9. NC2 Prospectus p. S-11.

10. FCIC Report (2011), chap. 7, p. 105.

11. For the central role that money market funds played in the securitization machine, see Zoltan Pozsar, Tobias Adrian, Adam Ashcraft, and Hayley Boesky, "Shadow Banking," *Federal Reserve Bank of New York Staff Reports* 458, July 2010.

12. Note that in finance jargon, the terms "special purpose vehicle" or "special investment vehicles" are ubiquitous; however, in law they are structured like the good old trust we encountered in chapter 2 already.

13. In 2003, the total amount of securitized residential mortgages amounted to $2.98 billion, of which only 10 percent were subprime. By 2004, the total volume had increased to $7.2 billion, of which 34 percent were subprime, and by 2005 had reached $18.4 billion with 45 percent subprime.

14. Adam J. Levitin and Susan M. Wachter, "Explaining the Housing Bubble," *Georgetown Law Journal* 100, no. 4 (2012):1177–1258, p. 1192.

15. On the role of foreign sovereign wealth funds in stabilizing the global financial system in the fall of 2007, see Katharina Pistor, "Global Network Finance: Institutional Innovation in the Global Financial Market Place," *Journal of Comparative Economics* 37, no. 4 (2009):552–567.

16. See FCIC, *Financial Crisis Inquiry Report*, p. 116 and documents uploaded to the commission's web page.

17. Sudip Kar-Gupta and Yann Le Guernigou, "BNP freezes $2.2 bln of Funds over Subprime," August 9, 2007; available online at www.reuters.com.

18. NC2 Prospectus, p. S-9.

19. The safest, AAA rated, assets in the NC2 pool accounted for 78 percent of the total assets. The riskiest tranche at the lowest end of the spectrum accounted for less than 2 percent. See the NC2 Prospectus.

20. NC2 Prospectus, p. S-75.

21. Marilyn Blumberg Cane, Adam Shamir, and Thomas Jodar, "Below Investment Grade and Above the Law: A Past, Present and Future Look at the Accountability of Credit Rating Agencies," *Fordham Journal of Corporate & Financial Law*

17, no. 4 (2012):1063–1126, p. 1112ff.; and Caleb Deats, "Talk that Isn't Cheap: Does the First Amendment Protect Credit Rating Agencies' Faulty Methodology from Regulation?," *Columbia Law Review* 110 (2010):1818–1864.

22. In the first half of the nineteenth century, only land was eligible, and government bonds and corporate shares were only gradually added to the mix. See chapter 2. On this point, see Kenneth C. Kettering, "Securitization and Its Discontents: The Dynamics of Financial Product Development," *Cardozo Law Review* 29 (2008):1553–1726.

23. See Hyman P. Minsky, *Stabilizing an Unstable Economy* (New Haven, CT: Yale University Press, 1986), p. 279, describing the credit process as an endogenous destabilizer.

24. This is the essence of what lawyers call the "holder in due course doctrine." See James Steven Rogers, *The Early History of the Law of Bills and Notes: A Study of the Origins of Anglo-American Commercial law*, Cambridge Studies in English Legal History (Cambridge: Cambridge University Press, 1995), pp. 2–3 and 126.

25. James Steven Rogers, *The Early History of the Law of Bills*, p. 218; emphasis added.

26. Following Minsky, Perry Mehrling argues that all credit (the flip side of debt) is money, labeling this approach "the money view." See his *The New Lombard Street: How the Fed Became the Dealer of Last Resort* (Princeton, NJ: Princeton University Press, 2011).

27. For a history of anti-usury rules, see Mark Koyama, "Evading the 'Taint of Usury': The Usury Prohibition as a Barrier to Entry," *Explorations in Economic History* 47, no. 4 (2010):420–442, and Elaine S. Tan, "An Empty Shell? Rethinking the Usury Laws in Medieval Europe," *Journal of Legal History* 23, no. 3 (2002):177–196.

28. See Rogers, *The Early History of the Law of Bills and Notes*, p. 73.

29. Lynn A. Stout, "Derivatives and the Legal Origin of the 2008 Credit Crisis," *Harvard Business Law Review* 1, no. 1 (2011):1–38, showing how legal limits on wagers and other speculative transactions were undermined in case law, but even more important, by legislative change.

30. See Emily Kadens, "The Myth of the Customary Law Merchant," *Texas Law Review* 90 (2011):1153–1206 and Albrecht Cordes, "Lex Mercatoria," in *Handwörterbuch der deutschen Rechtsgeschichte*, ed. Albrecht et al. Cordes (Berlin: Schmidt Verlag, 2015).

31. City after city enacted special statutes on bills of exchange, including Rotterdam (1635), d'Anvers (1667), Leipzig (1682), Hamburg (1711), Bremen (1712), Braunschweig (1715), Augsburg (1716), Frankfurt (1739), and many others. Merchants were well represented on city councils in major trading centers, thus facilitating the passage of these statutes. In France, the Grand Ordonnance Française du Commerce 1673 created rules for the bills that were later incorporated into the Code de Commerce (1807). In England, courts forged the rules governing bills in case law as discussed in Rogers, *The Early History of the Law of Bills and Notes*.

32. Convention Providing a Uniform Law for Bills of Exchange and Promissory Notes (Geneva: League of Nations, 1930), available online at https://www

.jus.uio.no/lm/bills.of.exchange.and.promissory.notes.convention.1930/doc
.html (last accessed August 8, 2018).

33. Ronald J. Mann, "Searching for Negotiability in Payment and Credit Systems," *UCLA Law Review* 44, no. 4 (1997):951–1008.

34. On the history of early banking, see Richard Tilly, "Universal Banking in Historical Perspective." *Journal of Institutional and Theoretical Economics* 154, no. 1 (1998): 7–32; Richard Sylla, John B. Legler, and John J. Wallis, "Banks and State Public Finance in the New Republic: The United States, 1790–1860," *Journal of Economic History* 47, no. 2 (1987):391–403; on the long-term implications of early choices in the design of banking, see Charles W. Calomiris and Stephen H. Haber, *Fragile by Design: The Political Origins of Banking Crises and Scarce Credit* (Princeton, NJ: Princeton University Press, 2014).

35. The full plan in English translation is available in D. M. Frederiksen, "Mortgage Banking in Germany," *Quarterly Journal of Economics* 9, no. 1 (1894):47–76.

36. Ibid., p. 51.

37. As Büring put it in the plan put before the king, quoted in Frederiksen, "Mortgage Banking in Germany, *p. 48.*

38. Frederiksen, "Mortgage Banking in Germany," p. 57.

39. The Federal Housing Finance Agency (FHFA) took the two GSEs into conservatorship on September 6, 2008. For details, see https://www.fhfa.gov/Conservatorship.

40. Urban Institute, *Housing Finance at a Glance* (2018), p. 10.

41. REMIC is not a thing; it is not even a legal entity; rather, it is a conduit that can take various forms, including a trust or a corporate entity, or comprise only a set of assets. Only certain assets, such as securitized mortgages, qualify for REMIC treatment, and other contingencies apply, including the requirement that assets are transferred to the REMIC on the startup date and that the conduit may not change the composition of mortgage assets. No pre-approval was required for acquiring REMIC status; instead, the law allows sponsors of REMICs to self-select into them provided they meet the relevant requirements and imposes a 100 percent tax on prohibited assets or transactions. See 26 U.S. Code § 860D(a), F(a), and G(a) for details.

42. *U.S. Bank National Ass'n v. Ibanez*, 458 Mass. 637, also at 941 N.E.2d 40 (Mass. 2011) (hereinafter *Bank v. Ibanez*).

43. *Bank v. Ibanez* at recital 641.

44. No additional involvement by the judiciary is required at this stage: whoever holds a mortgage properly assigned may foreclosure without the need of obtaining judicial authorization.

45. *Bank v. Ibanez*, recital 640.

46. Ibid.

47. Riles, *Collateral Knowledge*, pp. 62–63; Vincent Antonin Lepinay, *Codes of Finance: Engineering Derivatives in a Global Bank* (Princeton, NJ: Princeton University Press, 2011), chap. 4, "The Memory of Banking."

48. Adam J. Levitin, "The Paper Chase: Securitization, Foreclosure, and the Uncertainty of Mortgage Title," *Duke Law Journal* 63, no. 637–734 (2013).

49. Leading banks created a holding company, which in turn set up a limited liability company named MERS. It resembled the Deposit Trust Corporation that Congress had created by statute in 1968 as the formal title holder to shares in publicly traded companies. MERS, in contrast, was a private arrangement; financial intermediaries had to opt in and they had to rely on private law arrangements, such as agency law, for the system to work. For details, see Levitin, "The Paper Chase," p. 677.

50. Miguel Segoviano et al., "Securitization: Lessons Learned and the Road Ahead," *IMF Working Paper* 2013, no. 255 (2013), p. 38.

51. See Levitin, "The Paper Chase," p. 705.

52. Note, however, that a close cousin, Collateral Debt Obligations, or CLOs, have been on the rise, so much so that some observers predict they will cause the next crisis sooner rather than later. See Matt Philipps, "Wall Street Loves These Risky Loans. The Rest of Us Should Be Wary," October 19, 2018, available online at www.nytimes.com.

53. FCIC Report, p. 129. In 2004 about half of all securities in CDOs were backed by mortgages. See ibid., p. 130.

54. Ibid., p. 131.

55. England is an important exception to this practice. The landed elites resisted dilution of gold coins, because they were paid their rents in gold. See Christine Desan, "Beyond Commodification: Contract and the Credit-Based World of Modern Capitalism," in *Transformations in American Legal History: Law, Ideology, and Methods: Essays in Honor of Morton J. Horwitz*, ed. Daniel W. Hamilton and Alfred L. Brophy (Cambridge, MA: Harvard University Press, 2010).

56. Reuters Staff, "IMF projects Venezuela inflation will hit 1,000,000 percent in 2018. Reuters Business News, July 23, 2018, available online at www.reuters.com (last accessed August 8, 2018).

57. Kim Oosterlinck, "Sovereign Debt Defaults: Insights from History," *Oxford Review of Economic Policy* 29, no. 4 (2013):697–714; see also Carmen Reinhart and Kenneth S. Rogoff, *This Time Is Different: Eight Centuries of Financial Folly* (Princeton, NJ: Princeton University Press, 2009).

58. M. Aycard, *Credit Mobilier* (Brussels, Leipzig, Livourne: A. Lacroix, Verboeckhoven & Cie, 1867).

59. Merton as quoted in McKinsey Global Institute, "Mapping Global Capital Markets" (New York: McKinsey Global Institute, 2008), p. 136.

60. The structure is an example of what Minsky would later call "Ponzi finance"—in reference to Mr. Ponzi, who ran one of the most audacious Ponzi schemes in the 1920s. See Minsky, *Stabilizing an Unstable Economy*, pp. 230–232, where he compares hedge, speculative, and Ponzi finance.

61. Johann Plenge, *Gründung und Geschichte des Crédit Mobilier* (Tübingen: Verlag der H. Laupp'schen Buchhandlung, 1903); the book includes the articles of incorporation of the bank.

62. For a short definition and the description of the original Ponzi scheme, see https://www.investopedia.com/terms/p/ponzischeme.asp (last accessed August 8, 2018).

63. Robert Lenzner, "Bernie Madoff's $50 Billion Ponzi Scheme," December 12, 2008, available online at www.forbes.com.

64. Karl Marx, "Crédit Mobilier," *New York Daily Tribune*, part III, July 11, 1856. Available online at http://marxengels.public-archive.net/en/ME0978en .html (last accessed August 28, 2018).

65. Ibid.

66. Greece and Portugal could be listed here as well. However, their problems stemmed at least in part from excessive government borrowing. For a new, illuminating account of the Euro crisis in the context of the global financial crisis, see Adam Tooze, *Crashed: How a Decade of Financial Crises Changed the World* (New York: Viking, 2018), Part III, pp. 319ff.

67. A detailed history of the evolution of option pricing theory can be found in Donald MacKenzie, *An Engine, Not a Camera: How Financial Models Shape Markets* (Cambridge, MA: MIT Press, 2006).

68. Franklin R. Edwards, "Hedge-Funds and the Collapse of Long Term Capital Management," *Journal of Economic Perspectives* 13, no. 2 (1999):189–210, p. 199.

69. Perry Mehrling, "Minsky and Modern Finance: The Case of Long-Term Capital Management," *Journal of Portfolio Management* Winter 2000 (2000):81–89.

70. The banks involved in the rescue included Goldman Sachs, Merrill Lynch, J. P. Morgan, Morgan Stanley, Dean Witter, the Travelers Group, Union Bank of Switzerland, Barclays, Bankers Trust, Chase Manhattan, Credit Suisse First Boston, Deutsche Bank, Lehman Brothers, Paribas, and Société Générale. See Edwards, "Hedge-Funds," p. 200.

71. Recent data suggest an upward trend in pensioners filing for personal bankruptcy in the United States, which has been attributed to the costs of health care. See Tara Siegel Bernard, "Too Little, Too Late: Bankruptcy Booms among Older Americans," *New York Times*, August 5, 2018, available online at www .nytimes.com (last accessed August 8, 2018).

72. Some central banks, the Fed among them, operate under the dual mandate of price stability and full employment. See Sec. 2.a. of the Federal Reserve Act, available online at https://www.federalreserve.gov/aboutthefed/section2a.htm.

73. For a useful overview of the scope of regulatory reforms in the United States, see Viral V. Acharya et al., *Regulating Wall Street: The Dodd-Frank Act and the New Architecture of Global Finance* (Hoboken, NJ: Wiley, 2011). For a critique that targets primarily the discretionary powers of regulators, see David A. Skeel, *The New Financial Deal* (Hoboken, NJ: Wiley, 2011); and on the shortcomings of the Dodd-Frank Act in terms of remodeling the financial system, see Arthur E. Wilmarth, Jr., "Turning a Blind Eye: Why Washington Keeps Giving in to Wall Street," *University of Cincinnati Law Review* 81, no. 4 (2013):1283–1446.

Chapter 5. Enclosing Nature's Code

1. James Watson and Francis Crick, "A Structure for Deoxyribose Nucleic Acid," *Nature* 171 (1953):737–738.

2. https://www.genome.gov/10001772/all-about-the—human-genome -project-hgp/.

3. The legislative history of the 1952 reinstatement of the Patent Act is summarized in *Diamond v. Chakrabarty*, US Supreme Court, March 17, 1980, 447 U.S. 303.

4. *Int'l News Serv. v. Associated Press*, 248 U.S. 215, 250 (1918) (Brandeis, J., dissenting, p. 248ff.).

5. James Boyle, "The Second Enclosure Movement," *Renewal: A Journal of Labour Politics* 15, no. 4 (2007):17–24.

6. *Diamond v. Chakrabarty*, p. 313.

7. *Association for Molecular Pathology v. Myriad Genetics, Inc.*, 569 U.S. 576 (hereinafter *Molecular Pathology v. Myriad*).

8. 35 U.S.C. § 101.

9. *Molecular Pathology v. Myriad*, p. 590.

10. Quoted in *Molecular Pathology v. Myriad*, p. 595.

11. *Molecular Pathology v. Myriad*, p. 596.

12. Angelina Jolie, "My Medical Choice," May 14, 2013, available online at www.nytimes.com.

13. Jacob S. Sherkow and Christopher Scott, "Myriad Stands Alone," *Nature Biotechnology* 32, no. 7 (2014):620.

14. A number of authors have pointed to the obvious parallel between the first and this "second" enclosure movement. See Boyle, "The Second Enclosure Movement," and Ford C. Runge and Edi Defrancesco, "Exclusion, Inclusion, and Enclosure: Historical Commons and Modern Intellectual Property," *World Development* 34, no. 10 (2006):1713–1727.

15. The facts for the summary that follows can be found in the district court's ruling, *Association for Molecular Pathology v. United States PTO*, 702 F. Supp. 2d 181.

16. The company was incorporated in Delaware. For the ability of companies to choose their place of incorporation, see chapter 4.

17. Jeff M. Hall et al., "Lineage of Early-Onset Familial Breast Cancer to Chromosome 17q21," *Science* 250, no. 4988 (1990):1684–1689.

18. Sec. 282 Patent Act establishes the presumption that once granted, patents are valid, and the burden is on the party that claims invalidity.

19. Philippe Aghion et al., "The Public and Private Sectors in the Process of Innovation: Theory and Evidence from the Mouse Genetics Revolution," *American Economic Review* 100, no. 2 (2010):153–158.

20. Sherkow and Scott, "Myriad Stands Alone," p. 620.

21. Myriad Genetics Corporation, Annual Report for the Financial Year Ending in June 2017, available online at http://investor.myriad.com/annuals-proxies.cfm.

22. US Constitution Art. 1 Sec. 8 Clause 8.

23. This is nowhere more apparent than for the development of copyrights in the United States. For a careful history of the evolution of statutory copyright law in the United States, see Jessica Litman, "Copyright Legislation and Technological Change," *Oregon Law Review* 68, no. 2 (1989):275–362. Litman suggests that copyright law is a "web of interdependent bilateral and trilateral deals" by the

industries with consumers, but also the original authors, mostly absent from the negotiations. Ibid., p. 361.

24. See patent statistics of the US Patent Office, available online at https://www.uspto.gov/web/offices/ac/ido/oeip/taf/apat.htm#PartA1_1b.

25. Haskel and Westlake, *Capitalism without Capital* (Princeton, NJ: Princeton University Press, 2018).

26. Ibid., table 3.1, p. 44.

27. *Molecular Pathology v. Myriad*, p. 596.

28. See the discussion in chapter 1.

29. See, however, Ugo Pagano, "The Crisis of Intellectual Monopoly Capitalism," *Cambridge Journal of Economics* 38, no. 6 (2014):1409–1429, who emphasizes the critical importance of legal monopolies in the case of the asset class knowledge.

30. As quoted in Carol Corrado, Charles Hulton, and Daniel Sichel, "Intangible Capital and U.S. Economic Growth," *The Review of Income and Wealth* 55, no. 3 (2009):661–686, p. 661.

31. The saying is attributed in slight variations to different authors, including Peter Ducker (a business economist), Peason (a mathematical statistician), or Thomas Monson.

32. Corrado et al., "Intangible Capital," p. 683. Leonard I. Nakamura, "Intangible Assets and National Income Accounting," *Review of Income and Wealth* 56, no. S1 (2010):S135–S155. For a summary of this literature, see also Saskia Clausen and Stefan Hirth, "Measuring the Value of Intangibles," *Journal of Corporate Finance* 40 (2016):110–127.

33. Haskel and Westlake, *Capitalism without Capital*, figures 2.1 and 2.2, pp. 24–25.

34. Ibid., chap. 5, p. 91.

35. Pagano, "The Crisis of Intellectual Monopoly Capitalism," p. 1419. On secular stagnation see also Lawrence H. Summers, "U.S. Economic Prospects: Secular Stagnation, Hysteresis, and the Zero Lower Bound," *Business Economics* 49, no. 2 (2014):65–73.

36. Pagano, "The Crisis of Intellectual Monopoly Capitalism," p. 1420.

37. See Joseph A. Schumpeter, *Capitalism, Socialism and Democracy* (New York: Harper & Row, 1942), p. 82–83.

38. P. J. Frederico, "Origin and Early History of Patents," *Journal of the Patent Office Society* 11 (1929):292–305.

39. Ibid., p. 293.

40. Jeremy Phillips, "The English Patent as a Reward for Invention: The Importation of an Idea," *Journal of Legal History* 3, no. 1 (1982):71–79, with an English translation of the Venetian decree, pp. 75–76.

41. Quotes are from Phillips, "English Patent," pp. 75–76.

42. Daron Acemoglu and James A. Robinson, *Why Nations Fail*, chap. 7, p. 182, where they describe the quest for a patent by the inventor of an automated knitting machine, which was refused by Elizabeth I and her successor.

43. The text of the Statute of Monopolies is available online at http://www
.legislation.gov.uk/aep/Ja1/21/3 (last accessed August 28, 2018).

44. Susan Sell and Christopher May, "Moments in Law: Contestation and
Settlement in the History of Intellectual Property," *Review of International Political Economy* 8, no. 3 (2001):467–500, p. 484.

45. Ibid.

46. Susan K. Sell, *Private Power, Public Law: The Globalization of Intellectual
Property Rights* (Cambridge: Cambridge University Press, 2003), chap. 4 on the
"domestic origins of a trade-based approach to intellectual property," p. 75.

47. See Trade Act of 1974, 19 USC, Chapter 12, Sec. 301.

48. The current members of the renamed Advisory Committee for Trade
Policies and Negotiations can be found online at https://ustr.gov/about-us
/advisory-committees/advisory-committee-trade-policy-and-negotiations
-actpn. The only non-CEO or non-owner of a business is the president of a small
business association.

49. John Braithwaite and Peter Drahos, *Global Business Regulation* (Cambridge: Cambridge University Press, 2000), p. 467.

50. Ibid. See also Michael A. Heller and Rebecca S. Eisenberg, "Can Patents
Deter Innovation? The Anticommons in Biomedical Research," *Science, New Series* 280, no. 5364 (1998):698–701.

51. Amy Kapczynski, "Harmonization and Its Discontents: A Case Study of
TRIPS Implementation in India's Pharmaceutical Sector," *California Law Review*
97 (2009):1571.

52. See chapter 6 for a discussion of these international treaty instruments.

53. Tim Büthe and Walter Mattli, *The New Global Rulers: The Privatization
of Regulation in the World Economy* (Princeton, NJ: Princeton University Press,
2011).

54. Braithwaite and Drahos, *Global Business Regulation*, p. 96.

55. Peter Drahos, "Global Property Rights in Information: The Story of
TRIPS and the GATT," *Prometheus* 13, no. 1 (1995):6–13, p. 12.

56. As quoted in Sell, *Private Power, Public Law*, p. 94.

57. Joseph Stiglitz, *Making Globalization Work* (London: Norton, 2006); see
also Dani Rodrik, "The Global Governance of Trade: As If Development Really Mat-
tered," *United Nations Development Programme (UNDP) background paper* (2001).

58. Drahos, "Global Property Rights."

59. For a summary of the process, see https://www.wto.org/english/tratop_e
/dispu_e/disp_settlement_cbt_e/c6s1p1_e.htm

60. See Sell, *Private Power, Public Law*, p. 114.

61. The history of trade secrets can be traced back to the early seventeenth
century and has been a core feature of rules governing guilds and their quest to
monopolize skills. See Sean Bottomley, "The Origins of Trade Secrecy Law in
England, 1600–1851," *Journal of Legal History* 38, no. 3 (2017):254–281.

62. Brenda M. Simon and Ted Sichelman, "Data-Generating Patents," *Northwestern University Law Review* 111, no. 2 (2017):377–439.

63. Ibid.

64. This background history is recounted in the decision of the district court of this case; see *Ass'n for Molecular Pathology v. Uspto*, 702 F. Supp. 2d 181, p. 201.

65. Simon and Sichelman, "Data-Generating Patents," p. 377.

66. Ibid.

67. Sean Bottomley, "The Origins of Trade Secrecy Law."

68. See chapter 2.

69. Bottomley, "The Origins of Trade Secrecy Law," p. 261.

70. Evidence from business organizations that are organized in a similar manner to guilds as clubs suggests that they can put these mechanisms to quite effective use. See Lisa Bernstein, "Opting Out of the Legal System: Extralegal Contractual Relations in the Diamond Industry," *Journal of Legal Studies* 21, no. 1 (1992):115–157.

71. Karl Polanyi, *The Great Transformation*, esp. chap. 5, pp. 56ff. and 65.

72. Ibid., chap. 19.

73. Catherine F. Fisk, "Working Knowledge: Trade Secrets, Restrictive Covenants in Employment and the Rise of Corporate Intellectual Property, 1800–1920," *Hastings Law Journal* 52, no. 2 (2001):451–535, p. 451.

74. Ibid., pp. 468ff. for a detailed account of the Du Ponts' practices at the time.

75. John Duffy, "The Death of Google's Patents?," *Patently-o Pat. Law Journal* 2 (2008):3–7, available online at https://patentlyo.com/media/docs/2008/07/googlepatents101.pdf.

76. Christine MacLeod, *Inventing the Industrial Revolution: The English Patent System, 1660–1800* (Cambridge: Cambridge University Press, 1988).

77. This, at least, is the result of recent case law developments. See *Mayo v. Prometheus*, 566 U.S. 66 (2012) and, most recently, *Alice Corp v. CLS Bank Int'l*, 573 U.S. 134 (2014).

78. AnnaLee Saxenian, *Regional Advantage: Culture and Competition in Silicon Valley and Route 128* (Cambridge, MA: Harvard University Press, 1994).

79. The case, *Waymo LLC v. Ueber Techs Inc.*, was filed in 2017, but settled in February 2018 only a few days into the trial. Ueber paid Waymo 0.34 percent of its equity, worth $245 million, and promised not to use Waymo technology for self-driving cars. Daisuke Wakabayashi, "Ueber and Waymo settle Trade Secrecy Suit over Driverless Car," February 9, 2018, available online at www.nytimes.com.

80. Charles Duhigg, "Stop Thief," *New Yorker*, October 22, 2018, 50–61, p. 61, quoting a spokesperson for Waymo, the Google subsidiary: "We comply with law-enforcement requests where there is a valid legal process, and this case is no exception."

81. An example is the US Defend Trade Secrets Act of 2016, available online at https://www.congress.gov/bill/114th-congress/senate-bill/1890/text.

Chapter 6. A Code for the Globe

1. Mary Beard, *SPQR* (New York: Norton, 2015), p. 465.

2. A summary of the patterns of diffusion of Western legal systems can be found in Berkowitz, Pistor, and Richard, "Transplant Effect."

260 NOTES TO CHAPTER 6

3. For a succinct history of Japanese law, see Hiroshi Oda, *Japanese Law*, 2nd ed. (London, Dublin, Edinburgh: Butterworths, 1999); see also John Haley, *Authority without Power: Law and the Japanese Paradox* (Oxford: Oxford University Press, 1994) for a critical assessment of how Western legal transplants operate in a very different culture. After World War II, the United States occupied Japan and transplanted some of its own laws, with mixed success.

4. Alan Watson, *Legal Transplants: An Approach to Comparative Law* (Edinburgh: Scottish Academic Press; London: distributed by Chatto and Windus, 1974).

5. Katharina Pistor et al., "Legal Evolution and the Transplant Effect," *World Bank Research Observer* 18, no. 1 (2003):89–112.

6. The text of the Convention is available online at https://www.hcch.net/en/instruments/conventions/full-text/?cid=72.

7. Bradley Crawford, "The Hague 'Prima' Convention: Choice of Law to Govern Recognition of Dispositions of Book-Based Securities in Cross Border Transactions," *Canadian Business Law Journal* 38, no. 2 (2003):157–206.

8. Under the US Uniform Commercial Code (UCC), the applicable law for financial assets can be determined by the jurisdiction of the issuer, but also by an agreement between an entitlement holder and a securities intermediary. See Sec. 8-110.e UCC, available online at https://www.law.cornell.edu/ucc/8/8-110.

9. Julian Arato, "Corporations as Lawmakers," *Harvard Journal of International Law* 56, no. 2 (2015):229–295; Lise Johnson, "A Fundamental Shift in Power: Permitting International Investors to Convert Their Economic Expectations into Rights," *UCLA Law Review Discourse* 65 (2018):106–123.

10. Lucian Arye Bebchuk, "Ex Ante Costs of Violating Absolute Priority in Bankruptcy," *Journal of Finance* 57 (2002):445–460.

11. Christoph Kaserer, "Der Fall der Herstatt-Bank 25 Jahre danach. Überlegungen zur Rationalität regulierungspolitischer Reaktionen unter besonderer Berücksichtigung der Einlagensicherung," *VSWG: Vierteljahrschrift für Sozial- und Wirtschaftsgeschichte* 87, no. 2 (2000):166–192.

12. A new, single resolution board for the Banking Union—the member states who opted into the Eurozone and whose larger banks are now supervised by the European Central Bank—was established at the beginning of 2018. For details, see https://europa.eu/european-union/about-eu/agencies/srb_en.

13. Note, however, that the EU has standardized bank resolution law. See the EU's Bank Resolution and Recovery Directive (BRRD) of May 15, 2014, available online at https://eur-lex.europa.eu/legal-content/EN/TXT/?uri=celex:32014L0059. In addition, a new single resolution mechanism has been established for eligible banks from member states that participate in the Eurozone. See the EU's Regulation on the Single Resolution Mechanism of July 15, 2014, available online at https://eur-lex.europa.eu/legal-content/EN/TXT/?uri=CELEX:32014R0806.

14. Morris R. Cohen, "Property and Sovereignty," *Cornell Law Quarterly* 13, no. 1 (1927):8–30, p. 8.

15. Ibid., p. 29.

16. See Cynthia M. Ho, "Sovereignty under Siege: Corporate Challenges to Domestic Intellectual Property Decisions," *Berkeley Technology Law Journal* 30, no. 1 (2015):215–304.

17. *Eli Lilly & Co. v. Government of Canada*, Case UNCT 14/2 of March 16, 2017, available online at http://icsidfiles.worldbank.org/icsid/ICSIDBLOBS /OnlineAwards/C3544/DC10133_En.pdf, recital 65, paraphrasing the language of the Act, which states that invention is "any new and useful art, process, machine, manufacture or composition of matter or any new or useful improvement." Hereinafter "*Eli Lilly v. Canada*."

18. Canada's supreme court denied "certiorari"—a writ in an appeal process that determines whether the highest court will hear a case or not.

19. The details of the case and its history are available in *Eli Lilly v. Canada*.

20. An introduction to NAFTA and the treaty text can be found on the home page of the NAFTA secretariat, online at https://www.nafta-sec-alena.org /Home/Welcome. The new USMCA is available online at https://ustr.gov/trade -agreements/free-trade-agreements/united-states-mexico-canada-agreement /united-states-mexico.

21. All international human rights tribunals require the exhaustion of domestic remedies before filing a claim. Note that the Maya obtained a hearing at the IACHR without having done so, because the domestic courts refused to grant them a hearing at all and the IACHR deemed this a denial of justice. The IACHR decision on the case the Maya brought against the Toledo district of Belize is available online at http://www.cidh.oas.org/annualrep/2004eng/Belize .12053eng.htm.

22. For the latest statistics on investor-state-dispute-settlement (ISDS), see UNCTAD, "Special Update on Investor-State Dispute Settlement: Facts and Figures," November 2017, available online at www.unctad.org.

23. See Art. 60 of the Canadian Patent Act, available online at http://laws-lois .justice.gc.ca/.

24. *Metalclad Corporation v. United States*, CASE No. ARB(AF)/97/1, 30 August 2000, available online at https://www.italaw.com/cases/671.

25. See *Eli Lilly v. Canada*, recital 223.

26. Ibid., recital 25.

27. Ibid., recital 331. The costs of arbitration, including fees and expenses totaled US$750,000; the sum total of the lawyers' fees for both sides amounted to US$5.3 million. *Eli Lilly v. Canada*, p. 143.

28. Bankruptcy Act of 1705, 4&5 Anne c 17.

29. Markham V. Lester, *Victorian Insolvency* (Oxford: Clarendon Press, 1995).

30. For an overview of the development of insolvency law in the UK from 1820 to 1914, see Michael Lobban, "Bankruptcy and Insolvency," in *The Oxford History of the Laws of England: 1820–1914 Private law*, ed. William Cornish, et al. (Oxford: Oxford University Press, 2010).

31. Information about ISDA is available on the association's webpage (www .isda.org). For a summary of its history, see Glenn Morgan, "Market formation

and governance in international financial markets: The case of OTC derivatives," *Human Relations* 61, no. 5 (2008):637–660.

32. Others include the International Capital Market Association, which provides documentation primarily for bonds that are issued transnationally, and the Loan Market Association (LMA), which does the same for loans that are transferred internationally. Unlike derivatives and bond issuance, LMA contract documentation makes extensive reference to French and German law. See Agasha Mugasha, "International Financial Law: Is the Law Really 'International' and Is It 'Law' Anyway?," *Banking and Financial Law Review* 26, no. 3 (2011):381–450.

33. On the link between standardization and liquidity, see Bruce Carruthers and Arthur L. Stinchcombe, "The Social Structure of Liquidity: Flexibility, Markets, and States," *Theory and Society* 28, no. 3 (1999):353–382.

34. See https://www.isda.org/membership/.

35. Joanne Braithwaite, "Standard Form Contracts as Transnational Law: Evidence from the Derivatives Markets," *Modern Law Review* 75, no. 5 (2012):779–805, and Bruce Carruthers, "Diverging Derivatives: Law, Governance, and Modern Financial Markets," *Journal of Comparative Economics* 41, no. 2 (2013):386–400.

36. See the most recent statistics for global OTC derivatives compiled by the Bank for International Settlement (BIS) at http://www.bis.org/statistics/d5_1 .pdf. Not all derivatives have made a comeback, however.

37. See, however, Jeffrey Golden, "Interpreting ISDA Terms: When Market Practice Is Relevant, as of When Is It Relevant?," *Capital Markets Law Journal* 9, no. 3 (2014):299–307, referring to the ISDA MA as a "relational contract."

38. J. P. Braithwaite, "OTC derivatives, the courts and regulatory reform," *Capital Markets Law Journal* 7, no. 4 (2012):364–385 shows that there were fewer than 100 cases in the years prior to the financial crisis.

39. The web page of the panel is www.primefinancedsiputes.org.

40. See Sec. 6 of the 2002 MA.

41. The rules that govern insolvency procedures vary considerably across jurisdictions. English law, for example, allows creditors of an insolvent debtor to set off reciprocal claims without complying with the automatic stay. For a brief overview over the differences between set-off and netting in insolvency, see Matthias Haentjens and Bob Wessels, *Research Handbook on Crisis Management in the Banking Sector* (Cheltenham, UK: Edward Elgar, 2015), p. 331.

42. For a critical review of conflicts with US bankruptcy law, see Edward R. Morrison and Joerg Riegel, "Financial Contracts and the New Bankruptcy Code: Insulating Markets from Bankrupt Debtors and Bankruptcy Judges," *American Bankruptcy Institute Law Review* 13, no. 2 (2005):641–664.

43. Morgan "Market Formation," p. 650.

44. Morrison and Riegel, "Financial Contracts," for a discussion of the evolution of bankruptcy safe harbors in the United States.

45. Technically, repos transfer ownership over an asset from one party to another, and back. This would suggest that the holder of the property right can pull out its asset if the other party defaults; however, courts in several countries

have treated Repos as functionally equivalent to secured transactions, giving their holder only a claim to enforce against the asset, not the right to claim the asset itself. However, in practice, repos were frequently re-used, thereby exposing parties to the risk of a position of unsecured creditor. For details, see Edward R. Morrison, Mark J. Roe, and Christopher S. Sontchi, "Rolling Back the Repo Safe Harbors," *Business Law Journal* 69 (2014):1016–1047.

46. See the definitions in Sec. 101, 11 USC, subsection 53 A (ii).

47. ISDA, "Collateral Arrangements in the European Financial Markets, The Need for National Law Reform," (London: ISD, 2000). Available online at https://www.isda.org/book/collateral-arrangements-in-the-european-financial -markets/.

48. See Directive 2002/47/EC of the European Parliament and of the Council of June 6, 2002 on financial collateral arrangements. *Official Journal L 168, 27/06/2002 P. 0043–0050*. Note that under EU Treaty law, the European Council has the power to adopt secondary law, which has binding effects on member states. For a critical review on the impact of this directive on English collateral law, see Louise Gullifer, "What Should We Do about Financial Collateral?," *Current Legal Problems* (2012):1–34.

49. Several studies have documented a strong correlation between the expansion of safe harbors for derivatives and the rise of these markets. See, for example, Franklin R. Edwards and Edward R. Morrison, "Derivatives and the Bankruptcy Code: Why the Special Treatment?," *Yale Journal on Regulation* 22, no. 1 (2005):91–122.

50. Braithwaite, "Standard Form Contracts," p. 789.

51. CPSS, "OTC Derivatives: Settlement Procedures and Counterparty Risk Management," *BIS Report* (1998).

52. A brief history of the Financial Stability Board can be found online at http://www.fsb.org/about/.

53. David Geen et al., "A Step Closer to Ending Too-Big-to Fail: The ISDA Resolution-Stay Protocol and Contractual Recognition of Cross-Border Resolution," *Futures and Derivatives Law Report* 35, no. 3 (2015):1–17, p. 7.

54. The original protocol from November 2014 was relaunched in November 2015. The latest text can be found online at http://assets.isda.org/media /ac6b533f-3/5a7c32f8-pdf/.

55. For details see the US Federal Reserves, 12 CFR Parts 217, 249, and 252 available online at https://www.gpo.gov/fdsys/pkg/FR-2017-09-12/pdf /2017-19053.pdf.

56. Cardozo defined the contents of fiduciary duties as follows: "Not honesty alone, but the punctilio of an honor the most sensitive, is then the standard of behavior. As to this there has developed a tradition that is unbending and inveterate." *Meinhard v. Salmon*, 249 NY 458, p. 464. Subsequent case law in Delaware and elsewhere has relaxed this standard.

57. See, for example, Transparency International's Corruption Perception Index, where Canada ranks 8 out of 180 countries, available online at https://

www.transparency.org/, or the Worldwide Governance Indicators published by the World Bank, where Canada equally ranks among the top countries, available online at http://info.worldbank.org/governance/wgi/index.aspx#home.

58. There is a voluminous literature on the rise of "private regulation," which shows that private agents often assume regulatory functions over other private agents. See only Fabrizio Cafaggi, "New Foundations of Transnational Private Regulation," *Journal of Law and Society* 38, no. 1 (2011):20–49.

59. The full title of the convention is "The Convention on the Recognition and Enforcement of Foreign Arbitral Awards." The text of the convention is available online at http://www.newyorkconvention.org/.

60. Choudhury Barnali, "Recapturing Public Power: Is Investment Arbitration's Engagement of the Public Interest Contributing to the Democractic Deficit?," *Vanderbilt Journal of Transnational Law* 41, no. 3 (2008):775–832.

61. https://icsid.worldbank.org/en/.

62. See Arts. 50–52 of the ICSID Convention, available online at http://icsidfiles.worldbank.org/icsid/icsid/staticfiles/basicdoc/partA.htm.

63. The full list of member states is available online at https://icsid.worldbank.org/en/Pages/about/Database-of-Member-States.aspx (last accessed August 28, 2018).

64. Available online at https://treaties.un.org/doc/publication/unts/volume%201155/volume-1155-i-18232-english.pdf.

65. Note that the United States never ratified the Vienna Convention, but largely adheres to the principles laid out in it, as they are accepted as *ius commune*, the international common law of states.

66. Anthea Roberts, "Clash of Paradigms: Actors and Analogies Shaping the Investment Treaty System," *American Journal of International Law* 107, no. 1 (2013):45–94.

67. The EU has worked hard to ensure that member states abandon their own BIT in favor of EU law for matters among EU member states and treaties the EU adopts with other parties. It has adopted a special regulation that requires member states to notify the Commission and cooperate with it when opening negotiations on such treaties. See the EU's "Bilateral Investment Agreement Regulation," available online at https://eur-lex.europa.eu/legal-content/EN/TXT/?uri=CELEX:32012R1219.

68. While some of the arguments advanced in this book can be read to favor democratic self-governance over private interests, they do not support any form of nationalist backlash.

69. Joint Interpretative Instrument on the Comprehensive Economic and Trade Agreement (CETA) between Canada and the European Union and its Member States, October 27, 2016, available online at http://data.consilium.europa.eu/doc/document/ST-13541–2016-INIT/en/pdf, p. 5. CETA entered into force provisionally on September 21, 2017.

70. See Art. 8.27 CETA Treaty, available online at http://ec.europa.eu/trade/policy/in-focus/ceta/ceta-chapter-by-chapter/. The treaty specifies that the

Tribunal must have diverse membership, with an equal number of panel members from Canada the EU and other countries, who will serve a five-year term.

Chapter 7. The Masters of the Code

1. Quoted in Eileen Spring. "Landowners, Lawyers," p. 58.

2. Thomas Merrill and Henry Smith, "Optimal Standardization in the Law of Property: The Numerus Clausus Principle," *Yale Law Review* 110 (2000):1–70.

3. The *Wall Street Journal* reported in 2006, that the US$1,500 hourly rate had been crossed. See Sara Randazzo and Jacqueline Parlank, "Legal Fees Cross New Mark: $1500 an Hour," *Wall Street Journal*, February 9, 2016, available online at www.wsj.com. James Fontanella-Kahn, Sujeet Indap, and Barney Thompson, "The Dawn of the Superstar Lawyer," *Financial Times*, April 8, 2018, available online at www.ft.com.

4. For a blistering review and assessment of these practices, see only the ruling by the US District Court of the Southern District of New York against Nomura Holding America, Inc., *FHA v. Nomura*, December 18, 2014, 11cv6201-DLC.

5. The firm Milberg & Weiss, for example, was indicted in 2006 for paying kickbacks to plaintiffs in securities class action suits. See Julie Creswell, "Milberg Weiss is charged with Bribery and Fraud," *New York Times*, May 18, 2006, available online at www.nytimes.com; still, the case against the firm was eventually dismissed.

6. Rande W. Kostal, *Law and English Railway Capitalism* (Oxford: Clarendon Press, 1994), p. 46.

7. There is an elaborate literature on the internal organization of American law firms. See in particular Marc Galanter and William Henderson, "The Elastic Tournament: A Second Transformation of the Big Law Firm," *Stanford Law Review* 60, no. 6 (2008):1867–1929. On the global legal profession and its English origins, see also Marc Galanter and Simon Roberts, "From Kinship to Magic Circle: The London Commercial Law Firm in the Twentieth Century," *International Journal of the Legal Profession* 15, no. 3 (2009):143–178.

8. Maureen Cain, "The Symbol Traders," in *Lawyers in a Postmodern World*, ed. Maureen Cain and Christine B. Harrington (New York: New York University Press, 1994), with references to Weber and others who have studied the relation between law and capital.

9. On the rise of the large US firm, see also Anthony T. Kronman, *The Lost Lawyer: Failing Ideals of the Legal Profession* (Cambridge, MA and London: Belknap Press of Harvard University Press, 1993).

10. William D. Henderson and Arthur S. Alderson, "The Changing Economic Geography of Large U.S. Law Firms," *ssrn.com abstract 1134223* (2008) table 2, p. 8.

11. Stacey Zaretsky, "The Largest Law Firm in the United States," *Above the Law*, April 16, 2018, available online at https://abovethelaw.com/2018/04/the-largest-law-firm-in-the-united-states/ (last accessed August 29, 2018).

12. Ibid.

13. Ronald J. Gilson, "The Lawyer as Transaction Cost Engineer," in *Palgrave Encyclopedia of Law and Economics,* ed. *Peter Newman* (New York: Stockton Press, 1998), 508–514.

14. Ronald J. Gilson, "Value Creation by Business Lawyers: Legal Skills and Asset Pricing," *Yale Law Journal* 94, no. 2 (1984):239–313, p. 297.

15. This device emerged only in the mid-1980s. For a history of the poison pill and details on its legal structure, see Marcel Kahan and Edward B. Rock, "How I Learned to Stop Worrying and Love the Pill: Adaptive Responses to Takeover Law," *University of Chicago Law Review* 69, no. 3 (2002):871–915.

16. Lipton is a senior partner at Wachtell, Lipton, Rosen and Katz in New York. See http://www.wlrk.com/.

17. At the beginning of the 2000s, more than 60 percent of all publicly traded companies in the United States had poison pills in place. The numbers have since dropped to less than 10 percent in the Fortune 500. See www.sharprepellent.net for annual updates.

18. Elisabeth de Fontenay, "Law Firm Selection and the Value of Transactional Lawyering," *Journal of Corporation Law* 41, no. 2 (2015):394–430, p. 397.

19. Stephen Magee, "How Many Lawyers Ruin an Economy?," *Wall Street Journal,* September 24, 1992, Op-ed page.

20. See Charles Epp, "Do Lawyers Impair Economic Growth?," *Law and Social Inquiry* 16 (1992):585–623; followed by Stephen P. Magee, "The Optimal Number of Lawyers: A Reply to Epp," *Law and Social Inquiry* 17, no. 4 (1992):667–693, which was followed by another rejoinder by Epp.

21. See Piketty, *Capital,* especially chap. 5, and Alvaredo et al., *World Inequality Report.*

22. Alvaredo et al., *World Inequality Report,* p. 19 and 69; see also fig. 2.3.2a, "Top 1% vs. Bottom 50% National Income Shares in the United States and Western Europe, 1980–2016," p. 70 of the report.

23. Carol Silver, "States Side Story: Career Paths of International LLM Students, or I Like to Be in America," *Fordham Law Review* 80 (2012):2383–2437; as Silver explains, data are difficult to come by, but statistics from the International Education Institute suggests that the number of foreign students who study law abroad has increased from 3,500 in 1985 to almost 9,000 in 2009. Ibid., p. 23. Silver also reports that nearly 30 percent of all persons who sit for the New York bar exam have a foreign legal background. Ibid., p. 22.

24. The reference to the "old comparative economics" is to the comparison of capitalism and socialism. After socialism's demise, it now seemed time to compare different capitalist systems, but with a focus on law and legal institutions. See Simeon Djankov, Edward Glaeser, Rafael La Porta, Florencio Lopez-de-Silanes, and Andrei Shleifer, "The New Comparative Economics," *Journal of Comparative Economics* 31, no. 4 (2003):595–619.

25. Rafael La Porta, Francesco Lopez-de-Silanes, Andrei Shleifer, and Robert Vishny, "Law and Finance."

26. In their tenth anniversary paper, the authors emphasize that their findings are not about growth, but about financial market development; put differently, they reflect greater value of private assets but not necessarily enhanced economic well-being across the board. See Rafael La Porta, Francesco Lopez-de-Silanes, and Andrei Shleifer, "The Economic Consequences of Legal Origin," *Journal of Economic Literature* 46, no. 2 (2008):285–332.

27. Holger Spamann, "The 'Antidirector Rights Index' Revisited," *Review of Financial Studies* 23, no. 2 (2010):467–486; and with a focus on historical data on financial market development, Raghuram G. Rajan and Luigi Zingales, "The Great Reversals: The Politics of Financial Development in the 20th Century," *Journal of Financial Economics* 69 (2003):5–50.

28. Quoted in Benjamin R. Twiss, *Lawyers and the Constitution: How Laissez Faire Came to the Supreme Court* (Princeton, NJ: Princeton University Press, 1942).

29. Paul Brand, "The Origins of the English Legal Profession," *Law and History Review* (1987):31–50 esp. p. 35.

30. Harry Cohen, "The Divided Legal Profession in England and Wales—Can Barristers and Solicitors Ever Be Fused?," *Journal of the Legal Profession* 12 (1987):7–27.

31. Ibid., p. 11.

32. There is some dispute about the exact timing and location of the find, but that need not concern us here.

33. See Peter Stein, *Roman Law in European History* (Cambridge: Cambridge University Press, 1999).

34. Lucien Karpik, *French Lawyers: A Study in Collective Action 1274–1991* (Oxford: Clarendon Press, 1999), p. 16. See also David Bell, "Barristers, Politics and the Failure of Civil Society in the Old Regime," in *Lawyers and the Rise of Western Political Liberalism*, ed. Terence C. Halliday and Lucien Karpik (Oxford: Clarendon Press, 1997), 65–100.

35. Karpik, *French Lawyers*, p. 33.

36. See ibid., p. 59, who describes the classical bar that emerged in the eighteenth century as "a legal and political actor dedicated to liberal action." But see also Bell, "Barristers, Politics," who argues that lawyers did not just turn to politics; rather "lawyers and politics turned to each other" (p. 100), thus reinforcing a long tradition of lawyers in the service of the state. Also see Bell, p. 86.

37. The official translation of this Article reads "In the cases that are referred to them, judges are forbidden to pronounce judgments by way of general and regulatory dispositions." Available online at https://www.legifrance.gouv.fr /Traductions/en-English/Legifrance-translations.

38. Germany became a unified state only in 1871. On the country's relative economic backwardness, see Alexander Gerschenkron, *Economic Backwardness in Historical Perspective* (Cambridge, MA: Harvard University Press, 1962).

39. Dietrich Rueschemeyer, "State, Capitalism, and the Organization of Legal Counsel: Examining an Extreme Case—the Prussian Bar, 1700–1914," in *Lawyers*

and the Rise of Western Political Liberalism, ed. Terence C. Halliday and Lucien Karpik (Oxford: Clarendon Press, 1997), pp. 207–228.

40. Ibid., p. 208; the second quote is attributed to A. Weissler.

41. Kenneth F. Ledforth, "Lawyers and the Limits of Liberalism: The German Bar in the Weimar Republic," in *Lawyers and the Rise of Western Political Liberalism,* ed. Terence C. Halliday and Lucien Karpik (Oxford: Clarendon Press), p. 228.

42. The German Law on Judges (*Deutsches Richtergesetz, DRIG*) stipulates that the study of law at a university followed by two state examinations are the basic requirements for an appointment as judge (Sec. 5 DRIG); and according to Sec. 4 of the *Bundesrechtsanwaltsordnung (BRAO),* the Statute that regulates the legal profession, access to the legal profession is conditional on being eligible for a position as judge.

43. Robert W. Gordon, "The American Legal Profession, 1870–2000," chap. 3 in *The Cambridge History of Law in America,* edited by Michael Grossberg and Christopher Tomlins (Cambridge: Cambridge University Press, 2008), 73–126, p. 76. Note that a few years later, in 1874, the American Bar Association put the number of lawyers at 64,000. This is when formal legal education began to take off and numbers of practicing lawyers were recorded.

44. Justin Simard, "The Birth of a Legal Economy: Lawyers and Development of American Commerce," *Buffalo Law Review* 64 (2016):1059–1134. Historic data on the size of the US population are available online at https://www.census.gov /history/www/through_the_decades/fast_facts/1870_fast_facts.html.

45. Edward J. Balleisen, "Vulture Capitalism in Antebellum America: The 1841 Federal Bankruptcy Act and the Exploitation of Financial Distress," *Business History Review* 70, no. 4 (1996):473–516.

46. Andrew Abbott, *The System of Professions: An Essay on the Division of Expert Labor* (Chicago and London: University of Chicago Press, 1988).

47. The first woman admitted to a state bar in the United States was Belle Babb Mansfield, in 1869. See American Women, online at https://memory.loc .gov/ammem/awhhtml/awlaw3/women_lawyers.html (last accessed August 9, 2017). Harvard Law School did not admit women until 1950. See Robert W. Gordon, *The American Legal Profession,* p. 80.

48. See Kronman, *The Lost Lawyer,* pp. 113ff.

49. Gordon, *The American Legal Profession,* p. 74.

50. Ibid., p. 99.

51. Data are based on a historical data compiled by the *Wall Street Journal* and published online on "The Faculty Lounge" blog. See http://www .thefacultylounge.org/2013/02/historical-data-total-number-of-law-students -1964–2012.html (last accessed November 4, 2017).

52. These statistics are publicly available online at the website of the American Bar Association. See https://www.americanbar.org/resources_for_lawyers /profession_statistics.html (last accessed August 29, 2018).

53. Lincoln Caplan, *Skadden: Power, Money, and the Rise of a Legal Empire* (New York: Farrar Straus Giroux, 1993), p. 126.

54. Today, 36 percent of all active attorneys are women, but the share of minorities, including African Americans and Hispanics, has remained at a stable low of only 5 percent. See the ABA statistics, available online at https://www.americanbar.org/resources_for_lawyers/profession_statistics.html.

55. The history of the new style of firms is well captured in the story about the rise of Skadden. See Caplan, *Skadden*. On the persistence of the WASP cliché in blue-chip law firms, see Eli Wald, "Big Law Identity Capital: Pink and Blue, Black and White," *Fordham Law Review* 83 (2015):2509–2555.

56. See Caplan, *Skadden*, pp. 63 and 207.

57. See Stuart Anderson, "Changing the Nature of Real Property Law," *The Oxford History of the Laws of England: 1820–1914 Private Law*, ed. William Cornish et al. (Oxford: Oxford University Press, 2010), 1–54, p. 30, quoting T. S. Williams from 1909.

58. Bankruptcy law is a partial exception, because it exists at the state and federal levels.

59. On the political choices that shaped the history of banking in the United States, see Calomiris and Haber, *Fragile by Design*.

60. For a critical assessment of the competition for corporate law in the United States, see Mark Roe, "Delaware's Competition," *Harvard Law Review* 117 (2002): 588–624. He argues that competition between Delaware and the federation was at least equally important.

61. "The Global 100: Firms Ranked by Headcount," *American Lawyer*, September 25, 2017, available online at https://www.law.com/americanlawyer/almID/1202798544204/ (last accessed November 4, 2017).

62. As of September 2017, this included Freshfields Bruckhaus Deringer (Rank 14 by gross revenue). See "The Global 100," available online at https://www.law.com/americanlawyer/almID/1202798543572/.

63. GVA measures the value generated by any unit engaged in the production of goods and services.

64. For the contribution of the legal services sector to the UK economy, see The CityUK, "Legal Services," 2016, available online at https://www.thecityuk.com/assets/2016/Reports-PDF/UK-Legal-services-2016.pdf (last accessed November 4, 2017). Data on the contribution of the financial sector to the economy are available in the House of Commons Library Briefing Paper, "Financial Services, Contribution to the UK Economy," No. 6193, March 2017, p. 5. According to these data, the contribution of the financial sector peaked in 2009 at 9.1 percent of GVA.

65. Ibid., p. 10.

66. Other foreign firms in London originate primarily from Continental Europe and Australia. See City UK's "Legal Services," p. 6.

67. Ibid., fig. 14, p. 19.

68. Daniel Sokol, "Globalization of Law Firms: A Survey of the Literature and a Research Agenda for Further Study," *Indiana Journal of Global Legal Studies* 14, no. 1 (2007):5–28, especially chart I on p. 10 and accompanying text from which the following data are drawn.

69. Ibid.

70. See also the discussion in chapter 6.

71. On the transformation of the American legal profession in particular, not so much as a result of globalization but growth and the internal reorganization of these firms, see also Marc Galanter and Thomas Palay, *Tournament of Lawyers: The Transformation of the Big Law Firm* (Chicago and London: University of Chicago Press, 1991).

72. For a similar point, see Steven Shavell, "The Fundamental Divergence of Social and Private Benefits of Litigation," *Journal of Legal Studies* 26, no. S2 (1997):575–612.

73. Florian Griesel, "Competition and Cooperation in International Commercial Arbitration: The Birth of a Transnational Legal Profession," *Law and Society Review* 51, no. 4 (2017):790–824.

74. Ibid., p. 791.

75. See, for example, the UNCITRAL Model Law on Arbitration, which was first adopted in 1985 and was last amended in 2006; available online at http://www.uncitral.org/uncitral/en/uncitral_texts/arbitration/1985Model _arbitration.html.

76. For details, see https://www.consumerfinance.gov/arbitration-rule/.

Chapter 8. A New Code?

1. Lawrence Lessig, *Code 2.0* (New York: Basic Books, 2006) (the original book was published in 1999).

2. For a good introduction about how blockchain works, see Primavera De Filippi and Aaron Wright, *Blockchain and the Law* (Cambridge, MA; London: Harvard University Press, 2018), especially the introductory chapter.

3. Soviet legal theorists have struggled with this notion, because they faced the reality of a complex economic system that required some guidance, or governance, as we would say today. Evgeny Pashukanis, the Soviet legal theorist, explained the paradox of smashing the old order, yet adopting a civil code during the subsequent period of the "new economic policy," as a necessary step in the evolution of socialism toward communism. See his *The Marxist Theory of Law and the Construction of Socialism*, Revoliutsiia prava (1927), no. 3, pp. 3– 12, available online in English translation at https://www.marxists.org/archive /pashukanis/1927/xx/theory.htm.

4. This summary of the views of some of the digital coders is based on my own interactions with them at workshops and conferences, including a workshop on cryptocurrencies I organized at Columbia Law School in September 2017.

5. De Filippi and Wright, *Blockchain and the Law*.

6. Oliver Hart and John Moore, "Foundations of Incomplete Contracts," *Review of Economic Studies* 66, no. 1 (1999):115–138. See also Cooter and Schäfer, *Solomon's Knot*, who argue that the inability to firmly commit is at the heart of the poverty of many nations.

7. Kieron O'Hara, "Authority Printed Upon Emptiness," *IEEE Internet Computing* 19, no. 6 (2015):72–76.

8. Nick Szabo, "Formalizing and Securing Relationships on Public Networks," *First Monday*, September 1, 1997, available online at https://firstmonday.org /article/view/548.

9. Oliver Hart and John Moore, "Foundations," and Eric Maskin and Jean A. F. Tirole, "Unforeseen Contingencies and Incomplete Contracts," *Review of Economic Studies* 66, no. 1 (1999):83–114. See also chapter 9 for a detailed discussion of incomplete law.

10. Frank Knight has coined the term "fundamental uncertainty." See Frank H. Knight, *Risk, Uncertainty and Profit* (Boston: Houghton Mifflin, 1921), p. 232 and chapter 8, pp. 233ff.

11. See Ronald J. Gilson, Charles F. Sabel, and Robert E. Scott, "Contracting for Innovation: Vertical Disintegration and Interfirm Collaboration," *Columbia Law Review* 109, no. 3 (2009):431–502. The authors make the case that the design of contracts for inter-firm collaboration have become more incomplete to leave room for mutual agreed adjustments over time.

12. For details, see De Filippi and Wright, *Blockchain and the Law*, at Loc. 1626 (Kindle edition).

13. This includes the doctrine of "frustration" of contracts in the common law, and a fundamental alteration of the basis of the transaction, in German law. See J. P. Dawson, "Judicial Revision of Frustrated Contracts: Germany," *Boston University Law Review* 63 (1983):1039–1098; and also his "Judicial Revision of Frustrated Contracts: The United States," *Boston University Law Review* 64 (1984):1–38.

14. Philip Ashton and Brett Christophers, "On Arbitration, Arbitrage and Arbitrariness in Financial Markets and Their Governance: Unpacking LIBOR and the LIBOR Scandal," *Economy and Society* 44, no. 2 (2015):188–217.

15. Katie Martin, "Scrapping LIBOR leaves 500bn of Bond Contracts in Limbo," *Financial Times*, October 10, 2018, available online at www.ft.com. On the push-back against the new benchmark Alex Harris, "LIBOR Refuses to Die, Setting Up $370 billion Benchmark Battle," Bloomberg, May 7, 2018, available online at www.bloomberg.com (last accessed August 1, 2018).

16. See De Filippi and Wright, *Blockchain and the Law*, Loc. 721 (Kindle edition).

17. This is a curious arrangement, because under general insurance regulation, it is prohibited to insure an asset one does not own. But for CDS it did the trick of exempting them from regulatory oversight; apparently the logic is that an insurance contract that is illegal cannot possibly qualify as one. Remarkably, the insurance regulators seem to have bought the argument.

18. Most CDS contracts and their credit schedules were governed by templates the International Swaps and Derivatives Association (ISDA) had standardized. For details, see chapter 6.

19. According to the materials collected by the FCIC, after not having had to pay collateral on a single CDS, AIGFP, the dominant player in the market, was

charged by Goldman Sachs to pay US$1.8 billion from one day to the next. See
http://fcic-static.law.stanford.edu/cdn_media/fcic-docs/2007-07-27_Goldman
_Sachs_Collateral_Invoice_to_AIG.pdf (last accessed June 21, 2017).

20. For details, see chapter 4.

21. Nick Szabo, *Secure Property Titles with Owner Authority*, 1998, publications
of the Satoshi Nakamoto Institute, available online at https://nakamotoinstitute
.org/secure-property-titles/.

22. See Coase, *Problem of Social Cost*, p. 15.

23. Szabo, *Secure Property*.

24. Ibid., p. 3.

25. Ibid.

26. Ibid., p. 7.

27. De Soto, *The Mystery of Capital*, p. 179.

28. For a survey of the effects of formalizing property rights in the developing
world in recent years, see Klaus Deininger, *Land Policies for Growth and Poverty
Reduction*, World Bank Policy Research Reports (Washington, DC: World Bank,
2003).

29. The concept of the decentralized autonomous organization (DAO) is illustrated on the Ethereum website: https://www.ethereum.org/dao. For a useful account of The DAO's brief existence, see Muhammed Izhar Mehar et al.,
"Understanding a Revolutionary and Flawed Grand Experiment in Blockchain:
The DAO Attack," available online at ssrn.com/abstract=3014782 (2017).

30. See the SEC's press release of July 25, 2017, available online at https://
www.sec.gov/news/press-release/2017-131, about its investigative report that
concluded that ICOs of the kind The DAO had issued were securities and as such
subject to regulations and supervision.

31. This is the fundamental problem of the "separation of ownership and con-
trol" that Berle and Means identified. See Adolf Augustus Berle and Gardiner
Means, *The Modern Corporation and Private Property* (New York: Council for
Research in the Social Sciences, Columbia University, 1932).

32. The nexus of contract theory of firms is associated with Jensen and Mack-
ling, "Theory of the Firm," as noted earlier; but see also Frank H. Easterbrook
and Daniel R. Fischel, *The Economic Structure of Corporate Law* (Cambridge,
MA: Harvard University Press, 1991).

33. See Mehar et al., "Understanding a Revolutionary and Flawed Grand Experiment," section 3, "The Organization of The DAO," where they describe this
feature as follows: "The DAO can split such that minority users who disagree with
a proposal are able to receive their portion of Ether on that investment prior to
the formation of a new DAO where the users who agree with the proposal can
spend their Ether."

34. For a detailed discussion, see chapter 3.

35. See, e.g., Nathaniel Popper, "A Venture Fund with Plenty of Virtual
Capital, but No Capitalist," *New York Times*, May 21, 2016, available online
at https://www.nytimes.com/2016/05/22/business/dealbook/crypto-ether

-bitcoin-currency.html; "The DAO of Accrue," *The Economist*, May 19, 2016, available online at https://www.economist.com/news/finance-and-economics /21699159-new-automated-investment-fund-has-attracted-stacks-digital -money-dao.

36. See, e.g., Emin Gun Sirer, "Thoughts on The DAO Hack," *Hacking, Distributed*, June 17, 2016, available online at http://hackingdistributed.com/2016 /06/17/thoughts-on-the-dao-hack/.

37. Mehar et al., "Understanding a Revolutionary and Flawed Grand Experiment in Blockchain," section 4, "Attack on The DAO."

38. Ibid.

39. Stan Higgins, "From $900 to $20.000: Bitcoin's Historic 2017 Price Run Revisited," available online at https://www.coindesk.com/900–20000-bitcoins -historic-2017-price-run-revisited/. Hannah Murphy, "The Rise and Fall of Ethereum," *Financial Times*, October 18, 2018, available online at www.ft.com.

40. "Craig Stephen Wright Claims to Be Satoshi Nakamoto. Is He?" *The Economist*, May 2, 2016, available online at www.economist.com.

41. A debate about the sources of money has been raging for quite some time. Carl Menger and other representatives of the "Austrian" school suggest that money emerged spontaneously and in a bottom-up fashion to facilitate exchange; while others, also labeled "chartalists," have asserted that true money is a creation of states. For a good overview of these alternative theories of money, see Geoffrey Ingham, *The Nature of Money* (Cambridge: Polity Press, 2004); and Christine Desan, *Making Money: Coin, Currency, and the Coming of Capitalism* (Oxford: Oxford University Press, 2015). See also Roy Kreitner, "Legal History of Money," *Annual Review of Law and Social Science* 8, no. 1 (2012):415–431.

42. Robert Sams, "Blockchain Finance," a PowerPoint presentation of March 2015, available online at https://www.slideshare.net/rmsams/blockchain-finance (last accessed August 31, 2017).

43. For a critique of cryptocurrency coders on this point, see Perry Mehrling's blog, "Cryptos Fear Credit," available online at http://www.perrymehrling.com /2017/09/cryptos-fear-credit/.

44. Satoshi Nakamoto, *Bitcoin Manifesto: One CPU One Vote* (Heterodoxa collection edited by Stefano Tombolini, 2014), p. 5.

45. They were admitted in October 2017. See the CME's press release online at https://www.cmegroup.com/media-room/press-releases/2017/10/31/cme _group_announceslaunchofbitcoinfutures.html. Meanwhile, futures trading has picked up, and the CME reported in the summer of 2018 that futures trading volume had increased by 93 percent.

46. Minsky did not advocate the nationalization of all banks, but he argued for stringent capital requirements and for a big role of the government in the economy to ensure stability. See the policy principles and agenda for reform set out in chapters 12 and 13 of his *Stabilizing an Unstable Economy*. For an excellent summary of Minsky's thinking of how to stabilize an inherently instable financial system, see Mehrling, "Minsky and Modern Finance."

47. Described by De Filippi and Wright, *Blockchain and the Law*, at Loc. 449 (Kindle edition).

48. Gerard, *Attack of the 50 Foot Blockchain: Bitcoin, Blockchain, Ethereum & Smart Contract (Creative Commons*, 2017) at Loc 202 (Kindle edition).

49. De Filippi and Wright, *Blockchain and the Law*, at Loc. 800 (Kindle edition).

50. See also Desan, *Making Money,* who argues that money is grounded in constitutional law.

51. Mark J. Flannery, "Contingent Capital Instruments for Large Financial Institutions," *Annual Review of Financial Economics* 6 (2014):225–240.

52. On how CoCos might perform under stress, see Thomas Hale and Dan McCrum, "Why CoCo Bonds Are Worrying Investors," *Financial Times*, February 9, 2016, available online at www.ft.com.

53. Charles Tilly argued that protecting one's friends and their clients is a core feature of emergent states. See Charles Tilly, "War Making and State Making as Organized Crime," in *Bringing the State Back In*, ed. Peter Evans, Dieter Rueschemeyer, and Theda Skocpol (Cambridge: Cambridge University Press, 1985), 169–191; see also the discussion in chapter 9.

54. Chuan Tian, "The Rate of Blockchain Patent Applications Has Nearly Doubled in 2017," July 27, 2017, available online at https://www.coindesk.com /rate-blockchain-patent-applications-nearly-doubled-2017/ (last accessed September 1, 2017).

55. See http://appft.uspto.gov/netahtml/PTO/search-bool.html (last accessed August 1, 2018).

56. Mark A. Chen, Qinxi Wuy, and Baozhong Yang, "How Valuable Is FinTech Innovation," ssrn.com/abstract=3106892 (2018); see especially figures 4 and 5B.

57. See Chuan Tian, "Goldman Sachs Granted 'SETLcoin' Cryptocurrency Patent," July 13, 2017, available online at https://www.coindesk.com/goldman -sachs-granted-setlcoin-cryptocurrency-patent/ (last accessed September 1, 2017); Christine Kim, "Barclays Seeks Twin Blockchain Patents for Banking Services," July 19, 2018; and Kim, "Mastercard Wins Patent for Speeding Up Crypto Payments," July 17, 2018; both available at www.coindesk.com (last accessed August 1, 2018).

58. For details, see https://www.r3.com/about/.

59. Cohen, "Property and Sovereignty," labeled private entrepreneurs captains of industry and finance; see ibid., p. 13.

Chapter 9. Capital Rules by Law

1. The title of this chapter is borrowed from Rawi Abdelal, *Capital Rules* (Cambridge, MA: Harvard University Press, 2007), but he refers to the capital adequacy rules used for prudential regulation of banks, including the Basel Accords.

2. Max Weber, *General Economic History* (New Brunswick, NJ: Transaction Books, 1981), p. 277.

3. Weber, *Economy and Society*, Vol. II, Chapter 8, p. 880.

4. Adam S. Hofri-Winogradow, "Protection of Family Property from Creditors in the Enlightenment-Era Court of Chancery," ssrn.com 1104385 (2008).

5. Michael Lobban, "Bankruptcy and Insolvency," in *The Oxford History of the Laws of England: 1820–1914 Private Law*, ed. William Cornish, J. Stuart Anderson et al. (Oxford: Oxford University Press, 2010), 779–833.

6. See chapter 4 for details.

7. Margaret Levi, "The Predatory Theory of Rule," *Policy and Society* 10, no. 4 (1981):431–465.

8. Christoph Menke, *Kritik der Rechte* (Berlin: Suhrkamp, 2015), especially chap. 5.

9. Ibid., p. 311. The German original reads: "Daher gilt: Ohne die Form der subjektiven Rechte kein Kapitalismus."

10. This is the case in the United Kingdom and the United States. In other countries, competing principles, including that of a social welfare state, have been used to balance the power of subjective rights, Germany being one example. But over time, the balance has tilted toward the latter.

11. Sanford J. Grossman and Oliver D. Hart, "The Costs and Benefits of Ownership: A Theory of Vertical and Lateral Integration," *Journal of Political Economy* 94, no. 4 (1986):691–719; Oliver Hart, and John Moore, "Property Rights and the Nature of the Firm," *Journal of Political Economy* 98, no. 6 (1990):1119–1158.

12. Katharina Pistor and Chenggang Xu, "Incomplete Law," *Journal of International Law and Politics* 35, no. 4 (2003):931–1013.

13. On the rules vs. standards debate, see Louis Kaplow, "Rules versus Standards: An Economic Analysis," *Duke Law Journal* 42 (1992):557–629.

14. For a full exposition of the different sources of incomplete law, see Pistor and Xu, "Incomplete Law."

15. *In Diamond v. Chakrabarty*, 447 U.S. 303; see also chapter 5.

16. Boyle, "The Second Enclosure Movement and the Construction of the Public Domain," p. 38.

17. There is substantial variation in the rules about who bears the costs of litigation in different countries and different areas of the law. However, even if the loser has to pay all the costs, the plaintiff faces a substantial probability that it will be he or she who will have to pay up.

18. For first steps taken by Congress against class action suits, see Stephen B. Burbank, "The Class Action Fairness Act of 2005 in Historical Context: A Preliminary View," *University of Pennsylvania Law Review* 156 (2008):1439–1551. And on the change in perception of victims and vulnerabilities, see Christine P. Bartholomew, "Redefining Prey and Predator in Class Actions," *Brooklyn Law Review* 80 (2015):743–806.

19. In economic terms, this would be a classic externality; but constitutional law is not about policing externalities, but about policing rights and wrongs.

20. Levi, "The Predatory Theory of Rule"; but see also Douglass C. North, John Joseph Wallis, and Barry R. Weingast, *Violence and Social Orders: A Conceptual Framework for Interpreting Recorded Human History* (Cambridge: Cambridge

University Press, 2009), who argue that law-bound public orders have become open-access orders; the public order sets the rules of the game that allows private parties to pursue their own interests, but marvelously, without affecting open access.

21. On the "new property rights," see Charles A. Reich, "The New Property," *Yale Law Journal* 73, no. 5 (1964):733–787; for a normative claim to extend the concept to the "new, new property rights," geared explicitly toward the most vulnerable members of society, see David A. Super, "A New New Property," *Columbia Law Review* 113, no. 7 (2013):1773–1896.

22. Menke, *Kritik der Rechte*, p. 321.

23. See, for example, Rafe Blaufarb, *The Great Demarcation: The French Revolution and the Invention of Modern Property* (Oxford: Oxford University Press, 2016).

24. In a meeting of August 4, 1789, less than a month after the storming of the Bastille, the General Estates abolished all feudal forms of property and announced a new property regime based on individual rights. See Blaufarb, *The Great Demarcation*, p. 12.

25. This was done in the laws that implemented the bold political proclamations about the abolishment of old rights. For an insightful account, see Horst Welkoborsky, "Die Herausbildung Des Bürgerlichen Eigentumsbegriffs," in *Eigentum Und Recht: Die Entwicklung Des Eigentumsbegriffs Im Kapitalismus*, ed. Wolfgang Däubler (Darmstadt und Neuwied: Luchterhand, 1976), pp. 11–74.

26. See Michael P. Fitzsimmons, "Privilege and the Polity in France, 1786–1791," *American Historical Review* 92, no. 2 (1987):269.

27. Tilly, "War Making and State Making."

28. Mancur Olson, "Dictatorship, Democracy, and Development," *American Political Science Review* 87, no. 03 (1993):567–576.

29. The final chapter in Polanyi's book *The Great Transformation* (see also chapter 1) suggests a new great transformation that assures society primacy over the market for a new postwar order.

30. As noted earlier, Schumpeter argued that competition is the motor for social and economic change. See Schumpeter, *Capitalism, Socialism and Democracy*, p. 82.

31. Harold J. Berman, *Law and Revolution*.

32. Albert O. Hirschman, *Exit, Voice, and Loyalty*.

33. Harold Demsetz, "Toward a Theory of Property Rights."

34. See the quote by Rudden in chapter 1.

35. For a sweeping critique of the rise of financial capital and its relation to the real economy, see Rana Foroohar, *Makers and Takers: How Wall Street Destroyed Main Street* (New York: Crown Business, 2016).

36. See *Financial Times*, "A Better Deal between Business and Society," editorial, January 2, 2018, available online at www.ft.com.

37. Some exceptions apply in the EU, where conflict-of-law rules have been harmonized for contract and tort law. In addition, several international treaties have promoted the standardization of law.

38. This would also be compatible with Tsilly Dagan's argument that more rather than less tax competition might be advisable. See her *International Tax Policy*.

39. Gary S. Becker, "Crime and Punishment: An Economic Approach," *Journal of Political Economy* 76, no. 2 (1968):169–217.

40. Stout, "Derivatives." See also Glenn Morgan, "Reforming OTC Markets: The Politics and Economics of Technical Fixes," *European Business Organization Law Review* 13, no. 03 (2012):391–412, and Frank Partnoy, "ISDA, NASD, CFMA and SDNY: The Four Horsemen of Derivatives Regulation," in *Brookings-Wharton Papers on Financial Services*, ed. Robert E. Litan and Richard Herrig (Washington, DC: Brookings Institution Press, 2002).

41. Edward R. Morrison, Mark J. Roe, and Christopher S. Sontchi, "Rolling Back."

42. Note, however, that some medical schools have eliminated school fees in order to encourage graduates to pursue not only the most lucrative doctoral careers, but to consider family practice and other, relatively less-paid positions in the medical profession. See David Chen, "Surprise Gift: Free Tuition for All N.Y.U. Medical Students," *New York Times*, August 16, 2018, available online at www.nytimes.com (last accessed August 29, 2018).

43. For a similar point, see Robert L. Hale, *Freedom Through Law*, especially chapters 1 (Economic Liberty and the State) and 2 (The Legal Basis for Economic Inequality).

44. The official representative of the open-source community just celebrated its twentieth anniversary. See https://opensource.org/ (last accessed August 28, 2018).

45. Eric A. Posner and Glen Weyl, *Radical Markets* (Princeton, NJ and Oxford: Princeton University Press, 2018).

46. The subtitle of *Radical Markets* is "Uprooting Capitalism and Democracy for a Just Society."

47. Menke, *Kritik der Rechte*, p. 265 (in English, *Critique of Rights*) (my translation). The German original reads, "Das Subjekt der bürgerlichen Rechte zahlt für seine politische Ermächtigung den Preis der Entmächtigung der Politik."

48. See also the excellent critique of *Radical Markets* by Hanoch Dagan, "Why Markets? Welfare, Autonomy, and the Just Society," *Michigan Law Review* 117 (forthcoming).

49. The latter is Amartya Sen's position. See Amartya K. Sen, *Development as Freedom*, 1st ed. (New York: Random House, 1999).

50. This joke circulated widely in the former socialist countries when they sought to replace their old with a new order.

51. See Jean L. Cohen, *Globalization and Sovereignty: Rethinking Legality, Legitimacy and Constitutionalism* (Cambridge: Cambridge University Press, 2012) for a refreshing restatement of sovereignty in the age of globalization.

INDEX

AAA rating, 86, 99–100, 251n19
ad hoc privileges, 119, 218, 223, 228
Advisory Committee for Trade Negotiations (ACTN), 121–24
Amazon, 130
American Civil War, 41, 50, 138, 174
American College of Medical Genetics, 113
American Express, 50
American International Group (AIG), 191
American Society for Clinical Pathology, 113
anti-usury rules, 90, 236n26
Apple, 72
arbitrage: optimizing legal, 67, 161; RASCAL and, 73–75; regulatory, 48, 56, 73–76, 90–91, 226; tax, 48, 56, 73
arbitration: as alternative to slow courts, 181–82; capital rule and, 215, 217, 223, 226; code masters and, 161–62, 178, 180–82; corporations and, 48, 56, 67, 73–76; digital code and, 190, 204; empire of law and, 15, 18; global code and, 136, 139–43, 146, 152, 154–57, 261n27; lawyers and, 161–62, 178, 180–82; minting debt and, 90–91; private, 143, 146, 152, 154, 157, 162, 180–81, 217, 223, 226
Arendt, Hannah, 243n40
Arruñada, Benito, 239n56
artisans, 118–19, 128
asset-backed securities (ABS), 85, 87
assets: bearer, 198; Bitcoin and, 197–202; capital rule and, 205–34; cloning legal persons and, 47–75, 247n24; code masters and, 158–61, 164–69, 174–75, 177, 180–82, 267n26; coding land and, 23–26, 30, 35–46; Debt Recovery Act and, 39–40; digital code and, 187–94, 197–204, 271n17; empire of law and, 2–22, 235n9, 238n51; eviction and, 41, 233; exclusive use rights and, 35, 209; foreclosure and, 39, 95–98, 253n44; genetic knowledge and, 109; global code and,

132, 135–38, 142–50, 154, 260n8, 262n45; homeowners and, 59, 80–84, 86, 88, 94–98, 100, 106; intangible capital and, 13, 24, 115–21, 143, 212, 216; landowners and, 24, 34–39, 42, 45, 56, 78, 128, 158–59, 166; legal coding and, 2–8, 11–12, 15, 19–24, 40, 52, 87, 92, 107–8, 116, 118, 132, 143, 168, 177, 180, 205, 208, 211–12, 215–18, 222–27, 233; legal personality and, 55; lock-in and, 15, 47, 65–67, 77, 81, 117, 196; MBS, 82–83, 86–87, 94–95, 97, 99, 101; Medici empire and, 57–58, 247n21; minting debt and, 77, 251n19, 253n41 (see also minting debt); monopolies and, 17, 41, 66, 91, 109, 111, 114–26, 257n29; partitioning and, 48, 52, 54, 56–57, 59, 107, 238n51; pooling of, 13–14, 16, 19, 45, 47, 52, 55–56, 66, 83–84, 86, 93, 96, 164–65, 211, 251n19; property and, 1–5 (see also property); rating agencies and, 80, 86–87, 98–100, 251n6, 251n19; scalability of, 145; securitization and, 43, 45, 78–86, 91–101, 165, 251n11, 251n13, 253n41; self-interest and, 6, 8–9, 18, 232, 236n18; shielding of, 3, 14, 20, 22, 44, 47–48, 51–63, 65, 67, 71, 78, 84, 86, 99, 107, 129, 161, 165, 205, 215, 238n51, 246n16, 247n20; stage-contingent, 41; titles and, 13, 25–27, 30–35, 37, 43, 46, 75, 96–97, 110, 125, 194, 206; toxic, 86, 100, 167; trade secrets and, 126–31; tranched, 83–87, 94, 98, 101, 251n19
Association for Molecular Pathology, 113
attorneys, 21, 32, 143, 160–62, 171–74, 181–82, 217, 269n54
Australia, 29, 33
Austro-Hungarian Empire, 120
autonomy: capital rule and, 209, 212–13, 215, 218–20, 232, 272n29; coding land and, 33; corporations and, 50; digital autonomous organizations (DAO) and,

autonomy (*continued*)
194–97, 272n29, 272n30, 272n33; digital
code and, 194–97; global code and, 134–
35; lawyers and, 171–73

bailouts, 55, 62, 64, 84, 104–5, 151, 226,
247n17
Baldwin, Simeon E., 169
Bank for International Settlement (BIS),
149–50
bankruptcy, ix–x; capital rule and, 207, 209,
211, 227; cloning legal persons and, 48–
49, 51, 55, 62–63, 73, 75; code masters
and, 160, 168, 269n58; coding land and,
27; derivatives and, 144–52; empire of
law and, 3, 13–14, 16, 21; global code and,
137, 144–53, 262n42; ISDA and, 147–51;
law and, 3, 13, 16, 21, 73, 78, 87, 107, 137,
144–52, 160, 168, 209, 239n55, 262n42,
269n58; Lehman Brothers and, 48–58,
61–65, 70–75, 80, 85, 96, 101, 103–4, 106,
135, 149, 175, 190, 245n4, 246n6, 248n33;
minting debt and, 78–80, 83–84, 87, 107,
255n71; safe harbors and, 63, 145, 148–50,
152, 207, 211, 227, 262n44, 263n49;
United States and, 55, 148, 239n55,
255n71, 262n44
Banque de France, 104
Barclays, 203
barristers, 169–70
Bayerische Landesbank, 85
bearer assets, 198
Bear Stearns, 64, 83
Belize: British colonialism and, 26–27; coding
land and, 23–29, 230, 241n7, 261n21;
Constitution of, 25, 28, 241n7; courts and,
23–24, 27–29, 126, 230, 261n21; global
code and, 261n21; independence of, 26–
27; Maya people and, 23–29, 230, 261n21;
mining and, 25–27, 29, 37; Privy Council
and, 27–29, 126
beneficiaries, 43–45, 53, 81, 115, 164, 181–82
big data, 126–31
bilateral investment treaties (BITs), 140, 155,
264n67
bilateral trade, 122, 132, 136, 140, 154–56,
256n23
bills of exchange, 57, 78, 88–92, 108, 198–99,
252n31
Bitcoin, 197–202
Black Act, 243n42
blacklisting, 73, 225
Blackstone, William, 46

blockchain, 184, 187–90, 192, 195, 197–98,
203–4, 270n2
blue-chip corporations, 83, 175–76, 269n55
BNP Paribas, 85
Bonaparte, Louis, 104
Bonaparte, Napoleon, 133, 242n27
bourgeoisie, 10, 208
Brandeis, Louis, 109
Braudel, Fernand, 9
Breast Cancer Susceptibility Gene (BRCA),
111–14, 116, 127, 130, 214
Brexit, 179
bright-line rule, 224–25
Bristol-Myers, 124
Bruges, 57–58
bubbles, 59, 247n26
bugs, 185, 188, 196

Campbell, Lord, 158, 170
Canada: coding land and, 29;
Comprehensive Economic and Trade
Agreement (CETA) and, 156–57,
264n69; Eli Lilly and, 138–43, 152–55,
261n17, 261n19; Federal Court of, 139;
global code and, 138–43, 156–57, 261n17,
261n18, 263n57, 264n69; intellectual
property and, 138–43, 152–55, 261n17,
261n19; NAFTA and, 124, 138, 138–42,
155, 261n20; USMCA and, 139, 261n20
Canadian Patent Act, 140, 261n23
Cancer Genetics Network Project, 113
capital: attributes of, 3–4, 11–15, 21, 39, 78,
161, 183, 205, 211–12, 233; coding land
and, 24, 26, 29, 34–45; Commons on,
12; convertibility and, 3–4, 11, 13, 15,
19, 77–78, 183, 193, 199, 211, 229, 233;
corporations and, 47–48, 52–53, 56–57,
64–67, 70, 73–76; digital code and,
183–86, 189, 195–200, 203; durability
and, 3, 211, 229, 233 (*see also* durability);
economic growth and, 2; empire of law
and, 2–22; enigma of, 9–13; global code
and, 132–38, 143, 149, 152–57; intangible,
8, 115–18; intellectual property and, 108,
112–20, 126, 130; labor and, 2, 9–11, 116,
160, 169, 217, 237n37; legal attributes and,
13–15; legal codes and, 2 (*see also* legal
code); Levy on, 12; Marxism and, 9–11;
minting debt and, 77–79, 83, 92, 100–102,
107; Piketty on, 4–5; priority rights and,
206–7, 215 (*see also* priority rights); in
service of, 152–57; Smith on, 6, 46, 134,
220, 240n68; state power and, 15–19 (*see*

also state power); universality and, 3–4, 11, 13–14, 19, 21, 54, 211, 229, 233; venture, 112; wealth and, 12–13 (*see also* wealth)

capital gains, 235n9

Capital in the Twenty-First Century (Piketty), 4–5

capitalism: capital rule and, 205–9, 212, 217, 222, 224, 228–29, 234; cloning legal persons and, 47; code masters and, 168, 179, 182, 266n24; coding land and, 26; digital code and, 199–200; empire of law and, 2, 4, 8, 10–14, 17–21, 238n44; free markets and, 4, 19, 106–7, 128–29; global code and, 132–33; historiography of, 10; nature's code and, 112; substance of, 238n44

Capitalism without Capital (Haskel and Westlake), 115–16

capital rule: arbitration and, 215, 217, 223, 226; autonomy and, 209, 212–13, 215, 218–20, 232, 272n29; bankruptcy and, 207, 209, 211, 227; bright-line rule and, 224–25; capitalism and, 205–9, 212, 217, 222, 224, 228–29, 234; coercive power and, 220, 232–33; collateral and, 224; contracts and, 209–18, 222–27, 231, 276n37; convertibility and, 211, 226–27, 229, 233; corporate law and, 209–11, 224; costly externalities and, 226; courts and, 206–7, 211–18, 221–24, 227, 230; creditors and, 206–7, 211, 216; debt and, 206–7, 209, 219, 228; derivatives and, 211, 227; durability and, 211, 229, 233; elitism and, 218; enclosure and, 229; enforcement and, 210, 220, 223; enigma of capital and, 9–13; feudalism and, 5–6, 205, 211, 223, 276n24; first-mover advantage and, 214–15; global code and, 152–57; globalization and, 219–23, 277n51; governing the code and, 222–29; growth and, 220; harmonization and, 227; inequality and, 223; intangible capital and, 212, 216; International Center for Settlement of Investment Disputes (ICSID) and, 154–55; investment and, 225–26; knowledge and, 229; law's inherent incompleteness and, 210–13; lawyers and, 206–16, 221, 224, 227–29, 234; legal attributes and, 13–15; legal code and, 205, 211–13, 216, 218–20, 225, 227, 230; legal structures and, 225; Marxism and, 207–8, 216, 234; mortgages and, 206–7, 211; New York Arbitration

Convention and, 154; partnerships and, 228; patents and, 211–15, 230; priority rights and, 206–7, 215; private code and, 20, 209–19; private law and, 209–15; property and, 206, 209, 212–20, 222, 224, 230, 276n24; public power and, 216–19; reform and, 218, 231; regulation and, 211, 213, 216–17, 221, 224–27, 274n1; resurrecting limitations and, 227; risk and, 207, 226, 229; roll-back strategies for, 224–29; roving, 219–21; safe harbors and, 63, 145, 148–50, 152, 207, 211, 227, 262n44, 263n49; shareholders and, 213, 229; slavery and, 205; sovereignty and, 234, 277n51; state power and, 15–18, 205, 208–9, 212, 216, 221–23; treaty law and, 225; United Kingdom and, 228, 234; United States and, 219, 227–28, 234; universality and, 211, 229, 233; veils and, 8, 13, 48, 207, 246n16; wealth and, 205–9, 215, 217, 221–22, 224, 230; Weber and, 206; without law, 229–34

Cayman Islands, 50, 71, 99, 135, 249n53

central banks: code masters and, 167; empire of law and, 6; global code and, 151; minting debt and, 77–78, 89, 102–6, 255n72

Chase, 64, 83–85, 248n32, 255n70

Chicago Mercantile Exchange, 200

China, 178

China Investment Corporation (CIC), 85

Chrysler, 247n17

Citigroup, 60, 248n32; foreign help for, 84; Kleros clones and, 100; NC2 and, 79–87, 94, 98–100, 106–7, 135, 251n4, 251n19

Citigroup Mortgage Realty Corporation (CMRC), 80–85

City Group Global Markets (CGGM), 85

civil law, 42–43, 133, 168–73, 178, 249n48

civil rights, 232

claims to future pay, 78, 84, 88

cloning legal persons: bankruptcy and, 48–49, 51, 55, 62–63, 73, 75; capitalism and, 47; collateral and, 51; contracts and, 47–48, 52–55, 58–60, 64–65, 68–69, 247n24; corporate law and, 47–56, 60–62, 65, 67–72, 74, 76, 246n14, 246n16, 248n30; courts and, 58, 68–70, 73–76, 247n24; creditors and, 47–48, 51, 54–67, 71, 73, 75, 246n16, 247n24; debt and, 47–53, 56, 59–60, 67, 73–74; durability and, 47, 54–55; elitism and, 66, 75; immortality and, 50, 55, 65–67;

cloning legal persons (*continued*)
incorporation theory and, 69–70, 74, 136, 246n10; investment and, 48–53, 60–65, 67, 72, 75, 248n39; Kleros and, 99; labor and, 49; lawyers and, 48, 52, 70; legal entities and, 51–53, 55, 57, 65, 69–71; Lehman Brothers and, 48–58, 61–65, 70–75, 80, 85, 96, 101, 103–4, 106, 135, 149, 175, 190, 245n4, 246n6, 248n33, 250n59; limited liability and, 60–61; loss shifting and, 55, 59–64, 67; monopolies and, 66; NC2 and, 79–87, 94, 98–100, 106–7, 135, 251n4, 251n19; priority rights and, 55–56, 63; private law and, 68; property and, 47, 68; regulation and, 249n46; risk and, 48, 54–56, 59, 63–66, 70, 74–75; Roman law and, 51; slavery and, 49, 54, 57, 60; universality and, 54; wealth and, 48, 56, 59, 64, 66–67

Coase, Ronald, 45, 192

code masters: arbitration and, 161–62, 178, 180–82; assets and, 158–61, 164–69, 174–75, 177, 180–82; bankruptcy and, 160, 168, 269n58; capitalism and, 168, 179, 182, 266n24; central banks and, 167; coercive power and, 177, 180; collateral and, 160, 177; common law and, 168–73, 176–78; contracts and, 159–60, 172, 178, 181–82; corporate law and, 159–60, 163–64, 168, 174–79, 269n60; courts and, 159–64, 168–73, 177, 180–82; creditors and, 158–59, 168; debt and, 158, 167, 174; durability and, 159, 161, 182; elitism and, 158, 162, 164, 175–77; enforcement and, 168, 180; globalization and, 176–79, 270n71; growth and, 166, 175, 267n26, 270n71; inequality and, 167; investment and, 160–61, 165, 167–68; labor and, 160, 169; legal code and, 158–59, 167, 177, 180; legal origin of, 167–76; Lehman Brothers and, 175; partnerships and, 162–63, 166, 175–78; poison pills and, 163–64, 266n15, 266n17; priority rights and, 158, 161; private law and, 169–73, 182; private money and, 175; property and, 158–60, 164, 172, 177; reform and, 158–59, 171; regulation and, 160–63, 168, 171–77, 182, 267n37, 268n42; risk and, 161–62, 165; securitization and, 165; shareholders and, 164, 168; sovereignty and, 160; United Kingdom and, 168, 178–79; United States and, 162, 168, 171, 174–79; wealth and, 159, 162, 164–67, 174, 176

coding land: acquired rights and, 45–46; autonomy and, 33; bankruptcy and, 27; Belize and, 23–29, 230, 241n7, 261n21; British colonies and, 39–42; capitalism and, 26; collateral and, 30, 35–36; common law and, 31–32, 40, 243n43; common use and, 29–30; contracts and, 41–42; Conveyance Act and, 38–39; corporate law and, 24, 35, 37, 44; courts and, 23–34, 38–45, 244n63; creditors and, 24, 30, 35–45; debt and, 30, 35–42; decoding the trust and, 42–45; digital code and, 183–90, 194, 197, 203–4; discovery doctrine and, 34–35; durability and, 24, 39, 42–43, 46; elitism and, 8, 40–41, 75, 158, 164, 254n55; emerging land market and, 32; enclosure and, 29–35, 39, 229, 256n14; eviction and, 41, 233; important role of land and, 23–24; inequality and, 46; investment and, 25, 37, 45, 241n13; landowners and, 24, 34–39, 42, 45, 56, 78, 128, 158–59, 166, 254n55; lawyers and, 24, 31–32, 35, 37–38, 40, 43–45, 164, 240n6, 242n29; legal code and, 24, 39–40, 43; legal title and, 24–29, 33–34, 45–46; Maya people and, 23–29, 230, 261n21; monopolies and, 41; mortgages and, 35–38, 43; ownership and, 30, 34–35, 136; priority rights and, 24–25, 29, 37, 39, 46; property and, 23–39, 42–46, 240n2, 241n10, 241n13, 242n27, 242n36, 243n41, 245n75; protecting spoils and, 35–39; reform and, 38–41, 244n58, 244n64; regulation and, 44; risk and, 35, 41; securitization and, 43, 45; Settled Land Acts and, 38–39; settlers and, 33–35, 42, 125, 192–93; shielding and, 44; slavery and, 39; sovereignty and, 26–27, 33–34; state power and, 23, 46; Statute of Enrollments and, 44; Statute of Uses and, 44; titles and, 25–27, 30–35, 37, 43, 46, 125, 194; trust law and, 42–45; turning land into private, 29–35; usage and, 24–29; wealth and, 24, 27, 35–46

coercive power: capital rule and, 220, 232–33; code masters and, 177, 180; digital code and, 187, 193; empire of law and, 4, 7, 15–21, 239n60; global code and, 132, 154; minting debt and, 90; trade secrets and, 126, 129; World Trade Organization (WTO) and, 125

Cohen, Morris, 137–38

Coindesk, 203
collateral, ix–x; capital rule and, 224; cloning legal persons and, 51; code masters and, 160, 177; coding land and, 30, 35–36; digital code and, 187, 190–91, 271n19; empire of law and, 3, 7, 11–13, 16, 21, 238n49; global code and, 144, 148, 263n48; minting debt and, 78, 81, 86–87, 92, 97, 99, 103, 107; mortgages and, 13–14; slavery and, 11–12
collateralized debt obligations (CDOs), 87, 99–101, 108, 165, 211, 254n53
Columbia Law School, 270n4
Commerce Clause, 70, 177
commercial codes, 13, 238n48, 260n8
common law: code masters and, 168–73, 176–78; coding land and, 31–32, 40, 243n43; digital code and, 271n13; empire of law and, 5, 8; English law and, 27, 38–40, 43, 146, 178, 262n41; frustration of contracts and, 271n13; global code and, 133, 264n65; law schools and, 243n43; nature's code and, 119; New York State laws and, 8, 76, 80, 132–33, 135, 143, 146, 150, 168, 178; Roman law and, 30, 42, 132–33, 135, 170, 177, 242n27, 243n43; United Kingdom and, 176–77
Common Pleas, 32
Commons, John, 12, 238n44
Companies Act, 61
competition: free trade and, 38; guild barriers and, 128–29; intangible capital and, 118; investment banking and, 50, 91–92; lawyers and, 174, 176; private rights and, 122; property and, 121; regulatory, 68, 135, 221, 227; Schumpeter on, 118, 276n30; state power and, 221; tax shelters and, 72; trade secrets and, 128–29
Comprehensive Economic and Trade Agreement (CETA), 156–57, 264n69
conflict-of-law rules, 9, 68–69, 134–35, 212, 225, 249n48, 276n37
contingent convertibles (CoCos), 202
contracts, ix–x; blockchain and, 184, 187–90, 192, 195, 197–98, 203–4, 270n2; capital rule and, 209–18, 222–27, 231, 276n37; cloning legal persons and, 47–48, 52–55, 58–60, 64–65, 68–69, 247n24; code masters and, 159–60, 172, 178, 181–82; coding land and, 41–42; credible enforcement and, 1–2; digital code and, 183–92, 195, 198, 203, 271n13, 271n17, 271n18, 272n32; empire of law and, 2–8,

13, 15–16, 21, 238n48; enforcement of, 2, 16, 203; frustration of in common law, 271n13; global code and, 135–37, 139, 145–53; insurance, 190, 271n17; minting debt and, 78–81, 86, 88–89, 107; nature's code and, 129; nexus of, 48; rise of West and, 4; Roman law and, 187; smart, 187–91; theory of firms and, 272n32
convertibility: capital rule and, 211, 226–27, 229, 233; debt and, 3, 15, 77–78, 87–91; digital code and, 183, 193, 199; empire of law and, 3–4, 11, 13, 15, 19; state money and, 3
Conveyance Act, 38–39
copyright, 11, 115, 256n23
corporate law, ix–x; asset partitioning and, 53; capital rule and, 209–11, 224; choosing, 69–71; cloning legal persons and, 47–56, 60–62, 65, 67–72, 74, 76, 246n14, 246n16, 248n30; code masters and, 159–60, 163–64, 168, 174–79, 269n60; coding land and, 24, 35, 37, 44; digital code and, 185, 189, 196, 202; empire of law and, 3, 5, 8, 11, 13, 21, 238n54; enabling, 55; global code and, 135–36, 155; incorporation theory and, 69–70, 74, 136, 246n10; international private, 68–69; international treaty, 9, 120, 136–39, 225; legal personality and, 55; minting debt and, 78, 80, 86, 91, 98–102, 107, 252n22, 253n41; nature's code and, 108, 115, 122, 125; seat theory and, 53, 69–70; shopping for, 67–69; sunset provisions and, 76; treaty law and, 70; veils and, 8, 13, 48, 246n16
corporations: arbitration and, 48, 56, 67, 73–76; autonomy and, 50; blue-chip, 83, 175–76, 269n55; bonds and, 5, 16, 44, 48–49, 83, 86, 102–5, 108, 128, 195, 198, 202, 211, 252n22, 262n32; choosing tax rate and, 71–73; coding modern, 54–56; conflict of law and, 9, 68–69, 134–35, 212, 225, 249n48, 276n37; contracts and, 47–48, 52–55, 58–60, 64–65, 68–69; durability and, 47, 54–55; essence of, 52; immortality and, 50, 55, 65–67; incorporation theory and, 69–70, 74, 136, 246n10; legal entities and, 14, 51–59, 65, 69–71, 249n46, 253n41; legal structures and, 48–51, 54, 58, 70–71, 76, 80; Lehman Brothers' bankruptcy and, 48–58, 61–65, 70–75, 80, 85, 96, 101, 103–4, 106, 135, 149, 175, 190, 245n4,

corporations (*continued*)
246n6, 248n33; limited liability and, 51, 53–54, 60–61, 63, 99, 254n49; loss shifting and, 55, 59–64, 67; mobility and, 68, 70; ownership and, 59, 67, 92, 118, 136; partnerships and, 65 (*see also* partnerships); poison pills and, 163–64, 266n15, 266n17; PRIMA and, 136; put option and, 55, 64, 226; RASCAL and, 73–75, 250n60, 250n62; rating agencies and, 80, 86–87, 98–100, 251n6, 251n19; regulation and, 47–48, 50, 56, 68, 73–76, 226, 249n46; risk and, 48, 54–56, 59, 63–66, 70, 74–75; Roman law and, 51, 54; shareholders and, 48–56 (*see also* shareholders); shielding and, 3, 14, 20, 22, 44, 47–48, 51–63, 65, 67, 71, 78, 84, 86, 99, 107, 129, 161, 165, 205, 215, 238n51, 246n16, 247n20; sovereignty and, 53, 66–70; subsidiaries and, 50–53, 58–59, 61–64, 70–74, 84, 131, 135, 149, 151, 191, 196, 247n17, 250n59, 259n80; United States and, 139, 142, 148, 151, 156; US Supreme Court and, 68
cotton, 41, 49, 246n5
courts: appeals and, 26–27, 72, 113, 139, 143, 155–56, 261n18; arbitration and, 180–82 (*see also* arbitration); Belize and, 23–24, 27–29, 126, 230, 261n21; Canada and, 138–43, 152–57, 261n17, 261n19; capital rule and, 206–7, 211–18, 221–24, 227, 230; cease and desist orders and, 113; certiorari writ and, 261n18; cloning legal persons and, 58, 68–70, 73–76, 247n24; code masters and, 159–64, 168–73, 177, 180–82; coding land and, 23–34, 38–45, 244n63; Common Pleas and, 32; Comprehensive Economic and Trade Agreement (CETA) and, 156–57; digital code and, 187, 204; discovery doctrine and, 34–35; empire of law and, 7–8, 12, 15–20; equity rule and, 31–32; European Court of Justice and, 70, 156; first-mover advantage and, 214–15; genetics and, 109–16, 127, 211, 214; global code and, 133, 136, 138–46, 150, 152–56, 261n18, 261n21, 262n45; Ibanez case and, 95–97; Indian Removal Act and, 34; indigenous rights and, 126; Inns of Court and, 242n29; International Court of Justice and, 125, 146; ISDA and, 146; jingle rule, 247n24; King's Council and, 27, 31; landowners and, 38–39; minting debt and, 87, 90–91,

96–98, 104, 252n31; nature's code and, 110–16; patents and, 120; plaintiffs and, 32, 58, 69, 113, 142, 214, 265n5, 275n17; Privy Council and, 27–29, 126; property and, 17, 23–28, 30, 38–39, 43–44, 96–97, 126, 136, 140, 143, 159–60, 172, 214–15, 218, 262; Star Chamber and, 31; sunset provisions and, 76; trade secrets and, 127–31; tribunals and, 18, 136–43, 146, 152, 155–57, 261n21, 264n70; US Supreme Court and, 34, 68, 110–13, 116, 127, 211, 214
credit cooperatives, 93–95
credit default swaps (CDS), 190–91, 271nn17–19
credit derivatives, 78, 145, 165, 227
Crédit Mobilier, 102–6
creditors: bailouts and, 55, 62, 64, 104–5, 151, 226, 247n17; capital rule and, 206–7, 211, 216; cloning legal persons and, 47–48, 51, 54–67, 71, 73, 75, 246n16, 247n24; code masters and, 158–59, 168; coding land and, 24, 30, 35–45; Debt Recovery Act and, 39–40; digital code and, 187–88, 202; empire of law and, 3, 13–16, 20; eviction and, 41, 233; global code and, 144, 147–50, 262n41, 262n45; landlords and, 206–7; Lehman Brothers and, 61, 63–64, 71, 73, 103; limited liability and, 51, 53–54, 60–61, 63, 99, 254n49; lobbying by, 207; minting debt and, 77–79, 88–89, 92–93, 95, 103–5, 107; reciprocal claims and, 262n41; Roman law and, 54; shareholders and, 14, 48, 55–56, 60–67, 71, 104, 168, 202, 246n16; shielding assets from, 14, 20, 47–48, 54–61, 63, 65, 67, 71, 107, 247n20; Statute of Enrollments and, 44; Statute of Uses and, 44; tort, 55, 59; trade secrets and, 128
Crick, Francis, 108–10
Critique of Rights (Menke), 209, 231
cryptocurrencies, 15, 192, 196–203, 238n53, 270n4, 273n43, 274n57

debt, ix; bills of exchange and, 57, 78, 88–92, 108, 198–99, 252n31; capital rule and, 206–7, 209, 219, 228; cloning legal persons and, 47–53, 56, 59–60, 67, 73–74; code masters and, 158, 167, 174; coding land and, 30, 35–42; convertibility and, 3, 15, 77–78, 87–91; credit cooperatives and, 93–95; Crédit Mobilier and, 102–6; creditors and, 3,

13 (*see also* creditors); default and, 14, 35–36, 38, 42, 56, 62, 81–83, 88–89, 92, 96–97, 100, 102, 105, 137, 146–48, 151, 153, 170, 174, 180, 187, 190, 223, 233, 262n45; derivatives and, 78, 81, 86, 91; digital code and, 187, 190, 198–203; empire of law and, 3, 13–16, 20–21; foreclosure and, 39, 95–98, 253n44; global code and, 144, 147, 149–50, 262n41; Kleros clones and, 79, 86, 98–100, 107, 135, 165; minting, 77–107 (*see also* minting debt); NC2 and, 79–87, 94, 98–100, 106–7, 135, 251n4, 251n19; notes and, 78, 88–92, 98, 108, 198–200, 202; private money and, 86, 89, 92, 101–7, 147, 202; regulation and, 85, 90–91, 99–100, 103–7, 251n6, 255n73; risk and, 78–87, 90–95, 98–100, 104–5, 251n6, 251n19; securitization and, 78–86, 91–95, 98–101, 251n11, 251n13, 253n41; state money and, 77–78, 88–93, 106; unsecured, 79

Debt Recovery Act, 39–40

Deposit Trust Corporation, 254n49

derivatives: Bank for International Settlement (BIS) and, 149–50; bankruptcy and, 144–52; capital rule and, 211, 227; collateralized debt obligations (CDOs) and, 87, 99–101, 108, 165, 211, 254n53; comeback of, 262n36; complex credit, 165; digital code and, 189, 202; empire of law and, 5, 8; Financial Stability Board (FSB) and, 150–51; global code and, 143–53, 262n36, 263n49; International Swaps and Derivatives Association (ISDA) and, 145–53, 261n31, 271n18; Lehman Brothers and, 63; Loan Market Association (LMA) and, 262n32; Master Agreement (MA) and, 146–47, 150–51, 153; minting debt and, 78, 81, 86, 91; paving way for, 143–52; PRIME and, 146; safe harbors for, 263n49; transnational, 150–51

De Soto, Hernando, 14

digital autonomous organizations (DAO), 194–97, 272n29, 272n30, 272n33

digital code: arbitration and, 190, 204; assets and, 187–94, 197–204; autonomy and, 194–97; Bitcoin and, 197–202; blockchains and, 184, 187–90, 192, 195, 197–98, 203–4, 270n2; bugs and, 185, 188, 196; capitalism and, 199–200; capital rule and, 205, 208–9, 212, 216, 221–23; "code is law" and, 183, 196;

coercive power and, 187, 193; collateral and, 187, 190–91, 271n19; common law and, 271n13; contracts and, 183–92, 195, 198, 203, 271n13, 271n17, 271n18, 272n32; convertibility and, 183, 193, 199; corporate law and, 185, 189, 196, 202; courts and, 187, 204; creditors and, 187–88, 202; debt and, 187, 190, 198–203; derivatives and, 189, 202; durability and, 183, 193; elitism and, 186; enclosure and, 183, 203; enforcement and, 187, 190, 203; exogenous shocks and, 188; hierarchy and, 185–86, 201–2; immutable ledgers and, 188–90; investment and, 195–97, 200–202, 272n33; knowledge and, 183; lawyers and, 183–86, 188, 204; legal code and, 183–90, 194, 197, 203–4; legal entities and, 195; Lehman Brothers and, 190; LIBOR and, 190; Marxism and, 185; as meritocracy, 186; mining and, 200–201; patents and, 203–4; priority rights and, 193; private code and, 198; private money and, 198–99, 202; property and, 184–86, 191–94, 198, 203–4, 272n28; realists and, 184–86; reform and, 273n46; regulation and, 185–86, 190, 271n17, 272n30; replacing law by, 183–84; residual rights and, 191–92; scalability and, 184; shareholders and, 195–96, 202; state money and, 198–203; state power and, 184, 193, 197; Szabo on, 192–93, 198; United States and, 202; utopists and, 184; wealth and, 198, 200

discovery doctrine, 34–35

dividends, 11, 53, 61–62, 103

DNA (deoxyribonucleic acid), 108–11, 114

Drahos, Peter, 124

dry exchange, 90

Du Pont, 124

durability: capital rule and, 211, 229, 233; cloning legal persons and, 47, 54–55; code masters and, 159, 161, 182; coding land and, 24, 39, 42–43, 46; digital code and, 183, 193; empire of law and, 3–5, 11, 13–15, 19, 21; intangible capital and, 117; minting debt and, 78

Dutch East India Company (VOC), 65–67, 196

East Asian Financial Crisis, 105

Economist, The (magazine), 37

Edward III, King of England, 118

Egypt, 133

Eichengreen, Barry, 240n64
elephant curve, 1, 8
Eli Lilly, 138–43, 152–55, 261n17, 261n19
elitism: capital rule and, 218; cloning legal
  persons and, 66, 75; code masters and,
  158, 162, 164, 175–77; coding land and, 8,
  40–41, 75, 158, 164, 254n55; digital code
  and, 186; empire of law and, 2, 8; global
  code and, 133; gold coins and, 254n55;
  Goldman Sachs and, 175; Lehman
  Brothers and, 175; minting debt and, 85,
  254n55; Roman law and, 132–33; WASPs
  and, 176
Elizabeth I, Queen of England, 32, 119
empire of law: arbitration and, 15, 18;
  bankruptcy and, 3, 13–14, 16, 21;
  capitalism and, 2, 4, 8, 10–14, 17–21,
  238n44; coercive power and, 4, 7, 15–21,
  239n60; collateral and, 3, 7, 11–13, 16,
  21, 238n49; common law and, 5, 8;
  contracts and, 2–4, 7–8, 13, 15–16, 21,
  238n48; convertibility and, 3–4, 11, 13,
  15, 19; corporate law and, 3, 5, 8, 11, 13,
  21, 238n54; courts and, 7–8, 12, 15–20;
  creditors and, 3, 13–16, 20; debt and,
  3, 13–16, 20–21; derivatives and, 5, 8;
  durability and, 3–5, 11, 13–15, 19, 21;
  elephant curve and, 1, 8; elitism and,
  2, 8; enforcement and, 2, 9, 12, 16–19,
  239n60; enigma of capital and, 9–13;
  globalization and, 2; growth and, 1, 4, 8,
  20, 235n10; inequality and, 1–3, 6, 21–22,
  235n9, 240n69, 240n70; inheritance
  and, 238n48; intangible capital and, 13;
  investment and, 12, 14, 16; labor and, 2,
  9–11, 237n37; law's guiding hand and,
  6–9; lawyers and, 3–4, 6, 8, 15, 19–20,
  22, 165, 236n26; legal attributes and,
  13–15; legal code and, 2–15, 19–22;
  legal entities and, 14; legal norms and,
  16–17; legal structures and, 4, 6, 9, 18, 21;
  Marxism and, 2, 9–11, 22; monopolies
  and, 17; mortgages and, 13–15; patents
  and, 11; priority rights and, 13–14, 16, 18;
  private law and, 20–21; property and,
  1–5, 11–14, 17, 19, 21, 238n44, 238n48,
  238n50, 239n56, 240n68; reform and, 1;
  regulation and, 7; risk and, 14, 17; self-
  interest and, 6, 8–9, 18, 232, 236n18;
  shielding and, 3, 14, 20, 22; slavery and,
  11–12, 237n38, 237n40; state power and,
  4, 14–19; universality and, 3–4, 11, 13–14,
  15, 19, 21; wealth and, 1–8, 12–14, 17–22

enclosure: capital rule and, 229; coding
  land and, 229; digital code and, 183,
  203; intangible capital and, 117, 256n14;
  knowledge and, 35, 108–9, 115, 117, 131,
  183; nature's code and, 109–12, 115;
  property and, 29–35, 39, 229; trade
  secrets and, 131
Enclosure Acts, 29–30, 242n22
enforcement: capital rule and, 210, 220, 223;
  code masters and, 168, 180; contract,
  2, 16, 203; digital code and, 187, 190,
  203; empire of law and, 2, 9, 12, 16–19,
  239n60; global code and, 134, 139–40,
  147, 152, 154; International Court of
  Justice and, 125; law, 16–19, 125, 152,
  154, 168, 180, 187, 220, 259n80; minting
  debt and, 88; priority rights and, 16;
  trade secrets and, 130; World Trade
  Organization (WTO) and, 125
Engels, Friedrich, 185
English law. See common law
entitlements, 44–46, 212, 217, 219, 222–24,
  260n8
entrepreneurs, 7, 59–60, 93, 114, 163, 179,
  206–7
equity rule, 31–32
Ethereum, 195–97, 201, 272n29
European Central Bank, 79, 260n12
European Commission, 79, 148
European Court of Justice, 70, 156
European Union (EU), 224; bilateral
  investment treaties (BITs) and,
  264n67; capital adequacy and, 73–74;
  Comprehensive Economic and Trade
  Agreement (CETA) and, 156–57,
  264n69; corporations and, 72, 249n51;
  debt and, 106; global code and, 134, 137,
  140, 156, 263n48, 264n67; International
  Swaps and Derivatives Association
  (ISDA) and, 148
eviction, 41, 233
exclusive use rights, 35, 209
exogenous shocks, 118, 188

Facebook, 130
Fannie Mae, 84–85, 94
Federal Home Bank of Chicago, 85
feudal calculus, 5–6, 129, 223
feudalism: capital rule and, 5–6, 205, 211,
  223, 276n24; France and, 276n24; legal
  code and, 5–6, 10, 30, 36, 128–29, 158,
  205, 211, 218, 223, 276n24; property and,
  30, 36, 128–29, 158, 218

fidelity, 85
Fifth Amendment, 241n9
Financial Stability Board (FSB), 150–51
Financial Times journal, 223
First Amendment, 87
Flemish Weavers, 118
Florence, Italy, 56–58
FMC Corporation, 124
Ford, 247n17
foreclosure, 39, 95–98, 253n44
Fourteenth Amendment, 25
France: Banque de France and, 104; bills of exchange and, 252n31; civil law and, 168, 171–72; Code de Commerce and, 252n31; D'Estaing and, 240n64; exporting law and, 133; feudalism and, 276n24; International Swaps and Derivatives Association (ISDA) and, 151; lawyers and, 170–71, 178; legal profession requirements and, 170–72; minting debt and, 85, 93, 102–4; Napoleon and, 133, 242n27; Péreire brothers and, 102–3; property rights and, 218, 242n27; skyrocketing lawyer fees and, 173; Société General and, 85; top global law firms and, 178–79
Freddie Mac, 94
Frederick the Great, 3
free market, 4, 19, 106–7, 128–29
free trade, 38, 121, 123–24, 138
Fuld, Richard, 62–63

General Agreement on Tariffs and Trade (GATT), 123
General Electric, 124
General Estates of the Netherlands, 65–66, 276n24
General Motors, 124, 247n17
genetics: BRCA and, 111–14, 116, 127, 130, 214; cease and desist orders and, 113; courts and, 109–16, 127, 211, 214; Crick and, 108–10; enclosure and, 109–12, 115; Human Genome Project and, 109–10; inheritance and, 109; intellectual property and, 107–16, 127–29, 214; legal code and, 108, 110, 114, 116; Mendel and, 108; monopolies and, 109–12, 115; Myriad Genetics and, 112–16, 127–29, 214; National Institutes of Health (NIH) and, 109, 112; nature's code and, 109–12, 115; patents and, 109–16, 230; privatizing, 111–12; risk and, 111–14, 116, 127, 130, 214; sequencing and, 109–13, 127–28; US Supreme Court and, 109–13,

116, 127, 211, 214; Watson and, 108–10; Wilkins and, 109
Germany, 13, 209, 246n7; Bayerische Landesbank and, 85; bills of exchange and, 252n31; civil law and, 168, 238n48; Constitution of, 241n10; credit cooperatives and, 93–94; exporting law and, 133; frustration of contracts and, 271n13; Herstatt bank and, 137; International Swaps and Derivatives Association (ISDA) and, 151; Law on Judges and, 268n42; lawyers and, 172–73, 178–79; Lehman Brothers and, 49; Loan Market Association (LMA) and, 262n32; private money and, 101; seat theory and, 70; state power and, 107; subjective rights and, 275n10; top global law firms and, 178; unification of, 267n38
Getzler, Joshua, 40
Gilson, Ronald, 163
Ginnie Mae, 92
global code: arbitration and, 136, 139–43, 146, 152, 154–57, 261n27; assets and, 132, 135–38, 142–50, 154; autonomy and, 134–35; Bank for International Settlement (BIS) and, 149–50; bankruptcy and, 137, 144–53, 262n42; Belize and, 261n21; bilateral trade and, 122, 132, 136, 140, 154–56, 256n23; Canada and, 138–43, 156–57, 261n17, 261n18, 263n57, 264n69; capitalism and, 132–33; capital rule and, 152–57; central banks and, 151; coercive power and, 132, 154; collateral and, 144, 148, 263n48; common law and, 133, 264n65; Comprehensive Economic and Trade Agreement (CETA) and, 156–57; conflict of law and, 134–35; contracts and, 135–37, 139, 145–53; corporate law and, 135–36, 155; courts and, 133, 136, 138–46, 150, 152–56, 261n18, 261n21, 262n45; creditors and, 144, 147–50, 262n41, 262n45; debt and, 144, 147, 149–50, 262n41; derivatives and, 143–53, 262n36, 263n49; elitism and, 133; enforcement and, 134, 139–40, 147, 152, 154; expanding private choice and, 134–37; exporting law and, 132–34; intellectual property and, 136, 138, 140, 143; International Center for Settlement of Investment Disputes (ICSID) and, 154–55; International Swaps and Derivatives Association (ISDA) and, 145–53, 261n31, 271n18; investment and,

global code (*continued*)
132, 134–42, 154–57; lawyers and, 135–36, 142–45, 154, 176–79, 261n27; legal code and, 132–33, 143; legal structures and, 134; Lehman Brothers and, 135, 149; Marxism and, 154; NC2 and, 135; New York Arbitration Convention and, 154; patents and, 122, 136–43, 152; priority rights and, 149, 156; private law and, 133, 136, 154; property and, 135–40, 143, 262n45; regulation and, 132, 135, 137, 141, 143, 145, 148, 151–54, 264n58, 264n67; risk and, 146, 262n45; shareholders and, 135; sovereignty and, 135–44, 148, 152, 155, 157, 277n51; state money and, 147; state power and, 138, 141, 154; treaty law and, 136–42, 154–57; United Kingdom and, 151
globalization: capital rule and, 219–23, 277n51; code masters and, 176–79, 270n71; empire of law and, 2; nature's code and, 121–22
global law, 8–9, 145, 166–67, 176, 178–79
gold coins, 254n55
Goldman Sachs, 49, 100, 175, 203, 248, 255n70, 271n19, 274n57
Google, 129–31, 259n80
government-sponsored entity (GSE), 84, 94, 253n39
Great Depression, 49, 106
Great Financial Crisis, ix–x; bailouts and, 55, 62, 64, 104–5, 151, 226, 247n17; car manufacturers and, 55; Lehman Brothers and, 48–58, 61–65, 70–75, 80, 85, 96, 101, 103–4, 106, 135, 149, 175, 190, 245n4, 246n6, 248n33; misleading information and, 161; put option and, 55; US Consumer Financial Protection Bureau and, 182
Greece, 255n66
Greenspan, Alan, 105
growth: capital rule and, 220; code masters and, 166, 175, 267n26, 270n71; elephant curve and, 1, 8; empire of law and, 1, 4, 8, 20, 235n10; minting debt and, 102, 106; nature's code and, 117; property and, 4
guilds, 128–29, 170, 206, 258n61, 259n70
Guinness brewery, 38

Hague Conference on International Private Law, 136
Harvard Law School, 175, 268n47
Haskel, Jonathan, 115–16
hedge funds, 64, 102, 105–6, 151, 251n5
Herstatt bank, 137

Hewlett-Packard, 124
Hindu law, 177
Hirschman, Albert, 221, 248n42
Hodgson, Geoffrey, 10
homeowners, 59, 80–84, 86, 88, 94–98, 100, 106
House of Lords, 38, 158
housing market, 5, 61, 94
Human Genome Project, 109–10
human rights, 29, 139, 228, 261n21

Ibanez, Antonio, 95–97
IBM, 124
immortality, 50, 55, 65–67
immutable ledgers, 188–90
imperialism, 17, 133
incorporation theory, 69–70, 74, 136, 246n10
India, 122
Indian Removal Act, 34
industrial policy, 118–21
inequality: capital rule and, 223; code masters and, 167; coding land and, 46; empire of law and, 1–3, 6, 21–22, 235n9, 240n69, 240n70
inflation, 15, 101, 106–7, 254n56
inheritance law, 238n48
initial coin offerings (ICOs), 195–96
Inns of Court, 32, 169, 242n29
insurance, 3, 100, 157, 178, 190–91, 271n17
intangible capital, 8; capital rule and, 212, 216; empire of law and, 13; enclosure and, 117; intellectual property and, 13, 24, 115–18, 120–21, 143, 212, 216; patents and, 143, 212 (*see also* patents); shareholders and, 117
intellectual property: abstract ideas and, 110; Austro-Hungarian Empire and, 120; big data and, 126–31; Canada and, 138–43, 152–55, 261n17, 261n19; capital rule and, 212–13; coding land and, 24, 241n10; copyright and, 11, 115, 256n23; digital code and, 186, 203–4; empire of law and, 3, 5, 11, 19; genetics and, 107–16, 127–29, 214; global code and, 136, 138, 140, 143; intangible capital and, 13, 24, 115–18, 120–21, 143, 212, 216; monopolies and, 109, 115, 120–24; Myriad and, 112–16, 127, 129, 214; nature's code and, 108–9, 115, 120–30; Netherlands and, 120; patents and, 11, 109–23, 126–30, 136–43, 152, 203–4, 211–15, 230, 256n3, 256n18, 257n24, 257n42, 274n54, 274n57; pharmaceutical industry and, 121–22,

124, 129, 138–42, 152–55, 261n17, 261n19;
shareholders and, 114–15; Trade Act
and, 121; trademarks and, 11, 115–16, 215;
trade secrets and, 126–31; tragedy of the
commons and, 109; TRIPS and, 123–25,
136, 138; United Kingdom and, 117–21;
United States and, 109, 112, 115, 121–24,
256n23; US Constitution and, 241n10
Intellectual Property Committee (IPC),
123–24
Interamerican Commission on Human
Rights (IACHR), 29, 261n21
interest rates, 80, 90, 190
International Capital Market Association,
262n32
International Center for Settlement of
Investment Disputes (ICSID), 154–55
International Court of Justice, 125, 146
International Monetary Fund (IMF), 64, 79
international private law, 68–69, 136
International Swaps and Derivatives
Association (ISDA), 145–53, 261n31,
271n18
International Trade Organization, 123
investment: capital rule and, 225–26;
cloning legal persons and, 48–53, 60–65,
67, 72, 75, 248n39; code masters and,
160–61, 165, 167–68; coding land and, 25,
37, 45, 241n13; digital code and, 195–97,
200–2, 272n33; empire of law and, 12, 14,
16, 112; entrepreneurs and, 7, 59–60, 93,
114, 163, 179, 206–7; global code and, 132,
134–42, 154–57; intangible capital and,
116–17; minting debt and, 77–86, 91–107,
251n12; nature's code and, 114; rate of
return and, 4–5, 147
invisible hand, 6–9, 225, 236n18
Ireland, 72, 104, 233, 250n57
ISDS (investor-state-dispute-settlement),
136–38, 140, 155–56, 261n22
Islamic law, 177

Japan, 51, 124, 133, 260n3
jingle rule, 247n24
Johnson & Johnson, 124
Johnson v. M'Intosh, 34
Jolie, Angelina, 111
JP Morgan, 62, 64, 83–84, 248n32
Justinian, 170

Kapital, Das (Marx), 9
Kempe, John, 118
King's Council, 27, 31

Kleros Real Estate CDO III Ltd., 79, 86,
98–100, 107, 135, 165
knowledge: capital rule and, 229; digital
code and, 183; enclosure of, 35, 108–9,
115, 117, 131, 183; expert legal, 162 (see also
lawyers); genetics and, 108–9, 113, 115–16;
global commons and, 126; industrial
policy and, 118, 121; intangible capital
and, 116–18; intellectual property and, 110
(see also intellectual property); lawyers
and, 162, 165; monopolizing, 117, 257n29;
trade secrets and, 126–31; utopists and,
184–86, 197, 200; wealth and, 40, 108–9,
118, 131, 165

labor: capitalism and, 2, 9–11, 116, 160, 169,
217, 219, 237n37; cloning legal persons
and, 49; code masters and, 160, 169;
coding land and, 34; empire of law and,
2, 9–11, 237n37; minting debt and, 94;
property and, 120; rights of, 217; trade
secrets and, 128–29; unions and, 219
land law, 95, 158, 177, 244n58
landlords: coding land and, 29–32, 35,
244n64; commoners and, 30–31, 112–13,
192, 206, 214; corporations and, 59;
creditors and, 206–7; digital code and,
192; gold coins and, 254n55; intellectual
property and, 112–13, 192; mining debt
and, 93; priority rights and, 30, 158–59,
206; titles and, 206
landowners: coding land and, 24, 34–39,
42–45; corporations and, 56; lawyers
and, 158–59, 166; minting debt and, 78,
128; trust law and, 42–45
Langdell, Christopher Columbus, 175
law merchants, 90–91
law schools, 25, 162–63, 168, 174–76, 228,
240n6, 243n43, 268n47, 270n4
lawyers: arbitration and, 161–62, 178, 180–
82; attorneys, 21, 32, 143, 160–62, 171–74,
181–82, 217, 269n54; autonomy and,
171–73; barristers, 169–70; capital rule
and, 206–16, 221, 224, 227–29, 234; civil
law and, 42–43, 133, 168–73, 178, 249n48;
cloning legal persons and, 48, 52, 70; as
code masters, 3 (see also code masters);
coding land and, 24, 31–32, 35, 37–38, 40,
43–45, 164, 240n6, 242n29; common law
and, 168–73, 176–78; competition and,
174, 176; courts and, 15 (see also courts);
cross-country analysis of, 168–82; digital
code and, 183–86, 188, 204; economic

lawyers (*continued*)
  growth and, 166; elitism and, 158, 162, 164, 175–77; empire of law and, 3–4, 6, 8, 15, 19–20, 22, 165, 236n26; exploitation of plurality of laws by, 177–78; first-mover advantage and, 214–15; freelance, 170; global code and, 135–36, 142–45, 154, 261n27; global law and, 8–9, 145, 166–67, 176, 178–79; global profession for, 176–79; income of, 163, 178, 265n3; indictment of, 162; Inns of Court and, 32, 169, 242n29; landlords and, 32; law schools and, 25, 162–63, 168, 174–76, 228, 240n6, 243n43, 268n47, 270n4; law's inherent incompleteness and, 210–13; legal knowledge of, 162, 165; as legal service providers, 159; Magee on, 165–66; making new laws and, 160; market for young, 228–29; minting debt and, 79–80, 82, 86, 252n24; mobility of law and, 167–68; plaintiffs and, 32, 58, 69, 113, 142, 214, 265n5, 275n17; poison pill and, 163–64, 266n15, 266n17; priority rights and, 158, 161; pro bono operations and, 163; regulation and, 160–63, 168, 171–77, 182, 267n37, 268n42; rules of property and, 160; specialization and, 162; trade secrets and, 129–30; transactions and, 161, 163–65, 169, 176–81; US demographics on, 162–63; wealth protection and, 166–67; women as, 174–75, 268n47, 269n54
legal code: acquired rights and, 45–46; ad hoc privileges and, 119, 218, 223, 228; assets and, 2–8, 11–12, 15, 19–24, 40, 52, 87, 92, 107–8, 116, 118, 132, 143, 168, 177, 180, 205, 208, 211–12, 215–18, 222–27, 233; autonomy and, 33, 50, 134–35, 171, 173, 194–97, 209, 212–13, 215, 218–20, 232, 272n29; blockchain and, 184, 187–90, 192, 195, 197–98, 203–4, 270n2; capital rule and, 205, 211–13, 216, 218–20, 225, 227, 230; centrality of, 8; "code is law" and, 183, 196; code masters and, 158–59, 167, 177, 180; coding land and, 24, 39–40, 43; complexity of, 19; conflict of law and, 9, 68–69, 134–35, 212, 225, 249n48, 276n37; decoding the trust and, 42–45; digital code and, 183–90, 194, 197, 203–4; discovery doctrine and, 34–35; empire of law and, 2–15, 19–22; exclusive use rights and, 35, 209; exporting law and, 132–34; feudalism and, 5–6, 10, 30, 36, 128–29, 158, 205, 211, 218, 223,

276n24; global code and, 132–33, 143; governing, 222–29; harmonization and, 123, 134–42, 179, 227, 250n58, 276n37; imperialism and, 17, 133; incorporation theory and, 69–70, 74, 136, 246n10; intangible capital and, 116–18; law's guiding hand and, 6–9; minting debt and, 79, 88, 92, 98; modules of, 3–7, 12–13, 17–21, 24, 29, 42–44, 52, 78, 86–87, 92, 101, 108, 116, 143, 159–61, 165, 168, 177, 180, 184, 203–15, 222–26, 229; nature's code and, 108, 110, 114, 116; New York State law and, 8, 76, 80, 132–33, 135, 143, 146, 150, 168, 178; power of, 8; PRIMA and, 136; private code and, 209–19; RASCAL and, 73–75, 250n60, 250n62; as social ordering technology, 17; trust law and, ix–x, 42–45; wealth and, 3
legal entities: asset partitioning and, 53; corporations and, 14, 51–53, 55, 57, 65, 69–71, 249n46, 253n41; digital code and, 195; empire of law and, 3, 14, 20, 22; minting debt and, 100; priority rights and, 14; property and, 24, 44–47, 136, 159, 217, 224; risk and, 100; tax rates and, 71–73
Legal Foundations of Capital, The (Commons), 12
legal structures, 266n15; capital rule and, 225; corporations and, 48–51, 54, 58, 70–71, 76, 80; empire of law and, 4, 6, 9, 18, 21; global code and, 134
legal title, 24–29, 31, 33–34, 45–46
Lehman Brothers: American Express and, 50; code masters and, 175; creditors and, 61, 63–64, 71, 73, 103; derivatives and, 63; digital code and, 190; early underwritings of, 49; elitism and, 175; founding of, 49; Fuld and, 62–63; global code and, 135, 149; Great Depression and, 49; Great Financial Crisis and, 48–58, 61–65, 70–75, 80, 85, 96, 101, 103–4, 106, 135, 149, 175, 190, 245n4, 246n6, 248n33; growth of, 49–50; Ibanez loan and, 96; immortality of, 65; incorporation of, 50; institutional autopsy of, 48; LBHI parent company and, 51, 53, 61–63, 71, 73, 250n59; legal structure of, 48–51, 54, 58, 70–71, 76; limited liability and, 51, 53, 63; loss shifting and, 61–64; Medici empire and, 58–59; minting debt and, 80, 85, 96, 101, 103–4, 106; New York Cotton Exchange and, 49; partnership of, 50; public offering of, 50; RASCAL

and, 73–75, 250n60, 250n62; regulatory arbitrage and, 73–76; special-purpose vehicles (SPVs) and, 51; subsidiaries and, 50–53, 58–59, 61–64, 70–76, 135, 149, 250n59; United Kingdom and, 50, 71, 73, 149, 250n59; use of corporate form and, 50–51; World War II and, 49

Lehman Brothers International Europe (LBIE), 73–75, 149, 250n59, 250n62

Lehman Brothers Switzerland (LBF), 73–75, 250n62, 250n65

Lessig, Lawrence, 183

Levy, Jonathan, 12

licenses, 44, 102, 113, 119, 122, 129, 136, 141

limited liability, 51, 53–54, 60–61, 63, 81–82, 99, 254n49

liquidity, 36, 57, 64, 90, 92, 104, 151, 199, 262n33

lobbying, 102, 148–50, 153, 211, 217

lock-in, 15, 47, 65–67, 77, 81, 117, 196

London Interbank Official Rate (LIBOR), 190

Long Term Capital Management (LTCM), 64, 102, 104–6

loss shifting, 55, 59–64, 67

Maastricht Treaty, 249n51

Madoff, Bernard, 103

Magee, Stephen, 165–66

Mansfield, Belle Babb, 268n47

Mansfield, Lord, 89

Marshall, Thurgood, 34

Marxism: capital rule and, 207–8, 216, 234; Crédit Mobilier and, 104; digital code and, 185; empire of law and, 2, 9–11, 22; global code and, 154; intangible capital and, 116; minting debt and, 104–6; withering of state and, 185

Master Agreement (MA), 146–47, 150–51, 153

MasterCard, 203

Maya people, 23–29, 230, 261n21

May Department Stores, 49

Medici empire, 57–58, 247n21

medicine, 109, 170, 189, 277n42

Meiji Restoration, 133

Mendel, Gregor, 108

Menger, Carl, 273n41

Menke, Christoph, 209, 217, 231–33

merchant banks, 8, 89–90, 199

Merchant of Venice, The (Shakespeare), 35–36, 198–99

Merck, 124

meritocracies, 186

Merrill Lynch, 100, 255n70

MERS, 254n49

Merton, Robert, 102, 104

Metalclad, 141

Mexico: Metalclad case and, 141; NAFTA and, 124, 138–42, 155, 261n20; USMCA and, 139, 261n20

Middle Ages, 128–29, 170, 206, 221, 258n61, 259n70

mining, 25–27, 29, 37, 103, 200–201

Minsky, Hyman P., 252n26, 254n60, 273n46

minting debt: arbitration and, 90–91; bankruptcy and, 78–80, 83–84, 87, 107, 255n71; capitalism and, 77, 107; central banks and, 77–78, 89, 102–6, 255n72; claims to future pay and, 78, 84, 88; coercive power and, 90; collateral and, 78, 81, 86–87, 92, 97, 99, 103, 107; contracts and, 78–81, 86, 88–89, 107; convertibility and, 77–78, 87–91; corporate law and, 78, 80, 86, 91, 98–102, 107, 252n22, 253n41; courts and, 87, 90–91, 96–98, 104, 252n31; credit cooperatives and, 93–95; Crédit Mobilier and, 102–6; creditors and, 77–79, 88–89, 92–93, 95, 103–5, 107; derivatives and, 78, 81, 86, 91; durability and, 78; elitism and, 85, 254n55; enforcement and, 88; FCIC and, 79–80, 83; France and, 104; gold coins and, 254n55; growth and, 102, 106; investment and, 77–86, 91–107, 251n12; Kleros clones and, 79, 86, 98–100, 107, 135, 165; labor and, 94; lawyers and, 79–80, 82, 86, 252n24; legal code and, 79, 88, 92, 98; legal entities and, 100; Lehman Brothers and, 80, 85, 96, 101, 103–4, 106; Marxism and, 104–6; monopolies and, 91; mortgages and, 80–88, 92–98, 251n13, 253n41, 254n53; NC2 and, 79–87, 94, 98–100, 106–7, 135, 251n4, 251n19; negotiability and, 89; notes and, 78, 88–92, 98, 108, 198–200, 202; Péreire brothers and, 102–3; priority rights and, 97, 107; private law and, 107; private money and, 86, 89, 92, 101–7, 147, 202; property and, 78, 86, 95–97, 107; reform and, 101, 106, 255n73; regulation and, 85, 90–91, 99–100, 103–7, 251n6; risk and, 78–87, 90–95, 98–100, 104–5, 251n6, 251n19; securitization and, 78–86, 91–101, 251n11, 251n13, 253n41; shareholders and, 99, 103–4; shielding and, 78, 84, 86, 99, 107; sovereignty and, 79, 84–85, 105; state money and, 77–78,

minting debt (*continued*)
88–93, 106; state power and, 107; titles
and, 96–97; United Kingdom and, 106;
United States and, 84, 87, 92–93, 95,
99, 106; wealth and, 77–79, 84–85, 106,
251n15
mobility, 18, 68, 70, 167–68, 225
monopolies: assets and, 17, 41, 66, 91, 109,
111, 114–26, 257n29; cloning legal persons
and, 66; coding land and, 41; empire of
law and, 17; genetics and, 109–12, 115;
intangible capital and, 117; intellectual
property and, 109, 115, 120–24; of
knowledge, 117, 257n29; minting debt
and, 91; nature's code and, 109, 111,
115; property and, 119–21; Statute of
Monopolies and, 119, 258n43; temporal,
121; trade secrets and, 126
Monsanto, 124
mortgage-backed securities (MBS), 82–83,
86–87, 94–95, 97, 99, 101, 103, 108
Mortgage Electronic Registration System
(MERS), 98
mortgages: capital rule and, 206–7, 211;
coding land and, 35–38, 43; collateral
law and, 13–14; empire of law and, 13–15;
Ibanez case and, 95–97; minting debt and,
80–88, 92–98, 251n13, 253n41, 254n53;
NC2 and, 79–87, 94, 98–100, 106–7, 135,
251n4, 251n19; subprime, 83, 251n13
Myriad Genetics, 112–16, 127–29, 214

Nakamoto, Satoshi, 198–99
National Institutes of Health (NIH), 109, 112
Native Americans, 34, 192–93
nature's code: capitalism and, 112;
common law and, 119; contracts and,
129; corporate law and, 108, 115, 122,
125; courts and, 110–16; enclosure and,
109–12, 115; genetics and, 109–16, 127–28;
globalization and, 121–22; growth and,
117; intellectual property and, 108–9, 115,
120–30; investment and, 112, 114; legal
code and, 108, 110, 114, 116; monopolies
and, 109–12, 115; priority rights and, 110;
property and, 108–9, 114–30; risk and,
111; wealth and, 109
NC2: ancestry of, 80; basic structure of,
79–84; China Investment Corporation
(CIC) and, 85; as Citigroup Mortgage
Loan Trust 2006–New Century 2
(CMLTI 2006–NC2), 80; Citigroup
Mortgage Realty Corporation (CMRC)
and, 80–85; complexity of, 86; conflict
of law and, 135; convertibility and, 87;
debt instrument of, 79–87, 94, 98–100,
106–7, 135, 251n4, 251n19; foreign
investment in, 84–85; global code
and, 135; homeowners and, 80, 83–84;
JPMorgan Chase and, 84–85; minting
debt and, 106–7; prospectus of, 80–83,
251n4, 251n19; shadow banking and, 79;
tranches of, 83–87, 94, 98, 101, 251n19;
trust law and, 43, 81–85, 95, 253n41
negotiability, 89
Netherlands, 65–66, 120
New Century, 80, 82–83
new comparative economics, 168, 266n24
New York Arbitration Convention, 154
New York Cotton Exchange, 49
New York State laws, 8, 76, 80, 132–33, 135,
143, 146, 150, 168, 178
New York Stock Exchange, 49, 137
New York University, 113
New Zealand, 29, 33–34
Nigeria, 27
Nobel Prize, 64, 102, 104–6, 109
Norman conquest, 30
North American Free Trade Agreement
(NAFTA), 124, 138–42, 155, 261n20
notes, 78, 88–92, 98, 108, 198–200, 202

Obama, Barack, 156
Olson, Mancur, 219–20
Option One Mortgage Corporation, 96–97
Option Pricing Theory, 102
ownership: Bitcoin and, 199; coding land
and, 30, 34–35, 136; corporations and,
59, 67, 92, 118, 136; ownership and, 59,
67, 92, 118, 136; separation of control and,
272n31; transfer of, 262n45

Pagano, Ugo, 118
PageRank, 129–30
Panel of Recognized International Market
Experts in Finance (PRIME), 146
parliamentary systems, 19–20, 29, 38, 61,
119–20, 158, 207, 222, 263n48
partnerships: capital rule and, 228; code
masters and, 162–63, 166, 175–78;
Goldman Sachs and, 248n39; immortality
and, 65; Lehman Brothers and, 50;
Medici empire and, 57–58, 247n21;
Roman law and, 54, 56–57; shielding and,
54, 56, 58–59; United Kingdom and, 60,
247n24; United States and, 247n24

Parvest ABS Euribor, 85
patents: artisans and, 118–19; Canadian
    Patent Act and, 140; capital rule and,
    211–15, 230; cease and desist orders and,
    113; copyright and, 11, 115, 256n23; core
    features of invention and, 126–27; courts
    and, 120; data-generating, 127–28; digital
    code and, 203–4; duration of, 118, 123,
    139; Eli Lilly and, 138–43, 152–55, 261n17,
    261n19; empire of law and, 11; England
    and, 118–19; genetics and, 109–16, 230;
    global code and, 122, 136–43, 152; Google
    and, 129–31, 259n80; industrial policy
    and, 118–21; intangible capital and, 116–
    18; intellectual property and, 11, 109–23,
    126–30, 136–43, 152, 203–4, 211–15, 230,
    256n3, 256n18, 257n24, 257n42, 274n54,
    274n57; monetary value of, 114, 127;
    Netherlands and, 120; novelty and, 126;
    pharmaceutical industry and, 121–22,
    124, 138–42, 152–55, 261n17, 261n19;
    property and, 118–22; trademarks and,
    11, 115–16, 215; trade secrets and, 126–30;
    United States and, 110, 113, 256n18; US
    Constitution and, 114–15; utility and, 126
Peabody & Co., 49
Pennsylvania University, 113
pensions, 63, 75, 83, 106, 255n71
Péreire brothers, 102–3
Pfizer Pharmaceuticals, 121–22, 124
pharmaceutical industry: Eli Lilly and, 138–
    42, 152–55, 261n17, 261n19; intellectual
    property and, 129; Pfizer and, 121–22,
    124; sovereignty and, 138; trade secrets
    and, 129
Piketty, Thomas, 4–5
plaintiffs, 32, 58, 69, 113, 142, 214, 265n5,
    275n17
poison pills, 163–64, 266n15, 266n17
Poland, 133
Polanyi, Karl von, 11, 19, 128, 133, 220, 228,
    276n29
Ponzi schemes, 103, 254n60, 254n62
Portugal, 133, 255n66
Posner, Eric A., 230, 232
power structures, 185, 206
Pratt, Ed, 121–22
PRIMA (place of the relevant intermediary
    approach), 136
priority rights: capital rule and, 206–7, 215;
    cloning legal persons and, 55–56, 63;
    code masters and, 158, 161; coding land
    and, 24–25, 29, 37, 39, 46; digital code

and, 193; durability and, 14; empire of
    law and, 13–14, 16, 18; enforcement of, 16;
    global code and, 149, 156; landlords and,
    206; lawyers and, 158, 161; legal entities
    and, 14; minting debt and, 97, 107; Native
    Americans and, 34, 192–93; nature's code
    and, 110; shielding and, 54–56, 107, 215;
    trade secrets and, 126
private law, ix; capital rule and, 20, 209–19;
    cloning legal persons and, 68; code
    masters and, 169–73, 182; contracts and,
    2 (see also contracts); crytocurrency and,
    198; digital code and, 198; empire of law
    and, 20–21; first-mover advantage and,
    214–15; global code and, 133, 136, 154;
    international, 68, 136; law's inherent
    incompleteness and, 210–13; minting
    debt and, 107; public power and, 216–19;
    trust law and, 3, 5, 44, 78, 211, 219, 226
private money: code masters and,
    175; Crédit Mobilier and, 102–6;
    crytocurrency and, 198–99, 202; digital
    code and, 198–99, 202; future growth
    and, 102; Germany and, 101; minting debt
    and, 86, 89, 92, 101–7, 147, 202; Péreire
    brothers and, 102–3; risk and, 187, 198–
    99; state money and, 15, 238n52
Privy Council, 27–29, 126
productivity, 39, 79, 117, 244n64
property: absolute, 30, 33; acquired rights
    and, ix–x, 42–45; capital rule and, 206,
    209, 212–20, 222, 224, 230, 276n24;
    cloning legal persons and, 47, 68; code
    masters and, 158–60, 164, 172, 177; coding
    land and, 23–39, 42–46, 240n2, 241n10,
    241n13, 242n27, 242n36, 243n41, 245n75;
    Cohen on, 137–38; Conveyance Act and,
    38–39; courts and, 17, 23–28, 30, 38–39,
    43–44, 96–97, 126, 136, 140, 143, 159–60,
    172, 214–15, 218, 262; Debt Recovery Act
    and, 39–40; digital code and, 184–86,
    191–94, 198, 203–4, 272n28; discovery
    doctrine and, 34–35; as dominium, 138;
    emerging land market and, 32; empire
    of law and, 1–5, 11–14, 17, 19, 21, 238n44,
    238n48, 238n50, 239n56, 240n68;
    enclosure and, 29–35, 39, 229, 256n14;
    Enclosure Acts and, 29–30; eviction
    and, 41, 233; exclusive use rights and, 35,
    209; feudalism and, 30, 36, 128–29, 158,
    218; foreclosure and, 39, 95–98, 253n44;
    France and, 218, 242n27; general, 30;
    global code and, 135–40, 143, 262n45;

property (*continued*)
growth and, 4; industrial policy and, 118–22; intangible capital and, 13, 24, 115–21, 143, 212, 216; intellectual, 3, 138 (*see also* intellectual property); ISDS and, 136–38, 140, 155–56, 261n22; labor and, 120; landlords and, 29–32, 35, 59, 93, 112–13, 158–59, 192, 206, 214, 244n64; landowners and, 24, 34–39, 42, 45, 56, 78, 128, 158–59, 166; legal entities and, 24, 44–47, 136, 159, 217, 224; legal title and, 24–29, 31, 33–34, 45–46; Maya people and, 23–29, 230, 261n21; minting debt and, 78, 86, 95–97, 107; monopolies and, 119–21 (*see also* monopolies); Native Americans and, 34, 192–93; nature's code and, 108–9, 114–30; Norman conquest and, 30; *numerus clausus* and, 160; occupancy and, 31; ownership and, 30; patents and, 118–22; residual rights and, 191–92; rise of West and, 4; securitization and, 43, 78; Settled Land Acts and, 38–39; settlers and, 33–35, 42, 125, 192–93; sovereignty and, 26–27, 33, 120–21, 135–43, 160; squatters and, 34; Statute of Enrollments and, 44; Statute of Uses and, 44; Szabo on, 192–93, 198; titles and, 13, 25–27, 30–35, 37, 43, 46, 75, 96–97, 110, 125, 194, 206; treaty law and, 120; trust law and, 42–45; turning land into private, 29–35; US Constitution and, 25; wealth and, 4–5, 12, 14, 19, 21, 24, 36, 42–43, 46, 108, 130, 209, 217, 222, 224, 237n38, 240n68
Prussia, 93–95, 172–73, 242n27
public power, 216–19
put option, 55, 64, 226

Qatar, 84
Quarterly Journal of Economics, 94

radical markets, 230–33
rate of return, 4–5, 147
rating agencies, 80, 86–87, 98–100, 251n6, 251n19
rational choice theorists, 208, 216
real estate mortgage investment conduits (REMIC), 95, 253n41
reform: capital rule and, 218, 231; code masters and, 158–59, 171; coding land and, 38–41, 244n58, 244n64; digital code and, 273n46; empire of law and, 1; English land law and, 158, 244n58; minting debt and, 101, 106, 255n73; TRIPS and, 124–25

regulation: arbitrage and, 48, 56, 73–76, 90–91, 226; capital rule and, 211, 213, 216–17, 221, 224–27, 274n1; code masters and, 160–63, 168, 171–77, 182, 267n37, 268n42; coding land and, 44; convertibility and, 226–27; corporations and, 47–48, 50, 56, 68, 73–75, 249n46; digital code and, 185–86, 190, 271n17, 272n30; empire of law and, 7; global code and, 132, 135, 137, 141, 143, 145, 148, 151–54, 264n58, 264n67; insurance, 271n17; lawyers and, 160–63, 168, 171–77, 182, 267n37, 268n42; minting debt and, 85, 90–91, 99–100, 103–7, 251n6, 255n73; private, 264n58; REMIC and, 253n41; US Securities and Exchange Commission (SEC) and, 103, 195
Regulation and Administration of Safe Custody and Global Settlement (RASCAL), 73–75, 250n60, 250n62
regulatory arbitrage, 48, 73–76, 90–91, 226
religion, 90, 236n26
repurchase agreements (Repos), 74, 76, 145, 148, 211, 262n45
residential mortgage-backed securities (RMBS), 87, 94, 103, 108
residual rights, 191–92
retirement, 65
R. H. Macy & Co., 49
Richard III, King of England, 44
risk: BRCA and, 111–14, 116, 127, 130, 214; capital rule and, 207, 226, 229; code masters and, 161–62, 165; coding land and, 35, 41; corporations and, 48, 54–56, 59, 63–66, 70, 74–75; digital code and, 187, 198–99; DNA and, 108–11, 114; empire of law and, 14, 17; genetics and, 111–14, 116, 127, 130, 214; global code and, 146, 262n45; legal entities and, 100; minting debt and, 78–87, 90–95, 98–100, 104–5, 251n6, 251n19
Rockwell International, 124
Roman law: Anglo-American civil law and, 42; corporations and, 51; creditors and, 54; early English treaties and, 30; elitism and, 132–33; expanding private choice and, 135; Justinian and, 170; law schools and, 177, 243n43; *pacta sunt servanda* (contracts are to be honored) and, 187; partnerships and, 54, 56–57; *peculium* and, 54, 56, 60, 164; Prussia and, 242n27; shielding and, 56; slavery and, 54, 57, 60
Rose Mortgage, 95–97
Rudden, Bernard, 5

rule by law: autonomy and, 33, 50, 134–35, 171, 173, 194–97, 209, 212–13, 215, 218–20, 232, 272n29; capital without, 229–34; roots of, 208–9
Russia, 93, 103, 105

safe harbors, 63, 145, 148–50, 152, 207, 211, 227, 262n44, 263n49
Savernake Forest, 38
savings, 62, 92, 101
scalability, 145, 180, 184
Scalia, Antonin, 116
Schumpeter, Joseph, 118, 276n30
Sears, Roebuck and Co., 49
seat theory, 53, 69–70
securitization: assets and, 43, 45, 78–86, 91–101, 165, 251n11, 251n13, 253n41; code masters and, 165; coding land and, 43, 45; credit cooperatives and, 93–95; Frederick the Great and, 93; Ginnie Mae and, 92; minting debt and, 78–86, 91–101, 251n11, 251n13, 253n41; onset, 83; private, 82–83, 86, 94–95; property and, 43, 78
self-interest, 6, 8–9, 18, 232, 236n18
Settled Land Acts, 38–39
settlers, 33–35, 42, 125, 133, 192–93
settlor (trust), 43, 47, 81–82
shadow banking, 50, 79, 211
Shakespeare, William, 35–36, 198–99
shareholders: bonds and, 5, 16, 44, 48–49, 83, 86, 102–5, 108, 128, 195, 198, 202, 211, 252n22, 262n32; capital rule and, 213, 229; code masters and, 164, 168; corporate form and, 48–56, 60–67, 71, 73, 76, 246n13, 246n16, 249n46; Crédit Mobilier and, 102–6; creditors and, 14, 48, 55–56, 60–67, 71, 104, 168, 202, 246n16; digital code and, 195–96, 202; dividends and, 11, 53, 61–62, 103; foreign law and, 7; global code and, 135; intangible capital and, 117; intellectual property and, 114–15; limited liability and, 51, 53–54, 60–61, 63, 99, 254n49; lock-in and, 15, 47, 65–67, 77, 81, 117, 196; minting debt and, 99, 103–4; poison pill and, 163–64, 266n15, 266n17; redeemable shares and, 246n13; shielding and, 14, 48, 52–56, 60–61, 63, 65, 67, 71, 99; veils and, 8
Shavell, Steven, 181
Shiedame, John, 118–19
shielding: of assets, 3, 14, 20, 22, 44, 47–48, 51–63, 65, 67, 71, 78, 84, 86, 99, 107, 129, 161, 165, 205, 215, 238n51, 246n16, 247n20; coding land and, 44; creditors

and, 14, 20, 47–48, 54–61, 63, 65, 67, 71, 107, 247n20; limited liability and, 51, 53–54, 60–61, 63, 99, 254n49; Medici empire and, 57–58, 247n21; minting debt and, 78, 84, 86, 99, 107; partnerships and, 54, 56, 58–59; priority rights and, 54–56, 107, 215; RASCAL and, 73–75, 250n60, 250n62; Roman law and, 56; shareholders and, 14, 48, 52–56, 60–61, 63, 65, 67, 71, 99; tax shelters and, 72, 225–26; trust law and, 44, 47, 51, 56, 84, 86, 107
shocks, 2, 42, 118, 188
Sichelman, Ted, 127–28
Simon, Brenda M., 127–28
Singapore, 84
Skolnick, Mark, 112, 127
slavery: auctions and, 39; capital rule and, 205; cloning legal persons and, 49, 54, 57, 60, 246n5; coding land and, 39; collateral and, 11–12; cotton production and, 49; empire of law and, 11–12, 237n38, 237n40; Roman law and, 54, 57, 60
smart contracts, 187–91
Smith, Adam, 6, 46, 134, 220, 240n68
socialism, 1, 102, 223, 266n24, 270n3, 277n50
Société General, 85
Solow, Roger, 117
sovereignty: bearer assets and, 198; capital rule and, 234, 277n51; code masters and, 160; coding land and, 26–27, 33–34; corporations and, 53, 66–70; global code and, 135–44, 148, 152, 155, 157, 277n51; as imperium, 138; minting debt and, 79, 84–85, 105; NAFTA and, 124, 138–42, 155, 261n20; pharmaceutical industry and, 138; property and, 26–27, 33, 120–21, 135–43, 160; USMCA and, 139, 261n20; World Trade Organization (WTO) and, 125
sovereign wealth funds, 84–85, 251n15
Soviet Union, 270n3
Spain, 103–4, 133
special-purpose vehicles (SPVs), 51, 83, 94, 99, 101
squatters, 34
Stanford University, 129–30
state money: convertibility and, 3; digital code and, 198–203; global code and, 147; intangible capital and, 117; minting debt and, 77–78, 88–93, 106; private money and, 15, 238n52
state power: blockchain and, 184, 187–90, 192, 195, 197–98, 203–4, 270n2;

state power (*continued*)
  capitalism and, 15–19, 205, 208–9,
    212, 216, 221–23; capital rule and, 205;
    coding land and, 23, 46; coercive, 17
    (*see also* coercive power); digital code
    and, 184, 193, 197; empire of law and,
    4, 14–19; global code and, 138, 141, 154;
    institutional legacy of, 184; minting
    debt and, 107; regulation and, 7 (*see also*
    regulation)
Statute of Enrollments, 44
Statute of Monopolies, 119, 258n43
Statute of Uses, 44
Strattera, 138–39
Structured Assets Securities Corporation, 96
subsidiaries: AIG and, 191; corporations
    and, 84, 131, 135, 149, 151, 191, 196, 247n17,
    250n59, 259n80; digital, 196; Google
    and, 131, 259n80; JPMorgan Chase and,
    84; Lehman Brothers and, 50–53, 58–59,
    61–64, 70–74, 135, 149, 250n59; US
    Federal Reserve and, 151
sunset provisions, 76
Szabo, Nick, 192–93, 198

tariffs, 38, 123–24
tax havens, 71, 73, 79, 86, 98–100, 107, 135, 165
tax rates, 7, 11, 68, 71–73, 225
tax shelters, 72, 225–26
Tilly, Charles, 219, 274n53
titles: coding land and, 25–27, 30–35, 37,
    43, 46, 125, 194; landlords and, 206;
    Massachusetts law and, 96; minting debt
    and, 96–97; patents and, 110; property
    and, 13, 25–27, 30–35, 37, 43, 46, 75,
    96–97, 110, 125, 194, 206
Tottenham Mansion, 38
trademarks, 11, 115–16, 215
Trade Act, 121
Trade Related Aspects of Intellectual
    Property Rights (TRIPS), 123–25, 136, 138
trade secrets: coercive power and, 126, 129;
    competition and, 128–29; courts and,
    127–31; creditors and, 128; enclosure and,
    131; enforcement and, 130; guilds and,
    258n61; intellectual property and, 126–31;
    labor and, 128–29; lawyers and, 129–30;
    pharmaceutical industry and, 129; priority
    rights and, 126; wealth and, 127–31
treaty law: bilateral investment treaties
    (BITs) and, 140, 155; capital rule and,
    225; corporations and, 70; European
    Union (EU) and, 70, 263n48; global code

and, 136–42, 154–57; Hague Conference
    on International Private Law and, 136;
    international, 9, 120, 123, 136–39, 225;
    ISDS and, 136–38, 140, 155–56, 261n22;
    property and, 120; Vienna Convention
    and, 155–56, 264n65
Treaty of Rome, 249n51
tribunals, 18, 136–43, 146, 152, 155–57,
    261n21, 264n70
Trump, Donald, 156, 182, 228
trustees, 43–45, 47, 75, 81–82, 95–96,
    243n52
trust law, ix–x; administrators and, 82;
    beneficiaries and, 43–45, 81; capital rule
    and, 211, 219, 226; coding land and, 42–45;
    empire of law and, 3, 5; legal constructs
    for, 244n67; limited liability and, 81–82;
    minting debt and, 78; NC2 and, 79–87,
    94, 98–100, 106–7, 135, 251n4, 251n19;
    securitization and, 43, 81–85, 95, 253n41;
    settlor and, 43, 47, 81–82; shielding and,
    44, 47, 51, 56, 84, 86, 107
Tudor dynasty, 118–19

Uber, 130–31
unemployment, 167
United Kingdom: Brexit and, 179; capital
    rule and, 228, 234; code masters and,
    168, 178–79; common law and, 176–77;
    exporting law and, 133; global code
    and, 151; gold coins and, 254n55; House
    of Parliament and, 29, 38, 61, 119–20,
    158, 207; incorporation theory and, 70;
    industrial policy and, 118–21; Inns of
    Court and, 32, 169, 242n29; intangible
    capital and, 117; intellectual property
    and, 117–21; International Swaps and
    Derivatives Association (ISDA) and,
    151; jingle rule and, 247n24; land law in,
    158, 177, 244n58; lawyers and, 169–70,
    176–79; legal professionals and, 169–70;
    Lehman Brothers and, 50, 71, 73, 149,
    250n59; LIBOR and, 190; minting debt
    and, 106; partnerships and, 60, 247n24;
    patents and, 118–19; subjective rights
    and, 275n10
United Nations, 29
United States: bailouts and, 55, 62, 64, 84,
    104–5, 151, 226, 247n17; bankruptcy
    and, 55, 148, 239n55, 255n71, 262n44;
    bubbles and, 247n26; capital rule and,
    219, 227–28, 234; car manufacturers
    and, 55; Citigroup and, 84; code masters

and, 162, 168, 171, 174–79; Commerce
Clause and, 70, 177; corporations and, 49
(*see also* corporations); Debt Recovery
Act and, 39–40; digital code and, 202;
English law and, 40; fragmented legal
system of, 177; global code and, 139,
142, 148, 151, 156; industrial policy and,
121–22; intangible capital and, 117;
intellectual property and, 109, 112, 115,
121–24, 256n23; International Swaps and
Derivatives Association (ISDA) and, 151;
Japan and, 260n3; land law in, 95; law
schools and, 240n6, 243n43, 268n47;
lawyer demographics of, 162–63; lawyers
and, 162, 171–82; limited liability and, 61;
minting debt and, 84, 87, 92–93, 95, 99,
106; monetary system overhauls in, 50;
NAFTA and, 124, 138–42, 155, 261n20;
Native Americans and, 34; partnerships
and, 247n24; poison pills and, 266n17;
powerful industry interests and, 125;
slavery and, 11–12, 237n40; subjective
rights and, 275n10; Trade Act and,
121; USMCA and, 139, 261n20; Vienna
Convention and, 264n65
United States-Mexico-Canada Agreement
(USMCA), 139, 261n20
universality: capital rule and, 211, 229, 233;
cloning legal persons and, 54; empire of
law and, 3–4, 11, 13–14, 15, 19, 21
unsecured debt, 79
US Bank, 82, 95–97
US Constitution: Commerce Clause and,
70, 177; Fifth Amendment, 241n9;
First Amendment, 87; Fourteenth
Amendment, 25; intellectual property
and, 241n10; patents and, 114–15;
preamble of, 236n21
US Consumer Financial Protection Bureau,
182
US Federal Crisis Inquiry Commission
(FCIC), 79–80, 83, 271n19
US Federal Reserve, 64, 105, 151, 248n38,
255n72
US Patent Act, 110, 113, 256n18
US Patent Office, 113–15, 136, 203, 211, 215,
257n24
US Securities and Exchange Commission
(SEC), 103, 195
US Supreme Court: Brandeis and, 109;
corporate dependence on state and, 68;

genetics and, 109–13, 116, 127, 211, 214;
Johnson v. M'Intosh, 34; Scalia and, 116
US Uniform Commercial Code (UCC),
260n8
usury, 90, 236n26
Utah Cancer Registry, 127
Utah Mormon Genealogy, 127
utopists, 5, 184–86, 197, 200

veils, 8, 13, 48, 207, 246n16
Venezuela, 101
Venice Statute, 119
Vienna Convention, 155–56, 264n65

Wall Street Journal, 166, 265n3
Warner Communication, 124
Watson, James, 108–10
wealth: capital rule and, 205–9, 215, 217,
221–22, 224, 230; cloning legal persons
and, 48, 56, 59, 64, 66–67; code masters
and, 159, 162, 164–67, 174, 176; coding
land and, 24, 27, 35–46; Debt Recovery
Act and, 39–40; digital code and, 198,
200; egalitarian, 40; elitism and, 8 (*see
also* elitism); empire of law and, 1–8, 12–
14, 17–22; hard work and, 4; intangible
capital and, 116–18; knowledge and, 40,
108–9, 118, 131, 165; legal code and, 3;
minting debt and, 77–79, 84–85, 106,
251n15; nature's code and, 109; property
and, 4–5, 12, 14, 19, 21, 24, 36, 42–43,
46, 108, 130, 209, 217, 222, 224, 237n38,
240n68; slavery and, 237n38; sovereign
wealth funds and, 84–85, 251n15; trade
secrets and, 127–31
Weber, Max, 17, 206, 265n8
welfare state, 275n10
Wells Fargo, 62, 248n32
Westlake, Stian, 115–16
Weyl, Glen, 230, 232
white, Anglo-Saxon, protestants (WASPs),
176
Wilkins, Maurice, 109
Woolworth, 49
World Bank, 33, 154–55, 242n33
World Trade Organization (WTO), 122–23,
125
World War II era, 49, 123, 134, 176, 260n3
Wright, Craig, 198

Zyprexa, 138–39

A NOTE ON THE TYPE

This book has been composed in Adobe Text and Gotham.
Adobe Text, designed by Robert Slimbach for Adobe,
bridges the gap between fifteenth- and sixteenth-century
calligraphic and eighteenth-century Modern styles.
Gotham, inspired by New York street signs, was designed
by Tobias Frere-Jones for Hoefler & Co.